Schoolboy to Soldier
1935 - 1945

Schoolboy to Soldier
1935 - 1945

Clement Hoyle

SERENDIPITY

Copyright © Clement Hoyle 2006

First published in 2006 by

Serendipity
First Floor
37 / 39 Victoria Road
Darlington
DL1 5SF

British Library Cataloguing-in-Publication data
A catalogue record for this book is available from the British Library

ISBN 1-84394-178-3

Dedicated to

Joan Lilian Hoyle

Girl

All is well
Death is nothing at all
I have only slipped away into the next room
I am I and you are you
Whatever we were to each other
That we still are.

and

to

Tony
and my wonderful family

Deepest thanks to
John Atkins who 'drove' my laptop and together with wife Chris
Proved that true friends are pure gold.

CONTENTS

Foreword

Unfortunately I only met Clement Hoyle, when he became an In-Pensioner of the Royal Hospital Chelsea, very shortly before my retirement as Lieutenant Governor. But during our short acquaintance I was taken by his positive attitude, spirit for life and sense of fun which is reflected in this delightful memoir, packed throughout with vivid memories and stories. It is an impressive recollection of a life full of variety. It contains immense detail and a wealth of stories about friends, colleagues and events.

CIement Hoyle joined the Royal Army Ordnance Corps in 1935 as a boy soldier and trained as an Armourer. The details of his apprenticeship [he grew into a fine craftsman as he learnt the skills of his trade] show the attention to detail that present generations seem to have lost today. Even boy soldiers in Clement's day had their hierarchy with the fight for the control of the wad racket.

On the completion of his training Mr Hoyle was attached to the 2nd Battalion, Hampshire Regiment and became fully involved in peace-time regimental life. This was soon shattered by the outbreak of the Second World War. He was sent to France as part of the British Expeditionary Force and evacuated from Dunkirk. His memoir illustrates the muddled confidence of the Phoney War and confusion that followed.

While in defence of the East Coast of Britain, Mr Hoyle displays his resourcefulness in obtaining sufficient Bren guns for the Battalion, but I am not sure that some would have written of their accuracy with a 2B pencil in displaying their shooting prowess, even if only to the Home Guard!

In October 1942, Mr Hoyle became a founder member of a new Corps, the Royal Electrical and Mechanical Engineers, and shortly afterwards the Battalion sailed for North Africa. Soon after arrival, the Battalion was engaged in a desperately fought battle for the Tebourba Gap in which Mr Hoyle was heavily involved. He continued to serve throughout the remainder of the campaign, before being posted to 30th Searchlight Regiment, Royal Artillery and then to 39th Light Anti-Aircraft Regiment, a period which he did not enjoy. Entry into the Italian campaign followed where he was attached to the Americans before moving to 8th Army Troops Workshops making (among other things) equipment for Popski's Private Army.

All in all this is a valuable account of the life of one more, remarkable British soldier learning his craft and doing his duty both In peace and war. How appropriate, therefore, that he should become a Chelsea Pensioner where these reminiscences will receive an appreciative and understanding audience.

MAJOR GENERAL JONATHAN HALL CB OBE

CHAPTER 1
SO IT STARTS

..Along to our left was a badly shot up to 15cwt, funny how flat tyres make a vehicle seem somehow sad. We walked across, the only sign of occupancy being an officers' map case hanging from the windscreen frame. Round to the back and once again 'unreal' or 'bizarre' are the only words to adequately describe what we found. The back was full of loose ammunition, just what we were looking for. But sprawled on top of it was a very dead Sergeant. The track of the burst that killed him could be clearly seen, smashing a hole through the side panel, ploughing a furrow through the ammunition and then through the Sergeant and on out. 'Not nice,' said Gaffer...

Born in Halifax of a family with no military connections or experience whatever, I had sort of drifted into the idea of going into the Army as a 'Boy Apprentice Tradesman'. After the various preliminaries such as exams, medicals, interviews etc. I was finally faced with a decision, do I or don't I? Encouraged by my parents and with great unease I decided to join, or more correctly to 'sign on', knowing full well that once in, there was no way back; only money could buy you out, which, for my parents, would have been impossible to find, I was never to regret this decision, though in those early days my resolve often faltered.

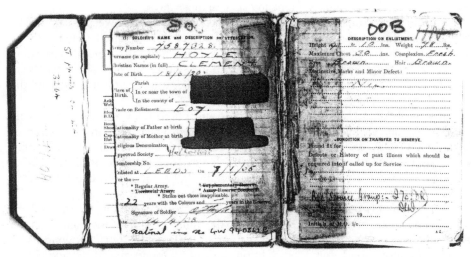

So to Leeds on 6 January 1935 where I was to be formally enlisted. I was accompanied by my Dad. I use this title rather than father because I was fourteen years old and he was quite simply 'my Dad'; we were very close. Even so, it was my Mum that I was missing. Why did we have to travel from Halifax to Leeds to enlist? Because one could only enlist in a Garrison Town and Leeds was and Halifax wasn't; I never understood the logic of this. After the formalities were complete my Dad passed on his only words of advice: 'Never hold the nail whilst somebody else hits it': quite profound really and to this day not a bad maxim. He then left me to the mercy of the Army and more immediately to the Recruiting Officer.

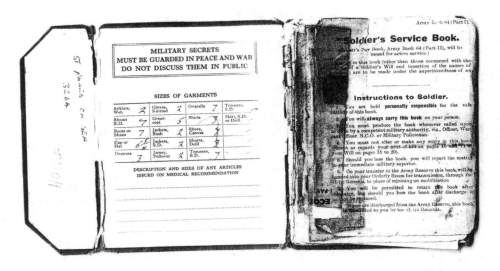

I spent the night in the recruiting office which proved an uncomfortable experience introducing the standard 'barrack bed' two pieces of iron and the three coir mattresses known as 'biscuits' to the soldiery. Come the morning I was despatched round the corner to a café and armed with the requisite authority, a voucher, was served a right royal breakfast of bacon, eggs and fried bread; oh what joy for a fourteen year old, fit and always hungry, no nanny state in those days.

And so back to the recruiting office, to make up my bed and sweep the floor. The making of a soldier had already begun, though I suspect it had started earlier with the cold water wash; It had been a bitterly cold night with a hard frost. Later that morning the Recruiting Sergeant and I made our way to the station on foot. The Army were still a few years away from mechanisation. My lasting impression of Leeds and the Recruiting Office was the cold.

I stood at the carriage window and as the train pulled out I was a pretty miserable would-be soldier yet the biggest step had been taken. I was now in possession of 'Army Book 64 Soldier's Record and Pay Book'. Amazingly I still have it in front of me. It says on the first two pages – 758732 Hoyle Clement, date of birth 18-6-20, trade on enlistment Boy, height 4ft 10ins, weight 78lbs, maximum chest 30ins, no distinctive marks or defects; they were getting a very small package!

It was a lovely cold sunny day and I remember very clearly, as the train pulled out, the large poster on the platform: 'Come to the Sunny South'. Many hours later the train pulled into Cosham station five miles north of Portsmouth. It was snowing! With the help of a passer-by I found the right bus and soon found myself outside Hilsea Barracks, the Depot of the Royal Army Ordnance Corps. This was to be my home for the next four years.

I went through the gates and across a very colonial looking veranda to the open door. I stopped and peered in; it was a big room, six made up beds were lined up along the opposite wall. There were several soldiers dotted around and in the centre a well scrubbed table complete with a large steel jug, well polished, and several enamel mugs all looking spotless. The floor was some form of what looked like dull red tarmac with the most amazing shine. This was indeed a strange new world. I was scared and I remember feeling that I would never pluck up the courage to go in: somebody shouted 'For God's sake come in,' and I did. They pointed to a sort of office in the corner and told me to report to the Guard Commander.

I went into the office, passing an enormous full-length mirror on the way. I handed in my documents to the Corporal sitting there and stood as straight as I could. God, I was frightened. I was soon to learn that in the Army, soldiers with rank from L/Corporal upwards came in every shade of personality from fair and sympathetic to out and out shit. This Corporal was certainly one of the good personalities. He looked at my bits of paper, then, after mentioning that there had been a boy like myself through earlier he shouted and I mean shouted, 'Stick Man!' What on earth was a Stick Man? I was feeling increasingly tired and miserable and now I had caused the summing of this strange sounding genie.

He arrived in a crashing of impossibly polished boots and what I later learned was a walking out cane tucked smartly under his arm. Pausing briefly to check his appearance in the mirror, he came rigidly to attention in front of the Corporal and was told to take me to the cookhouse where the duty cook would feed me. I trailed after this Stick Man pausing only to allow the duty bugler through the door first, little realising that the bugle was about to become a very dominant timekeeper in my life.

As we passed the Barrack Square the bugler was sounding a call. On enquiring what it meant the Stick Man replied 'Jankers,' probably something to do with you. Oops, should I be flattered or frightened? I was already frightened anyway. The cook gave me a generous meal of bacon, chips, beans and a mug of tea. I mention this particularly because from then on the food was issued strictly according to the rations laid down by the Army and could best be described as 'frugal'; we were always hungry but very fit. I had been told to report back to the guardroom and this I did; whatever happened to me now would at least be on a full stomach.

Nothing had changed much except for the addition of four soldiers in overalls one of whom was detailed to show me to J4, apparently my allocated barrack room, outside which there was a small handcart filled with bedding. Hello again to my old friends the biscuits; those I did recognise. We set off back, past the square, through several barrack blocks, until finally arriving at what appeared to be a pretty old building. My helper said, 'Up the stairs, room on the left and when you find your bed and dump your case come back down and pick up your bedding.' He then said a strange thing: 'I cannot help you, I'm not allowed to enter a Boys barrack block'; here was an introduction to the Service's absolute discipline that separated Boys, anybody under eighteen, from the men.

Up the stairs, turn left and once again a door into the unknown and one thing was certain: whatever lay beyond the door was very noisy, but open it I did and like magic the noise stopped. The scene was chaotic but I felt every eye on me and now I really was scared. I was just a schoolboy and a small one at that, nor did I know at the time that the shambles I was looking at was entirely due to the fact that it was Wednesday. This was a half day supposedly given over to sport but in reality it was just a half day in which those who played for the various teams indulged and the rest, well, they just indulged. I found that my eyes had focused on one of the boys stood on his bed wearing a bright yellow goalkeeper's jersey, shorts, football socks and a vast amount of mud; in view of the fact that it was around six in the evening, this showed a total indifference to washing or changing. His name was Lambert; he was the first team goalkeeper and a very good one.

I was shown my bed, the usual two lumps of iron, and somewhat to my surprise I was helped by a couple of the boys to collect my bedding from the handcart and shown how to set up the bed irons and then how to make the bed. The room by this time had resumed its noisy normality and I was able to sit on the bed and try to gather my wits. After a while a boy came in carrying washing kit but like me wearing civilian clothes.

I had found Peter Hills who had arrived a few hours earlier and had been mentioned by the Guard Commander. Two things had been established at this moment. Peter and I had been divorced from the rest of the intake, or as they were called at Hilsea, 'batch', and accommodated in a barrack room occupied by the previous 'batch' who were now seasoned Boy Soldiers with a full year's service and were 'Barrack wise' to say the least. Secondly, we were occupying adjoining beds and did so for the next couple of years until promotion moved us into different rooms. The reason for our being separated from the batch was that we were both a day late reporting and the Barrack room set aside for the newcomers was full - there's always a simple explanation! Peter and I have recently come together after all these years, sixty-six to be precise, and not having met in all that time it was a memorable moment.

I have no memory of the rest of the evening but I did sleep well; sleep has always come easily to me. The morning was very educational. Reveille sounded at six, damned bugle, followed almost immediately by the Orderly Sergeant or Corporal apparently coming through the door without opening it, or at least it sounded like that, but preceded by his voice 'asking' us to get out of bed and to emphasise this he tipped the nearest boy out onto the floor and departed. Nobody got up and I wondered, if this was wise. I certainly wasn't going to move until somebody else did then the boy next to me, not Peter, said, 'Don't worry, this one won't come back.' I soon learned which ones did and which ones didn't. I shall come back later to the art of 'bed tipping'. So to the washhouse, four toilets, a wall type urinal, six basins, concrete floor, plenty of elbow room and all the cold water you could wish for, and remember this served two rooms, about twenty boys.

During all of this the occupant of a bed in the corner by the fireplace had remained fast asleep and apparently totally oblivious to any thing that was going on. Peter and I discovered at breakfast that this was Corporal McCollum, a 'man' no less, and he was in charge of the room, that he was seldom there but he was to quote, 'a smashing bloke'. So what was my 'jankers' friend of the previous evening on about when he said there was a strict segregation, men from boys? Here was one actually living with us, simple: it was the system making an exception to suit the fact that there was only one Boy Corporal at this time. It changed later.

Back in the room the scene was of orderly chaos, beds being assembled into a sort of armchair by pushing the bottom half of the structure underneath the top half and arranging two of the biscuits on the bottom with the third biscuit upright at the back and the sheets and blankets folded with scrupulous care then covered with the remaining blanket. Helped by one of the boys I had achieved much the same result. About this time the bugle sounded and there was a rapid exodus with everyone carrying their mug, knife, fork and spoon or in the vernacular 'eating irons'. I grabbed my own, found amongst the bedding the night before, remember the hand cart?

Breakfast! Porridge, two slices of bread, a small ladle of beans, margarine and absolutely no second helpings and so on for the next four years. The beans changed every day and could be two small rashers of bacon or a boiled egg or a fried egg or two small sausages and on Sundays bacon and an egg. Sundays were special! The pat of margarine was replaced by butter. No one lingered over breakfast and back in the room there was a mass cleaning and setting out of the 'room furniture'. Writing this I have to smile: a trestle table scrubbed to an impossible whiteness, two forms to match, a galvanised coal 'bunce' and bucket, how could a receptacle for coal shine like that? Mind you, I had seen the table and forms being brought in from the wash house; all was to be revealed soon enough.

Finally there were sundry brooms, scrubbing brushes and yes a 'bumper'. This strange implement was being swung backwards and forwards across the floor by one of the boys and was obviously heavy as was his language when anyone got in the way. But here was the answer to one of my constant queries about these impossible shines. For a floor, you needed a bumper and a cursing soldier. The activity gradually slowed down and the boys began to dress for the workshops, then guess what! The damn bugler again. Mind you, he had been sounding calls off and on ever since reveille, in fact he had sneaked one in fifteen minutes before reveille though it had not registered, but this time the boys all left for the parade ground. Peter and I hung about feeling that we should know what to do next but no one had mentioned the next move on this long journey.

We were soon to learn, as one of the new (us) batch came in and said we were to parade downstairs in front of the block; this we did and reported to one of the drill Corporals and met the rest of our batch. They had of course been together for two days and I think they regarded us with some suspicion. For Peter and I to join a parade that was already formed did not present a problem because we had done it many times before. Peter had come from a Military Boarding School where they used Army drill, whilst I in my own small way had been a member of the Boys Brigade who likewise based their training on the Army drills so we were both well versed in the arts of 'falling in', dressing ranks, forming fours, and in this case joining correctly a parade already formed up i.e. in the' blank file'. Remember this was the old days and a parade was formed up in two ranks and an odd number would create a space one in from the right marker, this was the 'blank file'. I took the space and Peter created his own space next to me using a bit of muscle. Unlike me Peter was a big lad and anyway the boys we were joining didn't know what the hell was going on but very importantly the Corporal certainly did. It pays to get off to a good start.

We were shambled off, I nearly said marched, finally finishing up outside the Quarter Master's Store. Reading that title it strikes me how appropriate a title it was; every Quarter Master I ever met, and his staff, always regarded the stores and everything in it as theirs, certainly not to be issued if it were at all possible. There was a painful hour or so coming up for the QM, as twelve of us marched in to be fully equipped and kitted out. As the clothing and kit piled up I became more and more conscious of the enormous step I had taken. This was indeed a different world and I began to wonder if I would be able to cope. I was feeling pretty low, frightened, and a long way from home. Like all the others I was homesick and indeed this affected a small number of the batch quite badly during the coming weeks but everyone survived. This was a hard six weeks we faced and we were pressed all the time, but the drill instructors led by Drum Major Vick were always aware of the need to take care of the boys who were finding the separation from home very hard; they were very good at their job. They are all gone now but I am very pleased to make this small tribute,

There was, of course, a much more important and fearsome figure lurking in the wings: the Regimental Sergeant Major known nowadays to almost anybody who watches television as the RSM. The Queen's Birthday Parades have epitomised this superbly efficient component of the Army: being efficient not 'nice' was their trade. I never throughout my service met a RSM who didn't live up to this description.

The kit we were issued with was pretty comprehensive: two uniforms, two pairs of boots, three pairs of socks, one greatcoat. I can still hear the plaintive cries of the QM staff as they parted with their precious stores: 'Three shirts soldier's khaki size ten!' Gosh how it must have hurt. 'One housewife': hello what's this and where the hell is she?' Alas 'she' turned out to be a cotton holdall providing all the items necessary to sew and darn, what me? There were other strange items, 'puttees'; I had seen them in old photographs of the First World War. Kitting complete it was back to the barrack room, lay it out on our beds in some semblance of order, Peter and I breaking away from the batch to J 4, our own room, then on to the tailor's for alterations.

Anyone who was at Hilsea Barracks during the thirties and earlier will remember the two brothers, both dwarfs, sat on a large table busily hand sewing various items of uniform, surrounded by a litter of jackets and trousers. After the kit issue we had been told to return to the barrack room and put everything away, this meant in our locker and kitbag, then it would be lunch. We hadn't been back very long when the boys arrived back from the workshops and there was another chaotic period whilst they all changed into PT kit (physical training dress), vest, shorts and plimsolls, then paraded outside in the bitter cold marshalled by a couple of the PT instructors who called a roll then doubled them off in the direction of the gymnasium. At this point neither Peter nor I knew where the gym was. After about half an hour they returned mostly moaning about PT in general but mostly concerned with diving off for dinner and we quickly followed; needless to say the bugler had been at it again some five minutes before.

Dinner! Again reasonable helpings but strictly controlled by the size and type of ladle. None were considered of a small enough size to merit their having to be used twice. The quality was on the whole pretty good but of course, some things were looked forward to more than others. A great favourite was the Australian tinned rabbit, unless you got the rib cage with no meat at all whereas a total the back was thick with meat and quite delicious. The meat course changed every day and was accompanied in the usual way by vegetables. Potatoes were boiled, roast, mashed or yes chips; we used to count them sometimes, measure them and produce a total length of chip. It was a wonderful tribute to the servers (jankers again) that the total lengths were very consistently the same. The sweets followed a regular pattern, rice played a big part and so did bread pudding which also was a great favourite, I can't remember if it was the taste or the bulk but bread pudding was certainly OK. Come to think of it so was treacle pudding, almost certainly for the same reasons; bulk was certainly important and there was always the inevitable mug of tea.

After dinner the room was relatively quiet. Some just sat and relaxed on their made-up beds; others would make their beds and two or three would busy themselves taking the table, two forms and the brooms out into the wash house. I pondered this particular activity. I had thought that the table was for whatever tables are for and that the forms were for sitting on whenever this 'activity' was taking place: 'wrong', tables and forms were there to be scrubbed as white as possible then stacked out of the way in the wash house until next morning, always assuming that a bigger or tougher boy or several boys adding up to the same thing didn't need them. Peter and I along with the rest of the batch had been told to parade in their room, J5. The afternoon was to be devoted to putting on our uniform and what we were going to have to do to lick it into shape. I knew what our boots should look like, but the ones I had been issued with were stiff, covered with grease and certainly not meant to be worn by Homosapiens. Funny that, a few months later and they were supremely comfortable and oh that shine but that was all in the future; meanwhile everything was awful. There were problems of course as some had lost items to the tailors but there were enough boys with complete uniforms to enable the two Corporals to carry on.

I wonder how many old soldiers can remember 'puttees'. The First World War comes to mind but yes, they were still in use in 1935 and presented all sorts of problems mostly arising from the strict standards of smartness that were expected. They had to be wound on with an even spacing which depended on leg length, this was about ¾' to 1', finishing exactly on the centre of the outside of the leg where the tape was then wound round and tucked neatly in, again exactly central. To achieve this depended entirely on starting at the right point above the boot top. False starts were common even though you thought that you had it worked out: doesn't' sound too bad, just start again, and again, and again - this may be fine when you are practising, with all the time in the world but after the bugler (him again) has already sounded quarter for parade and it already seems ages ago then things get a bit fraught. I should explain the expression quarter for parade. Before a parade the bugler would sound three calls, 'half hour for parade', 'quarter hour for parade' and finally 'fall in'. Not many of us had watches in those days so time warnings were important. I am getting ahead at this point; all of this was still in the future.

So here we were with two increasingly exasperated Corporals trying to teach us to get the puttees to finish in the right place. Alas, this was only one aspect of this black art. Not only did they have to finish right they also had to collect the trouser leg on the way and in such a way that it could be folded neatly down over the top of the puttees. We did this and they looked awful, not like the neat clean 'hang' of the ones we had already seen in the Guard Room for instance. No one at this time had mentioned the other equally dark art, creases; these were the legal way to achieve that smart finish but there was another known as 'cut offs': the trouser legs were cut off and hemmed at exactly the right height which resulted in perfection of hang and obviously looked very smart. Very quick too. It was also a serious offence, funny that I never heard of anyone being charged for it. The RSM liked a smart parade and so did all the other non commissioned officers whilst I think that the commissioned officers just knew a good thing when they saw it. Who did the hemming you might ask - we did - the tailors wouldn't touch them. They may have had a price but when a penny bar of chocolate was a serious outlay we never found what it might be. Other things covered that afternoon were button cleaning, introducing the button stick issued earlier. I had wondered about that at the time. Getting the dubbin off the boots I had already decided was impossible; and trying to start a polish equally impossible; how to blanco webbing was something I came to hate though I cannot remember why; and finally the disposal of our civilian clothes, but that is for another day.

We finished about the time the boys got back from the workshops. We were all feeling very self conscious in our creased new looking uniforms and the ones still wearing their civvies more than a little conspicuous. No need to worry, the lads arriving back had only food on their minds yet when Peter and I arrived back in the barrack room our room mates took the trouble to make sure we got out of our khaki and into the overalls also issued that morning which were to prove to be the standard 'not doing anything else form of dress', and now? Grab eating irons and leg it to the cook house. I suppose I should refer to our place of eating as the dining room but it was always just the 'cook house'.

Tea! It was winter so the meals were hot and as I remember that evening I met the 'armoured car': this was a largish Cornish pasty reasonably well filled with meat and potato encased in a substantial pastry which for some reason was always tough hence the name, but delicious and very popular. Served with gravy, two slices of bread, the usual pat of margarine and of course a mug of tea it was filling and welcome on a cold day; and so back to J4.

The room was much as it had been left at lunch time and I realised later that they all had their own pattern of living so to speak or at least most of the time. I too was to develop a routine though it never seemed to be at the time; an example was making your bed, some made it at lunch time, others any time during the evening. Peter and I were now facing the prospect of trying to get enough of our kit in some sort of order so as to be at least presentable on parade the next morning. There had been a lot of ribbing by our roommates; at least we hoped that is what they would be, about the ghastly looking kit we were faced with, a good deal of laughter of the 'been there done that' sort of humour. I had noticed that they were all changing into their khaki, not in any great haste but with all the appearance of an imminent departure. On enquiring, I was told it was for a two hour school class every Monday, Tuesday and Thursday, six till eight in the evenings until you passed your first class certificate of education, how's that for a nasty carrot? I subsequently learned that this exam was far from easy.

There were pros and cons at being placed in a senior boys' room and one of the pros was about to be amply demonstrated. Several of them now took over the proper creasing of our trousers so that in addition to the normal creasing there was a crease across the legs providing a suitable fold where they would be turned down above the puttee. This creasing involved water, soap, shaving brush (mine) and large pieces of flat cardboard which were taken from their own beds. One pair of the trousers was carefully folded between two pieces of cardboard, the creases were damped with soap and water, the whole was then placed on top of the bed iron, and the bed made. This was the standard method for creasing trousers; indeed trousers lived permanently between the sleeper and bed iron not forgetting the cardboard. We were given a quick demonstration of how to clean buttons using the button stick, an old tooth brush, metal polish and the button brush, all previously issued, and promised to help us with the boots when they got back.

We had been scrubbing away at our buttons, carefully following advice, when Corporal McCollum walked in. After dumping some odds and ends on his bed he came over and formally introduced himself, shook our hands, asked how we were coping and then settled down to a long chat. Once again as we talked I was overwhelmed by the size of this step I had taken and the finality of it. At the end he told us that we were to come to him if we had any problems at all and that at the weekend he would allocate a room job for each of us to start on Monday. We knew now how all the work we had seen being done was organised. He did prove very elusive but there was never any doubt who was in control nor why he was so well liked by the lads.

It didn't seem long before the lads came clattering back in. Why was everything so noisy? Probably because I simply wasn't used to it; Peter never seemed troubled and it wasn't long before I too was oblivious. They flung their books down and resumed our education on the subject of boots, A word about these peculiar and very heavy items of footwear. They were covered in a thick grease like substance called dubbin which seemingly presented an impenetrable covering specially designed to prevent boots from acquiring any sort of shine but also to preserve them. What follows illustrates that the thinkers behind this preservation scheme needed to get up much earlier if they were to overcome the ingenuity of Boy Soldiers, who anyway were not much in to preservation except of course the 'self' type.

Things, even Army boots, are never what they seem but at this moment how were we to know? However help was at hand and amongst other things appeared to need the help of a candle (lit) and my table knife (steel). 'We are not allowed to do this, it's against regulations,' was the opening gambit by my helper, then he proceeded to do it. He removed as much of the grease as possible with bits of rag – source unknown - then we heated the knife handle over the candle and rubbed it across the leather, paying particular attention to the toecap meanwhile taking off the grease as it came out and of course constantly reheating the knife. When the leather became dry we caked it with boot polish, continuing to rub it as before with the hot knife handle till the semi-molten polish sort of disappeared; this process was known as 'hot boning'. It shortened the life of the boots, hence its illegality but anyway was only really necessary once.

From now on the same procedure was followed but preferably with an old bone handled knife or toothbrush, hence the term 'boning' when referring to the cleaning of boots. After the polish was well 'boned' in the toe caps were polished with a soft cloth and the uppers with a brush. During all of this a great deal of spit was also used. This then was the end of the second important and barrack wise lesson but we hadn't finished yet. There was the chinstrap to do; this was a small strap of leather which went round the front of the hat hooking onto two small buttons at the side (already polished). The leather was really well finished and quickly took a good polish, thank goodness something did. This was about it for the time and anyway it was nearly lights out. Another bugle call followed by a great deal of shouting from the Orderly Sergeant. 'Get those lights out,' just a few years ahead of that familiar sound which everyone came to know, 'Put that light out.'

Supper! I missed that, a mug of cocoa about seven which for some reason the lads didn't seem to bother with. I tried it some time later and all was clear but even so there was a bugle call for it; I was beginning to wonder if there might not be one for bowel movements. And so to bed, the first day was done. I was still reeling with the massive change to my life and the frightening future but I was still in there and come what may I would sleep well; I always did.

Friday and I hoped, as was the fashion in the life I had left behind, that it would be pay day and it was. The morning room routine followed the same pattern with the exception that Peter and I had to climb into our uniforms ready to parade but we soon discovered that we were not going to be allowed to do this unaided, another of those pros. The barrack room as a whole seemed to have decided that any remiss on our part would somehow reflect on them so we were carefully 'assembled' into our uniforms with special attention to puttees and the hang of our trousers; remember that funny crease across, well, here it was, functioning perfectly or nearly so. The final result was very good we didn't realise how much so until we arrived on parade and saw the rest of our batch, oh dear it was almost embarrassing – almost. The Corporals never batted an eyelid as if it was normal for them to turn up looking just like raw recruits, grease still on their boots, creased uniforms, nightmarish puttees and two of the batch looking like old soldiers - even our boots were shining, our puttees almost dead right and the hang pretty good. We formed up in the usual two ranks remembering that at this point we had not done any drill training just the basic rules to get us into some sort of order; as previously explained Peter and I at least knew what we were supposed to be doing and jogged the other boys along.

I think at this stage the Corporals had the task of eventually getting the batch presentable because so far we had not met either the RSM or Drum Major Vick who would be our direct boss during the coming six weeks nor had we done any formal drill, just enough to shuffle around in a reasonable way. So off we went to J5 to start our education into the mysteries of Barrack life and the protocol thereof, starting with the names of the Commanding Officer and the Adjutant (always a very important personage, indeed it would be fair to say that the Adjutant and the RSM pretty well ran any unit). We learned the name of the officer in charge of Boys and also, of more immediate relevance, the Sergeant in charge of us who occupied a bunk on the landing between our room J4 and the one opposite J3. Bit of a surprise this to Peter and me, as so far, he hadn't been mentioned by our roommates. There were other Officers and of course the RSM. All the names had to be memorised and during the next weeks we had to be ready to produce a name at any time. We were shown where the gymnasium and the riding school were, a run down of the various periods we were allocated for sport, showers or baths, when we could use the gymnasium on a voluntary basis, where and when our small branch of the NAAFI was and what were the opening hours.

This organisation was the Services' equivalent of the Co-op. It paid a dividend to units according to how much they spent but more than that, it followed wherever we went; even in dangerous active service areas they would never be far away, the recipients of much complaining and much affection. There was too a Garrison shop, I never fully understood its status but it was very useful and sold a good range of products from groceries to football boots.

There had been a break for a cup of tea and now at twelve o'clock we were taken across the square to the office block to collect our first pay - two shillings! This wasn't our total weekly pay but the Army decreed what we would actually receive in cash each week and what they would retain for leave periods, personal replacements of items of clothing worn out or mysteriously lost and that most disliked catch all item, Barrack damages. I think our starting total weekly pay was six shillings. Clutching our two shillings and with orders to parade again in J5 at the time the Boys paraded for work we scurried off to collect our eating irons and off to dinner. As we left the square the rest of the Boys were arriving from the workshops and forming up alphabetically under the veranda which ran the length of the Office Block. This, then, was the pay parade routine each Friday on arrival from work, If your name began with 'A' or "Z". you would be either first or last to the cookhouse; this reversal of parade order each week didn't matter a damn to me with a start time so to speak, of 'H'. There was a subtle change in the room during this lunch time, a sort of diving out and returning with such luxury food items as Cadbury's fruit and nut.

The first item of the Friday afternoon session was for those with alterations at the tailors to go across and collect them. This was followed by instructions to pack our civilian clothes into a parcel ready to post home: what on earth good they were ever going to be to us in the future I could not fathom, we would grow physically at a fast rate and mature even more quickly. We would eventually be marched round to the local Post Office to post them home, at our own expense of course. Personally I would have preferred a quick visit to the incinerator and a couple of fruit and nut bars. The batch spent another hour practising dressing whilst Peter and I were given some message or other to run and then fall out which gave us a bit of time to sit on our beds quietly for a change and chat before the peace was shattered by the lads arriving back from the workshops. Tomorrow would be different – it was Saturday.

Our orders were to once again parade in J5 so we spent much of the evening working on our kit, the second pair of boots for instance which were destined to be our second line or working boots, also our other pair of trousers which were creased normally. The rest of the room too were busy getting their kit ready for the Saturday parades as well as the normal polishing of boots, buttons and equipment brasses. Of course before one could tackle these particular brasses the equipment had to be blancoed; we had been helped the previous evening with this chore but it was illuminating to watch our room mates treating their webbing with this khaki block of blanco plus water and an old nail brush, certainly didn't do anything for the sinks. I couldn't help thinking this was one room job you didn't want the morning after Friday night. Guess who got it?

Saturday mornings meant nine o'clock drill parade for everyone in the Depot, unless of course you could somehow manage to arrange a good enough reason to be excused, not easy, believe me. The parade under the command of the RSM was attended by the Adjutant plus the Officers in charge of the various sections of the Royal Army Ordnance Corps Depot, recruits doing their training as store men or clerks, armourer trainees (us). Our official title as a body was the Armourer's Training Branch always shortened to ATB. There was also the Depot staff, drill instructors, training instructors, administrative staff: I suppose there were well over one hundred on parade all of whom were there because they had failed to conjure up the good enough reason as mentioned above. So what was in store? Drill for the next hour, ouch! But all of this was still in the future for us newcomers and indeed there was much more to Saturday mornings than the initial hour drilling, better known as square bashing .

Before going on I really ought to replace the term 'newcomers'. We had already learned that we were a different sort of animal and until the next batch arrived in a year's time our status was that of 'Nozzers' and when a senior boy said, 'Move, Nozzer, you moved and quickly; not to do so could be very painful indeed, either at the time or later but more of this more brutal aspect of our first year in later chapters.

Back to J5 or more accurately to outside J5 to be inspected then inside for a few repairs to appearance here and there, then back out for a little simple drill mainly aimed at getting us to march reasonably and so be less conspicuous when moving about as a squad. Our real introduction to 'square bashing' was due to begin on Monday; meanwhile we had a tea break and then joined the rest of the boys at Religious Instruction. This was a regular Saturday morning parade and followed morning break. Saturday mornings after Religious Instruction varied according to whether there was a full church parade on the following day which would mean an extra half hour on the square practising with the band. No formal church parade meant it would be one of two things, fallout nice and early or if someone who shall be nameless was bloody minded, then another half hour's square bashing, funny about the smile on the RSMs face.

Saturday mornings were followed by Saturday afternoons, a statement of the obvious you may well think but here was yet another regular format or even ritual that was constant in all the rooms no matter the seniority and indeed had followed the same patterns over many years probably since the ATB had been formed and the boys recruited, then much the same as they were now. Meeting Armourers in later years the same barrack room stories would be swapped whatever the difference in era. However for me it was yet another scene of apparent chaos: would I ever come to terms with this life? I was filled with doubt and foreboding,

Individually there were a number of options: 'out of barracks' though at this time this was not an option for us, only after completing our initial training would we be allowed a pass; 'sport', which was at this time of year football, some would organise a kick around on the sports field, others playing for one of the teams; 'sleeping', a popular 'activity', annoying these sleepers another popular activity, dangerous too in truth. The most important requisite when deciding what to do was that it didn't cost anything as not only were we always hungry we were mostly always broke. Mind you, there was always the fire! This does need some explanation and on this my first Saturday afternoon and in a senior boys' room, I watched it unfold with increasing bewilderment. At some time during the Friday a couple of the boys had taken the highly polished coal tub and arrived back with it filled with coal and a few sticks of wood; this I learned at the time was our ration and it had to last until Wednesday when we would be entitled to another one. I had certainly been impressed on the day I arrived by the massive fire in the grate and the lads sprawled around it on a collection of biscuits (remember mattresses).

This barrack block making up the five rooms, J1-5, was very old, dating back to before the First World War. The heating system too was pretty ancient the central heating depending on a smallish boiler in a smallish boiler house with a smallish ration of coke and indeed a smallish boiler man, small enough to be impossible to find when the pipes were cold in the depths of winter. Of course the boys could get in to feed the boiler but there had been a few crises, something to do with stuffing the boiler with coke then departing to sit on the pipes which soon became too hot to touch and the boiler, suffering severe indigestion, packed up. This took ages to fix and had not been popular with the boys, or more disastrously the Sergeant in charge of boys who shared the same heating system and had been forced to rely on the small open fire in his bunk.

The authorities seemed more concerned with how the boys broke in and who was responsible rather than whether or not the lads froze to death: lots of them out there I suppose; just run a few more exams. Those difficult letters would have made interesting reading: 'Brilliant in the workshops, excellent sportsman, superb school work, a thoroughly likeable lad, very popular with all he had contact with, great pity about the frost bite.'

Central heating or not, all was not lost: in each room there was a large open fireplace and, fed by the coal ration as previously described, would last two afternoons,

Saturday and Sunday, though it was rumoured that a fire had even been sighted on a Monday evening. It was a long time before I spotted a fire on a Monday evening, indeed this fire was a constant source of acrimony which varied from aggression to violence, and was always about who got there first and in the best position and later there was more jockeying for position after bringing back their two slices of bread and hopefully, cheese, to toast, using the coal shovel. I will say that after the initial sorting out of positions the toasters were left to get on with it, the others waiting their turn. Of course this respect was entirely due to food, even two slices of bread and margarine, no matter who they belonged to, being far too precious to put at risk. It is very difficult to convey the utter chaos that ensued during the afternoons and evenings of 'the fire', but with the indifferent central heating the fire was important yet I never saw a disciplined use of the fuel ration, just huge fires until the coal was gone - mind you it was great while it lasted!.

Sunday and Church Parade, nothing special this one as I remember; everyone paraded in khaki but with white belts; fell in on the square and were marched off to their various places of worship. They arrived back in the barrack room about half an hour before the bugler did his stuff, this time for dinner. Our batch were excused this first Sunday parade, again because we simply were not ready either dress wise nor drill wise; the rest of the afternoon and evening were carbon copies of Saturday. Peter and I kept well out of the way, somehow it seemed safer. During the day Corporal McCollum had told us what our room jobs would be, and, though it didn't register then, I can see from this distance in time that the choice was probably carefully thought out. Pete was given the floor, remember the bumper, well he was a big lad but more importantly he had done it before; meanwhile I had been given the wash house. Not as bad as it sounds because it was shared with a boy from across the landing in J3. Although he was two years my senior, almost an 'old sweat', he nevertheless had a vested interest in it being done well. Both of our names were listed for the wash house, so praise and pain would be equally shared especially the pain.

Eight thirty Monday morning and here we were, formed up in two ranks on the square. So this is where our transformation would really begin. Anxiously we waited for the Corporal to say or do something but he just stood there immaculately turned out. It wasn't long before two figures emerged from the office block and strode purposely in our direction. The Corporal went out to meet them, bringing back with him the Regimental Sergeant Major and the Drum Major. The Corporal brought us to attention, The RSM then introduced himself by name, Bennet, and introduced Drum Major Vick who was to conduct and supervise all our initial training, talked to us very briefly mostly on the lines of work hard, keep out of trouble being a recipe for happiness, especially with him. He then departed in the direction of his office and Drum Major Vick took over.

The first hour was devoted to simple basics, forming up in two ranks, numbering, needed to form fours, dressing (the art of getting the lines straight), turning right, left and about and finally the most difficult drill of all, marching! The first hour went very quickly and was quite enjoyable; mind you I seem to remember that at this stage no one was shouting at us, at least only the words of command. After a break for the inevitable mug of tea there was a tour of the various venues that would play a such a part in our future: gymnasium, bath house, offices, sick bay and finally the Riding School, more about this building later but, though the whole complex of buildings that made up the Hilsea Depot barracks has disappeared under a blanket of housing development, the Riding School is, or was until very recently still there because it is a listed building. Well, so it might be but in the next few weeks and indeed the rest of our stay at Hilsea, we were to grow to dislike this building intensely. The reason? When it rained we continued our square bashing in there and because the concrete floor was overlaid with a thick layer of peat for the horses, after five minutes we were choking with the dust. It was very unpleasant indeed.

The afternoon started with a classroom session and guess what, bugle calls! There were a lot of them from 'Reveille' to 'The Last Post'. Our days would be measured out by the duty bugler. Though I said from Reveille, in fact the first call of the day was jankers some fifteen minutes earlier at 0545 hrs. There was cookhouse, half hour and quarter for parade followed by fall in for parade, sick, pay, lights out, retreat and last post. Retreat carried its own laws; if you were walking anywhere in barracks you were supposed to stand still until the call finished; if you were passing across the square then stand very firmly and correctly to attention remembering as you did so, that the square was overlooked by the Sergeants' Mess; you could never be sure, the RSM might just glance up from the snooker table or even from his pint, the consequences could be fearsome.

All of these bugle calls were preceded by the Regimental Call which to this day I can still remember: sound it and I think my ears would probably alert themselves to whatever might be coming. 'Gs' were used to identify calls that were specifically for one group. For example if the 'Quarter' for parade was for the Armourers then at the end the bugler would sound the appropriate number of 'Gs'. I cannot believe that I have forgotten how many it was for us but I think it was three. There were also special calls using the simple 'G' to inform the depot of the progress of one of our sporting teams competing in a semi-final or final of one of the Army championships; we soon learned that sport and its intense rivalries between units of the British Army was almost top of the Army priorities. Oh, I don't know though, if it wasn't sport what the hell was it, certainly wasn't anything nasty like war. We quickly learned these calls but even months later they could still create anxiety. Was that half or quarter for parade? The call had been heard but hadn't registered so was it quarter or half and this while you were still wrestling with the those stupid puttees, but somehow I always felt an affection for the bugle calls; they were always there, a certainty you could rely on.

At this very early point in our training there was room for a certain amount of 'theory' and though the rest of the batch needed to be instructed in how to report sick, for example, Peter and I were very well informed on all these procedures including a complete and very informative rundown on the medical centre staff. For example the Corporal nurse was not to be trifled with, didn't seem to like Boy Soldiers and remembering my early comments about the personalities of soldiers with rank he was definitely one of the out and outs. The Medical Officer, Colonel Ridout, was totally different, retired, gentle and sympathetic but could spot a scrounger almost before you reported sick; this involved seeing the orderly Sergeant and getting your name down for the sick parade at eight thirty. Having done this then you wouldn't be found absent at whatever you were supposed to be doing next. Very important that. Peter and I knew all this and much more already, another of the 'pros'; we were also much in demand from the rest of the batch for this sort of information.

The week carried on in much the same way. We marched off to the local Post Office with our pathetic little bundles of civilian clothes, and did our first Physical

Training (PT) sessions consisting of fairly straightforward exercises lasting half an hour; plenty of whistle but the staff seemed reasonably civil and provided you rushed about when told to do so everything was fine. The staff comprised a Sergeant Major Physical Training Instructor and two Ordnance Corps Corporals working towards a possible transfer to the Army Physical Training Corps. The Sergeant Major was a real old soldier and a few months after we started he finished his service and disappeared into the world we had just left. I hoped he wasn't as frightened as I was at the drastic change of lifestyles. We learned later that boxing was his forte and he was in his time a formidable Army champion. For Peter and me barrack room life began to gradually change as the lads started to assert their senior status; how innocuous that sounds, but believe me it was going to get a lot rougher.

About this time there had been a great deal of dental chat by our roommates directed, obviously, at us and we unhesitatingly passed it on to the rest of the batch. The theme was the horrific dental experience which awaited us starting with a trip to the Dental Centre in Portsmouth. OK so far, indeed it made a day out, always remembering that at this time we were confined to Barracks and that all we were going for was a checkup. Once this visit was over the stories became ever more lurid, the pain of extractions and massive fillings requiring an eternity of drilling all callously carried out without anesthetics which macho Army dentists didn't bother with in the early 1930s. How our room mates relished these terrifying stories. So what happened after all these dire warnings - they were all true! We couldn't wait for the next batch.

The third week was a disaster for me. It all started with a vaccination. I can't remember which day but I think it was a Wednesday because that was the 'wad racket' day which needs an explanation. A wad is the Army vernacular for any type of cake or bun and a racket is, well, a racket, a means of making money. It wasn't strictly legal especially the system of credit and its subsequent collection but it worked like this: Boy Corporal Dix (who sadly died recently) and whose 'racket' it was, had a contact with some sort of bakery. If you had ever eaten from one you would know exactly what I mean by ' some sort of bakery'. Anyway, he bought cheap and sold at a profit. I have no idea what the profit margin was and nor had anyone else. Boy Corporal Dix was a very big and quite ruthless lad and his number two, George Eastlake, was even bigger, but come Wednesday evening when they came round with the wads and a big book and even bigger smiles they were very popular and once again, I have to repeat, we were always hungry. Friday was not so popular because George turned up with the book, no smiles and very large muscles and collected; it was known for some to try and disappear during the payup period. Painful and a total waste of George's time and energy.

I had bought a couple of wads and somehow I didn't really enjoy them, funny, but I remember this very clearly. I woke during the early hours and was a very sick young soldier indeed, I was vomiting uncontrollably between bouts of diarrhoea, and I could hardly stand. I managed somehow to clean up a bit and finally get back to bed but couldn't sleep. A couple of the lads had helped me clean up. In the morning Corporal McCollum took charge, made sure I was placed on the sick parade list and eventually I found myself standing in the front rank of a small parade, whereupon I promptly fainted; to this day I can clearly remember starting to fall forward. I came to on one of the beds in the small Medical Centre Hospital. I thought I was dying and strangely enough I was convinced that I was a victim of the wads.

There followed the usual routine: temperature, and pulse, followed by a decision to send me to the Military Hospital at Netley near Southampton and as quickly as possible. I was hardly aware of what was going on though I had certainly grasped the hospital bit and I was not reassured.

Of the journey by ambulance and my admission I remember very little, just vague impressions but I do remember a doctor examining me after I had been put to bed, some form of medication and then I slept through until the following morning though I vaguely recall some form of treatment by a nurse during the night. It wasn't until the evening that I began to be properly aware of my surroundings and, I suppose, to feel a little better. A nurse brought me a hot drink, fussed around me and then I went back to sleeping only interrupted by treatment and the usual bodily necessities. The next day showed a marked improvement. I began to eat and have a good look around. I was in a large ward which was full and though it didn't occur to me immediately the other patients were men. Hello, here we go again shifting the rules because there were no special wards for boy soldiers, a tribute maybe to our general health! One or two of the up patients came over for a chat, one of whom said, 'My goodness, they were worried about you when you first came in.' It's nice to be cheered up. I subsequently found out that when I thought I had simply been sleeping there had been quite a lot of nursing going on and two doctor's visits. So what the hell was wrong with me? Simple, it was called vaccine fever and for some reason I had reacted very badly.

The next few days were very interesting; here I was again, in a very different world indeed where discipline ruled with a rod of iron known more commonly as Matron, Lt. Colonel no less and a real tartar. All the nurses were of course Commissioned Officers and we had to pay them the normal compliments due to an officer. They were superbly dressed, looking every inch a nurse: careful though, is that a Lieutenant, a Captain or even a Major under that uniform? Of course like every other commissioned or non-commissioned rank they wore their badges of rank appropriately. Here I must confess they were a bit soft with me, obviously a mixture of my age and size and an onset of motherly love.

Mind you, what was the first thing I acquired when I got up, on I think, the fourth day, a room job! Ah well, I thought, nothing changes and in this case I had acquired responsibility for the sluice room, a glittering shining palace of spotless porcelain and polished brass and copper. In one corner was an equally pristine cupboard filled with metal polish, porcelain cleaner and neatly stacked polishing cloths. I was soon to learn that the Matron always homed in on this little cupboard. It had occurred to me when I first looked in that I had never before seen a metal polish tin with the same shine as its potential beneficiaries, nor had I seen polishing cloths that seemed to have been ironed before they were put away but then again I had not yet met the Matron. Still it certainly wasn't going to take a lot of cleaning which was fortunate because though out of bed I felt pretty poorly.

Being out of bed was not the happy road to recovery that one might imagine: the routine - wash and shave (not me of course) then breakfast brought by whoever had picked up this job and eaten at a large table in the centre of the ward, wash up and leave everything spotless, make your bed, oh dear! After a demonstration by one of the nurses I was left to get on with it but in the end a couple of the other patients did it for me. I really wasn't up to it and during this they explained about the Matron. I already knew that sometime during the morning she would appear and go through the ward with a fine-tooth comb, even sick as I had been I had watched this inspection, but what I didn't know was that she would check my ward job – the sluice room – and if she didn't like it might even put me on a charge but worse was the bed. The cover had a very distinctive geometrical pattern and the Matron had a specially made stick which measured whether or not you had arranged this pattern to her satisfaction. Of course we didn't have a stick, The lady duly arrived and to my surprise asked me how I was feeling and hoped I would soon be well again. My God, did I detect a little mothering? No, couldn't have been, I don't know though, even now I have trouble understanding the cerebral workings of the ladies.

Netley Hospital was a truly wonderful building with a fascinating history; famous for the length of the building, I believe. The corridors were a quarter of a mile long, an endless stretch of highly polished linoleum. It was purpose-built for the Army and situated with its own landing jetty enabling patients from wherever they were in the world and more importantly, casualties, to be off loaded at the jetty just a few hundred yards from the reception hall, itself a magnificent building situated exactly central and the whole set in really beautiful grounds.

Several days later I was passed fit and so back to the Depot and my roommates and of course rejoining my Batch. I had not missed much and indeed, apart from a sympathetic enquiry from the Drum Major I just slotted back in as if it had never happened. As in all cases of hospitalisation I was required to report sick on the first morning back where I met Col. Ridout for the first time, was passed fit and my sick report was stamped 'Medicine and Duty'.

And there was an end to a frightening and mostly unpleasant experience. It had also happened much too early for me to really cope. I was very homesick and down during my stay in hospital. Also I had not told my parents until I was out but they told me much later that they had been notified by letter almost immediately. And so the weeks passed: drill, sport, PT, lectures and the hours spent cleaning brasses, polishing boots and of course putting blanco on our webbing. It was several weeks before I bought another wad from the racket and to this day I always associate that illness fifty-fifty between the vaccine fever and the wad.

It took me a couple of weeks to get over my illness completely and though the time passed quickly enough there were times when I felt low, and more worrying, began to question why I had joined. During the first weeks there were instances of lads breaking down; however they soldiered on and the batch began to take on the appearance of soldiers. More importantly we had a become a fairly tightly knit little unit. My letters to my parents during this time concerned mostly my progress and were meant to reassure. I knew how worried they would be and anyway no way would I even suggest that the whole thing was a mistake. Apart from anything else I was determined not to lose face and possessed a stubborn enough streak to see me through the rougher patches. There were many of these but slowly the sense that this was a totally alien world was beginning to fade and more importantly both Peter and I were becoming barrack-wise; our situation in a barrack room of senior boys dictated this and mostly evolved into an ability to keep out of the way especially when our roommates had time on their hands and were looking to relieve their boredom..

As we approached the final weeks of our initial training we began to look forward to being free of the constant search for perfection in dress and on the parade ground and to being able to get a pass to leave barracks, and of course finally to start our technical training. We were certainly a very different bunch to the hesitant half scared lot that started five weeks ago – mind you we were still hungry, at least most of the time. During this period of training Peter and I had witnessed another facet of our lives, a regular event approximately every four weeks though this wasn't set in stone and much disliked; apart from anything else it could cost you money. I'm referring to kit inspections. These inspections had their own little rules and even a 'perk'. They entailed laying out all your kit on the bed where it would be inspected for smartness and also for any missing items. This inspection was carried out by the Officer in charge of Boys accompanied by Bill Ollier our own Sergeant (more about Bill later) and a representative from the Quarter Master, usually a Lance Corporal complete with his little notebook. I said it could cost you money.

This trio would go through your kit, having first taken in the general appearance; they would then inspect various items at random: boot studs, contents of housewife, socks for holes and even for a worn toothbrush. Any items deemed to require replacing and those lost would be entered in the Lance Corporal's little book and new ones issued the following week, the QM still reluctant to issue but mollified by the fact that we had to pay for it, this by some mysterious jiggery-pokery whereby it would disappear from our pay balance. There was, too, always the threat of being disciplined in some form or other, a loss of privileges such as being confined to barracks over the weekend; in the summer it could even result in having to roll the Sergeant's Mess tennis court with three or four other boys. This roller was easily the oldest in the country, the heaviest and the rustiest, never been oiled in its life; indeed to get it moving at all was a task of enormous proportion, to quote the old cliché 'been there, done that', and it was a real killer; even so there was one punishment where the reward made the work worthwhile, 'peeling spuds'.

To sit facing a huge sack of potatoes waiting to be peeled was pretty daunting but when you had done, the cooks would provide a whacking great plate full of bacon, eggs, chips, bread and 'butter' and a mug of tea. Have I mentioned before that we were always hungry? So what was the 'perk' for a smart kit? Simply to be excused the next kit inspection, worth much more than it sounds especially come the next inspection when you could couple it with a day pass; this was fine providing you had money in your pocket, if not, then you could always hang around the recreation room. Still it was better than laying out your kit! And how did they decide who might be the fortunate recipient of this prize? It was anyone whose kit they deemed to have that little extra; mind you it also depended on what side of the bed they had all got out on as to whether there was a perk for anyone. Minor infringements of discipline were always dealt with by 'fatigues', for example - spud bashing, Sergeant's Mess tennis courts, etc., or being confined to barracks over the weekend. More serious breaches of discipline resulted in being charged and depending on your glibness or the hopeful naivety of a young officer resulted in jankers. I know, we've seen that word before; never mind the laptop doesn't like it either; all will be revealed later.

All of this of course can seem trivial especially looking back so many years later but this sort of reward, and there were many others of the same, was based on one boy being a jump ahead of the rest. It was always generally assumed that 'bullshit' comes from above but really it originates at the bottom where 'poor innocent soldiers' were encouraged to compete with each other. I wonder who first thought it a good idea to polish the studs on his boots for a kit inspection, it certainly wasn't the RSM or indeed any RSM nor was it me though I have done it, wasted effort in my case. I never did get excused. There were other attempts to catch the eye: for example someone in the distant past had decided that the way to being excused was not only to fold your shirts neatly but to also pack them with carefully cut cardboard; this of course simply became standard practice. The inspecting Officers probably thought this showed an inherent desire just to be smart and was worth encouraging but the idea that they dreamed up this bullshit was ludicrous.

And so we approached the end of our initial training but were we now soldiers or still schoolboys? I am sure of one thing: we were not, at that time, wasting energy trying to arrive at an answer. Survival was still the game. Looking back we had changed, still prone to homesickness but considerably tougher and wiser. We could parade with the best and with great confidence and yet we were 'Nozzers', regarded as such by everyone and the status often hammered painfully home. No, there was still a long way to go before we could feel that we had become a real part of the Army and were indeed soldiers

I should at this point outline the system of discipline; this was common to everyone in the Army and was laid out in great detail in what was then 'Kings Regulations' from murder down to drunk and disorderly or even being late on parade. It was a vast document. I described earlier how minor breaches were punished by simple deprivation of privileges or some form of extra work. Moving onwards, we have the formal charge generally referred to as a 252. This was the number of the charge sheet. Beyond this were the Courts Martial, not of any concern to us at this stage. Apart from the minor breaches of discipline it was the formal charge which concerned us; there was no set type of offence which dictated whether or not you would be charged, but there were unwritten rules of behaviour which were well understood and you were well aware that stepping over this line would result in being charged.

Of course there was a huge grey area before this which depended entirely on the NCO making the decision, I would remind you of my remarks at the beginning: 'fair and sympathetic to out and out shit', so there was a big element of chance or at least up to a point, because as we became more and more 'barrack wise' if we felt it necessary to sin we would be careful to try and arrange it so if caught it would be by 'fair and sympathetic', not always possible but we were a canny lot and it was surprising how much we got away with. One of the pros for Peter and me as 'Nozzers' in a room of senior boys was to learn all this very much more quickly than the rest of the 'Batch'. Much of what I am trying to say about knowing your enemy was illustrated earlier, on my first reveille, when having been hounded unceremoniously out of bed by the Orderly Corporal we all got back in again and the boy next to me said 'He won't come back'; some did, with sneaky tactics, even so, though we had a sound dossier of their various methods they still caught us out and it was back to that bloody roller or worse.

This is probably the point at which I should talk about the Sergeant. In charge of boys, Bill Ollier, known amongst us as 'Spit in yer Eye Ollier' and I haven't the faintest idea why. He occupied the room on the landing between our room, J4 and J5. Looking back I can see he was something of an enigma; for example I never remember him charging anyone or even dishing out the minor punishments yet we were scared of him. Another feature of Bill was you could rarely find him but start a noisy skirmish on the landing and there he was in his room all the time. When we reached the sanctuary of our bed spaces the most common remark was, 'I didn't know

Bill was in,' somehow we never did. I think with hindsight he had delegated much of the discipline to Boy Corporal Reg Dix. Now there was someone to be frightened of: no charges, no minor fatigues but my God his brand of discipline could be very very painful. More of Reg, later, at this stage I hardly knew him apart from the 'wad' evening when he and his number one George Eastlake brought them round all smiles, civility and size as opposed to Friday when they were all size and menace. Whatever Bill's philosophy, it worked; he maintained discipline yet remained well liked by the boys. He was always approachable and yet one always felt that it would be a waste of time complaining about the brutal bullying that was part of our lives, inflicting or suffering. Yet who would complain; it would have shown a lack of 'moral fibre' or as it is known now being a 'wimp'. Loss of face was just as important in those days as it is now.

So here I was, square bashing behind me, entitled to apply for a pass to walk out; submit your application in the morning and if granted you would find it waiting for you at the Guardroom, but this was trivial compared with the anticipation of parading for work and being at long last introduced to the workshops.

I never did explain the shout of 'Stick man' that so frightened me as I stood in front of the Corporal Guard Commander long, long ago. When the Guard for the next twenty four hours paraded on the square they were inspected by the Orderly Officer who would select the soldier he judged to be the smartest and this was 'the Stick Man'. It was well worth the effort as it meant that he wouldn't be doing the marching up and down bit for two hours at a time; instead his job for the next twenty-four hours would be to act as the Guard Commander's messenger. A cushy number.

Writing this it becomes increasingly obvious how those first few months, even the first couple of years, were in essence a question of survival. So many pressures and in an already strange and often hostile environment. The Technical Training was very difficult and there were always the high standards to be met, often resulting in weeks of work being scrapped, the studies for the First Class Certificate of Education, ending only when passed, the constant intimidation and the need to be constantly wary and keep out of the way, not always easy. The bullying and often gratuitous violence were a constant threat. There was often much talk about 'working your ticket' by messing up your work in the workshops where upon you would be discharged on the grounds of 'no mechanical Aptitude'. I never saw it happen but what did happen was that you would be offered a posting to another Unit as a Band Boy. This I did see but not within my own 'Batch'.

So here I am, still battling on albeit a bit battered here and there, about to start my transformation into an Armourer but still a long way from being a Soldier. I have managed to grow a bit and, though still a small package, a pretty hard one. I no longer feel the weight of this alien environment, and with every day that passes this feeling of not belonging gets less and less. Monday will bring our introduction to the Workshops and goodbye to the worries about how smart you were for the first parade of the day and of course the square bashing. Hopefully, leaving the initial training environment will also improve our morale.

I suppose falling in for the march down to the workshops on that first Monday must have been something of a highlight but as always accompanied by that inevitable feeling of apprehension. It had arrived and here we were on our way, and plenty of time to think. It was a long march but I for one didn't care. Mind you, there would be many times in the future and the pouring rain when we had to double (run) back that I did care: it was further than I thought.

'Jankers.' This is a word known only too well by all who at sometime passed through the Services. Quite simply it is a punishment and could best be described as 'formal' as opposed to the casual awarding of tasks for minor infringements; remember the Sergeants' Mess tennis courts and the fearsome roller. As I said earlier, discipline was covered in great detail in 'Kings Regulations' or as it is now 'Queens' and to finish up on 'Jankers' meant that you had been formally charged by an NCO or Officer, the details entered onto a charge sheet 'Army Form Number 252', and you had subsequently appeared before an Officer at which appearance, having failed to talk your way out of it, you would be 'Confined to Barracks' for a specified number of days depending on the perceived severity of the offence. So for 'Confined to Barracks' read 'Jankers' 'How did you get on?' would be the standard query when you arrived back and the reply a simple figure such as seven days! meaning seven days 'Jankers'. So there is a summary of the word 'Jankers' but it dosn't end there. To be simply confined to Barracks for seven days would hardly constitute any sort of punishment but the reality was vastly different and varied throughout the Army. Every unit had its own version of what should happen to the soldiers serving a spell of 'Confined to Barracks'.

I can only speak for Hilsea Barracks and here your spell on Jankers would be dominated by the Bugle. Any duty NCO, Orderly Cpl., Orderly Sgt., Orderly Officer and of course the Guard Commander could summon anyone on Jankers by Bugle call. Remember my arrival and the Jankers call which so frightened me when the Stick Man said the call was probably something to do with me (it was to provide me with bedding etc. and of course to push the handcart and show me where to go). There were set times too when the Jankers call would be sounded where routine tasks would be waiting such as washing up in the cookhouse and scrubbing the floor. The first call for Jankers was at 0545 hrs and the last at 2200 hrs. This last was a killer as you were required to take all your kit down to the Guard Room and lay it out for inspection by the Orderly Officer. Irrespective of the set calls, you needed to have your ears constantly tuned because you were required to be at the Guard Room within minutes of any call. Jankers was certainly a pretty rough punishment.

CHAPTER 2
OH NO, NOT AGAIN

The workshops were situated about a mile away in the stores Depot and entailed a longish march including crossing the main Copnor Road. Cpl. Dix seemed to enjoy striding purposefully out into the road and holding up the traffic. There was a large gate and sign at the entrance with a security lodge on the left. Marching in to work we simply went straight through, but marching out, the party would sometimes be stopped and a percentage of us searched by the Depot Police.

As we marched through it was easy to relate to the history we had been taught during the preceding six weeks. The depot had been established in an area of former fortifications built in the mid 1800s to ward off possible attacks by the French. There were high earthworks lining the northern limits beyond which was a moat and the 'Creek' separating Portsea from the mainland. The earthworks were called 'bastions' and housed a number of storerooms, dank and unpleasant as I learned a couple of years later. Moving on through the depot, it was soon obvious that this was indeed a big area and in some ways, to me at least, a strange mass of sheds housing various stores, a main railway line and finally, at last, our training workshops: the Armourers' Training Branch or ATB. There were two large buildings with a large concreted area in front where we were halted. Our batch were ordered to stand fast whilst the remainder were dismissed. Looking around there were a number of smaller workshops into which groups of boys were disappearing. I remember noticing how these groups conformed to their particular seniority.

We were quickly marshalled into what was obviously a classroom where we were introduced to the Warrant Officer in charge of the ATB, Armourer Sgt Major (ASM) Dabbs who delivered a little welcoming talk, a modicum of advice -- work hard, keep your nose clean and all will be well. This type of advice travels very well, as I discovered many years later delivering it to a new batch at the ATB, long ago moved to Arborfield near Reading. We moved on to the large workshops and an area that was allocated to the first part of our training, learning how to use hand tools to a quite remarkable standard. The craftsmanship demanded was total and the learning was very hard physically and on occasions could be emotionally devastating as the senior lecturer dropped three weeks hard work in the scrap bin and even among barrack hardened boys tears were not unknown.

Once in the workshops we were divided between the instructors who would be responsible for our initial training. The name of my instructor was Bramble, Mr Bramble when speaking about him to another member of staff, military or civilian, but known amongst the boys as 'Oily Bramble'. Those of us allocated to Mr Bramble were considered to be unlucky: a hard taskmaster he certainly didn't suffer fools gladly but like the other instructors he was superb at his job. So here I was ready to start and as I had already learned, there was no time limit on this particular course. Each work piece that I would make needed to pass the Senior Instructor Mr Brickell; it was generally conceded that it really was easier to pass a camel through the eye of a needle than a work piece past Mr Brickell and without his little stamp, a star in the centre of a circle, stamped on the piece it was back to the bench with a vengeance. The time it took to complete my first course of training would therefore depend on how quickly I worked and what might be described as 'the turn back factor'. A good time for the fitting course was eleven months, a slow time fourteen months these factors, on all of the various courses, would set my final finishing date and indeed my seniority on the long promotion climb. It really was very important!

First then, my own vice on the bench with the height correctly adjusted (some of us needed duck boards to stand on), a collection of tools, mostly files but a square and callipers, a twelve inch rule, scriber, a tin of engineer's blue and of course a hammer and a cold chisel together with a box to put them in and the certain knowledge that losses would be paid for as always. There was also a very nasty looking length of square rusty looking steel bar plus a hacksaw with a well worn blade; nothing new here, we had all absorbed the horror stories from our peers, it had been a sort of 'blistering' tale. Mr Bramble described the steel in front of us as a piece of two by two inch bar of black mild steel and. the first thing we would do was to cut off a four inch length using the hacksaw. He then set a piece into the vice and taking his own hacksaw with what I suspect was a nice new blade he demonstrated how to use it. Gosh how nicely the blade cut. Now it was our turn and I couldn't wait to get started. I didn't at the time think about the significance of this start but it was the beginning of my real future, albeit a painful one; remember my remark earlier that the tales we had heard were inclined to be 'blistering' - well, here was the start of those blisters.

I had, in fact, some experience of hacksawing and filing and considerable experience of chiselling; this was due to my having worked for three months for an engineering company in their fitting department which involved a modicum of hacksawing and filing but the last month was spent cold chiselling the rough edges off castings, a process known as fettling and believe me by the time I left, handling a cold chisel was almost second nature and as the next piece we would make (a specialist rifle tool) involved our introduction to chiselling, I could hardly wait. Meanwhile I could recognise a worn out hacksaw blade when I saw it and promptly asked for it to be changed. This is when I learned that life might become difficult and went back to try and wear my way through two inches of steel.

It wasn't long before the blisters began to show whilst the cut deepened very slowly. I stuck it for the first day but fifteen minutes or so into the next day, I carefully broke the hacksaw blade. This may appear to be a small thing to do, in fact I thought it might be a rather dangerous act and I was in fact petrified at the thought of reporting my 'mishap' to Mr Bramble, especially as I had been the only one to complain the previous day. What followed left me surprised to say the least – nothing - Mr Bramble gave me a new one, muttered something like take more care but I was through that bit of steel just after the morning break. Once again I had made a good start and I little dreamed how good.

I was now ready to start on this the first project. The brief was simple: file it flat square and parallel but not to any particular size and using only files, a square and calipers. This turned out to be a savage introduction to the perfectionist standards that would be expected of us throughout our training; everything we did during our four years would be marked and the marks carried forward. We were next shown how to hold and use a file, finally starting to prepare one side, which would be the master from which all the other sides and ends would be squared. To this day I can remember the periods of utter despair trying to get that side flat but even more devastating was trying to get Mr Bramble to pass it and then the indescribable relief when it finally happened. Later there would also be a feeling of both achievement and pride. This struggle to satisfy went on until I was given permission to take it to Mr Brickell for his final approval, marking, and then stamping with the the little ringed star which in effect said I wouldn't see the damned thing again until the final day after saying my goodbyes. I think my time for the block was very good, about four weeks, five blisters and much improved profanity. Although this particular piece had no finished measurements I was soon to learn that all the others did, and that even using very basic tools, I would be expected to achieve measurements accurate to one or two thousandths of an inch. The little ringed star became ever more difficult to acquire.

Just after finishing my block and before I could demonstrate my skills with a cold chisel, disaster struck. I had been nursing an infection under one of my fingernails and the pain finally forced me to report sick. The doctor diagnosed a whitlow and prescribed hospital, Oh no, not again! I was devastated, just as everything was beginning to settle down and I was getting to grips with the routine of this new life, here I was sat (with the driver this time) in an ambulance on my way back to Netley hospital. As I sat there I was totally overcome with homesickness and was pretty close to tears. The driver tried to cheer me up but I felt sure he thought it was the pain that was getting to me never dreaming that what I really wanted was my Mum. Oh, how long ago it now seems. One thing I was spared, I didn't know what was in store for me on the following day. The ambulance driver took me through into the reception area where I was duly processed, ending up in one of the surgical wards on the first floor. Previously I had been on the second floor but I was too preoccupied feeling sorry for myself to care what the hell floor I was on but at least I knew the correct procedures for an 'up patient'. A few of the patients helped me sort my odds and ends and then I was collected by a young nurse, taken to her office where more paperwork was completed, then to a small surgery to have my dressing changed, a new sling, plenty of sympathy but most of all permission to go to bed directly after lunch.

I remember feeling awful at this time. I just couldn't stop shivering so I just went to bed. The nurse came along, gave me something for the pain, warned the other patients about noise. I smiled at that, no patient at Netley ever made a noise; it would have been a kind of suicide by 'Matron'. This was not strictly true, the occasional light but controlled scream was allowed on the surgical floor as was a discreet death rattle on all floors providing you didn't overdo it. They didn't encourage wimps at the Netley Military Hospital. Funny, somehow, the nurses seemed to fuss over me, I must have presented such a small pitiable imitation of a soldier that their usual brisk efficiency was overcome by a strange instinct called mothering, yet I wonder now, if they already knew about tomorrow.

Not a good night but one of the night nurses brought me a cup of tea about two o'clock with another couple of tablets and eventually I found myself returning from breakfast to be told they were going to fix my finger at ten o'clock and I was to go along to the treatment room, fifteen minutes before ten 'clock in pyjamas and dressing gown (they still hadn't found any hospital blues to fit me). Though very apprehensive, my finger was hurting so much that the surgery couldn't come quickly enough. A male orderly took me along and indeed into the operating theatre; here there were two more male orderlies, a more senior nurse, a Major I seem to remember and the surgeon all dressed for action. I was helped up onto the operating table which I certainly couldn't have managed myself, at least not without a ladder, I was still a pretty small package!

They arranged me in a sitting position with my hand laid palm down on a kind of packing; it felt rather like a sandbag covered with towels. The nurse took off the dressing and the surgeon looked at the swollen throbbing digit. One orderly tightened his grip on my wrist, the other on my shoulders. The surgeon said, 'Very nasty,' calmly sliced the nail down the centre, then tugged the two halves of the nail off working from the base. It was reasonably quick but not that quick. I had been badly hurt and I remember two things vividly: I really couldn't believe what had just happened to me and I was in a state of collapse. The surgeon said, 'Well done, lad,' the nurse seemed upset and the orderlies took me back to the ward where no one would believe me! The young nurse of the previous day came in and took me along to the treatment room, settled me in a comfortable chair, plied me with tea and loads of sympathy. I began to recover; my finger had stopped throbbing though it was still painful and I was already beginning to realise what a story this was and indeed I suppose, unbelievably, that I was feeling a little smug. Hell, I'm still telling it!

Back in the ward the truth was out and everyone wanted to know what it was really like to have a fingernail pulled out. For a little while I enjoyed the attention but as my stories became ever more lurid so the morning's events began to catch up with me, someone fetched the nurse and I was put to bed. 'Tomorrow' was over and I was glad.

In the morning, apart from a little pain I was my old self and once my bed was made (plenty of help there) and the Matron had been round I was free to explore the hospital, something I had not previously been able to do. This was to be the pattern until I was discharged, marred only by my once a day visit to the treatment room to have the dressing changed. There was plenty to explore. This was a very famous building. The corridors stretched for a quarter of a mile one end to the other, the floor covered in shining brown linoleum. It was never possible to get a clear view along the corridor as there were always people moving about but mostly there were small groups of patients who had fallen foul of the Matron and were bumping this linoleum (remember the bumper) known as 'MJ' or Matron's jankers. This architecture faded into insignificance compared with my next discovery: the notice board on the ground floor advertising a variety show in the hospital theatre a couple of days hence. The office clerk told me that all I needed was my Ward Sister's permission and with it an entrance card which she would give me. I lost no time seeking out this lady, a Captain by rank, and following a few sympathetic questions I had the card. I only vaguely remember the format of the show but it was very good or so it seems to have been, looking back.

The week passed quite pleasantly. I had been paid, much to my surprise, so it made a visit to the NAAFI worthwhile. I could walk in the grounds and this time I didn't have a ward 'job' but finally it came to an end with a visit to the surgeon, Major McVickers, who pronounced me fit and I was back in the ambulance on my way to Hilsea. In an autobiography like this names are the biggest problem but here was one name I have never forgotten and never will: indeed, some years ago, 1988 to be precise, whilst holidaying with my Girl in Portsmouth we went to Netley to see if anything remained. I knew the hospital had suffered a serious fire in 1963 and this lovely huge building, The Royal Victoria Hospital Netley, commissioned by Queen

Victoria in 1856 and opened in 1863, had been finally demolished in 1966 but the magnificent and very beautiful chapel survived and now serves as the Royal Army Medical Corps museum. Tucked away in the grounds on a wooded slope we found the poignant memories of this historic hundred years lying in the hospital cemetery, the graves dug randomly between the trees represented brave soldiers from many counties and shires and also from many countries. One of the volunteer ladies manning the shop was delighted to find an ex-patient from so long ago and unbelievably turned up my admission entries in a huge ledger. There I was, 7587328 Clement Hoyle, Boy Soldier, RAOC, not only once but twice. Asked what I remembered I said the name of the surgeon who tore my fingernail off without anaesthetic. Unprompted the lady said, 'That would be Major Mc Vickers,' we know a lot about the Major, a very good surgeon but not known for splashing anaesthetics about for your sort of problem.' Now she tells me! It was a very nostalgic afternoon.

Arriving back in J4, I had to start picking up the pieces again, not something to look forward to but first there was the same routine as last time: report sick and be passed fit for duty but when the Colonel had finished reading my discharge document, he looked over his glasses at me and simply said, 'I see Major McVickers has made a strong recommendation that you be granted sick leave, seven days suit you?' Funny but when I left the sick bay I hadn't the faintest idea what came next so I went to the Company Office with my news, still not really believing it. Three hours later standing on the platform waiting for the London train and ticketed to Halifax I believed it. When on earth was I ever going to get to grips with that cold chisel? –who cares, I was on my way home!

Though it was the last thing my parents expected after seeing me off only a few weeks previously, they were very pleased and I had a great week though I didn't enjoy wearing my uniform. At that time in Halifax any soldier seen out wearing a uniform would have been a great curiosity but a fourteen year old boy—come off it. As is so often the case, my parents thought it was wonderful.

All too soon the prospect of going back began to loom large in my thoughts and unfortunately they were all negative. I couldn't think of a single thing that I might be looking forward to but lots of things I was enjoying at home. I pushed open the door, dumped my stuff on my bed and looked round at the usual Sunday chaos: roaring fire, 'biscuits' scattered round, bodies everywhere, the usual hum of noise, someone shouting, 'Have a good time, Clem?' and suddenly I belonged; no matter how tough the future might be (and it was), this was to be my life.

Well, here I am once again at my vice, box of tools and a drawing of the 'Wrench Bolt Head' on the bench, clearly marked to show that four of the edges were to be chiselled – at last. After the preliminary preparation and marking out I was ready to be shown how to use a cold chisel. I think there were a couple more of Mr Bramble's class at the same stage. First make sure the head of the chisel was not damaged, that the blade was sharp, set it up in the vice and using the hammer in the box, chisel the steel away down to the line, this was a tapered shape where you had to pick up the cut a little way down and finish quite deeply to about a half inch. Mr Bramble demonstrated the first cut to be made then left us to it. By the morning break I had finished two of the edges completely whilst the other two lads were still struggling and were also suffering bruising and skinning of the thumb after missing the chisel and hitting their thumbs.I couldn't help them because I was using a totally different grip on the chisel which left the palm upwards and not the thumb. This grip was always used by boilermakers because it protected the thumb joint: a little more awkward to get used to but after my weeks of fettling castings it was natural and comfortable. I really shouldn't have felt so smug about it and retribution arrived immediately after break in a summons to Mr Bramble's desk. I still thought I was going to be praised for the speed and quality of my work - fool! After a thorough roasting I was told to go back and complete the job using the chisel as I had been shown. This I did but all those weeks of 'fettling' castings still asserted themselves and I was finished before lunch. This however turned out to be the last lucky advantage for me and, like the rest of the lads, from then on it was physically hard, very difficult and the blisters took a long time to heal. There was a sort of postscript to this chiseling episode: weeks later Mr Bramble was talking to me about the work generally and how we were all progressing when he asked me which firm I had worked for and how long had I been fettling castings. Apparently the way I had held the chisel was a sort of fettler's signature which he hadn't seen for a long time. I didn't think it wise to ask why he told me off at the time.

Meanwhile in J4 Peter and I were settling into the daily routine, a routine which probably hadn't changed since the 'Armourers Training Branch' opened at Hilsea. Blanco, Brasso and boot polish seemed to feature very large in most of our spare moments but I remember the thing we all hated most was the four evenings we spent in class, studying for our Army Certificates of Education. Passing our entrance exam had already qualified us for the third class certificate but we had to take the exam for second class and thence to the first class certificate. This latter was a vital qualification and was very important to my progress in the future and it was also very difficult, rating with the civilian School Certificate. The second class was relatively simple but introduced us to map reading as an academic subject, also a combined subject, history and geography and of course our old 'fiends' maths and English. Cleverly interwoven into this situation was a simple but very powerful carrot: when you passed the 'first', as it was known, you no longer had to go to school and believe me this was a powerful driving force and one I was much more conscious of than the future benefits to my career. The second class exam was held after a relatively short period of time and didn't present any real problems for the batch; the map reading had proven fairly straightforward and easy to pick up so it was then onto our studies for the first class certificate and a different kettle of fish this turned out to be; it needed hard work.

I suppose Saturday mornings were another of our pet dislikes; devoted to the RSM's parade the first hour comprised an inspection followed by drill, better known as square bashing. This in turn was followed by Religious Instruction, a kind of adult Sunday school. We were separated by our various denominations, each group marching off to their different venues. Now came morning break and a dash to the cookhouse for the inevitable mug of tea then back on parade for a final half hour. Sometimes the RSM would dispense with this and we were free to go. There were many theories as to why this should happen varying from the vulgar such as the RSM's success in bed that morning to the rather more prosaic one that he was anxious to get an early pint in the mess. Of course there was an official explanation, there always is, that he had been very pleased with the earlier parade. Ah well, as the saying goes, 'If you believed that, you would believe anything.' I myself found over the years and as I progressed through the ranks, heading for an early pint was almost certainly the winner. Of course the 'lucky in bed' was a non starter - oh, I don't know though - I think I'm treading dangerous ground here; after all my wife (63 years married plus three years courting) is editing this. As I move on through the years of this autobiography this wonderful lady will occupy much well deserved space and indeed could tell a story of her own about the conversion from Civilian to Army.

There was another ending to Saturday morning parades. Once a month there was a formal Church Parade complete with the Depot band. The whole of the Garrison were present and we marched off the square down to the church where the band played for the service, then back on parade where we marched back to Barracks taking in a couple of main roads and collecting quite a few spectators. Hello, was that my future wife I spotted? No, surely not. So this particular Saturday the last half hour was devoted to what was loosely referred to as practice for Church Parade, sometimes also serving to remind me that my white belt needed blancoing. The rest of Saturdays were our own, I could go out if I had applied successfully for a pass or I could just lounge about which could be risky for a Nozzer. Of course the football teams would be playing in the local leagues and I played right from the start having played good football at school and even Rugby League - they still got a small package but I was quick and experienced and pretty hard if I might say so. There was a recreation room, a few battered chairs, an even more decrepit table tennis facility, an old radio but it worked as far as I can remember; which reminds me that its principal use was for the football results which were well attended because of the sweepstake. I cannot remember who ran this but it was almost certainly one of the senior boys and if he was of normal stature but sharper to the main chance, then his number two 'collector and payer outer' would be big. Mind you, it wasn't rocket science: you paid your money, pulled out a team and if they scored the most number of goals you collected the Jackpot. Still, although the cost was very low, it was worth winning which I never did.

There were two other popular time fillers or at least popular among the more energetic. These were played on a large slab of concrete which backed onto the wall of the recreation room building. One consisted of two teams of three, four, or five with the goalposts chalked on the wall and stones for the other. The game was played with a tennis ball and was fast furious and somewhat dangerous especially during the disputing of a goal. It certainly sharpened up your reflexes, ball control and the ability to evade being jammed up against the wall. I still carry a scar to prove that my evasion wasn't always slick enough.

The other game was a kind of squash, this time played against the wall along which a line had been chalked, I seem to remember about head high. Again the game was played using a tennis ball and, quite painfully, a clenched fist. Usually contested between two boys but some times pairs, strangely, though bitterly fought out, there seemed to be much less acrimony. Although the first game was called 'Slab Football' and I'm sure that name will strike a chord amongst those ex Hilsea boys still battling the Slab Football of life, the other game never seemed to have a name. I can still feel the intense pleasure we derived from these simple games.

So this was Saturdays, certainly at this point in my new life, the evenings I've already described – big fire, and a crowd round it sprawled on 'biscuits' trying to toast our two slices of bread or even aiming at cheese on toast using the coal shovel and our tea time piece of cheese (always on Saturdays) sliced as thinly as possible. A dodgy manoeuvre this one, believe me, a bit like trying to barbecue a steak surrounded by vultures.

And Sundays! Once again I was settling in to a regular Sunday routine and again it wouldn't really change throughout my Boy Service. The mornings were taken up with Church; three weeks were on an informal basis, simply parading and marching down to the church, then after the service, the day, like Saturdays, was free. The leisure activities of course depended on the time of the year and this being winter they were the same as Saturday. Every fourth week there was a formal Church Parade with all the trimmings. One aspect of Sundays is worth recording: for our evening meal we got a pat of butter instead of margarine; speaking personally I could never work up any real excitement at the prospect of a small pat of butter instead of margarine but it was Sunday and so butter it was.

The other alternative on weekends was to apply for a pass. Again our status in terms of service meant that there were limitations on the type of pass we could submit. Later it was possible to get an all day pass for Saturday or Sunday and dodge the normal routine but even then there was a strict ruling that you must be out of barracks by nine thirty, this to prevent people putting in for a pass just to dodge the Saturday parades. Very crafty, but though passes had to be picked up at the guardroom on the way out there must have been a loophole somewhere because it was common practice not to be out in the morning and I never remember anyone including myself being nicked for it. During the winter there was not a lot to go out for unless you had a bit of money in your pocket and you could maybe go to the pictures (cinema). Money was always short so these occasions were rare and usually prompted by a windfall from home; this you kept quiet or risk being pestered by would-be borrowers.

Monday again and back to the workshops. I really looked forward to this, my work was going well and my first 'proper' job had gone through the senior instructor's fierce marking first time and had been stored away wherever Mr Brickell stored away the finished work. So there it was, I had made my first specialist Armourer's tool, a 'Bolt Head Wrench'. Mind you, that is not how the Army stores vocabulary works, so it would be correctly called a 'Wrench, Bolt Head', spot the difference? Yes backwards more or less. What can I say about Mr Brickell? He was a fine craftsman especially with a file, so much so that certain of his favourite files were described by the boys as 'putting on files'. Strict though he was, if he could squeeze a job through by a little touch here or there and he was in the right mood then he would do so. If you had been struggling for a couple of weeks trying to get a part of the work right and finally your own instructor had given permission for you to try and get it past Mr Brickell then prayers were definitely in order. If the work was well done except for a couple of dimensions, maybe two or three thousands of an inch or maybe a surface you couldn't get quite right, then you were in with a chance that Mr Brickell would work one of his miracles with one of his little 'putting on files' and there was his pass stamp, a star within a ring, looking out at you from the work. How important this pass mark became in our lives is difficult to describe but it was the definitive measure of how quickly you were progressing through the fitting course.

I feel that I ought to say something again about how exacting the standards were and how difficult to achieve. Fitting is a good place to start. Only hand tools were allowed; even rounds had to be filed by hand just as Armourers had done down through the centuries, and holes drilled using hand drills. This could be long and tiring and it could easily be ruined by whoever you asked to keep the horizontal plane correct. This he would do by bending down and using his eye to judge whether the drill was level or not. Of course we all did this for each other. All threads were cut by taps and dies. I suppose ninety per cent of my work was done with a file. All flat surfaces had to be absolutely flat as tested on a surface table. The level of dimensional accuracy was savage, one or two thousands of an inch and all with a file, the finish also had to be produced with a damned file. Writing this brings so many despairing moments back when I had convinced myself that I simply couldn't do it.

The weeks passed and the number of finished tools was slowly growing and more importantly I was getting ahead with a good chance of an eleven-month finish. Barrack life too was slipping by and I was becoming well integrated; schooling was going well though still top of my dislikes as it took so many evenings away and we were moving into the spring. Weather was warming up, evenings getting longer and routines were changing but not by very much. During these months I had been introduced to several methods that were employed by the boys in the room to combat boredom, not all of them to be enjoyed by 'nozzers'.

Room Olympics: now that will be well remembered by any old boys from Hilsea who might be reading this. Comprising mostly sprints and hurdling it was exciting and dangerous. I recall one of the sprinters, failing to stop, at least until the window intervened, meriting a good number of stitches and some very fast talking to the medical staff, but the real prime event was the table hurdling. How we enjoyed this, at least those of us not doing it, waiting for the inevitable crash and hopefully a broken limb or two. It never happened, plenty of crashes but just severe bruising and this was entirely due to the carefully thought out landing zone—the fireplace! There was a kind of cheating allowance in which they could start their run from across the landing; remember they were hurdling this table lengthways. Great if painful days and certainly not for the faint hearted and that's just the spectators. A boy called Barnard was the best exponent of this particular lunacy. I didn't ever see him miss and I somehow felt that he had a kind of rapport with the fireplace. The tremendous crash never seemed to bother him though it bothered the lad whose room job it was; you could hear his voice above the general cheering pleading with Barnard and the other competitors not to bleed in his fireplace. Please note that I said 'his fireplace'; we all regarded whatever our room job was as ours. In my case I owned the wash house or at least half owned it with one of the J3 boys.

There was another very risky activity, a real challenge this one even though it always ended in failure and if I might say so very painful failure. This particular event grew out of the design of our beds, made up of two completely separate halves that were designed in such a way that it was possible to tip the bed up, irrespective of whether it was occupied or not, by simply lifting the front high enough when the bed would collapse in the centre. Again the construction meant that no great strength was needed. As you can imagine this disastrous weakness in design meant that anyone passing my bed, especially when settled and me a Nozzer, could simply tip me out. It got very wearing after a time.

But back to the challenge. Timing was of the essence after lights out and when you judged the room next door, J3 were asleep. Why am I saying this? Hell, it didn't matter when you timed it, you would fail. These attempts were made in pairs and at a given signal you would fling open their door - shit! where did that obstruction come from? - and dash down the room, one each side, tipping beds then a desperate sprint back to get out before they realised what was happening, no chance! So here we were, my mate and I, trapped in J 3, who were very senior boys. Funny how the more senior they were the bigger they were. Only one thing could save you now and that was for Bill Ollier, Sergeant in charge of boys and occupying a room on the landing, to come storming out and chase everybody back to bed. Oh Bill, why were you always out when I needed you? Sitting for the next few days was going to be painful; yes, I know, you thought the walking out cane was for walking out - wrong again.

There was another strange sort of brutal game we played. It had a name but I can't remember what it was and I know it wasn't unique to Hilsea. A couple of lads had their backs against the fireplace (not the fireplace again); four or five others would then form a kind of scrum against these two and the final objective of the other side was to run in as far as possible, hurl yourself into the air and land on the scrum, each member of this attacking team gradually piling up until the scrum collapsed. How was it scored? Bumps and bruises, I suppose but maybe the scorers of the Eton wall game might know. Though I was small and lightly built I had always been very much involved in sport, football, cricket and even rugby, at least, rugby league, playing for my school teams. This in turn meant a certain amount of participation in these lunatic activities and to this day I still carry a couple of scars but then, didn't we all. Great if bruising days, certainly not for the faint-hearted.

Of course much of this was born out of boredom, especially on those blank evenings in the winter. During the week there was school and other pressing activities, workshop notes, for example, taken during the day in the rough and rewritten at night or at any time as long as it was your time. The big worry for us Nozzers was that this boredom often sparked a form of bullying always painful and totally unavoidable.

The ever popular favourite was the 'Court Martial'. This involved setting the scene to mimic a Court Martial room i.e. the table covered with a blanket, the form behind, and situated, yes, you got it first time, in front of the fireplace. There was a proper cast: Judge Advocate, Court Officers (really the jury) Prosecuting Officer, Defending Officer, oh and of course, a defendant (or if you prefer and I certainly do, a victim), plus the public or howling mob, again whichever you fancy. I was lucky enough to stand in the dock only once, charged with having a Regimental Number different to everyone else in the Army – no chance of an acquittal there! Punishments could vary including such old favourites as pushing a matchbox along a chalked line with a wallop from a 'walking out cane' every time you pushed it off the line. Mine was very clever, comprising a form and a fire bucket full of water. I lay along the form, quite voluntarily with just a token resistance, it was easier that way, head hanging face down over the bucket. Here comes the clever bit, tipping the form on end, feet up, head down and with a bit of luck and a lot of banging of my head and assorted bits you would eventually get ducked in the water. I did say it was clever, I never said that it was refined.

There was a more cruel punishment meted out assuming you had been caught doing something against the code which could include refusing to do something as a Nozzer when told to do so by a senior boy. Most people are familiar with the expression 'Catch 22' and assume it had its origin in the well known film of that name, but wrong, it originated at Hilsea, courtesy of the two most senior boys not too remote from the wad racket, and went something like this. You would be invited to present yourself in their room, sit on one of their beds and you would be asked a simple question by one or the other, 'Is George better looking than I am?' There were three answers: 'Yes' and a howl of protest from Reg followed by a whack from his walking out cane: 'No' and ditto from George; ah, you might think, go for diplomacy and suggest that they are both as good looking as each other: following loud protests about being compared with that ugly ape, a whack from them both. So there you have it, 'Whack 22'.

In the workshops I continued to keep up the pace and felt more and more confident of my growing skills; also there was the blacksmiths' and tinsmiths' course to look forward to. Apart from anything else this would provide a welcome break from the interminable filing. But this was still well into the future. A much more important event loomed, the Easter leave. This was a short leave of a week and whilst most of the boys got away home for it there were a handful of us who because of distance and cost and the inability of our parents to finance it – these were the depression years – were unable to go home. So we were moved into one barrack room, J1 as I remember. There being only four or five of us I presume it was to keep us together for general convenience but it also meant that no one was stuck in a room by himself. The really great thing about the rest of the leave was that we were left completely to ourselves: no bugle calls to answer, the bugler could sound reveille forever and we could just ignore it; day passes had all been issued allowing us out until ten o'clock at night and we had a little extra money in our pockets. This had been accumulated for leaves and was standard procedure for boys. Meals of course were the usual times but we really could just lounge about to our heart's content – I loved those short leaves.

Although the summer months did not change the pattern of workshops and barrack life it did have a major effect on our leisure time. Sport consisted mostly of athletics: I never understood why cricket was not played by the boys; maybe it had something to do with cost or even lack of any general enthusiasm. The recreation which dominated was swimming. I wonder how many of us are left who can remember diving off the railway bridge where it passed over the 'Creek', none of us at all perturbed by the fact that the line was electrified. The beach at Southsea was a possibility but too far away to be reached without the price of a bus fare or a bike. I did walk it a few times but it wasn't practical just for a swim. The other alternative was an outdoor pool at Stamshaw, free and within walking distance but it was kind of unsavoury. I'm probably striking more memory chords. Having painted this picture of much activity I must confess that mostly we were dedicated to lounging about and even a little sunbathing.

Well, here it was at last, the summer leave period and I wish I could remember how long this was, I'll settle for three weeks but something nags at my memory suggesting it was in fact two. A great aura of packing up, last day in the workshops, collecting that all important pay, the groans when it wasn't as much as expected, hell it, never was, those bloody barrack damages again, surely we hadn't broken that many windows packing our cases and finally arriving at the Portsmouth station and in the first two years claiming a child's fare but after that more difficult to get away with.

I went into a theatre as sober as could be,
They gave a drunk civilian room, but 'adn't none for me;
They sent me to the gallery or round the music 'alls,
But when it comes to fightin', Lord, they'll shove me in the stalls.
For it's Tommy this an' Tommy that, an' 'Chuck him out, the brute!'
But it's 'Saviour of is country' when the guns begin to shoot,
An' it's Tommy this, an' Tommy that, an' anything you please,
An' Tommy ain't a bloomin' fool – you bet that Tommy sees!

Rudyard Kipling.

Two of us, heading for the North, and in uniform, got into a carriage (non corridor) which was partly occupied, with four or five people, plenty of room, but as we sat down they simply got up and left to find another compartment. Somehow we both knew and at this distance in time I can only say, 'Bloody hell, we were barely fifteen years old.' We learned later that a Service uniform often provoked this reaction though I never encountered it in the north of the country. How ironic that in five years time those words of Rudyard Kipling would once again ring absolutely true. So what of the holiday? A wonderful time but all too soon I was standing outside the Portsmouth station looking for a bus.

Life in Barracks continued along the same well trodden paths, second class education certificate exams came and went, no one had problems there but now into study for the first and this was a different kettle of fish: no respite from evening classes until we passed with the addition of three set books to be read and studied for English Literature. One was a good read at any time called *Breathless Episodes from Fiction*, but the other two, Scott and Thackeray, were difficult in the extreme not helped by trying to read them in a barrack room though this problem was basically recognised by everybody. Anyway we, were all struggling with these two books.

At last our turn for the blacksmith's workshops came around. I cannot remember how many could be accommodated, I think it was six, and of course it depended on how many fires were available. And so to Monday morning and our first meeting with possibly the most popular instructor, certainly a great character and a wonderful blacksmith. To watch John Sullivan work could only be described as an experience. After the preliminaries we were shown how to light and maintain the correct fire for the type of forging we were doing and how to keep the hearth clean. Mr Sullivan then forged a taper onto the end of a piece of round bar showing us how to use the hammer and angle the work piece and most important of all how quickly he did it with a minimum number of times that the work was returned to the fire. The quality of any forging depended on this factor and though Mr Sullivan had emphasised it, we were to learn the truth the hard way as we later struggled to get that little ringed star stamped onto our work.

I feel at this time it might be worth while to dwell on this phase of our training. Firstly it was obvious to us that learning to be blacksmiths must be something of a waste of time; when the course came around there was always much discussion on this point. We all had some idea of the trade set-up of the Armourer's craft and as far as we knew the only place one would encounter a forge, portable or fixed, would be in a large base type workshop in which case they would have their own fully qualified blacksmiths already on establishment. There was the horse transport element;

remember, at this time the Army was still not mechanised and most of the day to day stores movement was by horse and cart. This meant lots of harness with lots of link steel chains which we were supposed to be able to repair by forge welding new links; maybe we did do it in the distant past but certainly not any more. My own personal feelings were very simple. I took to forging like a duck to water. I loved every minute of it and even sounded out the possibility of changing my trade to blacksmith, a non starter that, so when the 'it's a waste of time' arguments were being aired, I thought, 'Who cares?'

Is there a sequel to all this? I'm glad you asked. Thirty years later I started work as a Lecturer in Mechanical Engineering at the Carlisle Technical College and in the workshops I found a nice little blacksmith's forge needing maintenance but very well equipped. I could almost see John Sullivan fussing around in his little leather apron. It transpired that the students were required to forge two items, a cold chisel which was pretty straightforward and relatively easy but also one jaw of a pipe wrench and this was not an easy exercise, indeed without some training as a blacksmith I would suggest impossible.

I spent a couple of hours cleaning up the forge but most importantly re-forging many of the various tongs which couldn't possibly have held the work piece. I also made up a selection of rings to hold the tongs in place and under pressure whilst working the steel. I then worked out the correct method to achieve the shape of the awkward jaw and was ready to go. The next day I demonstrated to two students by forging both items, started them off on that old favourite of John Sullivan's – the taper - and left them to it. At various times during this one or two of the lecturers had wandered in to watch, resulting in my agreeing to take the students for forging, irrespective of which class they were from. Over the years I did a lot of forging some for myself some for other people and I never lost my enjoyment of bashing a red hot piece of steel into more or less the shape I wanted. So here was one Armourer whose blacksmith's course was not wasted.

Back to the blacksmith's and the other part of the course, learning to solder. This involved making a round tin box. For me it was just something that got in the way of the second half of the real course. This time we learned to forge weld, something of an extinct craft now. It was like learning to ride a bike: I think I got through fifteen feet of wrought iron before I got my first link to weld and after that they all welded, don't ask me why. All the boys had the same experience, the only difference was the length of wrought iron before the first success. I think in our batch the record was thirty-two feet. Mr Sullivan would discuss the forging and welding of a link during the last hour before lunch. I remember as if it were yesterday. He laid great emphasis on the cleanliness of the fire. 'A dirty fire makes welding much more difficult, and if you get lead in the fire it is impossible.' We were always expected to get our fires and Mr Sullivan's fire lit before he came back from lunch so we lit his fire, popped two sticks of lead solder in and stood back looking as if butter wouldn't melt in our mouths. 'Gather round,' and we did; the wily old fox then proceeded to forge a perfect link, put it in the vice and twisted it until it broke, but not at the weld and said, ' Right, get on with it; oh, and would one of you clean the solder out of the bottom of my fire.' Again we were following an age old trail where nothing was new.

The final part of the course was to forge more complicated shapes which included lock parts for a Vickers gun and spring blanks that would eventually be turned into 'V' springs for pistols. After completing the Blacksmith's course it was back to trying to finish the programme of specialist tools we were making, in as quick a time as possible. This still depending on getting the work right first time.

The barracks routine continued in much the same way, and as time went by I became more and more confident and 'barrack wise' but most of all I was feeling very much at home and looking forward to Christmas leave knowing that when I returned I would no longer be a Nozzer. One thing at this point that I haven't mentioned was the Physical Training, twice a week and fairly straightforward. During the summer some of the sessions would be done on the sports field where the staff took the opportunity to weigh up any potential athletes but basically it was a chore which we didn't enjoy especially as it took half an hour out of two of our lunchtimes although we did finish early in the workshops. The PT at this time consisted of straightforward exercises, pretty hard but mostly pretty boring and I think some of our dislike of PT had its origins here. However things were to change in the coming year with the retirement of the Sgt Major Physical Training Instructor or for short the PTI and the arrival of PTI Walker who would figure very largely in our lives later on.

A month before Christmas about six of the batch, myself included, reached the end of our fitting course and with great relief were ready to move on to what we regarded as the 'proper' training and went from the fitting workshop into the first of our rifle classes. Known as 'Rifle one' it entailed learning all there was to know about the .303' Short Magazine Lee Enfield Rifle which of course was the standard issue rifle, always shortened to SMLE. How to strip it down to the last nut and bolt and, surprise, how to put it back together - very useful this latter skill. Then there was the board. We were to get very familiar with these boards, not 'happy familiar' either. Each board had every component of whichever piece of equipment we were studying at the time, in this case the SMLE, fixed to the board and under each component the name or more correctly the 'nomenclature' was printed. These parts were all removable and yes, you've guessed, we had to learn them by heart. The instructor would jumble them together and you had to pick up each part then name it correctly and put it back on the board. Until we could each do this there was no way forward. We now had to learn how the mechanism worked, write the sequence out, then later copy it in to our number one notebook as we did with all subsequent notes and drawings. These notes were done in the barrack room and they were very important because at the end of our training and when we were doing our final exams these notebooks were marked and the marks counted towards your final result.

No repairs were taught or attempted in 'Rifle one' but the use of the various gauges was practised and also the correct way to view a barrel: both eyes open and look into it, not through it, the various blemishes were also described but no attempt was made to try to view these defects. I was to find this a very difficult art to master when we were finally introduced to it in 'Rifle two'.

Christmas came and went and it seemed no time at all before I was back in J4 again and my first year was over - just don't call me Nozzer, the heavy brigade was on my side now! I could hardly wait to send some Nozzer, preferably a big one, to the NAAFI for me. Not really, but it was a nice nasty feeling if you'll pardon the paradox.

During this year past there had been a sensational development involving the 'wad' racket. A couple of the Boys set up a rival racket involving buying branded chocolate bars from a cut price shop called the Chocolate King and like Reg and George selling them on tick, collecting on pay day. The chocolate bars were infinitely preferable to the wads and so they flourished for about three weeks and then as quickly as they had started they just stopped. No one ever knew why and it didn't pay to probe. As remarked before, the wad racketeers were big lads.

Life in the barrackroom changed very little. I felt that we were maybe a little more secure from the 'boredom' syndrome which inevitably led to some form of physical pain, and during the past year that had been nearly always us 'Nozzers'. I had carried my quota of bruises from time to time. The summer of course stopped the 'orgies' round the fire: apart from anything else there wasn't a coal issue in the summer. I think we all missed this ancient ritual. Late evenings could be tiresome, as the light nights induced a reluctance to go to bed though the Orderly Officer would sometimes attempted to interfere but they were just young Lieutenants and soon learned better.

Money, as always, was a constant problem but a few of the boys found a lucrative source by 'Adopting a S/Sgt'. During the thirties the RAOC had introduced a recruiting system whereby Engineers who had the appropriate technical qualifications and could pass a trade examination including practical and academic skills were invited to join the RAOC where they were fast tracked by starting their Army career as S/Sergeants Gosh, how we envied them.

They came to the Depot as raw recruits and completed their first few months as had we, being turned into soldiers. Unlike us and because of their rank they were accommodated separately, each having a 'bunk' or room to himself. They were a truly pathetic lot and somewhere along the line some bright lad had the idea of offering himself as a batman (no, not the flying type,but the uniform pressing, brass polishing blancoing type). I have no idea who started this but because of the strict segregation rules between men and boys it must have been pretty fraught, even dangerous. Anyway it soon became general and was known as adopting a S/Sgt. For five shillings a week (the going rate) you contracted to do all his uniform cleaning and pressing. Some of these raw recruits suddenly seemed to be older soldiers than was possible. I never did it myself, there were only a few of them and I don't think I knew how the approach was made in the first place. Mind you, I often wished I had; it was always difficult trying to borrow money from one of these entrepreneurs, but come to think of it, it was sometimes a damned sight harder paying it back.

But here was Christmas looming again and the end of another year. It hardly seemed possible. There were always difficult times when I felt low and would question what I was doing in this situation and more upsetting was the feeling that time was dragging much too slowly and then suddenly it was Christmas again. I still pondered the question 'Am I a Soldier yet'? Not by a long way. A little more barrack wise and pretty quick on my feet when boredom loomed amongst the lads of J4 but a Soldier? No.

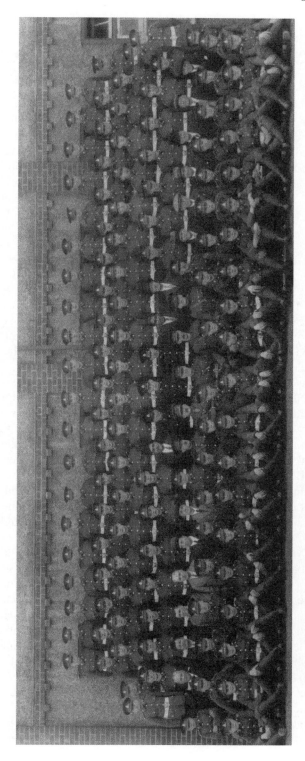

ARMOURERS TRAINING BRANCH
SCHOOL OF INSTRUCTION
RAOC HILSEA 1936

CHAPTER 3
AH WELL, NOTHING BLOODY CHANGES

As I sat on my bed surveying the chaos and listening to the chatter, the bugler sounded a familiar call, 'jankers'. Funny how at the first notes of the Regimental call the noise dropped quite noticeably until the call was finished then the chatter resumed. Someone shouted, 'Ah well nothing bloody changes,' and once again I was back but was I really a soldier yet? Not a good time to ponder this with the Christmas food and cosseting still so fresh in my mind and anyway how would I know and when? Mind you, there were a number of NCOs who were only too willing to offer an opinion, mostly profane.

Buglers and bugle calls have been something of a feature so far so I think it only reasonable that I should try and fill out this feature of our boy service at Hilsea. There were I think about six buglers and they were accommodated together in one room. Surprisingly we got on very well together with no more rivalry than existed between rooms. They were recruited as were we by competitive exam, and entered the RAOC for training as storemen or clerks; indeed this is what the RAOC did: supply the Army with equipment and repairs. I have no idea how the Regimental Bugler came into this equation but, whilst they learned their trade they provided the Depot with its Regimental Buglers.

They were trained by L/Corporal Bert Hollinsworth who was responsible for the drums and bugle section of the Depot Band. I think he came originally from the Brigade of Guards. I well remember this name but again the reason is in the future. Once they were considered proficient, they would be put on the twenty-four hour guard, firstly with another senior bugler and after that they would do the regular Guard duty, the interval between, of course, depending on how many of them there were to share this duty. Because of this regular duty they didn't do any of the other parades or barrack duties, only of course the monthly church parade with the band. Finally, if you were looking for the epitome of smartness then look no further than the bugler joining and the one coming off the twenty-four hour guard, immaculate! A bugler, by the way, went under the nickname of 'Badgie', I know not why.

So a new year stretched ahead. In barracks nothing much would change; there would be new batches of course but the tenor of our lives would follow the same pattern. The workshops though would be different, constantly changing courses as we moved from one type of weapon to another. An Armourer was basically responsible for the repair of all small arms from the 3" mortar downwards and also for bicycles and band instruments. The Armourer was also expected to look after optical instruments which included telescopic sights, angle of sight instruments, range finders, compasses and indeed, to show my age, heliographs, used for signalling and at that time doing sterling work on the North West Frontier - good heavens not Afghanistan again - and on the same lines Cavalry swords and lances, I nearly forgot those items.

Back to the workshops and having just completed 'Rifles one' we now moved onto 'machine guns one'. These comprised at this time only two types, the Lewis gun which was the standard Army light machine gun and had seen much service, (there was a new type on the way but it had not yet arrived), and of course the famous Vickers heavy machine gun. This gun is almost certainly still being used somewhere in the world, but of course it was used to devastating effect during World War One. So here were two battle hardened veterans waiting to test our powers of memory. The parts boards looked enormous but it was how they functioned and had to be learned by heart and recited back to the lecturer plus notes and drawings of the quite complex mechanisms that were to really put us under pressure, always remembering that everything we did was marked and the marks carried forward to our final examinations nearly three years hence.

We were at this time very busy. The workshops were straightforward enough but back in the barrack room there were so many chores to cope with, it always seemed that there was something waiting to be done. School in the evenings took a good deal of our time; there was kit to be cleaned, workshop notes and drawings to be written up as carefully as possible, the two set books for our English literature, *Old St Pauls* and *Woodstock*, really a difficult pair to read and, of course, our inevitable room jobs. A haircut once a week (Wednesday after work and before our half day for 'sports'), a shower or bath during the period when the bath house was open for Boys. Mind you, there were still room Olympics, courts martial, slab football, swimming and even sometimes going out. Looking back, it isn't easy to decide how happy or not I was during this second year but I certainly wasn't miserable.

Meanwhile I progressed through the various workshop courses from machine guns to pistols where in addition to our theory we were reunited with the spring forgings we had made during our blacksmith's course. These were to be made up into V-shaped main springs for the two types of pistol issued to the Army at this time: the big .45" revolver, a very long lived pistol with a distinguished pedigree, reliable and certainly packing a wallop, and its successor, a smaller version really of the big one, differences of course the calibre to start with, 38", and certain engineering changes. The two springs for example were different but not that much; anyway we were now required to make one of each. This part of it proved straight away the value of the previous year and the high standards that had been set; filing and shaping them to the correct V shape proved the least of our worries. Having completed the spring we hardened and tempered it (a new technique this but well tested) and submitted the finished article to the Pistol Instructor Mr Humphreys. Three things happened: first he would put the spring between the jaws of a pair of blacksmith's tongs and squeeze it flat and it would shatter into several pieces, but maybe not, so secondly he would release the pressure on the spring and the damned thing would just lie there, flat. Thirdly it would spring out to its correct shape and so would your hopes. Mr Humphreys still however had a killer move to deploy: he would put it into a pistol, cock it, compressing the spring fully, then lock it in his drawer until the following morning. Quite cruel, this.

And so to the next morning and there was a good chance your spring was OK. Great relief and it just remained to finetune the tension weight, then Mr Humphrey's 'pass' star stamped on and another quite tricky hurdle behind me. Many claimed that failures were due to the hardening and tempering process but the real cause was over-forging and as I said earlier it would catch up with you and here it certainly would. Myself? Well, I loved forging and in truth it was always my best discipline so my springs were fine first time and strangely enough the only thing I have left from all those hard years is my .38" main spring complete with Mr Humphrey's little 'star'.

On to bicycles. This too was a starter course, learning about the stripping and assembling, how the rear brake hub worked by simply back pedalling, in general use not a success. There was also the serious business of learning how to lace up a wheel given the rim, the hub and the spokes and then to true it; this art needed practice but it was not particularly difficult. The most interesting aspect of the Bicycle workshops, however, if you discount the eighteen hole golf course beautifully crafted on one of the very long benches by some long forgotten class and played with great seriousness using a spoke and a quarter ball bearing, was the instructor Mr Hull. He was unkindly nicknamed 'Jesus' because of his constant attempts to make us 'See the light' as he would express it. A gentle and tolerant, man sadly much put upon by the boys but I think we all had a soft spot for him. Once again the course had produced its quota of notes and drawings.

The range course was next and we were all excited about it; after all we were going to get to shoot a .22" calibre rifle. I don't suppose any of us thought of how much the ability to shoot well would be so important, I certainly didn't, I was just itching to get my hands on a rifle with real ammunition in it. This course was run by Mr Erskin. known throughout the Army shooting fraternity and the whole of the Ordnance Corps as ' Sandy'. He was an ex Staff/Sgt who left the Army with a wonderful record of competition shooting and came to Hilsea as the range instructor, and yes he was an Armourer and an 'ex Boy'. I was a little in awe of Sandy.

The training was run from the thirty-yard test range which followed the architecture of all the test ranges throughout the large Ordnance workshops at home and abroad. The Hilsea range did have a small extension which was to cope with the need for lectures. The length of the range was tightly controlled and this ensured uniformity of testing throughout the Army. The first day we spent familiarising ourselves with the general layout of a range: how the test targets on a continuous roll were set up and in the range house the very elaborate Enfield Rest designed to reproduce the effects of the human anatomy whilst never tiring. It was a huge and very heavy piece of engineering but again it ensured that all test results on the rifles were produced to the same parameters. Sighting was done with a telescopic sight specially designed for the Enfield Rest. We were allowed to sight a rifle and of course Sandy could easily check the accuracy of this by simply peering through the sight but all I wanted to do was test it by firing the damned rifle, not this time, sadly.

From this point on there were lectures on various aspects of zeroing weapons after they had been overhauled, which ensured that a gun would place five shots in a 1"x1½" rectangle proving that it would group to the set standard and the group would be central. Should a weapon fail then it went back to the workshops with a rejection slip but over and above all this were Sandy's safety lectures, leaving us all in no doubt as to the importance of conducting ourselves safely at all times. Tomorrow, however, we were to get our first taste of shooting; I could hardly wait!

At last here we were, .22" rifles laid out (these were the SMLE, rifle converted to shoot the smaller calibre giving a genuine feel of the 'real rifle'). The targets were scaled down versions of the full size targets, with the same colour and same aiming mark, a black half circle which gave rise to the name 'tin hat targets'. The scoring dimensions were also accurately scaled down and these targets were used throughout the Army on all thirty-yard ranges for training and serious target practice, not forgetting zeroing.

We each shot ten rounds using a sandbag as a rest, Sandy first demonstrating how to take up the correct position and use the sights. I fired my ten rounds and when the targets were checked they were in a tight group and all in the bull; I could hardly believe it. After the first shoot we shot a further five rounds each but this time without the sandbag. This was hard because of our physique coupled with the size and weight of the rifle. This time my group spread but still scored all five in the bull, I remember that Sandy said something mundane like 'Well done' but what I didn't know was that he had popped my name away as a possible future competition shot. We completed the week in a much less exciting mode though we were introduced to the Vickers gun on its heavy tripod mounting and also the Lewis gun and how it would be mounted on its bipod for testing but mostly notes and the constant reiteration of the importance of safety and that was the end of the first range course.

The year moved along, During the winter months I had established a place in the football team (Second XI) and in the summer a mixture of swimming and athletics kept me reasonably occupied and of course didn't cost me anything, and yes, I was still hungry most of the time but, I suspect, I was very fit. We had a great Easter holiday as before, about a dozen of us this time. The summer holiday was very enjoyable; I had scraped a few civilian clothes together and felt much more relaxed. I suspect too, that I was much more sophisticated; after all, I had just turned sixteen, time truly was marching on. We progressed through all the preliminary workshop courses and our school evenings were leading inexorably to the First Class Certificate exams. Suddenly it was Christmas and just as suddenly I was back in J4 and starting on my third year. Was I a soldier yet? I certainly felt like one. During the year there had been a group photograph taken and as I look at it now, well, I suppose we all looked like soldiers, certainly the older boys did. I had put on weight and height but I still looked a small package.

The First Class Certificate of Education Exams arrived. We were all agreed that none of us was ready in spite of our frantic revising over the last weeks; once again I remember those two damned set books as really difficult and I think we all viewed the prospect of the English Literature paper with foreboding. We filed into the classroom and waited.

It is interesting to dwell on the system that prevailed at the time for the Army. We had to take four subjects and to gain our Certificate it was necessary to pass them all. Combined Mathematics and Science, ditto History and Geography, also English and English Literature, finally Map Reading. For myself I found Map Reading the easiest, though at the start of the year it was a totally new subject. My Achilles heel as always was Maths and Science and I eventually scraped through by the skin of my teeth, but I had achieved good marks in all the other subjects, even the dreaded English Literature.

So there we were, sat in the examination room, each desk well separated. At the front sat an officer of Captain rank who would be invigilating. The examination was due to start at 0900hrs. Right on time we heard a motor cycle arrive. A few moments later there was a knock at the door and a dispatch rider, in full dispatch rider gear, carrying a large brown envelope with the most enormous seals. Marching smartly up to the Captain, he saluted, handed over the envelope, saluted again and marched out, leaving us to the mercies of the Examinations Board. The Captain quickly passed out the papers and we were off.

No one and the Army really meant no one was going to get an early glimpse at those papers. We were also sat well back, this I presume in case we had added the ability to read through large brown envelopes and even larger seals, to our many skills for evading Authority. These so called skills were, of course, purely mythical – oh, I don't know though. This ritual was re-enacted over the four days of examinations and I remember it was a little intimidating at the time. I never really felt at ease with it especially before the Maths and Science exam.

I still have copies of the question papers that I sat and feel that this map reading question might set a time scale.

Question 5. You are to send a driver with loaded horse-drawn wagon from Postling (Sq. 5857) to Acrise (Sq. 6360) and have to decide which of the following routes he will take:-

A – via Pts. 597580 ; 606576 ; 615581 ; 622587 ; 625596 ; 631504. Or

B – via Pts. 597580 ; 437879 ; 580643 ; 647654 ; 631604 ; 619602.

(1)   Which route will you choose?
(2)   As you cannot give your driver the map, write down in less than 100 words the instructions you would give him verbally, regarding the route to his destination.
(3)   Why did you not choose the other route?   (10 marks)

Or how about a Geography question !

Question 14. Write an account of the countries on the east coast of South America from the Amazon to Cape Horn, describing with sketch maps the physical features, climate and productions!

Where the hell is South America never mind its east coast?
During this year a group photograph had been taken including the lecturers. The photograph of myself on the front of the book was extracted from this large group and is testimony to the quality of the original photograph and the skills of my friends working in the British Telecom's Research Establishment just up the road from where I live. Looking at it after the many years it has been stored away and on top of what I have written so far, it was indeed nostalgic to see so many old friends. And I see Cpl. Reg Dix, he of the wad racket, is there showing off his stripes. The lecturers, Oily Bramble, Mr Brickell (without his putting on files), Mr Hull (Have you seen the light), and that great blacksmith and even greater character, John Sullivan.
So here we were well into our second year and of course into the workshop training, this time hands on and learning to carry out the repairs. I was moving along quite quickly and the work was increasingly more difficult but also much more interesting. Barrack life too was a lot easier, the only real tension that of waiting for the first exam results; would we ever be free of evening classes? A good summer meant many hours swimming in the 'Creek'. And course dicing with death diving off the electrified railway bridge.

Meanwhile, Christmas began to occupy our thoughts with the usual anxiety as to how much cash we might get subject to the usual deductions for barrack damages and whatever items of kit we had replaced. I used to wonder sometimes where it had all gone, the money I mean; was I serving in the Army or was I paying for it? But barrack damages were an age-old gripe and I suspect always will be. Never mind the 1930s, ask an ex-National Serviceman. However during this last year we had a pay rise. Technically this was really a skill at your trade award and for us seemed to just happen so I think that providing we kept our noses clean the trade weighting increases would just come along. How much was it? I just don't remember, maybe an extra fruit and nut bar?

So the year ended with another Christmas at home and back to what was to be a quite eventful year with plenty of unexpected variety, all of it very pleasant.

BUGLERS THREE
WILTSHIRE, HILLS, HOYLE
1938

CHAPTER 4
A BUGLE, A REAL TOY SOLDIER AND A GIRL

Another year ahead and I felt very comfortable about it. In the workshops we would be starting on our repairs and there were several new techniques to be learned. It is impossible to remember the exact sequence of the courses and indeed they varied between groups but a good place to start would be the short wood-working course. It wouldn't have been practical to go on to the next rifle course, without being able to 'patch' a piece of the woodwork where necessary. I cannot recall the instructor who taught these particular skills but I found it a very enjoyable course mostly devoted to cutting out the damaged piece - rifle butts were especially vulnerable - and then very carefully fitting a new piece of wood (Italian walnut), matching the colour as closely as possible. This was glued into place and the following day two holes approximately one-eighth inch diameter would be drilled through the unfinished patch and into the butt. Two suitable round pegs would be made and driven in with glue thus providing a superb support. Once these were dry the patch was cut and shaped to the correct form. This was a fraught moment because when it was finally polished the instructor demanded that the line of the join should be almost invisible. Success really felt good.

We also had to make two pairs of grips, one pair for the .45" pistol and another pair for the .38". Shaping these grips was not especially difficult but as in every other thing we seemed to do there was a snag, something that was not only difficult but needed to be just right to get it past the instructor. Known in the gun trade as chequering, this meant cutting the fine diamond shapes into the wood to provide a grip for the hand. For this we used a tool that we had already made, forged firstly then filed to the finished shape and hardened. These were entirely special to the art of chequering and were called chequering tools; the diamond shapes that were cut were referred to as chequers. The whole had to be contained within a set pattern drawn out on the wood and each chequer had to be crisp and unspoiled. I quickly discovered that not only did it require great skill, it also needed monumental patience. Much of today's chequering is done by machine but as in the past there are craftsmen who specialise and charge by the square inch. In our case we had to get our work approved and stamped which meant getting it past the instructor's enormous magnifying glass; we always felt this was a bit unfair.

The courses that followed were in many ways identical to each other, only the objects being repaired varied, though of course these were mainly weapons. There were anomalies, bikes for example, and other odd items: swords, lances and eventually instruments. The bicycle course was quite a long one and had its own workshop. I was looking forward to getting my handicap down! I might even take my own ball bearings this time; I already had a modified spoke hidden away.

So on to the next rifle course where we were given five rifles in very poor condition. These rifles were collected from one of the main storehouses in the depot. Some of them had been in store since the first World War and our task now was to restore them to a condition known by the Stores Section of the RAOC as 'Factory

Thorough Repair Standard', officially abbreviated to FTR which simply meant that when they left our hands they were recognised as new. At some stage thereafter they would be inspected by a 'Chief Inspector of Armaments' and would be taken back into store ready for issue as new.

This standard meant that everything not satisfactory had to be replaced and the rifles built up from scratch including the process of rust proofing known as browning. This gets a substantial paragraph later on. At Hilsea this was not so much a process as an ancient ritual whose origins had been lost in the mists of time; actually it was more like 'black magic'. And I mean black.

I started by stripping each of the rifles down to its smallest components. The barrel and body and the fore end were stood in my rack and the smaller components stored in numbered boxes on the bench. I now joined the rest of the class in a small group round Mr Shannon who showed us how we were to decide whether a barrel and body needed scrapping. This meant learning how to view the bore of the barrel by looking into it with both eyes, and much more tricky, how to identify the various faults which afflict barrels: bends, corrosion, erosion, pitting, bulges, puckers and wear. Which brings me to gauges and gauging: all weapons had their own sets of gauges the degree of which roughly depended on whether it was a large workshop with a thorough repair standard capability or a Regimental Armourer attached to a Battalion. Gauging was vital to ensure the function, safety and accuracy of the equipment.

We were then sent back to clean the barrels of the rifles we had been given, to view them and note what we thought we had found. Mr Shannon would come along and differ, at least that's what he did with my effort. I had found this viewing very difficult and indeed only one of my efforts was correct. As I remember it was severe pitting that according to Mr Shannon would have been easy to spot a mile away. I knew then that this particular and important skill was going to prove very difficult for me to master. Everything else was reasonably straightforward; we made a list of spares required, patched all the woodwork then scraped it down, sanded it and polished it with linseed oil. The components made of steel including the barrel and body were cleaned with emery cloth and the small components were wired and tagged for identity. This whole process of preparing the steel components was and still is called 'breaking down' and was the preparation required for the 'browning' process. Oh yes, musn't forget to plug the barrels. All of this activity reached a climax on Friday and the components were taken over to the Browning workshop to be 'Black Magic'd'.

This would take a full week and enabled all the woodwork to be ready in time to start final assembly when your components came back. All the screws were dealt with by a weird process called 'blanket blacking'. A small strip of unserviceable Army blanket (was there ever an Army blanket old enough or worn enough to be declared unserviceable?) was rolled tightly and tied with string. You then heated the component to a correct heat, fine judgement needed, the screw head was then rubbed with the end of the rolled blanket (you think I'm pulling your leg but it is true), finally quenching the component in oil. It works! Another method that works is simply to heat the component, or indeed several, using a small metal tray with drainage holes, drip oil onto the heated pieces, ignite this oil then keep dripping it at the same time keeping the oil burning, repeat a few times and finally quench in oil. These methods of blacking introduce considerable heat to the components many of which have properties of hardness which are sensitive to this, so the process has to be carefully monitored.

Preparing everything for the browning process involved repairing and replacing unserviceable components. With most, fitting was fairly straightforward except for the fore-end; this is the piece of the rifle that cradles the entire length of the barrel and body. The design of the SMLE rifle was such that its accuracy depended almost entirely on the fore-end being correctly fitted and this was a good test of the skills we had learned during our fitting and woodwork courses. Carelessly done, especially with a new fore-end, and the rifle would certainly come back from the range with a rejection slip, and, whilst this was not good anywhere, here at Hilsea the thought of all those marks that would certainly be deducted certainly kept your mind on the job. Strangely the ability of an Armourer to fit the SMLE rifle with a new fore-end quickly and well became a kind of benchmark.

Now with all the various components repaired, the woodwork patched, cleaned and polished, everything back from browning, it but remained to assemble the rifles, check the gauging limits were correct and the weight of trigger pulls were within their laid down parameters and the second pull was crisp with no 'drag', make sure none of the screw heads showed any sign of screwdriver damage, take a deep breath, then a quick prayer to the Goddess of 'No rejects and full marks' take the five rifles to Mr Shannon for marking. Fine, I stood them carefully in his rack, and I thought they looked great. Not looking at them he tossed a neat hand grenade at me saying, 'You are a bit ahead, young Hoyle, so I want you to go over to the Ordnance store. They have just got two hundred used barrels in and they want someone to go over and sort the good ones from the unserviceable. You know what to look for but especially for bent barrels; good lad, off you go.' What me?, I thought, me who only got one of my five rifle barrels correct and that one with massive pitting, My progress towards becoming a soldier was well advanced. I simply went.

My panic was very much calmed down by the hospitality of the storemen, mug of tea, cake? Eh, what's this? No mention of rifle barrels. It didn't last; they finally showed me into a room complete with a bench, a barrel viewing support (a length of timber with a v cut at the top and fixed to the bench), one needs a support to view properly and, oh, I nearly forgot, two hundred rifle barrels and an A4 clip board and pencil. Left alone I made a start. The first few I just didn't have the courage to make a decision but eventually after viewing them umpteen times I started my list. A few hours later and I could detect a bent barrel a mile away never mind the other defects, and so it has remained all my life: show me a rifle barrel and I'll give you chapter and verse in a few minutes. I wondered at the time and again now whether Mr Shannon had a crafty ulterior motive when he sent me on that job.

Our next move was to Pistols and this followed the same pattern. We were given five pistols of both types, .45" and .38", and were required to bring them up to a standard regarded 'as new'. These pistols had very much the same type of action and the function which turned the cylinder round (did I say previously they were revolvers?) bringing the next chamber into line with the barrel getting this right could be very frustrating. It depended on a curved pawl (we had to make one of these pawls, another old forging coming home to roost) coupled to the cocking mechanism and engaging a tooth on the cylinder thus ensuring that when the gun was cocked, the cylinder was brought into line with the barrel, because there were six chambers in the cylinder and wear on their teeth uneven. It was difficult to get each one in exactly the same position and held tightly; one or two would always be loose. For many years, even to this day, I never seemed to have the same difficulty that I did at Hilsea when Mr Humphrey was waiting to mark my efforts. I think it's called compromise.

But the Pistol course concealed an opportunity to demonstrate one's bravery - stupidity? One of the techniques used to clean a barrel was called lapping and first it was necessary to create a 'lap'. This was a piece of lead that had been cast around a cleaning rod which in turn was held at one end with a packing of cloth. When cool this left a lead plug exactly shaped to the inside of the barrel, which could then be covered with oil and a mild abrasive and worked up and down to polish the barrel, and very effective it was. Seems straightforward enough, even boring; well, we macho sixteen year olds were not at Hilsea or, come to that, in the Army, to be bored.

How many of you know that if you oil your hand, or any other portion of your anatomy and then pour molten lead over it the lead will simply run off harmlessly? Yes, yes, you are ahead of me now! I don't need to elaborate; suffice to say it works and we were all brave - stupid, but I suppose in one sense it was a rite of passage.

So what of barrack life during 1937 and what of the 'Bugle'? Well I must first emphasise that musically I was worse than hopeless; whatever talents I might have possessed music was not one of them. Let me talk about the band again especially how it was formed. The bandsmen came from various Regiments including the Guards; indeed L/Corporal Perkins in charge of the drummers was an ex Guardsman. They had various duties within the Depot but they were there basically to form a band. This was fine but there were holes to be filled, drummers and buglers to be precise who served to bulk up the band and looked good on the occasions when the band paraded, for example, on Sundays once a month. Speaking for J4 we were represented by Lambert (remember the goalkeeper), certainly a good keeper but a superb drummer and my old friend Peter, a good bugler. It hadn't taken me long to work out that being in the band, drummer or bugler, was a very fine thing if you could swing it; there were some unkind enough to describe it as a very fine way of dodging a lot of the more disliked duties, a super scrounge in fact. The trick was how to get in. There were very few vacancies and these only cropped up when one of the incumbents reached man service and had to give up 'music'. The trick turned out to be: get your name down early and keep your fingers crossed. Peter, of course, being from a Military School and already wise in the ways of avoiding tedious military duties, had his name down shortly after joining and he was already a member of the band but even so, for one so ignorant of things military, I had been pretty quick off the mark and suddenly out of the blue I was ordered to attend practice. This took place for one hour on Saturday mornings and that was it, one rehearsal with the full band in the band room before a Church Parade and from then on Saturday morning square bashing, kit inspections and sundry other unpleasant duties were a thing of the past.

I wasn't particularly hopeful. I had no idea how you played a bugle nor any idea what exactly would be required for me to be accepted for training. I stood around whilst one of the senior buglers took them through a couple of marches then they just drifted into their own little corners playing odd snatches of this and that, even a few scales, to say nothing of a little 'double tonguing' the art of which is still a mystery to me. One or two of the lads came over and they began to teach me how to produce a note. This is not straightforward nor is it a matter of just blowing but I began to get the hang of it until my top lip just sort of gave up. It was explained that as I progressed the muscle on my top lip would became stronger and harder and the whole thing would become easier, just needs lots of work. So I came to learn how to play a bugle and end up body building my upper lip; ah well, it takes all sorts.

Sometime later L/Cpl Hollingsworth, NCO in charge of Buglers and no mean performer on a trumpet, turned up, chatted to me for awhile about this and that but nothing about the band or even learning to play a bugle. Finally he gave me a bugle all my own, told me to look after it, use the mouthpiece to help me 'Get a lip' and was gone. I truly can't remember when I next saw him at bugle practice. This lack of interest or his love of lying in on a Saturday was a Godsend to me as I was pretty hopeless. A bugle only has five notes, much too many for me, but I did build up my lip and I could just about get by. The thing I dreaded was for L/CplHollingsworth turning up to actually conduct the practice because I had been told that when he did, he would make everybody play the marches that had been selected for Sunday, solo. I might just have got away with Last Post. I had practised that quite a lot as it was my lip builder. I might be a lousy bugler but I could still built the biggest lip – maybe in the whole country. Well, he did turn up in the end (something to do with finding a new bugle march in the bottom of the music pannier). I pleaded a bruised lip picked up in the Gym and as there was a lot of boxing going on at the time (at least so I had been told) he didn't query it; indeed he did an astonishing thing: he left me to run the lads through the practice and was gone. For the rest of my Boy service then, I survived as a voluntary bugler in the band. Believe me, this has to rate as a very great achievement.

And the girl? We met about this time, a fairly straightforward meeting. I had been playing rugby for the Boys' rugby team (don't excite yourselves, still a small package but very quick). My flank forward Harry Jeans and I stopped to chat up these two attractive young girls, what sophistication. I made a date and the young girl I dated some sixty-six years ago will be editing this chapter. I was besotted with her then and I still am. We went out together on my free evenings, with virtually no money, a trip to the cinema was a rare event indeed, yet for those years until I moved at the end of my training we were totally engrossed in each other, nothing else mattered. Her family liked me and in the years ahead of me my in-laws became very dear to me.

This liaison altered many aspects of my routine, one area of which was the writing up of workshop notes. Mostly this had been done during the evenings. I had learned early on that it was foolish to neglect them on the basis of I'll catch up later; these notes would eventually form part of my final examination marks and good marks were difficult to come by. Add to this that my final grading depended on the percentage of the total marks achieved throughout the course; these were then added to those gained during the final weeks of testing so it was imperative that these notes and drawings were well done. Things were indeed becoming complicated. Meanwhile there was sport, evenings spent in the gym (voluntary), and the normal chaotic barrackroom life and chores to cope with frankly. From where I sit now, I cannot envisage how I coped but I do know how I managed to write up my workshop notes. Simple, I normally got in after lights out and the only place with light that I could use was the ablutions so there you have it, the loos. Mind you I had a pretty sophisticated piece of board to fit my lap. Come to think of it the board would have been of about the same consistency as the Army loo paper of that era.

Looming up at this time was a very different and very enjoyable interlude. It had been decided (at the highest level I presume), that at the Tidworth Tattoo there would be a Toy Soldier display. Now this was a really prestigious event with enormous support from the public and it was Coronation year and who better to present this display than the Armourers Training Branch at Hilsea. Not only that but it lasted a whole week—we could hardly wait. So we started practising under the RSM. The whole was cleverly choreographed and performed to the tune of 'The Toy Soldier'. The climax was for the whole Company of toy soldiers to fall down one after the other to the sound of machine gun fire. It writes much simpler than it really was and there were many fraught moments between us and the RSM. A further complication: because of this falling routine (we were supposed to stay absolutely straight during our fall) the rehearsals could only be done on the sports field and it is more difficult to perform any sort of drill where you can't hear your feet.

The whole show of course was a theatrical production and as such there were a variety of parts to be cast: Cavalry with helmets, shakos and Guardsmen's bearskins. There were hobby horses, all of which went to the bigger boys; the rest of us were the Poor Bloody Infantry, better known through out the Army as the PBI. All the uniforms were in the style of nursery soldiers and to complete the illusion there were dolls, golliwogs, children; again these were selected from the tallest boys (no volunteers for these parts), a coachman (our tallest boy) and two drummers of which I was one complete with toy drums. All of this detail is in front of me in the form of the group photograph and I am meeting old friends again. Oh yes, there was make-up too a large red blob on each cheek, I never said it was the West End.

The show gradually took shape and following a full dress rehearsal on the sports field, Girl saw it and pronounced it good. We were scheduled to perform it for the first time at Fratton Park (home of the Portsmouth Football Club) as part of a mini Tattoo involving the local soldiery. One of the features of a Tattoo is the control of lighting. The idea was for us all to form up in total darkness. The display was then announced and on came the lights and there we were. I can remember how nervous we all were at the start of that performance but it went like clockwork and the applause was very satisfying, we had a good press too, but which of the Knights on a horse peed on the sacred turf and subsequently on all the turfs we performed on? I know and so do many others. When challenged he simply said, 'That's what horses do.' No argument there. Mind you, but he never managed the ultimate horsy challenge, no matter what we said about the benefits to roses.

And so to Tidworth. This really was an eye opener. In the first place the Tattoo was huge as was the Arena and we were just one part of a wonderful show. Packed out every night the audiences gave us all a wonderful reception and we enjoyed ourselves immensely. Earlier I mentioned that the lighting for Tattoos was important; here it was indescribable. At all times only the enormous 'stage' would be illuminated and the Royal Engineers could at any time draw a line of light down or across the Arena with everything and everybody behind it totally invisible, like a black curtain. Unfortunately we were never able to see this as the audience saw it but the finale involved the whole cast of hundreds forming up behind this line of light (a not easy thing to do, we all had our exact places to find quickly and quietly and all in total darkness) but when the lights came on revealing the entire cast of the Tattoo apparently conjured out of the dark there was a gasp from the crowds followed by enormous applause leaving us all in no doubt that the spectacle must have been really something. As just one small actor (not that again) I found the audience reaction quite overwhelming. After all these years I can still recall it vividly.

But behind the scenes where the nuts and bolts of the show were taking place, always in semi darkness, was another world. We were rubbing shoulders with the Kings Troop Royal Artillery with their immaculately kept guns and limbers and their beautiful horses contrasting starkly with a troop of armoured cars who had been performing a semi-humorous hunting sketch. The Kings Troop need no introduction. Their very dangerous ride is well known wherever there is a Military Tattoo. Indeed, during rehearsals, one of the riders was seriously injured after being unseated then run over by the gun and limber. There were mediaeval knights in armour waiting to perform their jousting demonstrations, strange to see a group of them minus helmets drinking tea in the NAAFI tent, horses tethered outside in full medieval Regalia. A small group of us met Earl Howe, the motor racing driver, in one of the refreshment tents, spending a fair while listening to him telling motor racing yarns. It truly was an exciting time. Finally in the early hours of the morning we had the long march back to where we were encamped, I suppose a good three miles: if not, it seemed like it. Going to the Tattoo was of course in daylight and it didn't seem so far but coming back, tired and ready for bed, it was hard but the organisers provided a small part of one of the massed pipe bands that had been performing and who were billeted near to our own area; this was a great help.

Our lives outside the actual show were very relaxed, because of the demands of the Tattoo. Arrive fairly early and something like three hours hanging about with our routine somewhere in the middle followed by the march back. We could get up late and the rest of the day was our own. We were in tents but eating in the cookhouse of one of the famous Cavalry Regiments who were stationed there at that time but which one? I find it hard to remember but I am pretty sure their motto was 'Death or Glory'. During the course of our stay the Regiment held one of their Regimental Gymkhana days. This was wonderful to watch and included tent pegging and many other competitions special to the Cavalry and their superb horses, a great day. We mostly lounged about, played a bit of cricket as I remember but what I do remember very clearly was the glorious weather we enjoyed throughout the week.

So it all came to an end, though not quite: we had many offers to perform the act around the country; it was even rumoured that there had been requests from as far afield as the Continent. We did two more, one a full weekend at Brighton and here we performed in a heavy downpour and after returning to the barracks we learned the downside of being a Cavalryman. The troopers who had been performing were still working on their horses and kit when we went for breakfast. As one of them said to me, there is only one thing in a Cavalryman's life - his horse - everything else comes a poor second especially the Trooper. We did one more show at Southend. This was a one off, there and back in the same day, but it was some sort of carnival day and part of the Arena was occupied by a fair and this made for a really good evening. We were there early and this gave us plenty of time before the show to enjoy the rest of the carnival. I have a feeling that we were given some sort of vouchers by the organisers which we could spend anywhere in the carnival but I'm not certain.

So there we were, a very enjoyable and at times exciting break from the normal routine, I wonder if our incontinent horse left any fairy rings on the various venues but the general consensus was just dead grass. The culprit claimed otherwise and vociferously so, until it was suggested that maybe a room Court Martial, charging him with bringing the equine of the species into disrepute, might be in order, and all was subsequently quiet, I think he was later heard bragging about his grass killing prowess; he certainly didn't need to brag about the 'hose' he used, communal showers suggested that he was indeed well cast as a horse..

As we returned to the rigours of Barrack life I should talk about the many other aspects of our lives which to us were very important. Sport for example was a very serious aspect of our daily lives and the various units of the Army competed ferociously to win the top trophies. Football and the Army Football Cup was one of the red ribbon events, closely followed by rugby, boxing, athletics, cross country running, cricket, tennis, tug of war and of course shooting. A feature of Army sport was how some units specialised. The Welsh Guards were consistent winners of the Boxing Championships and of course Rugby but here the Royal Signals often had a big say in the finals. There were many Regiments and Corps noted for their prowess at shooting and the Army Championships at Bisley were fiercely competitive.

So what was the speciality that our own Depot might be 'renowned' for? Tug of war! Not only were we always represented in the Army finals by both our teams, heavyweight and lightweight and regularly winning (I recall the finals were often battled out against the Middlesex Regiment) but we regularly reached the National Finals held at the White City. During my years at Hilsea the credit for this was down to Sgt. Ollier (remember the Sergeant in charge of boys), and the ruthless training regime he imposed on the luckless volunteers but most of all was his deep knowledge of the very considerable techniques needed for each member of the team. He really was a superb tug of war coach with few equals anywhere.

Many of us became quite knowledgeable about tug of war simply because their training area was situated on a piece of spare ground behind the Boys' block so we could watch it in the utmost comfort and watch it we did because we were seeing real suffering and of course this was irresistible.

On this piece of ground a large steel structure had been erected on which pulleys were suspended and so arranged that a rope finally emerged, the height of which was adjustable to suit the build of whoever was using it. As there were two classes of team, heavy and lightweight, pullers were selected on height and weight plus strength, courage and the inability to say no to Sgt. Ollier when he suggested they might like to try out for the tug of war team. I suppose, in all fairness to recruits still ignorant of the Depot's reputation in this field, tug of war had more of a pub team sound, the sort seen at the local sports day. How wrong can you be?

They started quietly enough with general fitness training, the techniques of position on the rope, the importance of keeping a straight rope and above all a straight body from the toes to the head and the use of the weight of the head. Room for a joke here but it was a much too serious a business. Eventually they arrived in front of a rope which was just the right height and told to pick it up and assume a start position, rope gripped correctly, tucked under the right arm, position upright. They had of course practised this during the theoretical training in the Gym but here it was different because fixed to the end of this rope was one of the big iron coal bunces filled with weights. Given the order to heave, the hapless trainee would now be expected to dig both heels in with a small jump, assume the correct body position and taking small steps backwards start to lift the bunce keeping it moving, working to Bill Ollier's commands. Everything developed from this; the successful and potential team members would spend many hours on this apparatus, working singly or as a team learning the many techniques: how to lock on the rope and hold it, how to drop at the knees whilst keeping a straight back and move backwards with small steps digging in the heels all to the command of the Coach, the various techniques to try to recover control if the other team started to move you. Amongst these were locking on the rope as a team, a move fraught with risk as you left yourself exposed to the alertness of the other coach during those seconds that you were moving into the lock position. Sometimes Bill would have the whole team locked on a ferocious weight for anything up to twenty minutes, hands blistering and skin being torn off the forearms. During the competitions teams have been known to be deadlocked like this for up to thirty minutes. Tug of war? Skill, strength and above all guts.

And you thought it was a pub sport usually played between villages at the local carnival.

During my time at Hilsea the boys' football team also covered themselves with glor,y winning the Boys' Army Cup three years in succession, no mean feat this, and whilst the boys were bussed to the final at Aldershot everyone left back in the Depot were eagerly listening for the goals and which team had scored. How? Telephone to the Guardroom and yes, you've guessed it, the ubiquitous bugler, fretting because he had drawn the short straw and wasn't with the rest of us at the Aldershot Stadium but ready to dash up to the square and sound the latest score. I emphasised earlier how big a part the bugle played in our everyday life and here is a fine example - Regimental Call followed by a' G' indicated that we had scored but a single ' G' by itself was the opposition. You were expected to keep your own tally. This routine was also used for the tug of war, each pull being signalled in the same way.

There were many other sports at which the Depot excelled and after the arrival of the new PTI, Sgt Major Walker, more time was devoted to gymnastics and fencing and less to the more boring exercises, I liked that! Sgt Major Walker worked on a system of a period on the boring exercise regime and when he was satisfied then you could select any of several disciplines to specialise in. Gymnastics and fencing were the ones favoured by Walker; strange that, I wonder if it was anything to do with him being a Member of the British Team at both disciplines. I went for fencing - a mistake; the preliminary exercises went on for weeks with never a sniff of a foil, épée or sabre so I changed to Gymnastics. Only a hand full of boys stayed with the fencing and in the end only three stuck it out to the competition stage and one of them, Frankie Ralls, won the Army foil championship whilst the other two made quite a name for themselves in local matches; indeed I remember the Boy who fought sabre being officially rebuked by the Police team for apparently hitting too hard in one of the bouts. Mind you he still won, it would seem that his opponent had difficulty fencing with a partly paralysed shoulder. 'It wasn't me Officer.' I am sorry but I can't remember the names of the two boys fencing épée and sabre.

During this summer there was a large open air swimming pool opened at the Lido (a smallish typical holiday type park with a boating lake and the usual holiday visitor attractions). This pool was quite superb with excellent diving facilities, spring board and a high board to Olympic standards. Three things conspired to lead me to a sport I frankly never felt I had the courage for. Firstly the Depot Adjutant retired and landed the job as the first Manager of the Pool, as a result of this he would a let a few of the boys in free but late in the evenings when the pool was virtually empty. Not a lot took this up; it was late and the evenings could be quite chilly. I and a Boy called Trott, who I think had been brought up in Australia and was a superb swimmer, had finished up one evening in the pool. I probably went along to keep Trott company, swimming didn't really enthuse me though I did like diving, I might add at this point that the Lido was just a five minute walk from the Barrack gate.

I had wandered up onto the high board platform to admire the view and watch Trott piling up the lengths with that lazy but fast crawl. A head appeared through the platform hatch, and the unmistakable voice of PTI Walker said, 'Good evening, Hoyle, doing a bit of diving?' Oops, I knew that PTI Walker was probably there to train because I also knew that he was a Member of one of the National High Diving Squads. We boys had come to know that there was no limit to Walker's gymnastic talents, I wonder if that is why he was so popular with the Boys. I hastily denied any intentions of diving from this height to which he replied, 'Wwell I'm damned if I know how you are going to get down." In that instant I knew just how I was going to get down, head first, in some semblance of a dive if my shaking legs would allow it. My panic must have shown and he was enjoying the moment but with the words, 'Come on, you might even enjoy it' (a macabre sense of humour), he led me to the edge of the platform and the first of many lessons began. I did dive off and when I hit the water believe me it is a considerable blow. I vowed never again but I stayed with Walker and became a reasonably competent high board diver. There is an end to this saga but for now it is in the future.

A final story about PTI Walker. One thing we had learned about him, he hated boxing, so imagine our surprise on asking where he was when he would normally have been in the gym; we were told that he had been summoned to Aldershot to fill in for one of the Army boxing team in a match against the RAF. On querying this against his dislike of boxing the Corporal PTI said, 'True, but he is bloody good at it, you'll see,' and we did. He knocked his opponent out in the second round and that with no preparation. It was never mentioned when he got back.

And so Christmas was once again very much in our thoughts. It was very hard to grasp that this was the end of my third year, yet was I finally a soldier. Who cares, I was in love and that's what mattered. My dad at this time was working for Mackintosh's, the high quality and expensive toffee and chocolate makers. I talked him into sending me a large tin of Quality Street. The tins in those days were works of art and this was a very impressive gift for Girl in those depression days; indeed, she has been known to mention it even now when the party chat has turned to romance. It was a few months before she found out that future father in law was the origin of the gift and in fact worked at Mackintosh's. Christmas arrived and of course leave which yielded a rare occurrence, indeed it had never happened before.

On the way home the whole country was under the influence of very bad weather, mostly snow plus foggy conditions. On arrival at King's Cross Station I discovered that most of the trains to the North had either been cancelled or were running very late (nothing changes). On enquiring from a porter when the next train to Leeds might run he replied that the only train guaranteed to pull out on time was the Yorkshire Pullman, a very famous train in its day, and it would be wise to pay the supplement of half a crown, enabling me to board it and thus being sure of reaching Leeds on time. This was a lot of money to me but I forked out and sure enough the Pullman pulled out exactly to the minute. What a beautiful train it was, lovely wooden veneers, luxurious seats. There were only two people in my compartment, an elderly couple on their way to Leeds. They were really nice and showed great interest in my life in the Army, especially at such a young age. I suppose very few people in those days knew about the recruitment of boys into the Army, Finally I was taken along for dinner with them. This was a real treat for me, in fact it was probably the highlight of my Christmas. As we approached Leeds the train was slowed down on several occasions and there was an air of unease more than justified when the Yorkshire Pullman pulled into Leeds Station twenty minutes late. At the time I simply did not appreciate the full implications but when I saw one of the stewards openly weeping and was told this was the first occasion that the Yorkshire Pullman had ever been late, I began to realise I had indeed been part of a sad episode in the life of this great train. Some things do change.

Another great Christmas at home being fed and cosseted once again but as I sat in the train moving steadily south once more I felt content. I would be back with Girl again and this was my last year give or take a month or two. Politically this was going to be a traumatic year, for the country with the infamous piece of paper and 'Peace in our time'. I cannot remember giving much thought to it but, my goodness, it was going to catch up with me in the very near future.

BISLEY 1938

CHAPTER 5
GOODBYE PUTTEES AND FOURS, HELLO CORPORAL

This year, 1938, saw two major changes in the life of every soldier, I cannot remember the exact timing but one caused great delight amongst the 'Soldiery'. In their infinite wisdom, them as decided these things ruled that puttees would no longer be part of our lives. Instead we were eventually to get a small webbing gaiter (had to be blancoed, again nothing changes) and for the time being we were issued with a small puttee simply wound round the ankle. The other change was very major indeed. The formation of soldiers on parade was to change from parading in two ranks and then forming fours for marching, to forming up in three ranks which would remain unchanged no matter what drill was being performed. This change meant very little to us personally and was slightly easier than the old way; none of us could quite fathom why they made this change but it certainly made a parade less cumbersome.

But by far and away the most important thing this year was the decision to create a proper Boy's rank structure. During the preceding two years there had been quite a growth in the numbers of Armourer Trainees and I felt this was what had prompted this radical change. Previously there had been just the one Boy Corporal mentioned before, Reg Dix, who I always suspected was there to ease the burden' on Bill Ollier. I cannot be certain of the exact establishment they started with, but if I say four Boy Corporals, two Boy Sergeants and one Boy RSM I won't be very far wrong. They started by filling one of the Sgt vacancies and the four Corporals; the other vacancies were filled some time later. Both Peter Hills and I were promoted to Boy Corporal There's glory for you but we were delighted and my parents even more so.

This promotion meant a big change in my barrack life in that I was moved from J4 to be put in charge of another room as the previous men NCOs no longer filled this role. It also meant that Peter also moved to take charge of a room so we no longer shared bed spaces, I did, of course, know the boys in the room. They were second year but taking responsibility for them and more importantly being responsible for the room discipline was a daunting prospect. Mind you I was seventeen so I just got on with it. This being in charge stretched to the rest of the boys and involved taking parades and marching them hither and thither wherever their next duty happened to be which was mostly backwards and forwards to the Workshops. Did we receive any training for this? No! A sort of just get on with it.

I had the previous year passed my first class certificate of education and so could look forward to freedom from evening school though we now had to attend a City and Guilds qualification class held on one evening a week. The lecturer came from the Portsmouth College and was a great character and very popular with the boys. He was also a very good teacher. Small and every inch the proverbial type professor we watched him arrive along the back of the administrative building driving a very old Rolls Royce with only a little of him protruding above the steering wheel. The first evening we were a bit wary, but early on, whilst writing up a problem on the blackboard, he quite casually drew a complicated illustration with his left hand whilst completing the necessary calculations with his right hand, both at the same time: the drawings on the left of the blackboard and the maths on the right. We were truly impressed. I just cannot remember his name but much as we disliked having to give up an evening a week to schooling we always treated him with respect and in return we all did well.

Meanwhile, I was trying to settle in and come to terms with my new responsibilities and learning that it is not easy. Take our old friend 'room jobs'. I certainly was off the list and could look to a little more free time but suddenly I was 'It'. It was me who would, from now on, allocate room jobs. Now I knew all about room jobs; after all I had been grafting for three years at one room job or another and one thing I had learned was that some of these jobs were better avoided if possible. How to avoid them was the question; well, they could lobby me and try to exert whatever pressure they might feel capable of, there was also of course, bribery! I seem to remember an offer to make my bed every day which was a ridiculous ploy; he should have known anyway that someone was going to make my bed every day and it would have nothing at all to do with room jobs. And there was also a little matter of blancoing which I hated anyway for some strange reason, indeed I still do but there's not much call for it now. Oh, yes, brasses, boots, etc., steady, Clem, sorry, Boy Corporal Hoyle, you'll be expecting to be carried down to work soon.

Reality soon intruded in the form of rostering the room jobs and the consequent acrimony, but I was learning and anyway the other four boys who had been promoted were all big lads and I had actually grown a bit myself. We were a sort of enforcement Free Masonry. Never a charge or a refused pass but just simple old fashioned discipline which everybody understood, especially the RSM. There had been a change of RSM during 1937, also a change of Adjutant. Now this really was a big change for the Depot; these two appointments of course are the real power in any Unit, nothing moved without their say-so and they could make life very hard for everyone. A soldier's phrase for this is being ''Regimental''. This time we were lucky, the new Adjutant was a larger than life character in every way, ex heavyweight Army Boxing Champion and Rugby Representative whose passion for Rugby still inspires me to spell it with a capital. The RSM too was big and came from the Welch Guards and was every inch the fearsome Guards RSM that one would expect.

So there we were, two newcomers to the Depot with the authority to change our everyday lives drastically one way or the other and they were both ''pussy cats'', at least where the Boys were concerned. Up to a point we could do no wrong and I think this was born of the comparison with us and the rest of the Depot who were basically all recruits, starting, in the middle of, or just finishing their training; they had not had the time to acquire the polish that we had built up over the years, so that when something special was required like the Inspection by the General Officer Commanding (once a year this) involving a large parade, drill and the many other things that might spin off from this orgy of inspection they both knew that the Boys section of the Depot were absolutely reliable and would ensure a favourable and often complimentary report. Another example of course was the Toy Soldier display. We just gobbled it up as if we had always been Thespians with a taste for odd drill movements, not only odd drill movements but also odd drill movements in the middle of a field. The RSM's name was Thomas and in common with all soldiers of that name this was always prefixed by Buffy.

The Adjutant's name was Clarke and he found it difficult to believe that here, in his new appointment, there were upwards of thirty strapping and very fit boys none of whom either boxed or played Rugby. Very shortly an order was posted asking for volunteers to box in a Boy's Depot boxing championship; full training and coaching beforehand would be given. I was less than enthusiastic. I had over the years met, so to speak, a number of these boys in one form of combat or another and I knew that it could only be wise to decline this voluntary form of sacrifice, after all kamikaze was still in the future. Chatting amongst ourselves it soon became clear that Major Clarke would quickly discover there was no possibility of putting on a boxing match with all the frills, including invited spectators and even the Depot Band in attendance, to say nothing of our small hospital medical staff: very great disappointment there, but even they conceded that they would need at least a few boys to spill blood before they could burst into medical activity. About this time we all noticed and even discussed the unusual signs of strange activities (other than people flinging themselves around) in the gym, culminating in a very smart and business-like boxing ring suddenly appearing in the middle to say nothing of seating all round.

Yes, we all agreed, there was to be some sort of boxing match: maybe the gym had been loaned out to one of the many units around Portsmouth, the TA perhaps! So here was something to look forward to and much of our chat was devoted to speculation. This came to an abrupt end following perusal of Depot Orders one morning where it not only laid out chapter and verse about a boxing tournament but as well as detailing officials, time of punch off (if that is the correct terminology), there we all were in a long list neatly paired off with our opponent. Hang on, somebody shouted I never volunteered for this caper! It was quickly pointed out that neither had any of us but here in all its 'gory' was the Adjutant's boxing tournament. My concern was who the hell was I fighting, sounds very macho at this distance but it quickly became apparent that there had been collusion somewhere along the line as we were all pretty evenly matched for size and weight but as I found to my cost later, not necessarily for aggression.

So fight night duly arrived and the gym filled up whilst the 'fighters' sat around the periphery of the ring in our PT kit and wearing boxing gloves. I do remember feeling very self-conscious and also taking sneaky looks at my opponent. I knew him well enough; after all, he was one of the boys in my room. I sat there trying not to look at my gloves and desperately trying to remember what room job I had dished out to him but he woudn't still be upset about that, would he? Finally we climbed up into the ring. Was I in the blue corner or the red? I can't remember but I do remember my second, PTI Corporal Dodd known as Darky Dodd. Always popular with the boys, I thought, at least I can trust good old Darky to look after me. Well, yes and no, as it turned out. At the end of the first round I thought I was doing OK, at least I hadn't been hurt, mind you I certainly hadn't hurt my opponent, but Darky seemed to think otherwise. 'You are going well and at this stage winning comfortably, just keep it up." Funny, that wasn't what I wanted to hear. I had worked out much earlier that winning would mean doing this all over again, you could get hurt at this game. End of second round and the whisper in my ear was another round in the bag. Ah well, stay away from his gloves for one more round, I did and this time no doubt, I had won comfortably? Well, Darky, why is the referee holding the other boy's arm up in the air? Maybe I had enjoyed a narrow escape from winning but I have a feeling that 'Darky' was a bit of a kidder really.

I never really knew what Girl thought about my not cleaning up the Boys' boxing championships especially as her father had been a professional and sometime

Southern Area Champion. Maybe I should have asked his advice but then again my name wasn't going to appear in a pairings list on some future Depot Orders, nor did I. Anyway Darky Dodd said I won and after all he was a real Corporal!

There was definitely a feeling of change in the air, hard to define but maybe it was the abandonment of puttees and the old fours drill or something more subtle, but what was certain was that this was a very important year for me as it was for the other three boys who had made up time on the workshops courses and we would be a group right through the remaining time until we finally qualified as Armourers and were split up to join the various units to which we had been posted. Our names? Peter Hills, now Boy Corporal Hills; remember we started together and shared a bed space for the first years; Ray Wilkins, Boy RSM; myself, Clem Hoyle, Boy Corporal; the three of us from the same batch and finally but by no means least Ginger Stratford, Boy, who was in fact older than us and part of an earlier batch. A great character, mind you; if you followed Ginger there was always trouble at the end. So this was the group of four Boys setting out on this final year together. Well not exactly, it was really four Boys and two Egyptian officers. I never said the Army was easy to understand, had they progressed a little more quickly through the workshops, I would also have needed to add two Royal Marine Sergeants Girl would have liked that, she always had a soft spot for the Royal Marines, Still has, she informs me, reading over my shoulder, which is rude but you tell her!

The names of the two Egyptian officers I can say but I doubt that I can spell them correctly. One slightly built and great fun - Essawy. The other big and very reserved who before the course finished married a local girl - Naguib. These two officers were part of the British Army's great tradition of training the soldiers of other nations technically as well as militarily. The Royal Marines always had one or two Sergeants passing through the workshops training to be Armourers.

The Barrack routine settled down with almost no variation. There were important changes to our everyday lives. As Boy NCOs we were entitled to permanent passes and allowed out to midnight and indeed to wear civilian clothes. Ginger achieved the same privileges by seniority and staying out of trouble for five minutes. There were other minor changes affecting everyone: we had always been entitled to a mug of tea during the morning, very welcome in the workshops because it meant we could put our files down and compare blisters; certainly in the early weeks of our first year when we were trying to convert a large lump of steel into a replica Oxo cube. Then out of the blue it was decided that for growing lads the tea would be replaced by a third of a pint of milk. I wonder where this decision was made, some high powered conference of the Army Council I suppose and like so many of this type of decision it produced different results in that we quickly discovered there were many boys who didn't like milk, couldn't stand it in fact which meant that those of us who liked milk simply drank up the surplus. Now, the milk arrived in crates of a dozen bottles and by the time it reached us each bottle had a fair top of cream. Yes, you are ahead of me, none of us milk loving gourmets would have dreamed of drinking milk when we could drink cream and sadly a great deal of milk went down the drain.

Funny, looking back like this I wonder if my love of cream over the years had anything to do with this decision and should I see a lawyer, as Girl says, 'Put a blob of cream on it and he will eat anything.' There were three new courses to occupy our attention, though one, the bicycle course, was only new in the sense that this time we would be required to build a complete bicycle from scratch having been given the various components, brazing the frame tubes together then trueing the whole frame, building the wheels and finally polishing everything with emery cloth prior to applying the enamel finish. This enamel paint was brushed on then baked in a large oven; get it right and you were left with a superb finish. We were also working on our handicaps round the difficult bench golf course. I remember my carefully worked custom built bicycle spoke let me down badly though the selected quarter inch ball bearings served me well. Enter the two Royal Marine Sergeants They too were beavering away on building their bicycles ready for enamelling and, I musn't forget, a couple of really nice guys, but in true Marine fashion drama lay just round the corner.

The oven used for baking the bicycle components was housed in an extension of the main building and was a simple structure of sheet steel, taking the form of a large box maybe seven feet high, five feet wide and five feet deep. There were steel bars inside, from which the freshly painted components were hung. There was a large door at the front which made it easy to walk into the oven. So far so good; however this was an oven which for the purposes of stoving needed high temperatures. Gas was used for this as in any gas oven except of course for the size. The gas burners went round three sides of the oven at floor level; switch on the gas and apply a flame to the burner and bingo away it went.

Well, that was the theory at least, but this oven had a strange will of its own. It just wouldn't light. The trick was to try and kid it that you weren't really bothered whether or not the bloody thing lit at all and starting on the right hand side of the oven and the end of the burner and with the gas switched on you ran whatever sort of flame you were using (piece of rolled up paper usually) as fast as you could round the burners in an anti clockwise direction. The burners would light with a satisfying little bang as each one came under the flame until you reached the end of the burner, now on the left hand side, when the whole lot would expire with a more than satisfying bang. The next move? Simple refresh your vocabulary of oaths and start again. This would go on for some time whilst you got steadily blacker with soot and your mates had learned to stop poking their heads round the corner to ask when the bloody oven would be ready as the paint on their bits was starting to dry. Suddenly it would work; the burners stayed lit and quickly shutting the door you would retire to the workshops to attend to your own 'bits', might even be time for quick round of 'golf' whilst waiting for the oven to reach the correct temperature, whatever that might have been. There was a sort of primitive thermometer fixed to the front of the oven door. The whole contraption was pretty primitive and yet only a few degrees of temperature change would alter the final colour out of all proportion.

So what happened if you were unlucky enough to get the temperature wrong? Well, if it had been your turn to tame this stupid oven then there could be a serious loss of marks to say nothing of friends as the frames had to be emery clothed again and the whole process repeated. And so to our two Royal Marine Sergeants

I cannot remember exactly when during the day but after checking the oven temperature I told the two Sergeants that it seemed OK and they could start to get their components in to bake. Not long afterwards, one came back and said the oven had gone out so I explained how to go about lighting it again and that you would need lots of patience. I went back to whatever I had been doing, when there was a pretty big explosion followed as always by utter silence whilst we all looked at each other and the Instructor, Mr Hull, a very religious gentleman, went off to check whether or not two Royal Marine Sergeants might have arrived at the heavenly gates a little early. The whole class followed of course and speaking personally I wasn't exactly enthusiastic about what we might find: what on earth would small pieces of Royal Marine Sergeant look like and would we be forced to look? It turned out to be a strange anti-climax. The oven was in a sorry state with the door blown off and there were bicycle components all over the place but not a sign of the Marines, not a trace anywhere. Had they really travelled to the heavenly gates on a hot blast of the Portsmouth's Gas Company's gas and would they be cross, the gas company I mean, not the Marines; after all the Royal Marines, as everyone knows, are a very special breed of soldier and they would have arrived for Peter's little welcoming chat totally unfazed by their strange travel arrangements.

It wasn't long before the main topic of conversation was quite simply, 'Where the hell are they?' There had been a lot of people of all ranks in and out of the workshops, Mr Hull, bless him, was feeling the strain of this mass gazing at his battered oven but my goodness, watching all this verbal activity and listening to it was obvious that there was much to discuss. Suddenly, and quite out of the blue, one of the investigative party suggested that it might be a good idea to notify the Depot Police and maybe instigate a search. I cannot remember who this might have been but he was obviously of high rank and importance because there was a rush to comply and this had not happened when one of the class had suggested it some hours previously.

A search of this nature was going to be a nightmare in the Depot and it was getting dark. It was a maze of large storage sheds, workshops, railway lines and platforms covering a huge acreage. We were, that is Peter, Ginger, Ray and I, deep in discussion entirely devoted to what the hell was our Commanding Officer going to tell the Royal Marines' Commanding Officer, was there maybe a form he could fill in and sign? or just blurt it out: 'Sorry, old chap, we seem to have lost two of your Marine Sergeants, frightful bore.' What then? Would we be expected to replace them with two of our own?

Ray said he couldn't think of anyone in the Depot that would fit the bill. Ginger thought that the new Adjutant would be perfect. He was as big as two Marines even if they were Sergeants, to say nothing of a superb broken nose. We imagined he was very fit, after all he was still breaking other people's noses somewhere in the bowels of various rugby scrums. The four of us agreed this was probably the best solution. I often wonder if Major Clarke ever knew how close he came to being two Marine Sergeants Ah well, ignorance is bliss.

At last a result: they had been found, wandering about a little battered but as I said earlier, not fazed. One was boasting a broken collar bone but the other as far as I remember escaped intact. I had suffered a few misgivings as we waited for news, mostly directed at thoughts of what Girl might have to say about our losing two Marines. You may remember I said previously that she had a soft spot for the Royal Marines: perfectly understandable, she is a Portsmouth girl and this was Portsmouth after all, home of the Royal Marines.

So back to the bicycles. Shame about the lost chance to swap the Adjutant. I must reiterate at this point that we liked the Adjutant, he was a superb officer. Meanwhile we continued to move on through the courses which eventually brought us inevitably to the black art of 'browning' the method by which small arms are rust proofed and given their blue-black finish. At Hilsea there was a set system to ensure that everybody did a turn in the browning shop. I cannot remember the exact number that normally made up what was referred to in orders as the 'Browning Party' but after two or three days were instantly recognisable anyway by their colour – black. In our case it was simply the six of us, the Boys and the two Egyptians; we were already a correctly sized group and moving together through our final test year it was doubly convenient.

As I have pointed out, during training every Boy did a stint on the 'Browning Party'. So when we arrived at our very own 'Browning Party' we knew exactly how to proceed. First let the cooks know; the business of Browning involved a very early start for two of the party who would get a special breakfast courtesy of the cooks and in these situations the cooks always did us proud hence there was never any problem finding the two volunteers for this early shift.

So how was this 'browning' or as some people wrongly refer to it 'blueing' achieved? Well it was a long tedious process almost totally labour intensive, and involving the use of various acids so requiring great care in protecting oneself. It also required at least two large tanks capable of boiling water and of course holding the larger components; finally it required a drying room which could be brought up to a reasonable temperature. The browning room at the ATB comprised a reasonable space, two tanks heated by wood fires underneath, a long bench, a small drying room equipped with racks to hang the components on and heated by a small coke stove which would be familiar to thousands of soldiers throughout the Army who have spent many hours huddled round one of these stoves on a cold winter's night.

A Boy NCO would be in charge of a Browning Party, a stint that I had already done and not one to be enjoyed. The final quality of the Brown was entirely down to me but this result depended entirely on the enthusiasm, or not, of the rest of the party. This meant a lot of chasing them up but mostly just worrying. This time it was different; we were all bound up in the final result and so we were well motivated. The process itself was very simple but as remarked earlier, tedious and very dirty and with no possible way of short-cutting any stage. All the components had been previously prepared by the Boy whose work it was. Small components were wired together and in larger parts rifle or machine gun barrels, for example, the barrels, and indeed any holes had been plugged to protect the important finish in the bores. All the components had to be degreased by boiling in water to which soda had been added and this repeated with clean water. Hence the two tanks and also the reason that two Boys had to be in very early to light the wood and coal fires and hopefully get the water boiling in good time for the rest of the party to start work. The stove in the drying room also needed to be lit in good time.

Once the components had been removed from the boiling water they were allowed to dry and barrels were dried out and cleaned using jute then re-plugged. The next stage was to mix the 'Browning mixture' to double the normal strength. I have absolutely no memory of the acids used though at this time we would all have known them by heart including the various strengths for the mixture. Nitric acid I remember as an ingredient and also Spirits of Nitre. No wonder this was regarded as a black art, even before we all ended up as black as the components. The next move was to coat the components with the double strength Browning mixture using small sponges and wearing rubber gloves, then into the drying room until the next morning and now clean up and we were ready for another early start tomorrow.

A feature of this part of the process was the awful appearance of the components, quite a shock the first time I saw it. The parts were covered in the most ghastly looking rust in an unbelievable number of colours. Now the components were boiled in clean water and the blacking could commence – not the parts but us. Each component must be thoroughly brushed, either bristle or wire though for optimal results the wire brushing was best. Surprise surprise, which was the more difficult and tedious? The wire of course.

Following the brushing the pieces were once again coated but this time with the normal strength solution and again hung in the drying room to dry. All of this was repeated over four days by which time the whole of the Depot had become accustomed to the sight of a small group of Boys, black from head to toe, whom nobody wished to be associated with and who were studiously avoided by officers, NCOs and even the RSM. We were indeed a privileged and mucky lot. Finally the components were immersed in oil, and so back to the workshops for assembly. Looking back it is hard to imagine anyone could come up with a process like this to rust-proof and blue small arms; what would happen if there were to be a war? We soon found out! They scrapped it.

One of our next courses was the final Range Course, eagerly looked forward to, when we would get to shoot the Vickers heavy machine gun (and at the same time be examined in our knowledge and dexterity in dealing with stoppages); this also applied to the Lewis light machine gun. Always there was the relentless examination and accumulation of marks.

I had during the early summer of this final year realised one of my great ambitions to be selected to represent the Depot at Bisley during the Corps Championships. Selection had followed many enjoyable hours of practice on the Tipnor Ranges, and though this intruded on my final workshop year I didn't really care. I was having the time of my life, I had even been issued with my own rifle, something that normally only occurred when you reached 'Man Service'; more on this later. The shooting team spent a week at Bisley in tented accommodation or 'under canvas' to use the correct expression. Unfortunately we didn't win anything but even worse I shot very badly and this fact weighed very heavily on me and certainly spoiled my Bisley Deput but there would be many more weeks at Bisley over the years and with much better results.

There were two other changes to my normal routine. Major Clarke had started a Boy's rugby team, and like all things new, an appeal appeared on Depot Orders asking for any boy or boys who were interested or better still, had played rugby, to hand their names in to the Adjutant. I had played Rugby League (the Northern code) at school so in went my name, taking great care to emphasise that my previous experience had been with the Rugby League code. There was one other Boy with previous experience, Jeans, who like me had played at school but unlike me, Rugby Union and unlike me he was a big lad and surprise, surprise, he was Welsh. We were an unlikely pairing around which to build a rugby team but build one Major Clarke did and within our capabilities a good one. The Adjutant saw me as an outside half or stand off as it was better known in those days. Harry Jeans was a very good flank forward, hard and with a wonderful knack of protecting his outside half when the going got rough. I loved that. I had also been made Captain because that sort of came with the position of stand-off half, or fly half or even outside half whichever you might prefer, still the same position though.

Sadly Harry died a couple of months ago so when the going gets rough now, I shall have to defend myself. The team flourished and we played a variety of teams around the Portsmouth area and indeed into deepest Hampshire. 'Churches College' at Petersfield was always very keenly contested and the food was great. We also played men's teams including the RAF at Thorney Island and the Fleet Air Arm at Gosport, but whilst we didn't disgrace ourselves the weight penalty and I suppose physical maturity took a heavy toll, I was still seventeen as were the other lads so faced with the massive communal bruising and a timely word from the Medical Officer, Major Clarke dropped these fixtures. I remember truthfully that they had become more painful than enjoyable but don't let Major Clarke read this wherever he may be; who knows he may be up there somewhere trying to argue his way out of becoming two Royal Marine Sergeants!

During this year Peter was making a name for himself as a footballer with the Boy's Army Cup winning team. Life was pretty good at this time. Girl and I were very, very much an item. I was getting in later and later at nights and spending more and more hours in the toilet trying to keep up with my notes and drawings. But in the background the sinister figure of Adolf Hitler was becoming increasingly threatening to all our futures. Then following the return of the Prime Minister Neville Chamberlain with the now notorious piece of paper our Test work came to an abrupt end as we were recruited into the general panic of trying to get the country in some sort of order to fight a war. Somewhere it must have been decided that the war would be fought using Army issue blankets. For some strange reason we Boys of the ATB were drafted in to load blankets onto lorries. This was interesting as none of us had seen an Army lorry before (internal combustion, I mean); previously the only form of transport we had been familiar with was the General Service Cart with four mules up. I can distinctly remember a Corporal Murleigh (Post Corporal) being charged with speeding in the Depot at the reins of a cart and four lively mules. Anyway we worked very hard into the early hours of the morning loading blankets; they seemed inexhaustible. I feel certain we must have covered Korea and the Falklands and that blankets are the secret behind the British Army's success in many battlefields.

During this period there was much digging of trenches going on and we picked up the task of digging a deep trench in the back garden of one of the senior officers. We paraded, gathered up our spades and pick axes and set off to Northend, a local shopping centre, always very busy. It was a march of about two miles but I remember it being a nice sunny day and by the time we got to Northend we were well into our stride. However this was the period of the film *Snow White* and we had been singing the hits from it as we marched along. I suppose all together there was about eight of us and shouldering our picks and shovels as we reached the main road we dropped into a crouching position and singing loudly, ' Heigh Ho ' we gave a very passable imitation of the Seven Dwarfs. The shoppers certainly enjoyed it, clapping our efforts and generally joining in.

It was a good day, the lady of the house fed us very well, we got a mention in the local press; pity about the trench filling with water. And so back to the exams.

The final examination that the four of us, Peter, Ginger, Ray, myself and of course the two Egyptians were deeply into by this time, I should try to explain. Firstly it was called 'Going on Test' and we then became officially the Test Party both in the Depot and the Workshops, a sort of protected status where we were excused many chores. The test itself was a mixture of everything we had done and was largely practical. It was sited in a smaller workshop and under the control of a Mr Honner, one of the very senior lecturers and not to be trifled with, believe me.

The' test' started, as all Army Trade tests seemed to start, with – a fitting test. Yes back to the blisters, this involved two blocks of metal which had to be filed flat, square and parallel and fitted and bolted together by means of a half inch by half inch slot cut in one piece (female) and a matching tongue cut on the other (male); the drilling both for the clearance hole in the male and the tapping hole in the female, both done with a hand drill, were critical if the two halves were to fit perfectly whichever way they were turned. The bolt was quarter inch diameter, leaving very little clearance. It was absolutely imperative that whoever lined up your hand drill by eye got it right.

It was a great tribute to the skills we had acquired that this seldom went wrong. As test blocks go, this one had a look of being reasonably easy but in practice it was very difficult and I musn't forget there was a time limit of eighteen hours to complete it from start to finish and of course we knew about it well enough from previous test parties and had already formed our method of approach before we even started on the long weeks of test. I personally found it reasonable as did the others with the exception of Capt. Essawy. We had already detected this weakness when called upon to perform this type of work and as Essawy was such a likeable character the four of us made a conscious decision to help him wherever we could. Now this wasn't going to be easy under Bertie Honner's eagle eye, but we did and he passed very well and now? I think maybe there was collusion somewhere at the top in the interests of Colonial Harmony.

Mind you, we loved it and it gave us a warm glow inside; indeed, worrying about our Egyptian friend sometimes took our own worries away. So how was I doing? Pretty well really, I just had one strange hiccup with the brazing test in which we had to braze two tubes together; for some reason I hadn't employed enough heat. One afternoon the Warrant Officer in charge of the workshops who did a great deal of the marking sent for me. Unusual this, what had I been guilty of this time? Lying on his desk were the two halves of a brazing test. He looked at me and said, 'Yes, it's yours and honest I only tapped it with a pencil.' Ah well, no marks there but I was lucky because amongst the hundreds of marks accumulating it was only worth fifteen and I would surely pull those back when we got round to the Blacksmith's test. I couldn't wait.

The Blacksmith's test was going to present a problem. There was no way that Essawy would get through this, so what to do? The six of us would assemble in the Blacksmith's workshop where Mr Sullivan would outline the jobs to be done and which anyway we knew well enough from past candidates. We had firstly to forge weld four harness links, three normal and on the end one large round link; next the forgings for two pistol springs. These were not going to be made up into the final springs but would be marked entirely as forgings. Additionally there were the fires to be made up correctly, forge tools to be repaired and reshaped (tongs for example); these were all finally laid out on whichever forge you had been allocated. Eventually the forge and the fire would be checked by Mr Sullivan and of course marked, then the links and spring forgings were taken over to the Test Workshop where both Mr Honner and Mr Sullivan would do the final marking.

There were six of us and six forges. The workshop itself was small, quite dark and always sort of cluttered, very much a Blacksmith's forge in fact. The key to our being able to help or I should say my being able to help Essawy because it had been decided that I would do any work that we thought we could get away with, would depend on what Mr Sullivan did during the period of the test. Like all the final tests this was also timed; I think the time allowed was forty-five minutes. So I just made up two sets of links and springs, fortunately not a problem for me. Mr Sullivan seemed to be keeping out of the way (Colonial Harmony maybe). Essawy made up his forge, laid everything out including the work I had done and we all stood back and kept our fingers crossed.

The two lecturers walked round the forge, chatting and making entries on their clipboards, sometimes picking up a set of links or peering at one of the spring forgings, then we were told to stamp our 'test number' on our work and take it over and put it on Mr Honner's bench. That was it. We didn't hear another word. This was normal with practical work as they never gave out the marks, hopefully they were accumulating somewhere secret and plentifully. There was a slight indication that our Colonies were in favour: Mr Sullivan remarked quietly to me as we left for the day, 'I see you've had a busy morning, Corporal'

There was much left to do, we had to complete five rifles and they needed to be as near perfect as possible, and this included their test firing at the hands of Sandy Erskine. A Vickers gun and tripod also subject to Range Testing, a Lewis gun ditto. Various woodwork tests embracing the most commonly found damage and in the bicycle shop two wheels to lace and true and everything done against the clock. How we all became obsessed by the minutes ticking away when something wasn't going just right. There were two pistols to be overhauled and a week on the Range. No picnic this one, plenty of theory and the very difficult art of recognising the cause of a stoppage on the machine guns and clearing it instantly or even sooner. Nerves and getting flustered could often be devastating to say nothing of embarrassing but we battled on and the end loomed ever nearer.

Eventually the last phase of all the written exams which also included delivering a lecture. Once this was over we then had the prospect of a Course on the various instruments we were also responsible for: binoculars, compasses, rangefinders, angle of sight instruments, telescopic sights, clinometers. Quite a formidable list and the course also included a great deal of optical theory. This course was held at the Artillery Optical and instrument school at Woolwich and we would be housed in the Cambridge Barracks. The duration of the course was four weeks and included a two day visit to the Royal Enfield Factory, a wonderful experience and also a visit to the Tower of London Arms Museum.

The name of the workshops where our practical training took place was the Rotunda and I'm sure this name will strike a few memories amongst old Artillery Gunners. We were still well short of this stage of our training but it was something to look forward to.

As I approached the final months, how was my conversion from Schoolboy to Soldier coming along? Well, the next few weeks were going to indicate not very well, Indeed, this applied to all four of us as we broke the cardinal rule of all real soldiers. Never, never volunteer for anything not even if they offer money. But before I talk about this there was a very serious landmark for me. I reached my eighteenth birthday and duly at midnight in accordance with the Army law I was a man and must instantly, if not sooner, move myself lock stock and barrel into a Men's block. This affected all the other members of our little group, so give a week or two we finished up in the same room. This was very convenient given we were steadily progressing through the final stages of our training as a group.

I have emphasised on several occasions the fixation of the Army to separate Men from Boys. This was of course a sexually oriented decision, its origins lost in the mists of time, a classic example of this paranoia. A few weeks before my eighteenth birthday there was a large Exhibition being arranged in Glasgow to celebrate some important anniversary and the Royal Army Ordnance Corps were taking the opportunity to mount a recruiting drive for Armourers and had taken a stand with the intention of staffing it with two Boys who would be showing examples of their work (mostly woodwork and including a pair of pistol grips) and at the same time working on repairs to various weapons, rifles mostly. What a glorious prospect for a break, it truly was exciting.

I was lucky enough to be selected as one of the Boys to go and as a Boy/Corporal could be given some responsibility. The Boy to share the duties at the Exhibition with me was not only a good friend but was also accommodated in my room, that is the one I was Boy/Corporal in charge of. Unbelievably, the day before we were due to leave was his eighteenth birthday and bingo he was a 'Man'. As we had been allocated a small room for accommodation at the Exhibition and I was still a Boy then suddenly I couldn't go. Typing this I am surprised at how the memory of this bitter disappointment and my anger at the time can still provoke a reaction, albeit a very minor one. Life was going to get a lot tougher than this and in the not too distant future. I remember too that Girl was very disappointed for me and that was nice as I would have been away for about a fortnight.

So 'never ever volunteer for anything' even if they offer you money, an absolute maxim for a 'real' soldier and never to be broken. Well, we did, the four of us, were we bored? Broke? Surely our finances couldn't be that low; after all we were now earning the princely sum, as Men, of ten shillings a week or was it that nice Medical Major who convinced us that it would be a truly good thing to do and might even save countless lives in the future; oh, and we would be paid five shillings per injection. Surely we couldn't have been that short of cash.

Apparently the Army Medical Corps were running trials with a new form of inoculation which would give protection against three types of tropical nasties. I know typhoid was one, the others escape my memory but every old soldier will remember the TAB jab; I see there are several dotted about my A.B.64 service book. The trick apparently for the Medical Chaps was to find the best solution in which to suspend the cultures in, hence the call for volunteers. I bet they were startled when they got four at once; after all it was rare indeed for a 'real' soldier to volunteer.

We paraded at the medical centre as ordered, rolled up our sleeves, tried to look nonchalant and were given the first of our two inoculations. We were excused duties and feeling quite virtuous popped into the NAAFI for a cup of tea and a game of snooker, then back to idle a few hours on our beds. This was probably the best thing we could have done. I never really knew, because very shortly we were four very sick volunteers, notice I didn't say 'soldiers'. For me it was almost a re-run of my vaccine fever symptoms: diarrhoea, vomiting and feeling really ill. I wasn't alone this time and the four of us could barely stand up. The whole thing was an awful mess and we couldn't even help ourselves but had to lie there in this mess until somebody turned up. Additionally there was a gradual swelling of the arm which had been used for the injection and it wasn't long before the elbow completely disappeared. I remember that my left arm was a continual swelling from the shoulder to the fingers; it was red and unbelievably painful to the touch. It became impossible to bear the weight of any clothes. We just didn't know what to do, eventually someone turned up and immediately contacted the medics who as I remember didn't seem unduly excited; they organised us into bed and properly cleaned up, fed us what were probably aspirins and said we were to report sick in the morning.

Unbelievable! following a terrible and painful night still being sick and convinced I was going to die a small posse of medics turned up. We were examined and told not to worry, the symptoms would ease off and we were to stay in bed, There followed three or four very miserable days and we began to feel less ill and were free of the diarrhoea and vomiting and our mates were bringing us food, the cookhouse having been alerted were putting themselves out so it was pretty good, pity about our appetites. As we began to get back to feeling normal, however, our arms got ever more painful even though the swelling was going down, so much so that it was totally crippling. If acute means anything this was it. Just remember, never ever volunteer for anything even if they offer you money.

On or around the third day one of our room 'mates' dashed in to tell us with great glee that a soldier in one of the Artillery Barracks who had volunteered for this experiment had just died. As by this time I, along with the others, had resigned ourselves to doing just that, the impact of this was, I remember, a little disappointing for the messenger but what the hell, you get to know who your friends are.

There was a programme for these injections involving a second one fourteen days after the first. As this particular 'D' day approached whatever improvement there was in our physical condition our arms remained both swollen and painful so we had sort of convinced ourselves that it wouldn't be possible to inject into the same arm again; in addition to the swelling and pain the area had become very hard. No place for wimps or sympathy for stupid people posing as soldiers, they'd had their money so roll up your sleeves, same arm please. Surprisingly the injection itself was OK but what wasn't OK was the exact repeat of our previous physical distress. What a mess we were all in and so ill. It was a nightmare and though it finally passed the painful arm lasted a very long time. Girl remembers grabbing my arm as we walked along the road weeks after the injection and the pain brought me to my knees as if I had been clubbed. I know that months later my arm was still very painful as were the others.

But it was back to the Test workshops and on with exams. There comes a time in a long drawn out test such as this when it settles into a routine pattern. One advantage of this is that you lose a great deal of the initial nervousness and apprehension. I felt this, and indeed needed to avoid getting over confident, or cocky whichever you fancy, same thing.

So it came to an end and whilst I felt relieved there was that faint niggle that it was too late now. The massive total of marks would have been added up and our individual classification as Armourers decided. From January 1935 it had been a long haul, sometimes good, often brutal and at times even vicious. I had endured a very fast learning curve, but at this time I was confident and very barrack-wise indeed, and we were all of us looking forward to our month at Woolwich and maybe a look at London. I should at this time say something about this final classification. It was of great importance to do well. There were two positive classifications one could attain, third class or second class; we were not allowed to be classified as first class until we had acquired at least one year's practical experience 'in the field'. There was also a dreaded negative classification, that of 'unclassified'. which meant starting the whole thing again, a frightening prospect. And so on to our Optical Course and the visit to Enfield. I was going to miss Girl. Ah well, you can't have everything.

We travelled up to London by train. I think this run from Portsmouth to Waterloo by electric train took around forty-five to fifty minutes and has never been equalled since.

When we arrived we were billeted in the Cambridge Barracks and, believe me, in those days one Army Barracks was the same as another. Looking round the barrack room I couldn't help thinking that in fact we hadn't moved at all and were still in our old Barrack block at Hilsea. And then the bugle sounded and we all knew we were in strange territory. No Regimental call, but most of all it wasn't even a bloody bugle, and I should know - just look at the muscle on my lip! Mind you, I still couldn't play anything, but I could manage a passable Last Post - always assuming a bit of time to practise. I had in fact survived my entire Boy Service as a member of the Band and I feel that this has to be possibly my greatest achievement. My goodness, I was indeed Barrack wise. So if it wasn't a bugle what the hell was it? A trumpet, Peter informed us, a bloody trumpet, and it was flat, thought it sounded odd (what's flat? I must have missed that bit during my long career in the band).

Trumpet, funny sound, strange barracks, it didn't make the slightest difference. We homed in on the cookhouse as if we had always lived in this Barracks and what joy, the food was both good and plentiful; we were going to enjoy our stay here and hopefully Peter would fill us in on the finer points of trumpet calls - 'flat'. I thought that's where people lived.

In fact we did need to come to grips with the new calls, trumpet or not. Here, like at Hilsea and anywhere else in the Army, the day was dictated by the different calls whatever the instrument and it wasn't wise to miss them. The next day was important for us to be up and prompt as it was the first day of our three-day visit to the Enfield Small Arms Factory. Our chaperon S/Sgt Dick Ford was from our workshops. An interesting memory here; we paraded on the square in the new threes formation for the first time, no more forming fours. A mixed feeling, this new drill was much easier but the old fours drill with its precision movement into the fours formation could be visually very effective. I suspect it was missed by every RSM in the Army.

And so to the Station where we fought our way on to the commuter train, an eye opener this (have I said before that nothing changes?). We were met at the factory and being a small party anyway were taken in hand by a gentleman who was to stay with us all day. What a wonderful two days these turned out to be: we were introduced to the manufacturing processes of all the small arms in service and which we had already worked on. There was a great emphasis on the manufacture of that great light machine gun the Bren, only just accepted by the Government. We had not seen this gun so we were genuinely delighted to be able to handle one and indeed strip and assemble it. Designed in Brno, Czechoslovakia, this gun was to become an old friend; every armourer would handle thousands of them throughout his career and as a professional and one who loved this gun I would class it as the finest light machine gun ever made. Later we saw it being tested to the limit on the factory range.

There was a strange manufacturing decision made at the outset of the Bren production. It had been decided that the body of the gun would be drop forged. At the time of our visit this proved one of the highlights; the body was a large component and it was being drop forged with one blow of the hammer. There was a follow-up drop to remove the metal that had been squeezed out. A large billet of almost white hot steel was introduced into the lower die and down came the hammer, the impact shaking the whole factory. Oh, we loved that, it was spectacular, but though we now had a very high quality forging duplicating the body dimensions, it was a really silly way to go about making a body for any gun. After this highly entertaining spectacle, the forging was taken away and when cooled it required some seventy plus machining operations to arrive at a body ready for assembly into a finished gun. I might add of the highest possible quality but of course this was not what the country, on the brink of war, wanted; the only thing that mattered was to get the gun rolling off the production line in massive quantities. This wasn't the way and indeed they quickly changed from forging to casting.

We still enjoyed that massive pyrotechnical thump though, and of course only now in old age have I given the production problems any thought, but my God I still remember that enormous hammer. The other major highlight was a visit to the pattern room where they stored at least one production model of every weapon classified as small arms and that had been accepted and produced for the British Army. Each model was sealed with a red authorising wax seal. They were there, of course, to provide a permanent reference in case of problems with manufacture or even dispute. They were almost all fully serviceable and capable of being fired. This pattern room is now located at Leeds and is open to the public.

Following our visit to Enfield we visited the Royal Armoury at the Tower of London, taking the opportunity to have a look at the Crown Jewels. We were now ready to start our Optical course at the Rotunda. The workshops were quite different to what we had been used to, being much cleaner to start with as befits an Optical repair workshop. The benches were quite high and certainly an innovation for us. We would be sitting down to work. We spent the days stripping, cleaning and adjusting the various instruments, all of which was fairly straightforward. None of us found any difficulty with this work; what we did find difficult were the masses of notes and drawings we had to complete each evening dealing with Optical theory. Was this, I now wonder, a ploy to keep us from the delights of London night life? If so it couldn't have been more futile; we could barely raise enough for a half each in the pub round the corner.

We were lucky though. Peter Hills had a brother or brother in law (I must phone him, Peter I mean) who was driving a Ministry car in London and was good enough give us a tour of the city one evening, certainly one of the highlights of our stay in London. Time once again for examinations where once again the marks would be added on to the grand total. My own result was not as good as I had hoped at 78 per cent but it was about average for the group.

I cannot close this account of our all too brief stay at Woolwich without bringing up the all too constant argument about the use of Spiders Webs in the instruments requiring what are called graticules. A telescopic rifle sight is an excellent example, everybody is familiar with the cross hairs lining up on the target to be assassinated. The marvellous educational benefits of television have made certain that we all know the mechanics of assassination. Well, the cross hairs that the rifleman carefully lined up were there, courtesy of the common house spider.

At this time nothing had been found to even approach the spun thread of a spider. It had massive strength allied to a superbly clear thread, so far found to be impossible to achieve in man-made attempts. So how was it done? Collect your spiders in August, this was the best month (please don't ask), then keep them in a healthy container, for the spiders that is, restrict their food (it says starve them in my notes). Finally, having prepared a rectangle made up of one-eighth diameter brass you shake out the spider gently, and carefully wind the rectangle, picking up the spider's thread by which it is now dangling. Success meant a brass rectangle which had two or three lengths of this thread stretched across it. Available was a special set of drawers designed to store these rectangles of brass until required, that is, until our exams. All sounds fiddly and indeed highly improbable but it was relatively simple. It but remained to toss the spider a handful of vitamin reinforced flies and set him – her, free. And the finale. Take your lens which has four small notches engraved at 90 degree intervals around its circumference, a minute touch of adhesive, lay one of the threads across, notch to notch, snip off to length, another handful of flies to our busy donor, preferably human flavoured, and hand your telescope in for marking. I know what you are thinking but I kid you not: there are pints to be won. Armed with this absolutely accurate knowledge. I've quite liked spiders ever since our Optical course.

Pack up and back to a proper bugle call, at least we could hear it. I would often, now with an air of nonchalance, remark, 'Sounded a bit flat to me,' very impressive that. Maybe I'll ask my old bugle master Corporal Hollingsworth one day, but then again he will probably be thinking who the hell are you so better not. After all, looking back, I think we only met that once when he put me in charge and dashed off. And as I remember snippets, I can hardly believe that I survived all those years as a Bugler in the Depot Band. So our old question, still unanswered. Am I yet a Soldier? Or still a Schoolboy? Well all those dodged horrible chores as a result of being in the band must count for something!

But I was back with Girl and experiencing that constantly recurring theme in a Serviceman's life, reunion, after being away for varying periods of time. One of nearly four years was just around the corner but we were blissfully unaware of the future. Our next worry, and it was very close, the Test results! This was combined with a visit to the Postings Office where both would be revealed together and the main reason for this was simply that with a number of postings to be sorted (in our case four) and all in different parts of the country, the one with the highest marks had first pick, a simple and fair way.

Before all this there was Christmas. Was my Dad going to produce the Quality Street once again? Of course he was and one extra for the family. No wonder I loved my Dad! Mind you, there is Mum's cooking to be entered into this particular equation. So another great Christmas and I could enjoy dwelling on going back with so much excitement to come: final results, a posting, Girl and nestling in my case *two* tins of Quality Street, Life couldn't get much better.

Lurking behind all this euphoria, sadly, the war clouds were gathering. I cannot remember that any of us were particularly concerned, at least it was never a subject for discussion, an odd word or two usually provoked by some news item or other. It somehow returns in my mind as a strange period of which I can remember very little. The truth probably lay in everybody's ability to tuck their heads in the sand, but to no avail, the pending disaster continued to gather momentum. I suppose that Girl and I were so engrossed in each other that even so serious a possibility as war didn't penetrate our idyll.

Finally the four of us stood in front of the postings officer and believe me, we were concentrating now. The great news was that we had all passed achieving second class classification so we were starting out as well as it was possible to do. I was the lucky one to have amassed the most marks so mine would be the first choice. In previous years an Armourer's initial posting would always be to one of the Command Workshops . These were scattered round the British Isles and could be as far away as Fort George in Scotland. This meant swapping the Barrack life of the Depot, with its parades, guard duties and discipline, for another Depot almost identical just in a different place. The work in these workshops was hard with long hours and so they were not popular. I was especially apprehensive as to the possible choices. I was hoping that amongst the Command Workshops might be Hilsea, with my first choice this would suit me well enough, just a change of workplace and of course I knew the Barracks routine backwards; but of course the important thing was that, Girl, lived just up the road.

But as so often happens in the Army our anonymous makers of decisions had been beavering away again and before retiring to lie down, had decided a change in the Establishment of the Infantry Regiments would be a good idea and this had been implemented. What they had changed was the number of RAOC Armourers attached to an Infantry Battalion from one Armourer Sergeant, to one Sergeant and a Private. This meant there were many vacancies among the Infantry for Armourer Privates and that meant our little foursome.

This of course was great news. We all knew that an Armourer's life with the Infantry was, give or take, pretty good. The Command Workshops were bad and we were free of that possibility. But which Battalions were on offer and more importantly where were they stationed? Yes, I know, I'm never satisfied! but it could be anywhere in the world virtually. I stood there with my thoughts in a turmoil. The postings officer, a retired Lt. Colonel, took his time in these situations, they always seem to take their time, but eventually he listed the Regiments and their locations that were to be our destiny and invited me to make the first choice.

Available to me were The Second Battalion The Hampshire Regiment, stationed at Aldershot; The Royal Scots also at Aldershot; The KSLI at Bordon and finally a Regiment whose name I cannot remember but who were stationed somewhere near Plymouth. There are in life a number of crossroads where one has to make a decision and in the services this can happen often and can be fortunate or even ultimately disastrous. One that often seems the more attractive may turn out to be a bad choice and of course vice versa. Unfortunately there is no crystal ball available, but for me the choice was pretty straightforward and went as follows. Girl lived in Portsmouth so the Plymouth posting was a non starter, much too far away, Bordon was regarded as the place to station a Regiment with a record of misbehaviour, it was also miles from anywhere, so it had to be Aldershot. Girl's Dad had served with the Second Battalion The Hampshire Regiment during the First World War so without hesitation it was The Hampshires. So two things came nicely together. Aldershot was ideal for commuting to Portsmouth and of course Girl's Dad would be delighted that I had joined his old Regiment and that couldn't be bad for my courtship of his daughter.

Peter went to The Royal Scots so this time we shared a town rather than a bed space; Ginger opted for the KSLI's at Bordon, and Ray went off to Plymouth. The sad thing is that I didn't see anything of Peter at Aldershot for various reasons, mainly I suspect because I was always in Portsmouth on our free days. Ginger came in a couple of times and we shared a drink and a yarn but I only saw Ray once and not to speak to. This was in Berlin when he captained a London Select Football team playing Berlin in the old Olympic stadium. He later turned professional and captained Brighton for a number of years.

Ray was the epitome of my crossroads theory. He was captured in France months later and spent the entire war as a POW. However I cannot remember whether Plymouth was a choice or whether he was last to choose and this was the only choice left. Ray was a wonderful athlete and somehow 'professional football' fits my memories very well.

So that was it: we were all committed and now just to wait for our posting date and another new start. Christmas was only just behind us and already 1939 had been mapped out but the old sense of apprehension kept nudging me.

So was my transformation from School Boy to Soldier complete after nearly four years at Hilsea? I certainly felt like a real soldier, wise in all the ways that a soldier should be. I could parade, immaculately turned out if necessary and super turned out if that was necessary. I could parade and drill a squad even though I had never been taught or trained to do so but most of all I never at any time thought of myself as anything other than a soldier. I was very comfortable with this and yes, I was definitely a soldier and a good one, at least that was my opinion; this would be severely tested during the next three years. When I left the Army twenty six years later I found the transition back to civilian life very difficult and some sixty years on from that frightening first day I am still at heart a soldier but more importantly an ex 'Boy Soldier'! Very special that.

We were sort of in limbo during the next few weeks. I was spending every moment I could with Girl and because we had a little more money to spend the cinema was very much a favourite evening; indeed I think for all of us it was a nice relaxing few weeks. During this period the Workshops were issued with a Bren gun, the 'Bren' as it became known to many thousands of soldiers. It almost rhymes with 'friend' and so it should a friend that never let you down or maybe in those early days of the War before it had a chance to settle down. This particular Bren was a very early model and was made in Czechoslovakia, the country that had developed it. I think it was number seven and beautifully finished.

As a result of this Bren turning up our little gang went back to the workshops to learn the basics, stripping and assembly, how the action worked, the inevitable drawings to be completed (too late for marks now) and that was that but we had at least handled it. Time was beginning to drag, but in a pleasant way. Our snooker certainly improved over these weeks but eventually we appeared on Depot orders requesting our presence in the Company Office. Here we were instructed to sort of close down our association with Hilsea Barracks. This, as it always does in the Army, means starting to hand everything in and collecting signatures on a large number of forms to prove we had done so.

Inevitably during this process I was reintroduced to my old friend the handcart, loaded and pushed if you remember by one of the unlucky soldiers who was doing his spell of 'jankers' during that traumatic evening some thousands of years ago. No help this time, load it up and push it round to the Quartermaster's store. He is almost smiling this morning; we are after all returning some of his property. No, it doesn't belong to the Ministry of Defence, at least only in some vague ' they paid for it originally way'; like all Army Stores it is the property of the Quartermaster and if you don't believe that, try getting something issued free just because it's worn out. Ah well, where next for a signature? Take your pick, Clem, NAAFI, gymnasium, cookhouse and of course the workshops.

Very mixed emotions when we finally marched down to the workshops. We had taken great trouble with our appearance; after all this was the only time our Instructors saw us dressed as real soldiers as opposed to working overalls and this was a courtesy they had well and truly earned over the last three and a bit years. We all had our favourites of course but they had without exception taught us well and in the process managed to look after us. I think we saw them as father figures. As we moved round from Instructor to Instructor I was surprised how emotional it was but remembering that I had spent four years with these gentlemen trying to absorb the knowledge and skills they had accumulated over a very long time it would have been a sad reflection if I hadn't felt a deep bond.

There was a good deal of advice flying around but to me the one I felt most appropriate came from the Instructor who taught machine guns. I had been, along with the others, chatting about the new postings that were now available to us and how we had all landed postings to Infantry Units. This Instructor, a very large gentleman I remember and one who didn't suffer fools gladly (I feel ashamed that I cannot recall his name), had been emphasising that we should always maintain the highest standards of workmanship and to remember that if you issued an Infantryman with a blacksmith's anvil he would bend it. How true !

And so it ended, four years of hard work, a lot of disappointments, a great deal of fun and always that feeling of being sort of special or maybe just different. 'Schoolboy to Soldier'? Oh yes, indeed, and proud of it.

What of my parents during these years? Very supportive, plenty of letters and I suspect after four years of worrying more than delighted that I had finally made it. There were times when I desperately needed them but I really was on my own so I gritted my teeth and got on with it. I know that they were very proud of that. On the next few pages is a letter that I sent them telling of my final results. Like so much of this sort of thing it turned up amongst my mother's possessions after she died. It had been lovingly stored away all these years by my parents and finding it was a moving moment.

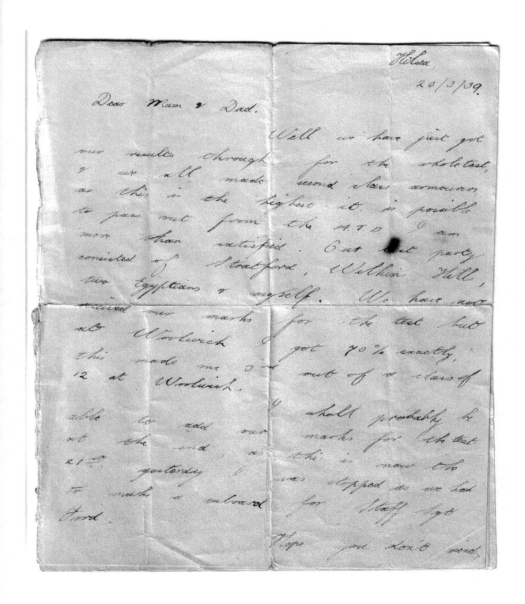

Hilsea,
20/3/39.

Dear Mum & Dad.

Well we have just got our results through for the whole test, & we all made second class armourers, as this is the highest it is possible to pass out from the A.T.D. I am more than satisfied. Our test party consisted of Stratford, Wilkins Hill, two Egyptians & myself. We have not received our marks for the test but at Woolwich I got 70% exactly, this made me 3rd out of a class of 12 at Woolwich.

able to add our marks for the test at the end, so this is now the 21st. yesterday I was stopped as we had to make a cuboard for Staff Sgt. third.

Hope you don't mind,

the letter being late, but I left
so that I could give you the results.
Our pay will be 3/6 a day now
or in weekly terms 24/6 a week.
Heaven only knows when we will
start drawing it though.

So far we have no
news of posting but I will let you
know as soon as possible. As for the
Rugger — the team has just about reached
up, officer & lost interest & now it
just a matter of playing when they
can get a team, so yours truly is
playing football regularly with the
mens second team, makes a nice change,
but I'm afraid rugger has got a little
something that football doesn't seem to
posess.

The weather down here

is pretty varied, bitterly cold one day & quite mild & warm the next.

Well I will close now waiting for the marks, love to all.

Love Clem

Results just come through, I came out top with 106½ marks out of 200 or 76%, this is well above average. Hill was second, Stratford & then Wilkins. pass marks for a second are 980

CHAPTER 6
THE 2ND BATTALION THE HAMPSHIRE REGIMENT

Another start and not unlike my first but now I was wise in the ways of soldiering and very Barrack wise indeed, so as the train pulled out of Portsmouth Station I knew that it did rain in the south but I also knew that Aldershot was a Garrison town and regarded as the home of the British Army and I was looking forward to being stationed there. To reach Corruna Barracks where The Second Battalion The Hampshire Regiment,(always shortened to 2nd Hants) were in residence, nice sounding phrase that and also perfectly correct in military circles. I was faced with a long trek up a steepish hill which I was to get to know well as Gun Hill. The Barracks was at the top.

This area of Aldershot housed most of the many Barracks and they were arranged off the main road along what were in effect streets. The barracks occupied either side of these streets in a very orderly and standard system. Corrunna Barracks was just over the crest of the hill then turn left down the first street. I wonder what sort of March day it was, must have been wintry I suppose but I have no recollection of it raining so it could have been a nice sunny day and that would have been very appropriate to herald a wonderful summer attached to this great Infantry Regiment and the start of a long stay with them.

I am to this day a member of their Staff Association and honoured at a dinner every year as one of the remaining survivors of the Battle of the Tebourba Gap. More of this battle later but to quote Lt. General Sir Brian Horrocks, speaking about the County Regiments and their qualities as Infantry soldiers: 'It was precisely these qualities which stood them in good stead during what I have always considered to be one of the epic battles of the last war, Tebourba Gap in North Africa.'

For the moment here I am, after struggling to the top of Gun Hill carrying all my goods and chattels distributed about my person as laid down by the Army for the 'PBI'. I'm not complaining, because when I can find the bloody Guard Room I shall be joining a crack Infantry Battalion and there will be a lot of miles to be covered in the not too distance future carrying much the same kit. Did I say that I have good feet? My God, I was going to be glad that I was so blessed. So past the sentry and straight through the open doors, report to the Guard Commander, ask the way to the cookhouse, I'm famished, pick up a defaulter (jankers doesn't change). A good tuck in, back to the Guard Room; they knew who I was by now, everything was all smiles and welcome. And I was revelling in this Barrack wise confidence. I really was a Soldier and behaving like one. Note there was no dithering at the door this time.

More and more that snowy afternoon when I arrived at Hilsea seemed a thousand years ago. Was I ever fourteen years old? Some things never change though. I had been allocated to a barrack room and when I opened the door it was very much 'Déjà vu'. Locate my bed, organise my kit then get down to introductions and a long chat with my new room-mates and of course paying my way into being included in the 'Gun Fire'. This is pretty common through out the Army and consists of a small group who have organised a system of making a bucket or two buckets of tea before reveille (courtesy of the cookhouse and fuelled by suitable bribes). This tea they would bring to your bedside and is known as 'Gunfire'. For this service everyone paid a regular amount into a kitty. I use a Teasmaid now!

During this first evening I learned that my immediate 'boss', Armourer Sgt Arnold, was away giving technical evidence at an enquiry in London to do with a shooting case. I also located the NAAFI, very important that. The next morning in the absence of Sgt. Arnold I duly reported to the Quartermaster, a Lieutenant Pullin, not popular as I discovered but I always got on very well with him. This was important because he was my boss.

I should at this stage outline as simply as possible the way that an Infantry Battalion was organised in 1939. There were four Rifle Companies. Each Company was lettered and this did vary between Regiments but was usually A B C and D Companies. However the 2nd Hants Companies were designated W X Y and 'Z'. Pulling all this together was the Headquarter Company, whose responsibilities were many and varied. They embraced the various specialist sections e.g. the Quartermaster, Band, Mechanical Transport, Mortar Platoon, Intelligence Platoon, Pioneer Platoon and of course there was the Company Office where the Adjutant and the RSM lurked, various clerks and finally but most importantly the Commanding Officer.

There were several attached personnel from other Corps: two Armourers, three Vehicle Mechanics and a Shoemaker all from the RAOC. I was filling the second of the Armourers' attachment, the other being Sgt. Arnold. There was a doctor from the RAMC (Royal Army Medical Corps) and last but by no means least, a Padre. At this time the Army was being brought up to strength by Reservists; these were somewhere but one sometimes wondered if they really existed, meanwhile in terms of solid flesh and blood. In the Barracks we were well short of the laid-down establishment for an Infantry Unit. This is best illustrated by the state of the attached personnel who were actually with the Battalion when I joined: out of an establishment of eight there were only two, the two Armourers.

The rest of the Battalion I would guess were at less than half strength, and only came up to strength for the annual manoeuvres when the Reservists were called up. Until then, for Arnold and me it meant plenty of time to ourselves. The workload was very light so tennis, cricket, shooting and in the case of Arnold learning to drive, were all occupying our time. Arnold was a top class tennis player and the backbone of the Sergeants Mess team. We did a certain amount of work but the weapons were all in excellent condition. I was also lucky that what is well known to Armourers as the Quarterly Inspection had been carried out before I arrived.

So to my first day. With Arnold away my initial duty was to report to the HQ Company Office and of course to the RSM. My documents were gobbled up into the system and the RSM said I would not be required for parades or Guard Duties, but on the following morning I would report, suitably dressed of course, to the Company Office for the Commanding Officer's Orders. CO's Orders, as they were commonly known in the Army, took place every morning and it is where the CO dispensed justice for the more serious offences that the soldiery were often prone to. There was also a welcome to be extended to newcomers like myself. It was all very formal so turn up, Clem, and be a credit to your Corps, stamp your feet at the right moments, the best salute you can muster and wait for the Commanding Officer to speak.

Remember this was totally new to me but with the RSM in charge then simply follow his orders and let matters take their course. How clearly I can picture it even now all these years later. Rigidly to attention, having produced a real corker of a salute and the RSM formally introducing me to Lt. Col. Lee, the Commanding Officer. The formality of it all had induced an attack of nervousness but Col. Lee's first words both surprised me and put me at ease. 'Welcome to the Battalion, I see you played cricket for the Ordnance Corps,' and at that point I seem to remember being invited to sit down. Funny how this made me feel even more nervous, I think that the formality was a kind of prop. Col. Lee then went on to discuss with the RSM how they might ensure that I played for the Battalion in the imminent Army Cricket Championships as the local RAOC Depot were bound to insist that I played for them.

I sat enthralled but was anyone going to ask about my possible qualities as an Armourer? They then covered my possible ability as a footballer, welcomed me to the shooting team, this without me firing a shot, and to finally cap my sense of the surreal, the CO said, 'You will enjoy being with this Battalion,' and to the RSM 'See that he is promoted to Acting Corporal, he will need Authority.' A warm handshake and Corporal Hoyle (acting) marched out a little dazed, to start what was to be a great adventure with this proud Regiment, good and bad and sometimes frightening beyond belief.

Outside the RSM told me to go to the tailers as soon as possible and get my stripes sewn on. Meanwhile he took me to the Armourer's Workshop which turned out to be an end room of one of the barrack blocks. I noticed that the other rooms were all empty. Using a room like this of course meant a big workshop and in one corner a shut off space had been created to make a living area. In this area there was already a proper bed set up and, I quickly noticed, already made, When I say 'proper bed', I mean one with springs and not easily tipped up, we always referred to them as 'Hospital beds'. There was also a cupboard and a bedside locker. Luxury indeed. The rest of the room was occupied by a large workbench and incongruous as it may seem a blacksmith's anvil plus rifle racks with a few rifles, cupboards containing general spares and a large desk.

All of this may seem a bit over the top but there were a couple of good reasons for this attention. Firstly security: a barrack room was not considered secure so by having me living in it, problem solved; the other reason is a little more delicate to explain. An Infantry Battalion, as previously explained, had on establishment one Armourer Sergeant. and leaving aside what he was actually there for, the care and maintenance of small arms (and bikes), he was a craftsman who hopefully could be relied upon to provide a little mechanical expertise, repair the odd typewriter, break into a Company Commander's cash box (lost keys for the umpteenth time), make crib boards for the Sergeants'. Mess and many other small tasks requiring a little mechanical knowledge and the requisite craftsmanship. Previously there had only been Sgt. Arnold but now there were two of us. This meant that when the tennis courts were busy someone could stagger down with a dodgy typewriter knowing that at least I would be there.

We were a great convenience. However, of much more significance to the way we were looked after was the more sinister aspect of our job and irrespective of rank the power we wielded when the Quarterly Inspection took place and our reports on all the Battalion weapons were submitted to the Commanding Officer, to the Assistant Inspector of Armourers RAOC (he was the one we Armourers feared) and finally copies to the Brigade Headquarters. The repercussions of a bad report were not pleasant.

Of course life was not quite like that. The troops knew how to care for their weapons and bad reports were pretty well unknown, just an odd niggle here and there. It is true one did notice that Company Commanders tended to show up in the workshops more frequently during the Inspection period but maybe only to chat about how the Inter Company cricket tournament was progressing, maybe a pat on the back following a good innings, I suppose to look at it crudely it was basically a back scratching situation but it made for a very pleasant Barrack life. For example pay parade, that is Arnold's and mine, took place in the workshops when the Pay Sgt. would *bring* the money, together with the appropriate documents for signature. I could get used to this, I thought.

All of these old barracks had an Armourer's workshop as part of the original architecture; unfortunately for some strange reason they were very small. The one at Corruna Barracks was, at the time I joined, being used as a secure storeroom. So the adaption of a barrack room to an Armourer's workshop made for plenty of room and as described provided accommodation for myself.

After the RSM left I lost no time in getting organised. A quick trip to the Quartermaster's store produced a couple of chairs and another locker, shuffle it all around and in no time at all it was just like home. I spent the rest of the day browsing around and looking through the paperwork, all of which I saw had been meticulously kept. This set me wondering what sort of person Arnold was going to prove to be. This was going to be crucial to the next few months, he was my direct boss and he would dictate my workload, both the amount and the type, or at least that is how I imagined it and so it proved to be.

March and the evenings drew in very early so I wandered down to the NAAFI, had a good supper and so to the end of my first full day, with much to mull over. Before falling asleep I cast a 'professional' (tone deaf ear) to the sounding of retreat and decided it was extremely well done, but I could have done without the next call which was of course Reveille. Breakfast and the food seemed good so back to start my first working day. But what the hell was I supposed to do? I didn't want to interfere with any of the part finished work lying about and after tidying the bench and the desk and sweeping the workshop for the second time, I put on my working apron and waited for something to happen.

At ten o clock I locked up and went over to the NAAFI where I discovered they did a very tasty kind of hot sausage roll; it was really good. Back to the workshop and finally something did happen. This in the form of a very large soldier wearing a long butcher's apron, not especially tall though believe me tall enough, and I would best describe him as 16 stone of bone and muscle, bare arms revealing a modicum of tattooing and with a waxed moustache with well developed spikes and as he strode up the barrack room towards where I was standing behind the bench I could see he was carrying quite effortlessly a bacon slicer.

Here was my first job and I remember thinking, 'We didn't do bacon slicers during our training', as the soldier in front of me put it gently down on the bench saying, 'You must be the new Armourer,' adding very correctly, 'Corporal'. Standing very straight he held out a large hand and said, 'I am L/Corporal Guyatt, the Regimental Butcher; call me Gaffer, everybody else does.'

I came out with some sort of greeting and said, 'They call me Clem.' 'I know,' he said, 'I had a look round the QM's desk before I came; it says 'Clement' on your documents.'

So started a long and close friendship with what I suppose could be lightly called a character, but Gaffer was much much more than that, an overwhelming presence anywhere, superbly intelligent and in action the best soldier I ever knew. He was very physical and very frightening and I learned quickly as I got to know him better that he had a fearful reputation among the frequenters of the local pubs. We all meet 'characters' in our lives but Gaffer was a very special person, much loved and much hated, but if he numbered you amongst his friends you were indeed lucky. During the three years of our close friendship he never ever called me Clem, to Gaffer I was always 'Tiffy'; this was and still is a shortening of the name 'artificer' which loosely means tradesman.

But here I am, bacon slicer on my bench! Hesitantly I enquire what's wrong with it to be told that the mechanism controlling the setting of slice thickness is faulty and keeps producing different thicknesses no matter what it has been set to. Our instructors at Hilsea had taught us well; faced with just this sort of situation they advised us to tell them to leave it and you will have a look at it later. This of course gives you a chance to have a look at it with no witnesses. An important facet of this charade is to appear authoritative as if you really did know what you were doing. Gaffer's reply to this was simple. 'Fine, if you fix it I'll be in the butcher's shop.' I suspected I hadn't fooled him for one moment. I also couldn't help wondering whether there was some sort of probing as to my abilities going on, was Gaffer sizing them up?

Before I could turn my attention to the bacon slicer another customer appeared at the end of the room bearing down on me. Oh no, I thought, not another 'character' but all was well. This was a Piper from the Royal Scots whose barracks was just down the road and whose Armourer was not available (where the hell had Peter Hills got to?). The Piper was in full regalia and magnificent he looked. He came to attention in front of me (I liked that) but after he had stated his problem in a very broad Scottish accent I was still totally in the dark until he produced the ceremonial dagger that is worn in the stocking called a Skean dhu (we had done this on the course.) It was a small problem that was causing the dagger to stick in the scabbard, easily fixed. There I was then, one down and one to go, the damned bacon slicer.

Struggling to move it around on the bench I couldn't help but remember Gaffer striding down the room carrying it effortlessly. Well, we all need a bit of luck. I found a loose screw on the feed mechanism and joy! It was fixed. Round to the butcher's shop, a very poky little room, hardly room to swing a cleaver: no Gaffer or cleaver come to think of it so leaving a note saying mission accomplished I hurried back to the workshop to maybe lie down for a little while.

Shortly after lunch the Corporal's Mess President came in and took me round to the Corporal's Mess. Introductions all round, a couple of beers and then snooker until the inevitable bugle announced it was tea-time. So ended my first day. Before locking up and closing down the workshop, I reported to the QM. We had a long chat then filling in the work book which Arnold kept so properly, I lay on my bed and tried to digest the day. I certainly liked the look of the future but of course there was that slight apprehension about meeting Arnold.

The third day and still on my own, so I made a start at the Quartermaster's, introducing myself and being introduced to the Staff with whom I would be working. I was to get to know them very well during the next three years. I tidied up the workshop for the umpteenth time, browsed through the spares cupboard and was contemplating a hot sausage roll at the NAAFI when Gaffer walked in carrying his rifle. After thanking me for the slicer we chatted about this and that, mostly how I was settling in and finally getting round to the rifle. It appeared that a couple of weeks ago Arnold had instigated a spot check on the Headquarter Company's rifles, that Gaffer's rifle had failed to impress and he was due to produce it in good order on Arnold's return, now very imminent. I also learned that Arnold and Gaffer did not get on too well, and would I please have a look at it.

A little dilemma here: although Gaffer had said very little about Arnold this was the first time anyone had really mentioned him and I was a little uneasy about upsetting my boss before we had even met. I would have been even more concerned if I had known the depths of this dislike between the two and unpleasant as it was I never ever found out what had started it. Anyway I looked at the barrel, found that it only needed a little professional attention, ten minutes and it was done, a thank you and off Gaffer went and off I went to my hot sausage roll.

The afternoon I spent browsing around Aldershot and ever since that afternoon I have always had a soft spot for this famous garrison town, always regarded as belonging to the Army. I don't know what percentage of the population were soldiers, but in this year 1939 it was very considerable. The geography of the town itself was of two separate entities: there was the town itself, a very typical English town with all the usual facilities but the suburbs were made up entirely of Barracks and walking around, you were conscious of one large Barrack parade ground after another. Incongruously dotted among these barrack blocks were patches of green. These were the various tennis courts, cricket and football pitches and here and there an athletics area. Fairly central to all this was a huge green park. Here they played polo and once a year the Aldershot Tattoo was staged. So back to my own little corner of this mass of Soldiery, Corunna Barracks, to find at the Guardroom that Arnold was back and would be in to work the next morning.

Sgt Arnold was married and living in married quarters adjacent to the Barracks so I judged he would be in reasonably early and so he was, nine o'clock give a minute or two. He was very pleasant and concerned about how I was settling in, also apologetic about not being here to welcome me when I arrived. Apparently a soldier shooting from a window in his own barrack room had shot another soldier in one of the other barrack blocks. Unluckily, Arnold had been the Armourer called as the expert witness to inspect the weapon and certify it as serviceable. For some reason the Civil Police were handling the case, hence Arnold's trip to London for the trial. This uncomfortable chore always fell to an Armourer and sadly came along much too frequently: indeed as my tale unfolds I shall recall the five Courts Martial at which I testified, all of them involving fatal shootings.

We spent an hour or so chatting and Arnold was suitably impressed by my entries in the work book, one bacon slicer and a Skean dhu. These provoked some merriment as I bemoaned the lack of bacon slicer training on the Armourers' training course. I hadn't mentioned Guyatt, just logging the job origin as QM ration stores. We had one thing in common, competitive shooting, and he was good, but Arnold's real love was tennis, honed in India. He was a top class player representing the Aldershot Garrison in the Service Championships and picking up trophies wherever he played. I felt that we would get on very well and I was feeling much relieved now we had finally met. He congratulated me warmly on my promotion though it was only an acting rank (this means among other things that I didn't get paid for the stripes).

Eventually Arnold went off to the Sergeants' Mess for mid-morning tea, saying he would be back around two o'clock and I of course was intending to head off to the Corporals' Mess on the same quest, except that coming down the room towards me was Gaffer. 'I thought you might like to have break with the lads.'

I had no idea what this meant, nor did I realise I was being invited into a very select group or that this group were not above bending the rules. One thing, there was no doubt about who was 'Godfather' to quote a well known film title. The location for this break was the ration store. Though I knew where it was I hadn't had cause to go in there up to now. I was surprised: it turned out to be very roomy; there was an odd chair here and there, plenty of cardboard boxes holding various rations, three or four tea chests and as far as I could judge most of the QM Staff.

I recognised the ration Sergeant, the QM clerk, his driver, the equipment repairer and what were they doing? Well, apart from the large mugs of tea they were nursing, they appeared to be breaking off lumps of what turned out to be hot bread and dipping it in opened tins (large) of cherries. I got stuck in and delicious it was too. I did not ask any questions and as I left, the ration Sergeant said, 'See you tomorrow, Clem' and that was that, not even a joining fee, though if there had been a card issued I assume it would have read 'accomplice'.

In the afternoon Arnold explained that my corner of the workshop was only a temporary measure, it had been constructed using Bren gun boxes but in fact they were building a totally new Armourer's workshop which would have proper accommodation for the Armourer built in. This conversion they were apparently carrying out in all Barracks on some modernisation scheme or other. We duly walked round and had a look at the progress; as in all things 'building' it was chaotic but Arnold learned that as it progressed he would be asked for suggestions as to layout etc. This pleased us both.

The next few days were very quiet and in truth I didn't see much of Arnold and why should I, his family was just around the corner and I had learned that Jean, his wife, was pregnant. I remember the two of us spent a week overhauling the Regimental Shooting Team's rifles. The Battalion were very much into shooting and each member had his own rifle. These in turn were kept in a separate store. It was very much 'a find something to do exercise' and with no Quarterly Inspection due the days began to settle down into a lazy routine. During this period I had been invited to dinner with the Arnolds and a very pleasant evening it was. Before joining the 2nd Hants, Arnold had done a tour in India some of it with a Gurkha Regiment and produced many superb photographs. These were of great interest to me because it was rumoured that the Battalion would soon be moving to India to replace the 1st Battalion who had been out there for a number of years. During the years before the war there were many postings throughout the world for the British Army, some better than others, and although India had been the favourite rumour, many were suggesting it would be Jamaica, I think it was wishful thinking. Jamaica was always known as the ultimate prize when it came to a posting.

Certainly I had learned that Sgt Arnold loved India and looked forward with eager anticipation to going back. I was learning a great deal about India. Both the 1st and 2nd Battalions had spent many years there. The North-West Frontier medal ribbons were very common in the Battalion: remember Afghanistan and the frontier wars? During the twenties and thirties the British Army were sustaining many casualties and on the

North West Frontier the Pathons and Afghans exacted terrible retribution on prisoners. Sadly nothing changes. But in all my service I never remember one Serviceman say a bad word about India and indeed most seemed to be only too keen to get back. Ah! those far flung out posts of the British Empire. How sad it is looking at some of them now, the British Tommy would never have allowed it.

On a day to day basis Arnold and I were getting on very well but the workload was very light. Meanwhile I was still playing my way into the Battalion, getting to know the Company Commanders, Company Sergeant Majors, Quarter Master Sergeants and as many of the Platoon Sergeants as possible. My judgement was that these were real backbone of what would be the sharpest end if and when we went to war and more and more it was shaping up that way. The next few years were to prove my judgement correct and all too many of the friends I was making during these early months would not survive. Competent, superb soldiers but when it came down to sheer stubborn courage, right or wrong, then this belongs with the officers and particularly the young ones, many killed whilst still learning their trade at the hands of experienced Platoon Sergeants I can see very clearly now how naïve we all were.

I was also spending my weekends with Girl. I suppose you could say I was commuting at the weekends but one thing I did know, my pay wasn't stretching very far. Luckily that Girl was working so we managed. Back at Aldershot there was the little matter of the 'Football Trophy'.

During the previous winter the Battalion had won the Army Football Cup. One day, one of the team appeared in the workshop bringing his individual trophy. This was a small figure of a footballer on a plinth and in the act of kicking a ball, the finish was a sort of gold colour and the name of the real footballer was Knight (Tacker Knight to his friends; mind you, all Knights were nicknamed Tacker certainly in this Battalion, except for the twins who were distinguishable by name from each other by being called 'Dark Knight' and 'Light Knight'. Sorry about that). Back to the Trophy which was missing an arm, broken off at the shoulder. I think he must have tangled with the 2nd Hants' centre half, big, and not given to finess and whose name, yes you've guessed, was Knight and I still haven't worked my way through all the Knights yet. Where was I? Oh yes, the trophy needing an arm replacing. It was a clean fracture (I'm already using medical jargon) but it seemed as if a little light soldering might do the trick and with no blood supply to worry about it should heal well, indeed almost instantly.

Tacker said could he come back tomorrow as he didn't have time to wait and this was the first of three lucky breaks that would establish my reputation amongst the lads as something of a miracle worker, technically that is. I warmed up my soldering iron not too hot. I reasoned that the material might be tricky and it was. I applied the soldering iron to the joint with the intention of putting a little solder on to start with and the shoulder and half the head disappeared into a misshapen blob. 'Oops,' I thought, knowing that I had been very stupid, also knowing that there was no way back and what the hell was I going to tell Tacker? Some surgeon! My first touch had been terminal. So I hid the body in my drawer glad of my first lucky break which had meant Tacker wasn't there to see his footballer die. Along came Arnold and said would I nip into Aldershot that afternoon and pick up a tennis racket which he had left for re-stringing. Second lucky break, heaven only knows when I might have next gone into Aldershot without this little errand. I walked in to give myself a chance to decide on the best of the many excuses I had been wrestling with. I had decided the only way of saving at least a semblance of face was a good excuse laced with technology. Miserably I turned into the sports shop and there in front of me in a large display case were what appeared to be thousands of these footballer trophies, all identical to the corpse in my drawer and priced 2s. 6d. each. Here was the third of my lucky breaks.

Clutching my 'living' footballer and 2s. 6d. lighter I hared off back to the workshops, handed over the racket to Arnold and once alone took out the dead footballer, removed the little brass plate from the base, which was only lightly pinned, transferred it to the new one and there I was off the hook. A trophy brought back to life. I felt sure that Tacker would not be too worried about the change and that my excuse would be better received. What happened next should I suppose be listed as a fourth lucky break depending on how honest I felt. I had put the trophy in the box Tacker had brought it in and left it on my locker. The next afternoon Arnold came in and said, 'By the way, Knight came in and picked up a job you had done for him. I assumed it was the box on your locker and he took it away saying he would come back and see you.'

Nothing happened for a couple of days, indeed I had almost forgotten about it when having my usual break with the QM staff Gaffer remarked that his mate Tacker had been on about this fantastic job I had done repairing his trophy. For a moment I couldn't connect, then it dawned that Tacker had been showing the new one around as his old one repaired. This was confirmed later when the Regimental Provost, Sgt. Jack Huggins, came into the workshops, a gentle giant if ever there was one, reputedly the best heavyweight boxer the Army ever produced, but in spite of his job as the Regiment's senior policeman he was popular and respected; he asked me if I could repair a large silver boxing trophy where the base had come loose from the cup. It was a superb trophy presented in India and made by true craftsmen. He remarked that he had seen Tacker Knight's trophy and hoped I could fix this one. It was an easy job and I was able to effect a permanent repair.

So, a reputation had been forged and the old saying 'Get thee behind me Satan' crossed my mind, but only very briefly! Tacker called in and offered to pay me, good heavens no, have it on me, still no sign of Satan.

As the months went by, Jack and I became firm friends and I never tired of his tales of India. I can still see his battered face lighting up when Gaffer came in and he would say, 'Now here's a rogue' whereupon Gaffer would ask him to come outside and say it and when the offer was declined would accuse Jack of pulling rank. Everything was settling down so well, summer was round the corner, I was generally recognised as I walked around the Barracks and was already beginning to identify with the Battalion. About this time my Dad came down and stayed for a day; this was a unique experience for him, seeing at long last, the results of all those long years of worrying. I think he was very pleased and we had a great day.

Meanwhile Arnold and I got on very well though truth to tell we didn't see too much of each other during the day, I held the fort more or less and he would pop in from time to time checking to see if anything interesting had turned up. We would maybe chat a while and that was pretty well it. However June was approaching and the next Quarterly Inspection was due. This would certainly be a busy period and needs explaining. Every Infantry Regiment was subject to a complete inspection of everything that came under the responsibility of the Armourer; this of course meant the small arms basically but remember from our training included odd items such as bikes, though they were not odd in themselves, just a bloody nuisance: what an Infantryman (bless him) could do to an Army bike beggars description.

This Quarterly Inspection was laid down in regulations and reported in considerable detail on special forms, copies to the CO Adjutant, Company Commanders, the Chief Inspector of Armourers and finally the Brigade Commander. There's glory for you! What a distribution for our little old Quarterly Inspection report. I couldn't really estimate the numbers of weapons involved, there were so many anomalies. The Battalion being under strength, many of the weapons were held in store to make sure that in the event of the Reservists being called up there would be weapons for them. There was a class of rifle known as Drill Purpose only; these were old and not serviceable but were used in training to save wear and tear. I do remember there were five bicycles, Why did I dislike the bikes so much? Never really worked it out but guess who got them to inspect on the Quarterly.

Indeed the inspection was far from evenly distributed as between Arnold and me. The weapons were brought in at nine o' clock and it was convenient for me to take them into the workshop, check them and see that they were racked; once Arnold arrived we both worked pretty well to lunchtime, less time off for a coffee. Inspection work was repetitive and massively boring and so all my service I disliked it, I wonder how many items (rifles for example) the average Armourer inspected during his service. Too many, but my goodness it was impressive to watch an Armourer process a rifle including barrel check and gauging. I was pretty slick myself.

So stop for lunch and then back to the grind but it wasn't long before I noticed I seemed to be on my own for most of the afternoon. Ah well, Arnold was senior and my boss so I suppose it was fair enough but he did do most of the paperwork and that was a big help. It was a very busy couple of weeks but passed quickly enough and it was back to the steady lazy days as the summer proved to be a good one.

About this time we had a small intake of recruits. I seem to remember it was nineteen. They were issued with a rifle and bayonet but unfortunately the bayonets were still in their new condition i.e. not polished, the blades still with their 'browned' finish. This presented a nightmarish prospect for these young lads to try and emery paper them to a shine. Arnold told me that there was a system whereby the recruits could pay a small sum to their Company Quartermaster and the Armourers would undertake to do it for them; the amount was 3s. 6d. and that is how I found myself polishing bayonets. It required hard work and it was of course a filthy job, shades of those browning parties at Hilsea. I completed the nineteen bayonets, returned them to the Company Quartermaster and that was it. Though nobody actually ever said it, I had assumed that the money would come to the Armourers and would be shared even though I had actually done the work. I decided that I had got it wrong and forgot about it; cricket was uppermost in my mind at this time.

I suppose if I had to list my sports at this time they would be cricket, shooting and football. We were moving into the cricket season and started with inter-Company matches. My Company team of course was Headquarter Company and the CO was our spin bowler and a very good one. I understood that he had played representative cricket in his younger days (sorry about that, Colonel Lee). Why am I building the Colonel up? Simple! He bowled underhand. My own cricket background had been a season with Yorkshire being coached by George Hirst; this was the product of a system operated in Halifax whereby any schoolboy who was considered to have the necessary possibilities would be sent to the Yorkshire cricket ground at Bradford and if they agreed he would be given regular coaching with a chance of a career in the game.

Strangely enough, because it simply wasn't played very much at Hilsea this season was like starting again and I quickly learnt in the nets that Colonel Lee required the utmost concentration. We got on well. At this time I was building what became a close friendship with a Corporal from the band, who was part of the Medical team. It was traditional for the band to supply the stretcher bearers and medical staff and Ben my friend was also a qualified chiropodist. Courses were open to the members of the band and Ben did his at a teaching hospital in Edinburgh, qualifying with outstanding marks; he had also done a nursing course and was to be found a couple of years later stitching up a nasty wound on my hand at two o'clock in the morning somewhere in North Africa. He was killed three weeks later at Salerno.

I find typing that very upsetting even though it was so long ago. Our common bond at Aldershot was cricket. Ben was a fast bowler and we were both selected to represent the Aldershot Command. Better still, in what was proving a great summer, we played in trials for the Current Army Team; these trials were played against the Territorial Army Team. Hosting these trials which lasted for two days was the Military Academy at Sandhurst and what a wonderful two days it proved. We were treated as officers. I remember a young officer bringing us back to Corruna Barracks at the end of the first day and picking us up the next morning in his car. The weather was glorious.

Old soldiers who played cricket before the war will recognise that to find two 'Other Ranks' playing in this sort of trial was indeed a rarity, comparatively so anyway. Most of the officers during the pre-war years came from University where they had been coached and a great many of them were County standard so it was a natural sort of progression. I was helped by my Yorkshire Club background and Ben was just too good for anyone to ignore.

And the match? From my school days I had always been an opening bat, indeed not only opening but a number one. We had won the toss; and our Captain elected to bat so here I was once again shaping up to the first ball of the match. Because it was important for me to do well (I fancied a place in the Army Team) I was nervous but not unduly so. I always enjoyed fast bowling, up to a point, and the point here was the bowler in question. To say that he was well known would be an understatement. I was aware of the first two deliveries, just. Thinking to myself, 'Come on, wake up,' I played the third ball with a beautifully crafted defensive stroke somewhere in the area I felt the ball might be, it wasn't! It took my leg stump past the wicketkeeper and God knows he was far enough back. As he walked back carrying the stump I thought briefly there might just be a record here, not many stumps get knocked back that far. Back in the dressingroom bags of the usual type sympathy. Not much of a help really so press on and look forward to lunch, bound to be good.

And who was this bowler who had so cruelly dashed my hopes (and my stumps of course)? The Reverend J.W.J. Steele, one of Hampshire's current opening bowlers. He commiserated with me at lunch and confirmed that I had indeed played a very elegant defensive stroke and that missing the ball was a little unfortunate – Halleluja!

The afternoon proved more fruitful and I managed a tidy innings somewhere in the seventies, I felt much better and the Reverend seemed pleased for me. Ben had a good game and was difficult to play all day so we arrived back in a reasonable mood though not in a particular hopeful one. The summer was certainly proving idyllic in many ways especially the weekends with Girl. The next few weeks were very busy for me and I spent a lot of time on the ranges with the Troops who were completing their annual range classifications: very important to them as it immediately affected their pay. I cannot remember exactly by how much but it was reasonably significant and of course a marksman classification carried a certain amount of prestige. I was involved zeroing the rifles, making sure they shot where they were aimed, at least technically. The ability of a given rifle to shoot a tight group never much bothered the average soldier, unless it produced unexpectedly wild shooting they trusted us, but the members of the shooting team were a very different kettle of fish. For a start they had a rifle which was kept just for their use and looked after by the Armourer and they knew what they were doing. Ah well, don't we all, pity the butt markers didn't always seem to know where our last shot had gone. Mind you, it was surprising how often when challenged the butt marker proved to be right: takes all sorts I suppose.

We all have our loss of form and this would often result in the shooter in question ending up in the workshop, unhappy with the performance of his rifle. As a member of the rifle team and a friend I would agree that it was time to have a look at the offending weapon, leave it (not that hoary old ploy again). I would strip it, have a good look at where a problem might have arisen but never find anything. Then I would hang on to it until collected, suggest I wasn't too happy with say the cartridge headspace (nice technical sound to that), but it will be OK now and sure enough it always was. Satisfaction all round! We are all psychologists and since watching an African witch doctor sort out a problem (more of this much later) I realised these practitioners were supreme masters from which modern psychology almost certainly descends. Not as effectively unfortunately, because now it lacks the one crucial ingredient. Fear!

Cricket was still playing a great part in my sporting life which leads me to a strange or even bizarre incident. The Battalion were playing The Royal Army Service Corps in what I remember was an important cup match. The match took place on their ground at Feltham. This sports field was bounded by a six foot high steel fence with, on the other side, an RAF airfield. A little research indicates that Feltham has changed names since then and is slightly more well known as Heathrow. The boundary of the cricket pitch where our game was taking place ran along inside this fence. It was a nice ground, the sun was shining, the wicket excellent and we were settling into the game very nicely. The RASC were batting and I was keeping wicket (a position I enjoyed and could be described as competent at but not much more). Somewhere from the direction of the offside boundary came this terrible sound of tearing metal and before we had time to gather our wits or try to take cover there was a battered RAF Gloucester Gladiator fighter plane lying on its back at about third man. We learned later that the pilot had overshot the runway and on coming through the fence turned over.

We rushed across to find the pilot trapped by his safety harness and soon had him free and on to the ground. He was basically unhurt though judging by the profanities he was none too happy about what had happened. I remember he was a very tall man wearing a white overall which Persil would have been proud of and in spite of his massive loss of face he was very gracious, thanking us and shaking hands with everyone then disappearing in a car which had come across to pick him up, giving us a cheerful wave as they roared away. The only anxiety he had shown was in making sure we didn't drop him as he wriggled free from the harness; necks get broken that way.

The fact that none of us actually saw the aircraft hitting the fence and flipping over gave the incident a surreal feeling. One second nothing, the next a large aircraft upside down just inside the boundary but we were more than aware that if we had been fielding someone at third man he could well have been killed, certainly seriously

injured. When things had settled and our hearts were back to normal the umpires walked slowly across to the stricken aircraft, looked at it carefully, conferred, then declared it an obstruction and we got on with the game. We learned later that the pilot was part of an RAF display team who performed aerobatics tied together and I can only assume looking back that they were probably returning either from a display or practice.

GLOSTER GLADIATORS DISPLAY TEAM 1939

Sadly this episode was only one of several. I seemed to be dogged by stricken aircraft even on the very first day of the 'real war' as we moved up to Brussels, in fact within the first two hours. I often feel that there was a strangeness about it somehow and as I write this the feeling returns.

Who won the match? For the life in me I cannot remember! But the summer was moving on and with it the Annual Field Exercises were beginning to loom large. A totally new experience for me, and the Armourer or Armourers would be moving into the 'Field' with the Battalion, complete with tools and spares and a rather ingenious collapsible bench, complete with vice which I seemed to remember bore the RAOC title of Toolbox, Armourer, Mk 13. There's glory for you. I was going to become very familiar with the vagaries of this piece of equipment, humping it into lorries, setting it up, packing it up, often cursing it and yet I managed a great deal of work on it and in some pretty unlikely places. Truth to tell I was mostly very glad to have it and I called it 'Fred'; that won't come as any sort of surprise to Girl or even the rest of the family.

So we were busy getting my first 'Fred' ready for the big exercise. By the way Arnold had decided that as he was an old hand at Field Exercises he would stay behind and leave the field to me: fair enough, I needed the experience and he was the Boss but oh dear, how apt the reference to 'field' turned out to be. Days before the exercise was due to start the Reservists began to arrive for this was the fortnight where they would be back in 'action' and as the soldiery would say about time too. Reservists were of two distinct types, the first were members of the Battalion who had completed their Army service and on discharge were legally obliged to serve a fixed period on 'Reserve'. It varied for some reason but could be two or three years. During this time they were called back to do two weeks training once a year and of course were always liable to instant recall in the event of a war. The other Reservists were genuine volunteers who felt a duty to do this service.

The Battalion took on a very different aspect during this time. For a start, so many of the reservists were simply old mates and so were picking up where they had left off. I was meeting men whom I only knew by reputation, gained for many things including trouble; there were also the veterans of the Palestine problem. The Battalion had only just returned from Palestine when I joined, and it had been a nasty campaign with a fair share of casualties. Gaffer had served with considerable distinction during this campaign but never mentioned it, though our friendship had continued. So the NAAFI was always full and awash with beer and tall stories and indeed as was the Corporals' Mess. The exercise was a large topic of conversation, but the possibility of war? It was still heads well down and bums in the air. All of this I struggled to relate to, nothing in my experience so far helped at all, but I was really enjoying it and Gaffer began to put a lot of it into perspective.

Gaffer had recently created a small legend. I suppose we could title it Corporal Guyatt and the Grenadier. He had been busily going about his business in the butcher's shop which, as mentioned before was a very small room; it also had a low entry door. The business Gaffer had been engaged in was cutting chops from a lump of some meat or other (sorry about that, Gaffer, you taught me war but never meat). Anyway he was swinging a large cleaver vigorously, both hands well behind his head when it met an obstruction. This was followed by a thud and looking behind, Gaffer found, as he put it, 'This large Grenadier Guardsman in best uniform lying on my floor bleeding briskly.' Gaffer always had a marvellous turn of phrase as Girl would testify.

Apparently our friend from the Grenadiers, living in the next barracks, had ducked under the low door as befits a large Guardsman and straight into the back of Gaffer's cleaver. A goodly number of stitches and a less goodly number of doubles later, our unlucky visitor tottered away, wondering I suppose what the hell hit him. (Always treat your enemies well especially if you have just clobbered one with a cleaver, and especially if a lot of his mates live in the next Barracks, all big lads. Gospel according to Cpl Guyatt.)

So the day of the move to camp arrived, interestingly. How were we going to get there, some twenty odd miles away at a place called Halt End? After all, we had not yet been mechanised. Our complement of vehicles amounted to several 15 cwt Morris trucks, six Bren carriers, six motor bikes and two water trucks. All was to be revealed when the RASC turned up with a reasonable number of Bedford three-ton trucks. We all piled in and the exercise was up and running, or was it? Did I say at the start of this paragraph how were we going to get there? proof indeed that I was a relative newcomer to the Battalion and I was shortly going to learn that faced with moving from 'A' to 'B' whether ten miles or twenty, you would normally check your socks, get to your feet, heap your worldly goods on your back and there you were, one foot in front of the other, regulation pace, three miles to the hour and a ten minute halt on the hour. This time though and I know not why, we were to be carried there in trucks; maybe the RASC needed the practice!

So here I was, in the back of a truck together with 'Fred', filled with sundry spares, and looking forward to the next few days. Oh yes, and it had started to rain heavily but so what, here were truckloads of tough, battle hardened, hairy-arsed soldiers ready to demonstrate their fitness for anything that might be slung their way!

Me? Oh I was just a beginner and attached at that. Keep a low profile and hope for the best. The Battalion Dispatch Riders were following our truck, dashing up to the front of the convoy occasionally, see everything was fine then back where we could insult them as we lounged in the truck. The rain had continued unabated and as we turned off into the field where our tents had been pitched it was obvious that mud would be the order of the day.

After de-bussing I quickly found the tent marked Armourer and supervised the unloading of 'Fred'. brought my own gear in and settled down to get comfortable. I thought I was lucky to have a tent to myself but it had also to serve as a workshop. However not long after settling in, one of the Pioneer platoon came along and banged another notice board in next to the one marked Armourer; a quick look and I found that I was to be joined by the Equipment Repairer. The tent itself was an old bell tent, probably First World War vintage but roomy enough. The Equipment Repairer was of course one of the QM's Staff like me and we were good friends, his name Joe Brown, and we later virtually shared the North African campaign together, slit trenches, bivouacs, rations, ammunition and even grave digging during the nastier parts. When we parted in Italy owing to my being posted, we were indeed the closest of friends. Joe like Gaffer will feature strongly as I move through the years.

You may be wondering what a Pioneer Platoon is and how does it fit into an Infantry Battalion? Very simply, they were a kind of DIY platoon responsible for repairs to anything of a building nature; they embraced carpenters, bricklayers, electricians and really they were a very useful and respected group of soldiers. Originally and historically their job was to make coffins, crosses and bury the dead, and before I forget, the Pioneer Platoon Sergeant. was the only soldier in the British Army allowed to grow a beard. Please don't ask.

Back to work, find the mess and wait for? - Yes, you are ahead of me again, the bugler; what on earth would we do without him? I fear time would have simply passed us by but the rain certainly had no intention of passing us by and continued torrentially. My wander round to locate the mess had left my boots covered with a thick clay and I was also pretty wet. Joe had been busy getting his tools and working equipment together so unlike me he was still sort of dry and pristine, nevertheless he set off with our mugs and quickly returned with them filled with hot tea. Here was my first intimation that Joe had that strange gift of disappearing, no matter where we were and coming back with some thing priceless at the time, a mug of tea, a tin of soup, even something as rare as one of the delicious tins of steak and kidney pie only found in Compo-rations and only one to a case. Nothing short of miraculous at times.

I was more than happy to stay close to Joe. But later in France I discovered that his hobby was aircraft recognition, that he belonged to a Spotters Club who apparently ran competition days and believe me looking at some of the printed silhouettes they were supposed to identify aircraft from it was no wonder that this hobby proved life-saving. Joe's dedication to this hobby never flagged. I spent many hours sharing a bivouac with Joe and turning over battered and dirty silhouette cards by a single candle. Funny really, though I learned the hard way to identify some aircraft, I basically couldn't tell one from the other; maybe it was being able to turn round to Joe and before I could ask he'd say quite calmly, 'Move your arse, Clem,' and believe me I did, he was never wrong.

Here we were then, both of us muddied up surrounded by a crack Infantry Battalion raring to go and the rain determined to make everybody earn their keep. Hang on a minute, the bugler was sounding a call summoning Company Commanders to conference at Battalion HQ (they *did* have a big tent to themselves). Not long now, think about checking your socks, make sure you've ditched as much from your fighting order as you think you can get away with and hopefully I'm ready for whatever this exercise may throw at me! Joe and I hung around chatting about this and that and especially the fact that though the Company Commanders had been summoned some time ago nothing seemed to be happening. Time for Joe to disappear which he did, coming back with two mugs of tea, a cheese sandwich and the news that we were going back to Barracks. Apparently it had been decided the conditions were too bad to proceed with the Exercise and we should be coming back to carry on when the weather eased. Of course it couldn't be true, Joe's winding me up; he wasn't and almost before I could finish my tea and my half of the cheese sandwich I was on my way back to Barracks. I did ponder the implications of all this come a real war (still head down and bum up you will have noticed, damn, I was beginning to look like an ostrich) and decided it had been decreed the next would only be fought in dry weather. 'That's comforting,' I thought, diving off to the Corporals' Mess for a beer and a discussion about my theory. 'Rubbish' was the verdict; I'd forgotten some of these lads had already fought a real war.

Three days later the rain had stopped and here I was again, climbing up into the same truck, and a little later climbing out of it and into the same tent still marked Armourer and Equipment Repairer. Joe was already there holding a mug of tea, what a mate.

So we got ourselves organised and went for a meal. It was still pretty muddy but not desperately so and it was certainly a beautiful summer's day. One thing was troubling Joe and me, there was a very nasty smell in the air and soon everybody was complaining about it. I couldn't fathom it as Joe and I were upwind of the latrines, so where the hell was it coming from. Come the morning it was still there and as the day warmed up it got worse. I couldn't wait for us to get out of the camp and on with the exercise. About four o'clock we did indeed get out of the camp, same truck, and unbelievably same destination, back to Barracks. I was beginning to lose sight of this exercise; it was all becoming a bit surreal. Two days later it got even more surreal, I remember I was in the Corporals' Mess playing snooker when the Orderly Sergeant came in with a pile of leave forms saying fill them in for a fortnight, leave starts tomorrow and he was gone. I suppose I should have said what about the exercise? But I was an old soldier now: fill it in, grab your money and off, don't look back just in case that bloody truck has turned up again.

Oh, there was a very simple explanation for the smell. The farmer on whose land we were camped had buried a large number of cattle some time ago and the heavy rain and a sort of disturbance by the trucks had brought this smell to the surface.

In the event I did not take any leave. I suspect, looking back, I was probably short of cash. Weekends with Girl were inclined to eat into the available funds. Arnold and his wife had taken off somewhere for a break so I had the workshop to myself for a few days, With the Reservists gone the Barracks was very quiet and there just wasn't any work, My snooker improved considerably and yet and yet, there was an uneasy feeling about, a sort of brooding, I was still enjoying my morning break with the gang in the ration store. Gaffer was busily arranging things for a RASC stocktake of the rations, which was imminent, a new one on me but I learned a great deal about the 'arranging things' aspect, but my lips were sealed.

During this period I spent more time with Gaffer, sometimes under his feet in the butcher's shop, one eye on the cleaver of course and when Arnold was not about he liked to chat in the Armourer's workshop. I knew Arnold didn't like any of this but I was making friends throughout the Battalion, not just the QM staff and I would be glad of it in the coming months and years. Joe Brown and Ben, my cricket companion, were already friends as they were both Bandsmen and we used to wander into Aldershot occasionally for a drink. Cricket seemed to have dried up but September was fast approaching, things would soon be moving and at a pace and in a direction none of us wished for; maybe we had a premonition and didn't recognise it for what it was.

By this time I had learned a great deal about Gaffer. By profession he was a burglar and claimed to have no education at all and as he put it, time ran out for him when the Magistrate offered a choice: 'Six months in jail or join the Army.' This was not uncommon in the twenties and thirties and well understood by Rudyard Kipling. So 'uneducated' Gaffer came to the Second Battalion and with them off to Palestine, where he distinguished himself during the fighting. He also managed to qualify as a First Class Arabic speaker. The QM told me once that listening to Corporal Guyatt arguing with an Arab in Arabic was a revelation. On the Battalion's return to England and Corruna Barracks, he applied for and went on a Master Butcher's Course finishing as a Qualified Master Butcher. Oh yes! Did I say? He also spoke fluent French. Mind you when he held his hands out towards you, palm down the top of the fingers read 'F---k you,' very neatly tattooed and I suspect the trigger for much violence to which Gaffer was always partial. Truly, wherever you looked, Gaffer was larger than life.

We were still in some form of limbo. The news was increasingly disturbing and quite definitely pointing to something nasty brewing for HM Forces. Then suddenly out of the blue we were ordered to parade outside the King George Military Hospital to collect suitable inoculations, one of which to my consternation was to be a TAB inoculation. I wondered if I should say anything about the trials I had been involved in with such disastrous consequences. In the end I said nothing and kept my fingers crossed. This time, unlike most of the lads who suffered various after-effects though nothing particularly virulent, I was fine. And so it proved over many TAB jabs throughout my service. I remember very clearly that Ben (feeling a bit groggy, and so he should; as a qualified Medical Orderly he had been wielding the needle vigorously all morning) and I went to the local variety theatre in town and so to bed. The next morning we awoke to the news that the Reservists had been called up and some form of mobilisation was taking place. Suddenly we were no longer in limbo; things were definitely happening. Us regular soldiers were none too pleased; after all we didn't sign on for nasty things like wars, more for the cricket and tennis and the postings to Bermuda and Egypt interspersed with a little light drill and gentle weapon training and cancelled exercises because it's too wet and smelly, but war! Oh Hell no.

Things really began to warm up with the arrival of the Reservists. Apart from the domestic disruption the old soldiers took it in their stride but for the volunteer Reservists, many of whom had never even worn uniform, it was a nightmare and to add to their discomfort it was raining throughout this period. Preparations for receiving these newcomers can only be described as chaotic and diabolical. Aldershot had a large RAOC Depot and Workshops where all the Volunteer RAOC Reservists were sent. There they were accommodated in tents and I remember it was raining heavily all this time. Once installed in a tent they were hounded and shouted at through a process of picking up their uniforms, equipment, rifles and quite astonishingly at this time, their quota of inoculations which quite predictably floored a lot of them; our old friend TAB still had a kick in it. Throughout this they were without exception wet.

My first intimation of what was going on at the Depot came as I walked across the road on my way to the Guardroom. Rounding the corner appeared an apparition wearing a greatcoat, the rest of his equipment strung haphazardly about his wet and bedraggled body. Being a nice sort of Corporal (remember? there are us and bastards) I went across to find out what on earth this lifeform might be and to my horror I found he was wearing an RAOC cap badge. I quickly found that he was pretty well out on his feet. Grabbing a handy soldier from the Guardroom I soon had him sitting in my bunk, everything wet stripped off and despatched via the unfortunate soldier (jankers of course) to be dried and pressed, boots properly cleaned etc. Maybe I wasn't always nice after all. Also a bed, sheets and blankets and the inevitable large mug of sweet tea.

Luck entered into this because a few weeks earlier we had moved into our new workshop and I into the purpose built accommodation, a very nice roomy bunk where there was ample room for another bed. My new friend, I had discovered, was one James Dunkley and he had been posted to the 2nd Battalion as one of the attached Vehicle Mechanics. Things were certainly beginning to move though I couldn't help thinking that the vehicle mechanics appeared to be arriving long before the vehicles. Jim was beginning to look very ill so I took the soggy envelope containing his documents over to the Guardroom and had him properly booked in, arranged for the Guard Commander to dig out Ben wherever he was and ask him to come over to my bunk. Whilst waiting, Jim explained about the system of posting going on at the Depot saying that there were two other RAOC fitters posted to the 2nd Battalion with him, but he had lost touch with them in the chaos.

Telling him to watch out for Ben who might start to attack him with a thermometer, I went back over to the Guardroom to check on the missing vehicle mechanics; no record or warning of their arrival appeared on his orders for the day, another measure of the chaos. I asked him to look after them well when they arrived and I would sort out accommodation and food etc. and get back to him as soon as possible. The friends I had made in the Battalion were beginning to come good. My next search unearthed Jack Huggins, the Provost Sgt. I explained the situation and Jack simply said, 'Don't worry, I'll fix them with a meal in the cookhouse and have them tucked up in bed before they know what's happened.' Back to the Guardroom nobody yet, but Jack had rung with full instructions. So feeling very virtuous I set off back to my bunk where Ben had fixed Jim up with the usual aspirin and said he had a high temperature, as had quite a few of the lads but sadly they would all be fit for parade in the morning.

Jim and I chatted for a while, little thinking at the time that this would be the start of a long and very close friendship. Come the morning, I located the other two still shattered by their VIP treatment the previous night and by a Provost Sergeant, no less. Jack had put them in a room occupied by the Motor Transport Platoon, very crafty that: once the drivers found out who they were they were guaranteed a great deal of help. An Infantryman is always alert to the main chance. Now seek out Jack and a big thank you, then back to the workshop, take a much improved Jim to breakfast and then wait for Arnold to turn up and make decisions.

All of the above meant that the Battalion were only one short of the Infantry Battalion Establishment for attached RAOC personnel: two Armourers, three Vehicle Mechanics and a Shoemaker who had yet to show. As explained by Jim the night before, the two other Vehicle Mechanics turned out to be 'alphabetical': Frank Day, Harry Drew and of course Jimmy Dunkley. Nice to know that at least somebody in the Depot could recite the alphabet. Finally arranging for Jim to be reunited with Frank and Harry and also arranging for his kit to be taken over to their barrack room, I went and had a word with Gaffer, explained the evening's events and left knowing that from now on there would be no worries about their future care or status.

Arnold proved strangely put out by these events, even annoyed. I think it might have been about this time that our previously good relationship began to slip. However we were about to be given a task that would keep us busy for the next few days and indeed into the small hours. Identity discs! Every soldier wore two and each one had to be stamped with name, initials, religion and Regimental number. The discs were different colours, red and grey, I understood the red one was meant to be fireproof but whatever, it was our job to stamp them and there were 1400 waiting to be stamped. I roped in Jim to help and we just got on with it: massively boring, quite painful and it wasn't long before the blisters began to appear. I must say Arnold more than pulled his weight and the job was eventually finished. I have my two discs here in front of me stamped 'Hoyle C. Meth. 7587328'. We have certainly come a long way together and the cords reflect that, being what can only be described as disgusting, at least that's what Girl says.

The next few days were hectic to say the least and indeed if it hadn't been for my old mate Joe Brown and Gaffer I would have been completely in the dark. Mind you, I was sort of filling up with sweet tea! God knows where Joe used to get it. Strangely during these days Arnold never imparted any information but as a Sergeants' Mess member he must have known as much as anybody did and for some reason preferred to keep it to himself and yet it is more than possible that my sources of information were more reliable than Arnold's would have been. Once this period ended Arnold and I sadly sort of tolerated each other. I never knew the real reason for this and at this time I didn't really think about it much; there were far greater worries on the horizon.

Sunday morning September 1939. I was in the workshops by myself listening to the radio when the fateful words were broadcast at 11.15 on a sunny Sunday. - 'No such undertaking has been received and that consequently this country is at war with Germany.' This was followed almost immediately by an air raid siren, and I set off for the nearest temporary air raid shelter. The all clear went and a little bemused by the enormity of what had been broadcast and the apparent instant commencement of hostilities, I went over to the Corporal's Mess. A very sober gathering indeed. I had never seen the Mess so quiet. There was an undercurrent of real concern; many of those present were married with families living in married quarters and they quickly left for home. I too had been thinking about Girl; I hadn't seen her for a couple of weeks, owing to the chaotic preparations along with the workload it was just impossible to get away.

What to do with myself at this time? I simply walked into the town and back. There was certainly a strange atmosphere about and I found myself discussing the events with perfect strangers. In the afternoon Joe (after all, we might need a mug of tea), Ben, Jimmy and his fellow vehicle fitters, Harry Drew and Frank Day, what one might call a strong RAOC presence, we were just short the Shoemaker who had not yet shown up. There was a lot of discussion and argument about what might happen to us all. Some of it proved wildly wrong, some of it was strangely accurate. To be absolutely honest we were all frightened of the future and, my goodness, we needed to be.

Gaffer turned up at one stage, and said we would be moving to France, probably within a week. This turned out to be accurate but considering our position as the First Guards Brigade, First Division, First Army it hadn't taken a lot of working out. Whatever, things would never be the same again for any of us.

The next few days were taken up with getting equipment together, checking stores, making sure that their weapons were in good condition. Wherever you went there were platoons with their equipment laid out in neat piles and the Platoon Sergeants checking and double-checking. The Mortar Platoon with its 3 inch mortars set up, Signal Platoon wrapped up in wire, radios laid out, (sadly they never worked) and as if in mockery there were signal flags been checked out. Though I never saw them I suppose they had packed their heliographs too; gosh; it must be further back in time than I thought, was this really 1939?

But the thing that I was eagerly awaiting were some form of large vehicles, we still weren't mechanised and at this time as I said earlier, there was the Bren Gun Carrier Platoon with six carriers, the six motor cycles and probably the same number of 15 cwt Morris trucks, oh yes and two water trucks rather like miniature petrol tankers. I didn't have long to wait; our heavy trucks began to arrive in the form of 'impressed' vehicles. These had been commandeered; the Army always used the word 'impressed. Probably something to do with accounting but my own opinion was that it had more to do with it sounding better, not quite so brutal.

What a wonderful hotch potch these vehicles were. Furniture vans seemed to have been a popular choice; there was a magnificent Lucas van still with its painted logos on the sides, pantechnicons too, these had the space inside extending over the driver's cab and it provided a nice cosy bunk for the driver; they were very popular! none of these vehicles had been painted over with Army Green so goodness knows what we were going to look like in convoy. I didn't think we would impress the Germans, lounging in their magnificent Mk 4 Tanks. Then again I didn't know anything at all about these tanks. We had been brought up to think they were all plywood mocked up to show off on manoeuvres. I find it hard to believe I am writing this but it is exactly as it was.

Even more bizarre was the next major problem! There were only a very few soldiers in the Battalion who could drive; in this day and age when almost every body can drive to find seven hundred men where maybe only fifty could drive is unbelievable. Some of the MT platoon had been attending driving courses in anticipation of eventual mechanisation and some of the reservists could drive but the fact was our vehicles had arrived and it was beginning to look as if we would have to push them. If you are thinking my imagination is working overtime, then, to use a well known phrase, 'You ain't seen nothing yet.'

All of this of course was simply going on around me. Arnold and I were pretty busy and although this was really just an extension of our Mobilisation each year for manoeuvres (remember our exercises), the truth was we were massively unprepared and I suspect everything was being played off the cuff. In the next day or two I was to get an insight into the desperate problem of finding drivers.

I was detailed to go to Winchester barracks, using one of the new trucks. I can't remember what I was supposed to pick up, but the Hampshire Regimental Depot was there so it must have been stores and would almost certainly have been weapons of some sort, hence the reason I had been detailed for the task.

By this time most of the new vehicles had been parked on the barrack square but my orders were to rendezvous with the driver and the truck outside the Guardroom. This I did and found that my driver was one of the older reservists who had served with the 2nd Battalion for many years and the vehicle was, if I remember correctly, a large Ford van. After the usual exchange of military greetings something like, 'Good morning Corporal I'm your driver, Pte Brown! Good, I expect you know we are picking up stores from the Depot at Winchester.' (Why did Private Brown seem so ill at ease?) 'Let's make a start.' I was really looking forward to this trip; after all, I had never ridden in any sort of vehicle other than public transport and the prospect of a pleasant drive to Winchester and back and also being in charge was very promising. I was already planning a long break somewhere en route.

We climbed in and not ever having driven or even sat with a driver before I waited for something to happen. Turned out to be nothing much. Brown was fumbling around as if he had never driven before: funny, that, it turned out that in fact he hadn't. After confessing, he explained how a non-driver like himself came to be detailed to drive the Armourer Corporal to Winchester. During this he was even more ill at ease but the story was that there was an item on Battalion Orders a couple of days previously which invited anyone with driving experience to report to the Mechanical Transport Sergeant the following morning at some ungodly hour to be tested as a possible driver. This would take place on the barrack square. I was beginning to see where this was leading.

I asked rather naively why he had put his name down if he had never driven.

Like a flash the reply came: 'I've got a motor bike which is sort of the same.'

I suppose one could stretch a point, some stretch.

'And how did you think that you would pass the test?'

I'm sorry but you may have to stretch your credulity to the limit now.

'My mate is a driver in Civvy Street and he told me what to do.'

You cannot claim that I didn't warn you; never mind, it gets better. I just had to ask,

'And what happened?'

'Well, there were these trucks at one end of the square and the Sergeant said get in, drive it to the top and back.'

'Hang on a minute, how did you start it?' silly sort of question really.

'When a truck got back the driver lined it up for the next bloke and left the engine running. I got in, my mate had told me how to put it in gear, just like a bike really. And I drove it up and back and the Sergeant said OK and put me down as a driver'.

'Oh dear, just one more question: how did you manage the gears?'

'I didn't have to, it was only a short distance.'

So what's all the fuss about these days, just leave it in first gear!

I was by this time full of admiration for this old soldier who come hell or high water, was not going to march the length and breadth of France or anywhere else. Alas, I still had to get to Winchester and I found myself infected by this madness, saying, 'Why not get hold of your mate, he can start the truck and we could maybe drive to Winchester in first gear.' This latter was wasted as Brown had already disappeared in search of his mate. My God, I was beginning to like this bloke Brown, the epitome of the crafty and intelligent soldier. I could certainly learn from him. Back he came, mate in tow, a very wary mate I might say; truck was started, a few last minute instructions and Brown and I were off. Once he mastered the technicalities of changing gears there were no problems, as a motor cyclist the roads presented no difficulties and the icing on the cake was that he knew the way, again the result of much motor cycling.

Looking back I was pretty foolish, but for the next few years I had more influence over the drivers than anybody. It always puzzled Jim; as for Private Jack Brown I just had to lift my finger and if it were possible it was done. Three months later he nearly killed me, but that's a later story.

On Sunday 10 September the Brigade moved off to France, seven days after the declaration of war. Organising and preparing had, in so short a time, been something of a nightmare but here we were, parading and ready to move off. Things had not worked out for me as I had expected; normally I would have travelled, with my 'Boxes tool Armourer', in the back of the QM's baggage lorry, with Arnold riding with the driver. The QM Section had of course been allocated a number of vehicles specifically for their use. This was a generous allocation as we had to carry the Battalion stores, clothing, blankets etc., oh yes, and the Battalion's rum ration. (After we got to France it was a toss up who found the rum first, Joe or Gaffer but Joe wasn't in Gaffer's class when it came to misappropriation; after all Gaffer was an ex-professional, at least I thought he was: ex, I mean.

As I said my position in the travel pecking order had been decided days ago but to my surprise when the day dawned, Company Orders decreed that at the appointed time I would be expected to parade with Headquarter Company fully dressed and equipped for war, which of course meant carrying everything I owned more or less, even my rifle. Mind you, they hadn't yet issued ammunition so I suppose that was something to be thankful for. The night before I had had this nightmare that I was marching down Gun Hill in the direction of the Station carrying all my gear including rifle but no ammunition. Come the next day I *was* marching down Gun Hill with all my gear, rifle but no ammunition finally coming to a halt with the rest of HQ Company in the station yard. I had also been issued with a 'haversack ration'; this culinary delight comprising two thick slices of bread with some sort of filling was always available to a soldier before being launched off into the blue where the prospect of being fed was sort of hit or miss. Not reassuring nor especially appetising. I did say that I was carrying all that I owned: well not strictly true. I was dressed in what was called 'marching order'. This comprised large pack, small pack, greatcoat, rifle and bayonet, and of course the necessary equipment straps etc. to support it all. What we put in our packs was whatever we thought we might want and leaving out whatever we thought we could get away with. The rest of our kit went into our kitbags which travelled by lorry and with which we would be united at the other end. This was the system. I think that served as a model for the present day airlines and their superbly reliable carousels and gave rise to the well known expression: 'Where the bloody hell are my bags?'

A strange thing happened at the station. We were joined by the RAOC Shoemaker looking very ragged and depressed and surprisingly old although many of the reservists looked old to us youngsters. I managed a brief chat but we were being chivvied onto the train and funnily enough it was on the boat that we next met, discovering that at least he had sense of humour. Much of the day and night that followed is very vague. We were assembled on the docks and I do remember it was very cold and it was raining. This rain was not popular with me; don't forget that not only did I have my own rifle to worry about I tended to worry about all the rifles and the Brens: mind you, not the bloody bikes!

It really was a foul night and sometime after midnight found Ben, Joe and me on the top deck, huddling as best we could under our groundsheets. It was pitch black, no lights showing at all and pouring with rain. Our thoughts and muted conversations were mainly concerned with 'U' boats; we were not happy bunnies. Suddenly a head poked through the ground sheets and in a hoarse whisper a voice said, 'I don't want to worry you, but the rats have left the ship.' All these years later I am finding as I struggle to remember detail, that there are some moments as clear in my mind as if they had just happened. In this case I can still feel the cold and the wet and hear the voice. It was the Shoemaker!

CHAPTER 7
A COLD COLD WINTER

After docking at Cherbourg we marched up onto the railway station platforms where we were allowed to fall out and make ourselves comfortable. As usual there was a total lack of communication so we just found ourselves a space, dropped our kit and discussed the lack of refreshment. Joe disappeared and returned empty handed, things were bad without a doubt, and all this time no sign of Gaffer. There was a whole Brigade on these platforms, The two Guards Battalions were together further along, with everyone sprawled about like us. At last the RSM appeared, heading our way purposefully. He ordered us to our feet, told us that food and drink were on its way, after that we would be paid in francs and the Colonel (remember our underhand bowler and all-round good guy) had ruled that we would be allowed out into Cherbourg, we would set an example whilst there and any one who missed the train would be Court Martialled. The train departure time was given and we were stood down again to await the food and drink whereupon Joe appeared from nowhere with a mug of hot sweet tea and I thought, 'Thank God, everything's back to normal, let's get on with the war – after we get back from Cherbourg of course.'

Collecting our francs was a bit of scramble. Heaven only knows how Col. Lee had organised this pay-out but it was noticeable that the Guards were simply getting on with the food and unlike us who were trying to tidy ourselves up a bit. They seemed to have settled down for a long wait and so it proved. We spent the evening wandering about Cherbourg and the Guards spent it on the station platforms. And very cold it must have been too. Then confirmation that things really were on the up and up, Gaffer turned up, said something about us needing a chaperon and we were off.

A drink together in a small café. Gaffer, chatting fluently to the lady, said, 'I'll see you on the platform, don't forget the time, Col. Lee always means what he says, I've arranged fried eggs and chips with the lady.' And he was gone. It was in the next hour that I discovered that the French couldn't cook to save their lives and so it proved so long as I was in France. They are still kidding the world. Eventually Joe took over the kitchen amidst strong protest and we enjoyed a good hot supper. The lady was all smiles again when we paid and left, not only that, she now knew how to fry an egg.

I never did find out where Gaffer got to but the three of us had learned that he spoke fluent French and that was going to be useful in the future. Joe did say at some time or other that he also spoke pretty good Arabic but we couldn't see a use for that. In fact as I said earlier he was a fully qualified Arabic translator. So back to the station, the rain had stopped and it was a clear but very cold evening, a clear memory this as I look back and think of the three of us, full of Joe's eggs and chips, finding our way back to the station. Nothing had changed, those of the Battalion who had not gone into town were still lying about surrounded by their kit as were the two Guards Battalions who had not been given the opportunity to go into town. We sympathised but not too much and anyway they were to have the last laugh before the night was done, and with a vengeance. Very much later in North Africa we lost out to these two great Regiments on the toss of a coin which cost us dearly. I'll tell this story eventually, always providing my GP keeps the tablets coming! Oh yes, there were two who missed the train and as promised they were Court Martialled and very severely punished.

Around midnight the trains pulled in and there we were, just as our fathers before: climbing up into the trucks marked '*Chevaux dix Hommes Quarante*'. Where's Gaffer when you need him, but even I know that is 'Ten Horses Forty Soldiers'. These railway trucks had indeed been used during the First World War and for French troops over the years but they had changed the straw! We were always far short of the forty when travelling in them and so could spread out with our kit, plenty of room for a card school, bit of brewing up or a good kip. Certainly on a long run they were far superior to a carriage.

We had not the faintest idea of where we were going, it was pitch black, so I, like the rest, stretched out and fell asleep. (I could still sleep anywhere.) I awoke to lots of shouting and general banging about. Half asleep and very cold it gradually dawned on me that I and all the others were being invited to get dressed (full marching order) and to parade on the platform, if possible before Christmas. None of this was easy as there were no lights anywhere and getting into full marching order under these conditions was something of a nightmare. The RSM sounded none too happy and Christmas was not that far away. Where were we?

Up popped Gaffer; where the hell did he come from, I thought? Unfortunately he was not bearing good tidings, We were on Arras railway station and our destination was an Agricultural College at a place called Tilloy where we would be billeted. The train now leaving platform four complete with the two Guards Battalions would end up at the College siding, the Guardsmen would be invited to go to bed and us? we would be marching out to Tilloy. Mileage? About twelve. Full marching order! I was suddenly frightened I might let myself down. I had never attempted anything like this before and twelve miles was a long way. I made it, I hated it but I found that I was, indeed, blessed with good feet.

During the march I had plenty of time to ponder a serious problem, Girl was pregnant. Those wonderful weekends but with a marriage arranged how was I going to get home? We were all beginning to realise that going to war was a very serious business that precluded things like leave even to get married. I was no nearer an answer when we finally limped into the Agricultural College but had decided to try and have a word with the Padre at the earliest.

The snoring we could hear as we searched for a free room could well have been described as a Guardsman's Chorus. You can't win them all, the rooms were equipped with six beds and to our weary bodies were more than inviting. Joe, Ben, the Shoemaker, Gaffer and I took over a room and even that early the four of us were beginning to form a separate group, though this was broken when the next day the Shoemaker was sent back to England because he had false teeth, please, please don't ask. A good night's sleep before being chased out by a combination of three buglers and one RSM. God, those Guard's buglers were superb. Gaffer thought they could be improved by ducking into the back of his cleaver, quieter at least. Ben objected on the grounds that he wasn't ready to start stitching though thinking about it he decided he probably needed the practice and what better than a dozen or so on a Guardsman's skull.

The lads were paraded and were busy checking their kit so our little group drifted off to look round the grounds and maybe wander into the small village that was

Tilloy. We had made our number back up to four by the addition of Corporal Prince, the Post Corporal Looking round the grounds we found ourselves wandering about amongst overgrown First World War trenches and picking up old cartridge cases: quite unbelievable and even more so when Prince said he could well have occupied these trenches as he had fought in one of the big battles around Arras, that he remembered Tilloy well enough and was looking forward to walking round the village. We of course had known that he was a veteran from his medal ribbons but this was quite exciting, so much so that Gaffer led us unerringly to the nearest estaminet the better to refresh Corporal, Prince's memory cells. I made another discovery that I didn't like the French beer.

Prince was able to describe the destruction and desolation of some of the areas, particularly one road leading out of the village which he said was almost certainly the road they moved along on the way to the front line but then of course it was a mass of shell holes and mud. I think Corporal Prince was happy to leave the village and everybody seemed a little subdued. The memory that sticks with me was Prince detailing the horrendous casualty figures for the particular battle that he had been part of around Tilloy, We in turn were left with much to think about: did a similar future await us, or would it be different this time? It was several days before I shook off this feeling of foreboding.

Back to reality where once again there was a feeling of not knowing what on earth was really going on. We mooched about amongst a great deal of activity, some of us even made friends with Guardsmen. As for the owner of the estaminet, the only one in the village, we seldom saw him, the theory being that he was just too busy counting his money. I bet that was one Frenchman sorry to see us go.

At this time the Battalion was not yet complete and would not be so until the B Echelon caught up with us or we with them. The B Echelon was made up of the Transport and Quartermaster's Sections and were part of Headquarter Company. An Infantry Battalion comprised basically Headquarter Company and four Rifle Companies and within this structure several specialist sections of which the B Echelon was the largest. Our B Echelon had left UK later than the Battalion and were driving the vehicles down to the port of embarkation and would eventually link up with the rest of us somewhere in France, I suppose somebody knew where they were but it was probably censored information. I did have an interest as all my personal tools (the ones made so laboriously at Hilsea) and my books, along with one or two extra personal items I had slipped in, were on the QM baggage lorry. To say nothing of my concern as to how Pte. Brown might be faring.

Things began to move again. When the RSM becomes unusually active it is a sure sign to get your kit together. As the war moved on you could substitute dispatch rider for RSM. Indeed you can find a mathematical equation forming here – Active RSM, get your kit together = Active dispatch rider, get your bowels together! A searing memory of this equation brings back a dispatch rider in the middle of the night and eight hours later we were in convoy to Casserine being savaged most of the way by Messerschmitts! Give me the RSM side of equation any day. But more of this later. Movement on this occasion meant forming up once again, best foot forward and soon we were settling down in the straw once again.

We finally 'detrained' in the middle of the night and our little group being part of B Echelon were separated and taken individually to our billet. Mine turned out to be a small shed in a garden, used for coal storage. Ah well, ground sheet and blanket down, snuggle up to the pile of coal briquets and yes, I know, I could sleep anywhere and I did - except. In the early hours of the morning I was herded out of the shed by the owners with much sympathetic chatter in French and bingo, I was stretched out in a gorgeous feather bed. Not exactly ' anywhere' but believe me I slept.

The next morning I was introduced to the continental breakfast which went down very well and in the evening a wonderful dinner. I might have to change my mind about the French and their cooking but not yet. The next day B Echelon arrived together with Arnold who was none too pleased at my cushy billet and promptly took it over and I joined the rest in a large café. I took time out to check the baggage lorry to see if my kit was OK. Whilst I was doing this Pte. Jack Brown scrambled up in to the truck wearing the biggest smile I had seen since landing. He didn't need to tell me that everything was going well, I was delighted. Oh God, the RSM is active again and in no time I am settling down in the straw with the other three. I had also caught up with Jimmy and the other two vehicle fitters, Frank Day and Harry Drew; happily they had been well looked after though I recognised the signs of home-sickness in Jimmy.

An Infantry Battalion is a tightly knit group of men obeying the orders of the Commanding Officer through the officers and NCOs. They live closely together the whole time, sharing barrack rooms, training, parading and playing hard and within this they look after themselves in a strange way; it is very difficult to explain. There were soldiers without any formal or official authority who wielded enormous power, I suppose you could say it was underground really and any officer worth his salt quickly made certain that he knew these people and kept them on side. All of this is to qualify my statement above: 'I had caught up with Jimmy and the other two vehicle fitters, Frank Day and Harry Drew; happily they had been well looked after.' This was no surprise to me. Weeks back at Corunna barracks Gaffer had said to me, 'Don't worry, I'll look after them,' which brought them into the orbit of this shadowy power. Throughout their time with the Battalion this 'looking after' would be with them and it makes me smile now to think they never knew.

Although I picked up these vibrations very quickly after I joined the Battalion I have just found it is impossible to describe. Some of these soldiers would die because they stopped to help a fellow member of the Battalion whom they might not even know. I'm still struggling to find a definition and will leave it at that. But here we were chugging along the French railways, tucked up in the straw and certainly not into philosophy, just wondering where the hell next. One thing that had begun to bother me was the cold. Although it was only late September it was certainly cold. Admittedly these moves had all been through the night but I hated the cold and I still do. Oh dear, is that the RSM's dulcet tones? It is and as the Americans would say, 'Move your arse.' Mind you, I'm getting pretty good at it, after all what more could you ask, three o'clock in the morning, a freezing cold station yard, pitch dark, half asleep. Good God here's Joe with a mug of tea, now I'm hallucinating.

And where were we? A largish village called Genech and we were to stay here for quite a while, certainly in relation to our in and out stops up to this point. I cannot recollect how long this turned out to be, several weeks at least, I remember getting through quite a lot of work whilst there but it wasn't that straightforward. After two or three weeks B Echelon moved out to a very small village some six or seven miles away and I moved with them. We were billeted in a large barn using palliases filled with straw and I found a chink in my 'sleep anywhere' boast: not if my feet were cold! and believe me that barn was cold. Gaffer solved the problem; were there no limits to his talent? He brought me a couple of large mail sacks which I pulled up to my waist and bingo, warm as toast; they call them sleeping bags these days. I have no idea where they came from and so kept them out of sight, especially when Corporal Prince was about.

During my stay there one of the drivers, Tug Wilson, suggested I might like to come out with him on one of his many trips for stores. A quick word with the QM (always go to the top) and as I wasn't particularly busy he gave me the OK. Once free of the village Tug Wilson pulled over and one of my pleasant chickens came home to roost. Apparently Jack Brown had suggested I ought to learn to drive and Tug had happily accepted the risk and here we were with my first lesson about to begin. In a sense we are back with that mysterious underground Freemasonry again. I was delighted and so my first lessons using a 15 cwt Morris truck began. They continued whenever the opportunity occurred and I became reasonably competent.

During this period I saw very little of Arnold who was billeted with a French family and living a very comfortable life. We had little or no work at this time. Tug and I became good friends. He had a good story to tell about his war in Palestine, turning over a truck like the one we were using. I had heard the odd story about Tug's reputation as a fast and reckless driver in Palestine, his brushes with authority, his L/Corporal to Corporal and back to Private again, finally culminating in the accident which nearly killed him. His face carried nasty scars. But he was still one of the drivers and well thought of. He will be back, believe me.

All of this was overshadowed by the birth of my son Tony on 16 October and I still hadn't got any sort of permission to go home and make an honest Girl of her. My application was somewhere in the system but things were so new that there wasn't any sort of organisation for sending just one soldier back. I personally felt that it was a 'Don't you know there's a war on syndrome' that I had been caught up in. All I could do was pester the life out of the Padre and anyone else who might be able to help. It wasn't until after Christmas that I was told that I would be on the first official leave to be approved; they still didn't tell me when that might be.

So this mixed interlude came to an end, happy because I was a Dad and Girl and the baby were fine and in good health but marred by my inability to get home. I was then sent back to Genech because the Battalion were about to embark on three weeks' range work which would include Brens and 3" mortars, an excellent opportunity to iron out the kinks and remind everyone what we were really here for. I had been moved back to cover this work and Arnold felt there was no need for two of us so he stayed behind to help the QM. The officers were billeted in a beautiful chateau and the rest of us in yet another barn but it was heated and not uncomfortable. The food at this point was very good so I have no complaints, except the facility for 'bowel movements'! The chateau was set in the middle of beautiful grounds which included a small fairly dense wooded area, the sort that, as my time with the Battalion increased, I would not see as beautiful but as a good tank trap, perceptions change. But back to the facilities. These had been constructed by the Pioneer Platoon (remember general factotums but main areas of responsibility, coffins, crosses and burial) if they happened to be handy. The Pioneer platoon I mean.

In a rush of carpentry and design genius they had dug a long deepish trench over which they had laid, between two cleverly designed wooden forks, a tree trunk of reasonably comfortable diametric proportions though one needed to exclude the rough bark when talking comfort. The length accommodated around six bums at once and proved an excellent platform for gossip and the planning of the next move in the war. There were no screens, just the trees, and it was bloody cold. I hated it. I have always been a bit embarrassed by this natural function especially when the nearest toilet might be a couple of hundred miles away and you knew sure as hell the German Artillery had your biological clock pinned on the side of their gun. Their air force too seemed to have a copy.

Ah, the spade and the stroll into the distance, no wonder my knees are useless these days. With all the present day furore about this kit or that kit, make sure you have got your mobile phone, make sure it's charged, plenty of money in it for these difficult calls to the RAF asking for close support, here is your rifle, useless, but never mind. The truth is most soldiers would settle for a pill that bunged them up until the end of hostilities. In hindsight I certainly would. But in the end it was, I suppose, just a pain in the arse. Sorry about that.

I wasn't long in the chateau barn, moving to another smaller barn at the other end of the village. Our little group were together in this barn and Gaffer had negotiated a deal with the owner of a small café opposite enabling us to use the washing facilities and yes, you have guessed, the toilet. This barn too was heated, and needed to be, the weather was getting very cold and this coincided with the first days of our range work. Just my luck, zeroing rifles became very painful as the day wore on and the lads weren't too happy either, then, disaster! The Brens simply wouldn't work.

This was the first time I had ever encountered a problem with this superb gun, baffling for a little while but the problem was quickly solved. The guns were well oiled and this had simply frozen. Solution – dry them out and away they went but under sustained fire they began to react to the lack of lubricant with a series of stoppages. The reason I was there of course was to sort out these problems: doubly difficult. First, I didn't have any lubricant suitable and second Joe hadn't shown up with a mug of tea. Was he losing his touch or my God, was he dead? No signs of the Pioneer Platoon so that's a good sign. I knew what I wanted, graphite grease, not issued unfortunately but with unaccustomed brilliance I quickly mustered piles of pencils and got the lads scraping the graphite onto the working parts where it mattered. No further trouble! My telling the Platoon Commanders to make sure they had plenty of pencils and a couple of penknives when they went into action wasn't well received, but we were all bloody cold as was the attempt at humour.

For myself a supply of correct lubricant was not a problem. I told Gaffer what I wanted and there it was, a couple of good sized tubes. French, but certainly graphite grease. This initiative wasn't really necessary as like myself Armourers all over the First Army were reporting the problem and the grease was quickly issued. Time was marching on and we were well into November and the cold was proving a problem especially on the roads where huge stretches of road would be covered in ice. I remember on one of my rare sorties with Tug us both pushing the 15 cwt up a slight gradient with the brakes locked. The road was totally impossible to drive on. About this time Gaffer left Genech to go back to B Echelon; the café and its clientèle certainly missed him. I think he was very close to taking the café over; he seemed to be spending more and more time behind the bar dispensing drinks or alternatively battling it out noisily with his French friends during their interminable card games.

Anyway we missed him. Now we were thrown back on our own feeble attempts at speaking French. Another indication of the severity of the weather was tragically illustrated in the deaths from hypothermia of two soldiers riding in the back of a truck with just a canvas cover. It was ordered after that, that there would always be two in the cab and on any long journey they would make frequent checks on any passengers. Hence I found myself detailed to accompany a driver to pick up stores from a distant Ordnance Depot. I think it was about fifty miles and a lot of it would be in the dark but there were no passengers because of the amount of stores to be picked up.

The truck duly turned up and smiling from the driver's seat was Jack Brown, not Winchester this time but he had been before and knew the way. We had a lot to talk about and I was brought up to date on how Jimmy, Frank and Harry were getting along. Apparently they were really good mechanics and very popular with the drivers. The outward journey was very straightforward, bitterly cold, a few odd convoys about but we made good time and were soon on our way back. The truck was a Dennis which in a previous existence had been a furniture removal van but its main characteristic was that the engine occupied the centre of the cab and Jack and I were snugly tucked either side, a perfect design for this cold weather.

As usual I was quickly off to sleep and this proved to be a near fatal mistake. I should have been sharing the long drive with Jack by chatting and generally keeping us both alert. My next waking was very abrupt and very painful and noisy. We had run into the back of an Artillery unit travelling in convoy and when I say run into the back what we had done in fact was to impale the truck onto the end of one of the gun barrels, I cannot remember which calibre gun it was, probably a 5.5" or 3.7 anti-aircraft but when being towed the barrel is locked down in what might be described as a 'being towed' position which leaves the barrel more or less horizontal and at just the right height to come into our cab and just above the engine. This always providing the point of entry was central.

Fortunately it had come in almost perfectly central, and because there was hardly any room between the seats and the front of the cab, we didn't have far to travel before hitting it, the front I mean. The other thing in our favour, we had been travelling slowly. The Artillery lads were excited about the paint on their gun, we were concerned with backing the lorry off the blasted thing and hoping the truck would get us back. This it did, the only other problem being the Mechanical Transport Sergeant, who I felt was bound to notice the hole. He did and tried to repair it with profane language but to no avail. It turned out to be much easier to write it off and turn the beautifully sculpted profanities in Jack's direction. That was it, there was a war on, the truck was replaced and there was an end to the incident. Jack and I were pretty sore for a few days but we were also very lucky, another foot either way and it doesn't bear thinking about.

About this time the Battalion travelled south to take part in some form of exercise. I moved with B Echelon, this time riding in the baggage lorry. We finished up in the inevitable farmyard sleeping in the barn. My lasting memory of this brief foray was the cold water we were washing in which led to my face becoming unbearably painful to shave. I wasn't alone! Sadly an unfortunate accident to the Carrier Platoon Officer when he tried to cut between two carriers on his motor cycle resulted in his death. The carriers I am referring to were the armoured tracked vehicles designed to carry a Bren gun, fast and very mobile.

Returning from the exercise was a very unpleasant experience. I had volunteered to travel with Jimmy who was going to try and keep a troublesome carrier going whilst on the move. It was dark. I kept a torch on the appropriate bit of the Ford V 8 engine and every time it began to fail Jimmy fiddled and it would come to life again. I said it was dark but my God it was cold, these carriers were wide open and I thought we would never get back. I was also of the opinion that I would never be warm again. Back to our little group in the barn and in this strange 'does anybody know what's happening?' sort of world we settled down to await the RSM's next bout of unusual activity.

Mid December and a strong rumour was gaining ground, I first suspected it might be coming from the vicinity of our old ' friend' the log and could only be a load of old 'crap'; once again sorry about that, I just can't resist it. I had never been back but sometimes wondered if the trench was full yet. I have often tried to relate the Pioneer Sergeants being the only ones in the Army allowed to grow a beard with the work they performed but never got anywhere. I don't think it could be anything to do with latrine construction or even design. And the rumour? We would be spending Christmas in the Maginot Line or thereabouts.

This was a strange turn of events if it proved to be true. I always thought that the Maginot Line was fully manned by the French soldiery. Anyway the rumour was very strong so we could only get on with what we were doing which was mostly trying to keep warm. Also at this time I was detached to an Artillery Unit to modify their Bren Gun Anti Aircraft tripods. It was a straightforward job and I was glad to finish, but I could not complain about the hospitality. The Gunners were a good crowd but I was keen to get back and catch up on the rumour, still persisting but losing strength as time passed and the RSM continued on his noisy way but with no sign of undue activity.

Again we entered a strange atmosphere of 'standing still' well known now as the phony war, which was described at the time as the period when adversaries glared at each other across Europe, each wondering what the other intended to do, a period of belligerent attitudes, of lassitude and slackness and of little real action. Training went on and Arnold and I did a fair bit of work on the ranges but the intense cold was affecting everybody and everything. Suddenly and with not a rumour in sight (I think the trench must be full), the RSM sprang into life so we got our kit together and sure enough it wasn't long before we were parading in the station yard, bitterly cold, pitch dark, waiting for a train and hoping the straw would be plentiful and clean. Par for the course really. I sometimes wondered what these stations looked like in daylight. Hello, here's Joe and guess what? Yes, absolutely right!

As we were scrambling up into our truck Gaffer turned up briefly and said we were on our way to Metz where we would be occupying a big French Cavalry barracks until moving on to the Maginot Line where the Companies would be doing reconnaisance patrols ahead of the Line itself. I asked if he had been sitting on the log recently but it didn't connect. So settle down, still our own little group together. We were becoming well organised: plenty of water, a good primus stove backed up by my blowlamp modified to cook or brew on, plenty of tea milk and sugar, bully beef and several loaves as well as little luxuries like chocolate, also two hurricane lamps.

I had plenty of things to think about and worry too. Girl and Tony were both well and he was really growing. Girl was also having a go at getting me home, tackling her local MP, and she felt there was a good chance that she would be successful whilst my application seemed to have gone to ground somewhere but the RSM had come into the struggle and somehow I found that reassuring, but I was pretty despondent during this period. I had started to write a letter every day and this I was to do whenever we were apart: indeed during the North African and Italian Campaigns I added the three air letters we were allowed per week.

How I wish I had them now! They added up to over a thousand letters. They were lost in a combination of circumstances. Girl of course was living in Portsmouth and when the raids got too bad she would move up to Yorkshire and stay with my parents until the situation improved and then back to Portsmouth. Somewhere in all this frightening chaos the letters just disappeared.

So there we were settling down for the night, Ben, Joe, myself and Don Raddon the QM clerk. Some one produced a pack of cards, and with two lamps to light our way we started a card school. This school lasted until we arrived back from the Maginot, maybe three weeks. During this time we played almost continuously, certainly every time we were free, often late into the night or early morning. The stakes were not high, a small amount to buy into the game at the start; if you won a hand then the school paid you, again a relatively small amount, and of course you took the kitty. If you went down then you simply paid the kitty, again a small account. In a serious school losing a hand meant paying the kitty and each player; the stakes would be much higher and a lot of money could be won, or of course, lost. These schools were very wide-spread and if you really wanted to gamble, they would certainly accommodate you. The game played was usually solo, sometimes called the poor man's bridge; it requires great skill and to enter a card school without this skill was asking for serious trouble.

Just as Gaffer had said we finally pulled into pulled into Metz, another station yard but a big difference this time: as we scrambled out of the truck, it was daylight. Then an even greater shock; we were taken out to the Barracks in trucks, the whole Brigade in fact. It was a huge Barracks and for the first time we were able to mingle with French soldiers who were already occupying parts of the huge dormitory blocks. Up to this point I couldn't remember seeing a French soldier at all. We were to spend several days at Metz, still doing nothing but normal chores and waiting for the next move, there was a lot of snow about by this time and Christmas was just round the corner. Ben and I were lucky enough to get a pass to go into Metz where we found that not only were we not popular but were actively disliked. We went into a restaurant, sober and in good order, and were immediately asked to leave, this in a very aggressive way. How lucky they were that I was with Ben and not Gaffer! We strangely finished up in a beautiful Olympic standard swimming pool. I talked myself into just one off the high board, simple pike and entry, done badly. I hurt my back and I have never been on a high board since.

Finally we were on our way to what proved to be a very pretty village on the side of a hill and overlooking one of the Maginot Line entrances. I was travelling in the QM baggage lorry along with Joe and we braced ourselves for the inevitable barn but instead found we were billeted in a sort of Community Hall which had a huge coke burning stove in the corner plus, oh joy! sacks and sacks of coke. At this time we weren't to know that we were in the middle of one of the worst winters France had seen for many years. No wonder I was suffering, I hate the cold.

Although there were overhead electricity lines we never seemed to be part of where it eventually went to. This was proving frustrating to our erstwhile vehicle fitters who were trying to work in the semi dark. Jimmy soon fixed this; having acquired a long pole I fixed two hooks on the end to his specification. There was a lot of wiring hanging about. Jimmy then hooked it over one of the power lines and bingo, we had light. Unbeknown to us RAOC engineers were doing this all over France, eventually resulting in an Army Order requiring this practice to cease forthwith.

Christmas came and went. I was pretty miserable and we seemed to be mired down in all this apathy, Anyway somebody had organised a celebration of sorts to take place in our billet; the 'of sorts' was mostly booze but we had plenty to eat and it all got pretty lively. All the QM staff were there and I remember the Quartermaster leading us in some filthy Army Ditty before falling off the table, not to be seen again till the following day.

The troops were forward of the Maginot line doing patrols and I went forward to their positions quite often. On the way out there I was fascinated to find that one of the stretches of road had huge camouflaged screens erected on the German side and running for half a mile or more. This was apparently so that the Germans could not see what we were up to. Nothing as it turned out, that is unless you count me meandering along in a 15cwt bound for one of the Company forward posts and already looking forward to a mug of tea, but not the possibility of having to do a job out in the open. There was a fair covering of snow on the ground, it was bitterly cold; indeed that describes exactly the conditions outside at the moment and I still hate the cold. Hang on whilst I turn the boiler up a bit. Ah here's Girl with a cup of tea; hello what's happened to Joe Brown?

During this period the three fitters, Jimmy, Frank and Harry, had moved into our billet purely on the warmth factor; the big stove really was efficient. In addition the fourth vehicle fitter moved in. Which leads me to Sgt. Joe Curley. Again jumping ahead to North Africa we were to share a nasty situation in which Joe was badly wounded. But back to the immediate pre war years. Not being mechanised the Battalion transport was made up of carts pulled by mules or suitable horses. This comprised the Horse Transport Platoon and Joe Curley was the Horse Transport Sergeant. and had been for many years. He was reputed to be second to none in his knowledge and rapport with mules and horses.

About the time that I joined the Battalion they were in the process of being mechanised, which had created a problem. Joe was out of a job and the Battalion now had a vacancy for a Sergeant vehicle fitter who would come from the Battalion as opposed to being attached from the RAOC Solution: send Joe to the Morris Motor Company to be converted to a motor mechanic, after all he was the Transport Sergeant, the activating power would be the same, just sort of different horses. I should at this point remind anyone who may be reading this that we did eventually win the war.

Jimmy, Frank and Harry all agreed later after working with Joe that he was a good motor mechanic but inclined to be rough especially with tools. Joe and I were already good friends. Like so many old soldiers he was a great character with a fund of good stories and a large family of five children. Like me he hated the cold and had a gift for getting some form of heat going. He certainly took over our stove quite brilliantly; indeed it wasn't long before we were actually shedding clothes when indoors.

So what about old soldiers' stories? Well, here is one for size. Gaffer spent most of his evenings in the estaminet almost opposite our billet and most of us popped over in the evenings. For one thing it was in effect the local for the French troops manning the Maginot so we got to fraternise with our allies though language was a barrier. This probably accounts for the fact that it was Gaffer who arranged for him and me to visit the Maginot Line and have a look round. From a professional point of view I was excited at the prospect, especially the prospect of seeing how they were deploying their small arms. We duly turned up at the large entrance that faced the village and were met by the Sergeant who had arranged the visit. We were led into the complex which as I remember had much the look of a ship; we were shown one of the galleries where the heavy guns were supplied and the ammunition came up.

Then on into what was obviously a Sergeants'. Mess. There were long scrubbed tables, plenty of tin plates, enamel mugs, plates of quite delicious bread hardly out of the ovens I suspected and plates of cheeses also delicious. We tucked in and I was introduced to the French Army issue wine, a pint mug full to be exact. It was at the best a rough wine and very dry. Another quickly followed and my next clear recollection was waking up on my palliase feeling like death and with not the slightest idea of how I got there. Gaffer came in later and I was flattered to see at least he looked like I felt nor had he any clear idea how either of us had got back. We were soon enlightened - on a hand-cart (yes, one of those) pushed by a couple of drunken French Sergeants End of story.

Was this their security system in action? It worked, I've been in the Maginot Line and this in wartime! Just don't ask me any questions except to do with bread and cheese and the first mug of wine. Fortunately for the drinking reputation of the British Army Gaffer discovered the French mess had been very hard pressed to find two Sergeants sober enough to push us back.

So eventually we retraced our steps but instead of back to Genech we had been relocated to Templeauve, a small but pleasant town where we were to stay for the rest of the 'Phony War'. The town was situated approximately half way between Lille and Douai and during our period there we could get a day pass to visit either of them but transport was hit or miss so not many of the lads bothered. The Battalion played several games of football against both local clubs and Army teams and I enjoyed these games on what was a very good local stadium. But the biggest thing that happened there was that I was given a provisional date for a week's leave to UK at the end of March! this really lifted my spirits. I will always have a soft spot for Templeauve.

The Battalion were very popular during our stay and this was primarily due to an ancient custom unique to the 2nd Battlion in that, whenever they were on active service and no matter where they were, the Pipes and Drums were required to beat Retreat at dusk every evening. This show was very popular indeed with the local citizenry who turned out in force every evening to watch and applaud. Well, it might have been popular with the public but it was not popular with lads of the Pipes and Drums. But from time to time I enjoyed it.

Then the great news. I was to go on a week's leave starting Wednesday 3 April. This resulted in a wedding day fixed for Saturday 6 April and my return date was Wednesday 10 April. It turned out to be a very long wait or so it seemed, plus the anxiety of something happening to stop it. How close I was to this eventuality! Another unexpected event during this wait: Arnold was posted to a Machine Gun

Battalion, I think it was the Middlesex Regiment, who were equipped with the Vickers heavy machine guns. This meant they had an establishment for an Armourer Staff Sergeant instead of Sergeant so the move was in effect to enable Arnold to be promoted. The really significant thing for me was that the way was now clear for the Battalion to promote me from acting Corporal (in effect Private) to Sergeant to fill the vacancy created by Arnold's departure. I couldn't have wished for a better wedding present. Apart from the extra comforts of rank there was a big increase in pay. How well it serves us, this inability to look into the future; there was the fantastic leave and our wedding followed by the nightmare of trying to survive to enjoy the marriage and this awful period was literally just round the corner.

The wedding suffered from the war. We were married in the Portsmouth Registry Office at eleven o'clock on Saturday 6 April 1940. Girl left to catch a bus for the Registry office together with her Mum and Dad; I was waiting together with my Mum for Bob Alexander, an old and close friend from the old Hilsea days and on this occasion to be my best man. My Dad had not been able to come which had been a big disappointment but Girl had enough relatives for both of us, not least plenty to share looking after young Tony for however long it took. The three of us (Mum, Bob and I)set off to catch a bus, calling in a jeweller's shop which was just round the corner, to pick up a wedding ring and so on to the Register Office. Not exactly Madonna and Richie but to us it was our dream come true and we couldn't have been happier.

There were drinks and food at The Rose in June, my father-in-law's favourite pub, then back to young Tony. Encouraged by Girls family to go out and spend the evening together we did! Unbelievably at the Carlton Cinema in Cosham watching *Destry Rides Again*, but we didn't see it through, and went home to bed. Watching the second half of *Destry Rides Again*, whenever it turns up on TV, has become a much loved nostalgic joke between Girl and me over the years. And Bob Alexander? I last saw him at Bisley in 1952, then we lost touch and now, incredibly, in the last few weeks we have traced him to Harare and are hoping that our letter reaches the address that we have been given. Apparently there is little in the way of a postal service left in Zimbabwe.

I arrived back to find that I was to sit my first class trade test in late April at a large Field Workshop and would be there for two weeks; this was good news as the qualification was very important. Otherwise nothing much was happening, the Pipes and Drums were still beating retreat every evening but most importantly the weather was warming up. This was mid April and it would soon be spring. Had I thought seriously about this I would have realised that this would create the perfect conditions for us to go to war, at least based on my experience of the last Battalion Exercise in England. The weather would be dry and the fields would be fragrant, no chance of a cancellation in favour of leave this time.

The workshops were basically accommodated in a large marquee and most of the living quarters were in empty houses. I was billeted in one of these and soon made myself comfortable. A good crowd of lads who were quite interested in what it was like to be with a front line Battalion, substitute barn for empty house and that was about it. They also had a very nice Corporal's Mess organised in one of the houses. An ASM (Armament Sgt. Major) or in another guise a Warrant Officer Class 1, the highest non commissioned rank would be directly supervising my test under the auspices of the workshop Officer, a Captain. The Commanding Officer was a Major.

The test itself followed set lines. I completed the fitting exercise, in this case a square into a square, quickly – I think there was an allowance of 15 hours. I overhauled a couple of Bren guns, a Vickers gun and Tripod, helped with the general work on Rifles, a brazing test and this completed my practical skills examination. A couple of fairly difficult theory papers, a machine drawing and with one bound I was free, finished. The Captain congratulated me on passing, the Commanding Officer ditto, whilst saying he would ensure the necessary paperwork was completed quickly, and it was off to the Corporals Mess to celebrate. I have researched the timing and this was Thursday 9 May. I must have been there longer than the proposed two weeks. It but remained to sort out how and when I was to get back but meanwhile enjoy the evening.

This I was doing when my celebrations were rudely interrupted by Bill Glair, our QM baggage lorry driver, with orders to return me to the Battalion as quickly as possible. What's up, Bill? was my first question, 'The Germans are moving into Belgium, and the Battalion is on standby to move'! I didn't have an answer to this, one assumes that something will certainly happen sometime but when it does it knocks the wind out of you. We were very quiet during the drive back, there just wasn't anything to say, and my thoughts were dominated by the fear that I wouldn't measure up.

CHAPTER 8
DUNKIRK

Why is it always dark? Arriving back things were indeed moving but once again the overall chaos seemed removed from my own immediate problems, it was almost like trying to operate in a space especially created for me. I had things to do and urgently. This I started to get on with. Some of it had been done, for example Gaffer and Joe had already loaded the QM baggage lorry and in doing so had made sure all my own tools plus the Armourer's Tool Box and my more personal items, including my technical books and old Hilsea Notes, were loaded. Checking through the truck I quickly realised that I had selected my friends well. An area partly covered with odd stores was hiding the distinctive basket in which the rum jars were packed, also there was a big stash of important items: tea, cases of tinned milk, sugar, the inevitable bully beef. Momentarily I wondered how on earth Gaffer had liberated a gallon of rum. Not to reason why, just settle down and wait for the next move. No one was saying anything and as I said we seemed to be in a vacuum; just sort out your own little responsibility and the orders would surely come along.

I contacted Jimmy, Frank, Harry and Joe and found they would be travelling behind us in the Transport Stores truck. Immediately behind us would be the QM stores truck, driven by Jack Brown and behind that the QM.'s small utility truck, a Hillman as I remember. We would be following two 15 cwts (these were primarily designed to carry ammunition) and in front of them one of the water bowsers; this was a converted 15 cwt. The RASC were transporting the troops. During this period waiting to move we didn't see much of Gaffer; his fluent French was in big demand as the townspeople were out in force and there was a lot of panic about. The news

DUNKIRK

Camarades!

Telle est la situation!
En tout cas, la guerre est finie pour vous!
    Vos chefs vont s'enfuir par avion.
A bas les armes!

British Soldiers!

Look at this map: it gives your true situation!
Your troops are entirely surrounded —
    stop fighting!
Put down your arms!

coming through on the radio was already looking menacing, prompting the citizens to pester us for serious news but sadly they were better informed than we were. I had lost all sense of time and I couldn't shake off this feeling of unreality. I didn't have long to wait before this feeling became a fact. Suddenly the large blocks of houses which had been home for our Headquarters burst into flames and the flames quickly spread along the block. The only fire appliance in the town was a very ancient hand pump that had to be pushed to the fire, then pumped by muscle power. The whole disaster

FAIREY BATTLE

was compounded by the Battalion beginning to move off and as we drove further and further away from the town the smoke was still visible. I feel that the whole block of houses must have been burnt down. We had been there for several months, sharing the 'Phony War' with them, and were

on excellent terms with the township in general. We were all very upset, compounded by the feeling of helplessness. There were going to be many times in the future when this feeling of helplessness coupled with a need to do something would leave us distraught. Indeed such a time was already just a few miles away along the road we were to travel.

About ten o'clock the convoy stopped for food and a stretch. So far the journey had been very straightforward if slow. This was suddenly shattered by four British aircraft flying very low, passing over the convoy. Joe immediately identified them as Fairey Battles, a light bomber. Against convoy orders, Joe, Gaffer and I got out. By this time the bombers had climbed away and were some distance from us when out of nowhere several German Me.'s appeared; we could hear their engines, the typical hard note that was to become so familiar. This was followed by the sound of machine guns but the cloud cover was pretty low and it was hard to pick the Battles up again until one appeared to our right, very low and in some trouble, no engine and losing height rapidly. The aircraft was swinging from left to right and at a point some 100 yds from where we were standing horrified, one of the wings clipped the ground and the Fairey Battle ploughed nose first in to the ground with great force.

We started to run over to what at that time was basically a huge cloud of dust. I was very shaken as I think was Joe. Gaffer as usual seemed unmoved as he led. I was frightened of what we would find and was feeling pretty ill but I kept going. It truly was a mess and there was nothing anyone could do. Gaffer tried to get in to retrieve identity but it wasn't possible, and eventually, becoming aware of being summoned in no uncertain terms back to the convoy, we rejoined and were once again moving. At this point I was a different person, very frightened and I couldn't stop trembling but as the miles disappeared I gradually recovered my composure and this just in time to be attacked for the first, but not the last, time by Stukas and their 'screaming bombs' and this, the

STUKA!

first time, I can assure anybody is frightful and nerve destroying beyond belief. The Stuka was a diabolically clever combination of death and fear with the strange ability of always appearing to have singled you out personally! Looking up at them was not to be recommended even to try and retaliate. Sadly we were not the sole target. We had for some time been having troubles with civilians fleeing the front and blocking the roads; they suffered desperately, nor could we stop to help. ' Welcome to the real war!'

The Battalion too suffered casualties but got away relatively lightly as did we, the B Echelon. Jimmy, Frank and Harry were like me pretty shattered, yet, like Gaffer, Joe Curley was strangely calm about it all. I can only put it down to the old soldier syndrome or alternatively they have seen it all before, or at least some of it. I wondered doubtfully whether I would ever be like that or much more to the point at this time, whether I would survive to be like it.

B Echelon were finally diverted off the main road onto a minor road which led into a large wood, several turns later and we parked up alongside the road, tucking our vehicles well into the side, I was tired and shattered so after getting a meal I was glad to get down to some sleep. No idea where we were except in some sort of wood. It was of course bloody dark again but I slept well.

STUKAS

Once light we were up and about sorting our kit, washing, shaving and watching Gaffer with great curiosity as he shaved with an old fashioned cut throat razor. Watching was a complete waste of time: he never cut himself. Breakfast, then the Quartermaster passed onto us what he knew which was not very much. The Battalion were digging in to stop the Germans, this about five miles further on from where we were and we would stay here and fulfill our role in support of the Battalion until told otherwise. This role was complex. We were responsible for feeding and watering, supplying any stores they might require, including ammunition, repairing their vehicles, their guns, their boots, sewing up their wounded. All of this of course involved a reverse supply: we had to arrange to pick all this up from various supply points. I remember thinking it would be a good idea if we could pick up a shoemaker, we had not had a replacement after losing the first one sans teeth and Joe was standing in. As equipment repairer the course leading to qualification had included basic boot repairs especially studs, but my worry was that it might interfere with his 'tea' magic. It didn't! Hello, here's Joe with a mug of tea. I'm hallucinating again.

So the three of us went to explore the wood and try and get some idea of where we might be. In fact the wood turned out to be an extension of the grounds of a large brewery. We had only a few yards to go before coming to a high brick wall. Moving along it we found a wrought iron gate and there was the brewery. Interesting and frustrating, the gate was well and truly locked. For the time being there was work to be done. 'Gaffer' of course was involved with rationing the Battalion, Joe and I joined in but the Quartermaster couldn't make the contacts we needed so eventually we simply waited. I remember trying to find out where Ben had got to but he was up with the Battalion Aid Post. Back to waiting and so the day passed. I was glad of the rest, I had been feeling quite ill all day, I wasn't the only one and we decided it was probably a hangover from the previous day. I suppose today it would be diagnosed as trauma. The nearest 'Councillor' was probably the RSM; there's a frightening thought.

A good night's sleep and the next day I felt fine. But somehow the quiet began to get to us. It just didn't seem right; after all the Battalion were in action just up the road. The QM was getting information in dribs and drabs and frustratingly we couldn't do anything. Gaffer had found a deserted farm on the edge of the wood and passed the afternoon butchering a pig, he had seen rations dry up before. Personally I kept well away from that, not my scene at all. Night, and we sat around listening to Vera Lynn on a portable radio but it made us more uneasy and intruded thoughts of home into our heads. I was pretty despondent thinking of Girl and Tony and I was also becoming fearful of where all this would end. The snippets we were picking up on the radio were frightening to say the least. The Germans were moving inexorably on; what was happening to the Battalion?

Why was it so quiet? Thinking about it was a mistake. It was about this time that the first shell arrived, another unwelcome first. We were well dug in, an unhappy Joe and an even unhappier Clem shared a slit trench for the first time but certainly not the last time. I'm told everybody reacts differently to real fear. I had already discovered my reaction which was a totally dry mouth making swallowing virtually impossible. The shelling was intermittent, no time pattern but not particularly heavy. The weight of shell was small so they were probably field artillery of some type. Looking back I realise now how naïve we all were; the seriousness of our situation still hadn't struck home. Suddenly it changed with the arrival of a dispatch rider; within minutes we were loading up to move, the shell-fire was wasting itself further into the wood and with great speed we were loaded up and moving out. When we arrived at the main road there were RMPs waiting to direct us and so there was little else to do but follow the directions as we went along. As always it was dark! During this hectic period Gaffer found time to moan about leaving the pig which he had prepared with loving care, but leave it he did. I wonder if the Germans enjoyed their bacon? The other well documented accounts of this time make great play with the dropping of parachutists in various disguises to try and confuse the movement of our transport, nuns, soldiers, civilians even RMPs. In fact history has shown this to be true. The Germans did employ parachutists to try and spread confusion, what a waste! We were up to our ears in our own confusion.

Looking back I find time very hard to pin down. Even days and dates are difficult to remember so I am just sticking to the sequences as they unfolded. Eventually we found ourselves in the suburbs of Brussels and somewhere along the way we had picked up a Royal Signals dispatch rider who began a desperate attempt to get us through the town. The roads were totally blocked with both military and civilian traffic; lorries and cars were stuck on the pavements. Finally the dispatch rider gave up and left to try and help somewhere else. I discovered later from the Quartermaster that he had said we were to head for Roubaix if and when we got clear. This we finally did but well after dawn. Again we tangled with both military traffic and civilians, many on foot, and by this time we were simply trying to follow the QM but significantly we had become totally separated from the Battalion.

I have used the words, unreal and bizarre before, and will certainly do so again but in the 'pickle' we now found ourselves it would take both of them together to do justice to our present situation. B Echelon at part strength acting on vague orders to make our way to Roubaix; fortunately we had a sensible officer in charge in the shape of the QM, and there was always Gaffer Guyatt. As a group we mustered three large lorries, the QM's baggage lorry, and two stores lorries. In addition there were two 15 cwt lorries, the QM's pick-up and strangely enough we still had the water bowser. This added up, counting Gaffer, Joe and myself and the QM plus the RQMS (a Warrant Officer and the Quartermaster's number two), finally, a Sergeant and L/ Corporal, to fourteen, hardly a force to create sleepless nights amongst the Panzer crews. We were armed! Thirteen rifles, one pistol, a Bren gun that I had been holding for checking, five Bren magazine boxes with magazines and plenty of ammunition.

Apart from the difficulty of threading our way through the people fleeing the Germans and trying to answer the thousands of questions hurled at us plus the hostility which grew with every mile, we slowly pressed on, hoping that we were heading in the right direction. During this phase Gaffer was quite magnificent, one second hassling and hounding the French people out of the way, the next cajoling and pleading and bribing with our rations. The QM had left finding our way entirely to Gaffer; I said we had a sensible officer in charge. Eventually about mid-day we pulled off the road into a large farmyard which could comfortably hold our vehicles. The farm itself was deserted; there were a dozen or so cows in the field adjoining the farmyard otherwise it was eerily empty. No chickens, in fact none of the livestock normally associated with a farmyard but nevertheless it was a well kept farm and the house was clean and tidy. We settled down to cooking a meal and just getting some rest. I remember quite clearly it was at this time that I began to feel very weary and desperately in need of sleep. The QM had taken Gaffer off to try and locate some information and also to find a route to Roubaix. I made myself comfortable in the truck and fell asleep. Joe was probably making mugs of tea.

I was awoken by the return of the QM who got us together to outline the position and what we were going to do about it. Firstly he had no news of the Brigade and this of course meant the Battalion. They had acquired a road map which showed Roubaix and the surrounding area so we would stay till later in the afternoon and then move on to Roubaix and hope we could find the Brigade HQ. Fortunately petrol was not a problem, our tanks were pretty full, so after we mulled all this over together we settled down to get some sleep. Though I found time to write a letter I had no idea whether it would ever get posted; indeed my thoughts were more and more haunted by survival.

They needed to be because within minutes we came under intensive shelling. The shells were of the air burst type, exploding some twenty feet above the ground and though initially falling short in the field and killing several cows it wasn't going to take them long to range on to us. This was easily deduced because the guns were located on the crest of a rise and I suppose maybe a mile or so away and we could see the flash when they fired. We had plenty of available cover by putting the farmhouse between us and the artillery, but that left the vehicles exposed. Unfortunately we had no choice and though they suffered some damage luckily none of it was terminal. The shelling went on for some time but it became intermittent until it finally stopped. We crept out keeping our heads well down; there was a great deal of activity where the battery had been which was easily seen because of the dust they were kicking up.

After waiting for quite a while the QM deduced that they had probably been moved to another location and a more important target and we too would move just as soon as we could load, or even sooner most of us thought but didn't say. As we drove out down to the main road we could hear Gaffer shooting the cows that had been wounded but not killed. Professional butchers have strict codes. It was not without risk as Gaffer exposed himself to the possibility that some Germans were still there. We eventually reached Roubaix. Again the journey was fraught with blocked roads and what seemed like the whole population on the move. The Stukas had been busy enough to leave us in a poor state of morale, and we were glad to reach our destination. It was noticeable that as we got closer to Roubaix the Stukas disappeared; they seemed to be concentrating on the roads.

This time we had parked in the grounds of a leather factory, and when we looked round inside the factory we found that they made the beautiful leathers used for cars and upholstery. These were stacked up in six feet high piles in all the colours of the rainbow and must have been very valuable. The QM set off again this time taking the RQMS with him and we all settled down to wait. This time we did get a reasonable sleep before they returned and the Quartermaster had been lucky making contact with the Brigade. We were to remain where we were until Brigade contacted us again by dispatch rider, but we could settle down until the following day; meanwhile the Battalion would be notified of our position.

The following day brought much of the same, but what it didn't bring was a despatch rider, so the QM disappeared again and arrived back very late in the afternoon with a route to be taken on the following day. At least we were beginning to feel less exhausted and tired; little did we realise that the next weeks were to test our strengths and our courage to the limits. We had begun to come to terms with the fact that we were retreating and heaven knows where to or when we might be stopping to fight, but come the next day we were once again underway. The QM seemed to know where we were heading and both the RQMS and Gaffer were riding with him in the utility truck. The journey became almost impossible at times. We were making hardly any progress on the roads choked with refugees and it was having an effect on our morale. Leaving them to fend for themselves, this feeling of helplessness was really upsetting and of course as the time passed the hostility became worse and worse.

But the nightmare had only just started. I have no memory of how long we had been struggling to keep moving when we came to a very positive halt courtesy of a strafing attack by Messerschmitts. We suffered quite a bit of vehicle damage and sadly lost one of our 15 cwt drivers. This was a shattering experience compounded by the casualties amongst the civilians and our need to simply keep moving. We continued to struggle on until finally we pulled off down a minor road which appeared to lead nowhere but eventually gave us the opportunity to stop and stretch our legs and, more importantly, eat. The strange thing about all this was the absence of German troops. We kept expecting them to come roaring into view but all we saw was aircraft. What the hell was going on? Things were indeed desperate. We seemed to be totally isolated.

There were two things keeping our morale from disappearing. The Quartermaster, though not really in possession of any real information, had stayed calm and reassuring and made his decisions firmly as if he knew exactly what was going on. The other was Gaffer, simply a tower of strength especially when things got rough. I sometimes found myself wondering why there are always people who seem to be totally impervious to danger or fear even when looking down the formidable barrels of a Messerschmitt. Believe me, I was getting very familiar with my dry mouth syndrome. We were obviously well off the beaten track so the QM decided to hole up for the night after spending some time trying to pin-point our exact position. I helped with this and in the end we felt that we were pretty sure of the road we were on and would move accordingly in the morning .

It wasn't a quiet night. Around one o'clock a motor cyclist, totally lost, turned up and we were able to pick his brains. He was from a different Brigade and had been sent out on a sort of 'free' reconnaissance to try and make any sort of contact and so far we were it, the only one and totally useless to him. But he supplied us with plenty of hard evidence that the German armour had broken through and indeed was moving very fast as was the whole front and our forces were falling back but to where? He didn't know. We fed him and he was gone. I wonder if he made it home?

The following day saw a great deal of activity on the road we had come down but it was entirely the inevitable locals fleeing to wherever they could. Gaffer talked to them and amongst a great deal of arm waving and sadly, tears, found they were mostly trying to reach relatives or friends but all were very very frightened. I certainly wasn't in the mood to be facetious but the predominant thought was, 'join the queue'. What on earth were we going to do next? Even getting a meal together was becoming impossible and anyway we were running out of food. Still plenty of tea, tinned milk and sugar, so Joe was continuing to pop up at the right moment with a welcome mug but this was coming to an end or at least would test his gifts to the limit. I was running out of paraffin for my blowlamp!

Finally in mid afternoon, after a fruitless journey trying to make contact, the Quartermaster decided that we would press on in the direction of Armentiers as this town had been mentioned when he had briefly contacted the Brigade earlier. God, how long ago was that? Just two or three days? It seemed much longer. The progress was becoming more and more difficult, the roads were packed and we frequently pulled off to the side hoping it might ease off and always looking out for a sight of British troops. It really was becoming more and more unreal, that word again but that's exactly how it felt to us. The whole of the British Army must be somewhere in the vicinity: how on earth was it possible not to bump into at least one; even an RSM doing his ' Get on parade' bit would have been welcome. Now, of course, history has given us the answers.

Our small convoy struggled on. We had lost one of the 15 cwts as I said earlier and in that attack we also abandoned the water bowser which was badly holed and leaked in no uncertain manner. We now had the Quartermaster's utility truck, the stores truck driven by my old friend Jack Brown, the QM baggage lorry driven by Bill Glair and a 15cwt the driver of which to my shame I cannot name. I think this adds up to ten of us.

Then at last British troops in the form of a Major, a largish number of RMPs and maybe twenty or thirty troops. There were a number of trucks in front of us so we parked up and waited for a sign. The QM had gone ahead to have words with the major which were to no avail. It had not escaped our notice that away to the right of us and at the bottom of a large open area of fields there was a very large fire burning and this fire was made up of trucks like ours. The troops under the skilled and noisy directions of a very large RSM were guiding trucks from the direction of the gate down the fields and into the inferno. Not good and our hearts sank. We had already identified the R.S.M as a Guardsman belonging to our Brigade so at least we were back in contact but what on earth was going on?

We were not left wondering for long. The QM soon returned and he was obviously both angry and concerned. The war was not going well and we were all in peril and now we were encountering our own 'scorched policy' which meant our trucks and their cargoes were to be destroyed. We would be allowed to salvage our personal possessions and anything we could carry, and whatever food we possessed should be taken. Our equipment order would be fighting, which meant small pack, ammunition pouches, groundsheet, rifle, washing and shaving kit, spare pare of socks, mess tin and as much optimism as we could muster. The three of us agreed to keep the Bren gun, sharing the burden as we went along and each of us would carry two loaded magazines in our ammunition pouches (the pouches had been designed for Bren gun magazines). This gave us a total of approximately one hundred and eighty rounds. We also had to squeeze in a reasonable amount for our rifles. In my case, no matter what was left behind it wouldn't be my writing equipment; letters to Girl were assuming massive proportions though it was beginning to look as though writing them would be a waste of time.

Mail at this time had dried up completely and I was desperate for news of Girl and son Tony. It was only going to get worse so I made a conscious decision that come what may I would somehow tough it out. Maybe I was whistling in the wind! Real fear can have a devastating effect especially when it is round every turn in the road and there is no way to fight back. It was decided by the Quartermaster that Joe and I would go down with the baggage lorry and with Bill Glair driving. Bill would come back and help drive the other vehicles down unless hopefully there had been a change of policy.

This seemed unlikely as more and more vehicles were beginning to pile up, and at the entrance to the field there were what seemed to be hundreds of troops. Joe and I were not happy to be losing 'Gaffer,' but in the event Gaffer and Bill Glair came back with the news that the Battalion had contacted the QM and as soon as the trucks were taken for burning we were to report back to him at the gate.

Losing the baggage lorry meant that I lost my personal tools, all those hard hours work at Hilsea and my books including again my handwritten notes. This was a blow. It was also goodbye to our old friend the Armourer's toolbox. Gaffer too had a worry: those gallon jars of issue rum, two to be precise. I suspect that a long and earnest conversation with the RSM in charge of burning so to speak, had something to do with the rum but he never said! That was it. We checked our kit and squeezed in as much in the way of rations as we could, substituting corned beef and tinned milk for an item of 'defensive' equipment (gas mask) that we hoped would never be required. It never was, either in this campaign or any other. Tea and sugar? Gaffer and I never gave it a thought; we had supreme confidence in our Guru and Joe was still with us. Unfortunately I had forgotten that we had also lost my little blowlamp set-up so even Joe was going to be hard pressed.

Without a backward glance at the inferno, Bill Glair resolutely keeping his eyes averted - drivers do get attached to their trucks. We trudged on back up the field to rendevous with the Quartermaster. He wasn't there! Nor the rest of the lads. We finally managed to speak to the, by now, harassed and I suspect despairing Major and his staff; even the RSM was losing his voice. The Major confirmed that Lt. Puleston had been contacted but that was the extent of his knowledge and suggested we make for Armentiers as there was a defensive line being assembled in this area and it was possible our Brigade would be part of it. Then looking at our little party of four (and a Bren gun) he quickly weighed up the stripes! two L/Corporals and a Corporal Looked me straight in the eye he said: 'You will be in Command and it is your primary duty to make contact with your Regiment. Good luck and if you bump into the German Army I suggest you form a square.' A slight grin; and he was gone. I hope he survived and writing this I can still see that grin there was something indomitable about it

I was far from happy at being in charge but that is how the Army works. Although a very small party I was senior and would have taken charge automatically anyway. So there I was with two old soldiers, both of whom had served in Palestine during the troubles and one young old soldier, that has to be an oxymoron. Two were old friends (Joe and Gaffer), Bill Glair as QM baggage truck driver and I were good friends and in turn he and Gaffer were old friends and had known each other a long time. Sounds cosy but nothing could be further from that; we were a million miles away from cosy.

Gaffer was stopping at regular intervals to gather any information he could from the refugees and to keep us going in the right direction. He decided after a lot of questioning over four or five miles that there probably was a defensive line being formed somewhere south of Armentiers and these people were desperately trying to get behind it, wherever it was. If we took Armentiers as a marker it looked like a twenty or thirty mile trek but we had time so I decided to break somewhere and try and find a barn. We were all very tired and weary and strangely enough hunger was beginning to make itself felt.

The weather was superb though we could have done with it being cooler; beautiful open countryside but it was too good to last as what seemed like hundreds of Stukas homed in on us. I still don't think they were picking our little group out but it bloody seemed like it. Shouting 'Form a square!' (I wasn't going allow a Major the only funny lines) we flung ourselves into the ditches alongside the road. Sod's law dictates that drive your car off the road, and ditches are always six foot deep, dive into one for a little protection from a naughty Stuka with you in his sights and you'll be lucky if it's six inches deep. I unshipped my rifle and said, 'Engage,' which we did. Though probably futile in terms of results it is easier to bear if you are at least retaliating. The trouble with that? You have to look up at them and that sight is quite capable of freezing your trigger finger - forever!

The attack lasted only a few minutes but it seemed ages and there were in fact only ten or so Stukas. Bill Glair had picked up a nasty little rip on his upper arm but was otherwise OK apart from deafness; the rest of us were unscathed, I personally felt that I would never swallow again; at least my pants were clean! But our nightmare was just beginning. The devastation among the refugees was immense and we were pretty helpless. What they needed was medical care and lots of it; this we did not have and they were simply going to have to cope. I decided we would move around as much as we could, trying to reassure and help with the more severe injuries but this didn't really help at all; indeed it was proving provocative so I formed up my army once again and we set off to find the Battalion.

And how did I feel as we trudged along? Frightened, upset, frustrated, angry, all come to mind but what I do recall very clearly was feeling strangely calm. My other vivid memory is of how tired I was - sleepy tired that is, I just couldn't wait to find a place where we could lay up. It was late afternoon when we found a farm. Situated almost at the top of a small hill with a substantial track leading up to it there was plenty of cover in the way of hedgerows along the track and we took advantage of this as we very cautiously approached the first gate. We hadn't seen any sign of the enemy on the ground so far but there was this strange feeling of apprehension all the time. The farm like the last one was totally deserted but with a clean dry barn and plenty of straw.

Scorched Earth

Joe disappeared into the kitchen and eventually returned with a mess tin of sweet tea. I decided we would open one of our tins of bully beef and share it, and so we dined. I detailed a watch, well we drew for it, a bit unmilitary I know but it seemed right at the time then. As soon as I stretched out I was gone. It wasn't a very satisfying night for sleep; we were working two-hour shifts so being woken and then have to struggle through your two-hour spell without falling asleep was a nightmare in itself. Though we could all have slept forever we were up just after dawn and after washing and shaving and trying to clean the worst of the previous day's attempts to help the injured refugees from our battledress, we took stock.

The farm overlooked a typical rural valley. We could pick out roads and there was still a lot of traffic on foot, easily seen because of the dust but most importantly there were groups of soldiers marching along in apparently good order. And unbelievably, over to our right, laid out before our very eyes was Armentiers: at least that was our judgement which later proved correct. Time for Corporal Hoyle to do his 'Commanding Officer' bit and make a decision. This was not

© R N Pearson 1999

HEINKEL H.E. 51

difficult. Breakfast! Same menu as the night before: a tin of bully and as much tea as Joe could muster. It was a lovely morning then as we sat eating our breakfast and admiring the view we were conscious of a loud and persistent hum which quickly revealed itself as several squadrons of small bi-planes; indeed they were blackening the sky. Joe instantly identified them as Heinkel He 51s and for good measure said they had been used in Spain. Apparently though essentially a fighter they could carry a very small bomb load. He also estimated there were well over a hundred of them.

This huge force of aircraft proceeded to bomb Armentiers. We watched it from our vantage point and again it didn't last long and though carrying only a small bomb load we could see that they had started a few fires but as the dust settled we couldn't see evidence of any major damage. Yet another awakening to the brutal realities of war. We were all very quiet, busy with our own thoughts, mine entirely around Tony and Girl and this knot of fear that seemed to have settled in my stomach; it was not going to go away, that much I knew. I decided we would get back onto the main road and moving south of Armentiers keep heading west and hope to pick up information as to where the Battalion was. With troops about I felt it was a possibility. Typically when we got onto the road the troops we had seen from the farm had somehow disappeared so once more we plodded on.

Later in the afternoon we stopped in a large village and found a sort of archway between two houses. This had a glass roof and it was off the road so we had a measure of privacy. There was a certain amount of bomb damage about but the village had so far escaped major damage. It was also pretty deserted. As we rested more and more troops began to go past in small groups, some of them with no equipment, just battle-dress. I remember one riding a huge farmhorse. There were also refugees mixed in. I began to question the soldiers as they came through but with no luck. Some of them had been bombed on several occasions and it was beginning to show; the only concrete information I got was that they were making for the coast but with no idea exactly where.

Throughout our journey so far ' Gaffer' had been a great asset. This fluency had sorted a few nasty moments and his physical presence had certainly quietened a few situations down. Joe and Bill had been what they were, bloody good soldiers! I was just about to be introduced to the two sides of Gaffer. Sometime during the afternoon three soldiers came into the arch carrying a typical Company cash box and asking if there was a 'Tiffy' about; very casually, as if not really interested, Gaffer pointed to me. I duly confessed to being a 'Tiffy' and was asked if I could open this cash box. I had, like most Armourers, opened a few of these cash boxes in my time: Company Commanders and their Lieutenants seemed to be chronically prone to losing their keys. All I needed was a decent but robust screwdriver and I was carrying one; no decent Tiffy ever ditched all his tools.

Gaffer held the box, the three soldiers hovered round hopefully. I sprung the lock and as always it gave way easily (I sometimes wondered if they hadn't been designed to be opened like this in anticipation of young Lieutenants and their penchant for losing keys). Gaffer stood up, opened the box, and lifted out the top tray. This was about three inches deep and divided into maybe three compartments in fact a typical cash box. He looked into the bottom of the box, pronounced it bloody empty, closed the lid, dropped the box carelessly at my feet, and handed the tray to the eager hands of the three soldiers. There was a couple of bundles of franc notes and a fair amount of coinage, enough to delight them. They quickly emptied the trays and were gone until a shout from Gaffer brought them scuttling back. After all, Gaffer was a L/Corporal and somehow people were always intimidated by his physical presence. 'What about something for the Corporal, lads?' They duly handed me a few notes, said, 'Sorry, Corporal,' and then were really gone. I idly picked up the 'empty' cash box, except that the bottom of it was stuffed with bundles of franc notes. Hastily closing the lid I studied Gaffers' face, a study in innocence plus a grin of professional competence! I gave him the box, he disappeared with it and indeed, I never saw the box again – but? And that's another story.

After this Gaffer disappeared for awhile. I sat and wrestled with the problem of what to do next. Joe and Bill stayed out on the road intercepting the odd troops coming through but without gaining any information that might help us. Gaffer came back and said, 'Come on, Tiffy, time to learn.' I duly followed him up the road through a garden gate into the back garden of a house where there was a huge bomb crater. The house was badly damaged and lying at the foot of this shattered wall was the body of a despatch rider. He was in a crumpled position and it was obvious that the blast from the bomb had flung him into the back wall head or face first. There was a nasty mark and a long smear where he had slid down. The weather had been very hot during the previous couple of weeks and he had been there long enough to present a sad and unpleasant task. I knew by this time what Gaffer had meant by ' Time to learn, Tiffy.' Helping the bombed refugees had I suppose started a hardening process towards injuries but this was something else and the victim was one of us.

I had not approached the body too closely and how clearly I remember all those years ago how I was battling to keep my stomach under control. I felt awful and I somehow felt that if I were sick it would be a kind of desecration; in extremities the mind plays strange tricks. It seemed an age before Gaffer spoke and this was to tell me he had found a shovel so we could get started on a grave and bury him correctly, head to the west and with the utmost respect, making sure his identity would be visible and protected. Starting to dig first where Gaffer had drawn out an outline I began to recover my composure. There was no real hurry so I made a good job of it. Gaffer never spoke. When I finished he simply said, 'Go and carefully turn him over so we can get a good look, take his pay book and identity tags, empty his pockets, then we will bury him.' These words are etched on my memory, I did as he said and it has to be the hardest test of my courage or fortitude ever. The head and face were destroyed beyond recognition and his left arm was raised as instinctively he had tried to save himself. And he was L/Corporal James Gent, of the Green Howards.

Gaffer came over as I finished and we carried James carefully to the edge of the grave where he gently straightened him out and so we buried him, leaving a wooden marker I had managed to make up showing his identity clearly. Gaffer stood and looked at the grave and said, 'Take it easy son,' and to me a simple, 'Well done Tiffy.' I had known all along that involving me had been a deliberate act, and now at nineteen and a half years old I probably was a soldier at last. Nothing I saw or did in subsequent campaigns, and some of it was grim, ever fazed me but I never came to terms with the smell associated with this awful business of war.

We made our way back to our little base where Joe and Bill had been holding the fort, but nothing helpful had turned up so I decided we should eat, I really felt the need to be careful as I think we were down to our last two cans of bully beef. There was plenty of water about in one of the houses and at that moment I was desperate to

ME 109

wash my hands but Gaffer had quickly opened one of the cans and slicing a piece off, offered it to me as he popped a slice into his mouth. I declined! The knife he was using had been one of our main tools during the last hour and he hadn't washed anyway so the fingers offering me a slice of bully I had last seen gently straightening out poor James. I still hadn't quite made Soldier.

I suppose today L/Corporal Guayatt, ex-professional burglar, Master Butcher, fluent French speaker, Class one Army Arabic translator and sixteen stone of bone and muscle, not to be trifled with physically, though he would have liked nothing better! would have been described as a complex character. We can discount the fluent French because he had been brought up as a young boy in the Channel Isles, Jersey to be precise and French came naturally. I had known him now for just over a year and was to know him closely for another two years. We were firm friends and yet what I have just written was all I ever knew about Gaffer or his past. Stories about him were legendary within the Battalion and as I think I have already said he was either liked or very much disliked. In my first week with the Battalion I had performed a small favour for him and he had repaid it in countless ways of which L/Corporal James Gent was one of the most important.

Reading these paragraphs again, I recall, and am still moved by that simple Benediction, 'Take it easy, son.' I close my eyes and I am back in that garden.

It was late afternoon by now and I decided we should move on; there was much less refugee traffic on the road outside and the sprinkling of military had petered out.

We started in the direction everybody had been moving. I had decided before setting out that I would turn off this road at the first opportunity; this we did about five miles after leaving the village. The new road was a quite minor road with open countryside on either side, where it led to heaven only knows. At the junction where we turned off there was the usual sign indicating a village and how far it was in kilometres. Without maps, it was useless to us. I was also becoming concerned about finding somewhere to break for the night. We were free of refugees but this of course precluded Gaffer from finding out where we were and more to the point where the hell we might be going.

The day was moving on and a little way along to our left there was a house set back from the road so turning off towards it would leave us very exposed should it be occupied by anybody who might be hostile. We had stopped on the edge of the road to discuss our next move when Bill spotted three planes, fairly low down but a good way off. This small reassurance was quickly destroyed by Joe who said quietly and briefly, 'MEs, better scatter.' We were in deadly trouble. We scattered pathetically, knowing that it was just us that they had in their sights and as I flung myself down I was totally consumed by fear and an overwhelming feeling of stupidity. Face down I had no idea where the planes were until they passed over us very close and loud and then total bewilderment as, without firing a shot they climbed away, finally disappearing into the distance. I felt very sick and shaken and also responsible. We had been caught in the open behaving as if there was no possibility of an attack from the air. If this was part of our learning curve how many more before a final lesson removed the need for further lessons?

We discussed endlessly why on earth the pilots had not fired but sixty-four years on I am still no wiser. But after that I don't think any of us took our eyes off the skies for more than a few seconds at a time, neatly shutting the stable door long after the MEs had gone. Getting back on the road I could only think about Tony and Girl and how near we had been to an end. Immediate problems soon began to intrude on our thoughts and mine was getting rid of the damn Bren gun. I was coming close to change-over time and with the best will in the world a Bren is not the most comfortable gun to carry though it is relatively light in weight. The carrying handle is no help at all and finding some way to carry it without developing a painful area is nigh impossible. We had been alternating this onerous task since burning our truck; whoever was carrying the Bren didn't carry his own rifle, the others taking care of it, and it had worked pretty well especially as Gaffer never seemed to remember when it was his turn to hand over and none of us rushed to remind him.

Time to find somewhere to hole up and rest and eat. How bizarre this was: here we were as far as we knew surrounded somewhere by the whole of the British Army, of whom we never saw anyone, just four of us and with two tins of bully beef, a couple of tins of evaporated milk, Joe still had tea and sugar and of course we had our Bren gun and it seemed the only people who knew where we were was the Luftwaffe, and to add insult to injury they didn't seem bothered, certainly not worth the ammunition.

So we kept on, finally turning off at a fork in the road simply because the road forking off to the right was lined with the tall poplar trees so common on French roads and would provide good cover from the air. There were still a couple of miles to go before we actually reached the trees but there is nothing like being frightened out of your wits to sharpen your learning curve. I remember saying we would carry on to the tree line then would stop and eat and possibly settle down for the night. Without a word Gaffer took the Bren gun from me and we set off once more. I was dog tired and hungry and though no one was complaining I knew we were all in much the same state, so, reaching the trees, I stopped and we made ourselves comfortable just off the tree line. Bill and Gaffer set off to see if they could find any sort of fuel to boil water and I sent Joe back onto the road to carry on the way we had been travelling, to reconnoitre and maybe find something of help. Bill and Gaffer had meanwhile arrived back, and we settled down to wait for Joe. We became increasingly concerned as the time passed and the light began to fade.

Then we were alerted, by the sound of a truck and bingo, there was Joe riding in the back of a 15 cwt. truck driven by a Sergeant with a Lieutenant in the passenger seat and wearing the First Guards Brigade flash on their battle dress. Eureka! we had found the Battalion because where there was a Guard's Brigade there was the 2nd Battalion the Hampshire Regt. And so it proved. I bet the Major would have been pleased and we managed without ever forming a square. Behind the first 15cwt. truck were three Bedford trucks. Apparently they were out trying to locate a supply point before dark so we climbed on board and showing no manners whatsoever we promptly fell asleep, waking only when they dropped us off at Battalion Headquarters. They had not located a supply point! The rest of the night we spent being debriefed by the Battalion Intelligence Sergeant, Le Soue, another Channel Islander and a great friend of 'Gaffers,' but it was us that did all the questioning and what we learned was pretty frightening: out of the frying pan into the fire comes to mind.

Le Soue was fascinated by our experience with the MEs but having wrestled with various possibilities we ended up no nearer to an explanation. He pointed out that had it been just one, there could have been a number of possibilities but three implied a formation and a leader, who must have made the decision for whatever reason. During the evening Joe was once more back to form and we didn't lack tea, but to our surprise when we were finding a corner to bed down Joe said when he went into the kitchen to make a cup he was politely asked to use his own tea and sugar. We left the documents and effects belonging to James and went to find a corner to sleep.

Yet again it was a broken night. There were a few alarms and we had to drag ourselves together and stand to in anticipation of an attack which never materialised then back to sleeping. Le Soue had given us a broad outline of the position but it wasn't until morning and after we had been reunited with B Echelon again, that the Quartermaster gave us a detailed summary of what was happening as it affected the Battalion. He also professed himself delighted that we had come through OK but the one question uppermost in my mind, was there any mail? And there wasn't. My morale sagged but we quickly learned that there wasn't much of anything and the convoy of last night summed it up perfectly. Supplies were badly disrupted and whilst this was having a serious effect on rations the really serious problem was lack of ammunition and where the hell to find it.

Le Soue had told us that there was to be an attempt to evacuate the British Army by sea from Dunkirk and now the Quartermaster began to dot the I's and cross the T's. The Brigade were to occupy a line south of a canal that formed a perimeter about fifteen kilometre's from Dunkirk and together with the natural defence that the canal posed we were to stop any attempts by the Germans to break through to Dunkirk. We would stay here no matter what and we would hold the ground until the evacuation was complete. It was in fact an old nightmare that troops had faced over many years summed up by the unspoken order:. 'Last man. Last round!' How melodramatic it sounds now but at the time it was stomach-churning drama for me. So began 'Operation Dynamo', the evacuation of our troops from Dunkirk. This then was late May 1940, though at the time I don't think any of our little group had any real idea of what day it was never mind what date. From now on most of our information came from the radio and it wasn't good. An example were the reports listing how many troops had been taken off so far and as the days passed, by statements that everybody had been taken off, not true! We were still dug in but Girl waiting for some positive news about me was pretty distraught. Add to this the lurid tales that were coming out, many of them true, made life unbearable for her. She was at this time staying with my parents in Halifax so though they offered support, they too were deeply worried.

At the end of our talk with the QM practicalities reared their ugly head and for me even more so. The QM had authority to promote me to Sergeant in a temporary capacity, this would enable him to form a B Echelon fighting platoon with me as Platoon Commander. Bloody hell! I was nineteen years old, my nerves were not in the best of shape and now they had decided I was to be in charge of winning the war, or at least that's how it seemed to my feverish brain. What was it I said about out of the frying pan into the fire? At least I would be allowed to select my own platoon from the B Echelon or at least what remained of it. Really? Just a minute, where were the RQMS and the Ration Sergeant? A Warrant Officer and a Sergeant? surely perfect for 'Platoon Commandeering'. They had been detached to Battalion Headquarters for other duties. Shit! no apologies; the word was made for the situation.

We were given a position on the edge of the village and behind a bomb damaged house. It had a good size garden and on the side away from the road there was a large field. I started by getting our little group together to discuss recruitment so to speak, I needed four more to make up the normal platoon strength of seven, so leaning very heavily on Gaffer we brought in L/Corporal Don Radden, the QM's clerk, Tug Wilson, my erstwhile driving instructor in better days but like Gaffer and Bill Glair with plenty of real experience, and Jack Brown, the other driver of course, if only to see how far his perpetual cheerfulness would last. 'Never mind, at least you've got a driving licence now,' I told him; he didn't offer a smile! We really were in trouble. Finally I scrounged one of the drivers from the MT section whose first name was Paul but I really, to my shame, cannot recall his second name.

I decided, after discussion with the platoon, that we would dig two-men slit trenches parallel to the garden and at a slight angle making sure of a decent field of fire and left them to it. I took the Bren and paired off with Joe Brown to dig our trench (Joe and I were to dig many slit trenches together as the war progressed, notably in North Africa). I asked Gaffer if he would try and locate the fitters, Jimmy, Frank and Harry to check whether they were all right, 'Done,' he replied, and they are fine.' I knew Ben was all right because they had established a Battalion first aid post about a mile from where we were and I sincerely hoped I wouldn't be seeing him. We stopped to eat, wonderful, the QM had produced tinned herrings and the inevitable biscuits and of course Joe produced the sweet tea. It was another lovely hot day and sweating from the digging but feeling calmer I settled down to eat. Tug Wilson had found a toilet in the house, usual hole in the ground and not too inviting but he reckoned quite usable. I started to contemplate a visit and that's when the shelling started and it never stopped until we moved out several days later. Fortunately it was sporadic. It would start up and then half a dozen or so erratic shells later it would stop but it certainly wore at our nerves. The house was hit on a regular basis but the toilet survived; we even cleaned it up a bit.

When we finally moved out I was able to report, 'No casualties,' and looking at the field in the vicinity of our defensive position, pockmarked with holes, I suppose somebody was looking after us. During this period the Brigade was in contact with the German Army on a regular basis and suffered a number of casualties but as history has shown, Hitler had decided not to commit his Infantry to attacking our positions and as a result our stay in defence of the perimeter was relatively quiet and I say this with the authority vested in me as a Platoon Commander. There's glory for you! To be truthful I was pretty frightened most of the time but another and even more important truth, I don't think that it ever showed and that truly was a massive victory for me.

Somewhere during this period I had to solve another puzzling Bren problem and not in the best of circumstances. The Bren gun carrier platoon were dug in very much forward of the Canal and had been heavily engaged with the German infantry on most days. They had three Brens and all were malfunctioning (posh word for not bloody working); this was leaving them very exposed and would the Armourer somehow come out and look at them, they would send a guide. 'Ere, hang on a minute, I'm a Platoon Commander now and a Sergeant to boot! Ah well, here I am following a guide who hopefully knows where he is going and did not endear himself to me by saying it was at least a couple of miles. As always it seemed a hell of a lot further; to add to my unhappiness the only tool I possessed was the screwdriver, already mentioned in an earlier paragraph and now with a criminal record (so to speak).

As we approached the Bren Platoon position there was a hell of a lot of shooting going on and my guide stopped, saying they were obviously under attack again so we would wait. Years later the shooting stopped. Trying to swallow I gathered up my stomach along with the screwdriver and shortly found myself lying under a Bren gun carrier and eyeing, very dubiously, three Bren guns. The Platoon had adopted a very standard defensive tactic for tracked vehicles, digging a large and deepish hole, driving the Bren carrier over it then creating a well protected field of fire from underneath. Crews, depending on the situation, would then deepen the platform underneath by either sloping it backwards or digging out the blunt end so to speak and creating a step. All of this to create headroom whilst the step often makes a good table. This table is where I took the Brens for a preliminary look. In a situation such as this, if you remove a machine gun it has to be replaced by extra riflemen. I simply cannot remember the proportion but we did this and laying out a groundsheet I stripped the guns. Basically the Bren gun never malfunctions and when it does there is usually some little stupidity involved; however everything seemed in excellent order. The guns were beautifully maintained so no wonder the crew were upset at finding themselves at grave risk because of this malfunction.

I fired the first one in the general direction of the enemy and sure enough it stopped and the stoppage was easily diagnosed as not enough gas to drive the mechanism fully back. But why? The gas driving the bullet is diverted through a small hole and into the piston chamber where it normally drives the mechanism back with the greatest of ease; indeed, on the early guns they were provided with different sized holes so the gunner could fine-tune them. Firing the other two provided the same stoppage; it also provoked a reply from the Germans which startled me to say the least. Bisley was never like this, at least I never remember anyone firing back at me. Mind you, the quality of my shooting sometimes certainly merited a few shots round my ears. The shooting stopped after a short while but interestingly enough I had heard their light machine gun for the first time and it obviously worked at a much higher rate of fire than the Bren. Not necessarily an advantage, guns need to be 'fed' and a high rate of fire will certainly get up the nose of the people who have to keep them supplied. Eventually anyway.

Back to my problem, this was a drastic situation and had to be solved but the cause turned out to be very simple. The holes for the gas escape were situated under a sleeve created by the bipod which slid over these holes effectually sealing them and making sure there was no loss of gas. The bipod was free to turn on this sleeve and might be a source of wear. I had never heard of this problem arising before so I was on my own. A new bipod to try would have proved my theory one way or the other, but my new bipods had been burnt to death with the demise of the baggage lorry. God, how long ago was that? How on earth could I seal this leak? Simple. I scrounged the silver paper from a packet of cigarettes (I was a non smoker, hence the scrounge), wrapped it carefully round the sleeve, put the bipod back on and away the gun went. What a relief. I couldn't put as many rounds through the guns as I would have liked; already the supply problems were closing in on us. A quick run through with the crew, no problems there, they were all smokers.

Grab the guide, and get out, I needed to get back as quickly as possible and brief all the Bren gunners. It was urgent and I suppose at that stage we probably still had twenty or thirty Bren guns and they had all been in service for the same time. The nightmare would be if they all started packing up at the same time and I hadn't been able to brief everyone. I left detailed information at Battalion HQ and as it was impossible to get everybody needing to know in, it was done by that unsung hero, the Company runner. I say 'hero' quite sincerely; the nature of their work ensured a high casualty rate. It was a long time before I got any sort of feedback on this problem and no one complained of trouble.

So what had my platoon being doing through the last few days? Well, standing to at daylight every day and reacting to warnings of attacks developing. There would be a flurry of activity whilst we hoped the attack would be contained before it reached our field of fire and on the rare occasions it did we would engage the Germans but they never seemed to be seriously pressing and after a short while when they returned our fire they would simply break off and retire. Much to our relief. These attacks were more frequent and determined at different points of the Brigade and there were many casualties but in our own little defensive area we continued to be lucky.

There was a good deal of air activity as the Luftwaffe made its way to the beaches. Junkers 88s and Heinkels were prominent according to Joe. We were also Stuka'd a couple of times and there were several aerial battles matching MEs with Spitfires and Hurricanes. Identification kept Joe very busy and then I would guess about the 25 May we were watching a relatively quiet sky and a Lysander, probably spotting and at a fair height. Joe had been listing technical details of this type of plane when a Me. came out of the sky above the Lysander, made one pass with guns firing and the Lysander turned onto its nose and with engine still flat out flew into the ground near enough to us to prompt evasive action into the bottom of our slit trenches. We scrambled over to what was simply a big hole - and I mean big – and lots of smoke from the remains of the Lysander, and we were faced with the awful task of trying to find some way down to what was left of the pilot and navigator.

Three hours later and we still hadn't succeeded. We simply could not get through the tangled wreckage to get even within touching distance of either of the crew. The QM had arrived about an hour after the impact; he had been told that there was a plane down in the vicinity of our position and was concerned that we were OK. By this time we were increasingly despairing of reaching the pilot and navigator. The QM joined in but it all proved futile and we were finally forced to abandon our efforts. The QM undertook to notify Battalion HQ and we were left exhausted and distressed. As I work through this story

LYSANDER

I am constantly reminded that there are times and incidents that have been deeply embedded in my memory. During this last paragraph the struggle and our increasing frustration came back to me with a clarity that is frightening: Gaffer using his great strength until he collapsed with exhaustion and near to tears. Joe dispensing tea and tears. Tug was another tower of physical strength but I clearly remember that he never spoke throughout. Only on the next day did he say anything, he simply said, 'I'm sorry'.

It was a lousy night, but stand to, then breakfast, and reality began to assert itself. We listened to the radio to find out how the evacuation was progressing and again we were all concerned about the references to the numbers already evacuated and suggestions that the perimeter was being held by troops who would stay to the last - us? All this added to the distress of Girl and my family as it did with the others. In truth we knew so little really about the overall picture and not knowing eats at your morale. Air activity had intensified and just to rub it in the shelling increased, so we were confined to our slit trenches. Of course sitting in a nice deep slit trench makes no difference to the way the sound of each shell arriving frightens you or stops you wondering if this one is going to land right in the trench. It is very wearing and I always put my constant weariness and feeling of exhaustion down to this almost permanent state of fear. I had decided to request permission to shift our position on the grounds that we were now too close to the remains of the Lysander. Indeed one of our slit trenches had collapsed with part of the crater intruding.

May was almost gone and when were we going to start moving back to Dunkirk? The news indicated that Operation Dynamo was complete so surely it was our turn. Reaching the end of my patience I told Gaffer to push off and come back with some sort of hard news. Increasingly I was becoming convinced that I would not be home for my twentieth birthday; with about three weeks to go to 18 June my thoughts were increasingly turning to thoughts of capture or worse. I am sure this faltering phase was due to the cumulative effects of my journey and responsibility. Though we had brief respites, the constant state of being in serious danger, my introduction to violent death, lack of food and sleep were beginning to destroy my morale and I certainly wasn't the only one amongst my own little group. We had become very close and again without the enormous presence of Gaffer I cannot imagine what the outcome might have been, and yet he too was beginning to fray at the edges! Maybe I was sensing this and it was also affecting me. One thing I am certain about, something favourable needed to happen. I was very much at the limits of my courage and God, I wish they would stop this constant shelling.

Gaffer failed to find out anything concrete except to confirm that the order to stay and hold the perimeter was still in effect. Two days later, 1 June, we were finally ordered back to Dunkirk. The tactic would be 'Leap Frog', whereby the Battalion would move back a Company at a time, each one in turn providing cover for the others in the event of the Germans following up our retreat. We gathered up our kit and our Bren; how we had cursed that gun at various times but to our credit we had stuck to it and by now had a love-hate relationship but not one round of ammunition. We were each carrying four empty magazines in our Bren pouches! The word bizarre leaps out again, though pitiful might be better. Maybe I was a better soldier than I thought. Again as I trudged on, now under the control of the RSM, I kept Girl and Tony firmly in my thoughts.

The Stukas had several goes at us as the Battalion moved at what seemed a snail's pace. I remember seeing a signpost as we set out saying 'Dunquerque 13 kilometres'. By this time that hardly seemed any distance at all. I still had good feet, no nerves left at all but definitely good feet! Anyway there was the RSM and when he shouted 'Move', as from time immemorial we bloody moved. Mind you, when the shout was 'Take Cover' we moved even faster. I think during these final kilometres to Dunkirk the Battalion suffered its worst casualties so far: too sadly, our little group lost Bill. Tug picked up a nasty wound but was still battling on when we reached the outskirts of Dunkirk. We had excused him his turn with the Bren. What a mess we were now confronted with as we entered the suburbs. We had been conscious of the burning oil for some time; it seemed like a black shroud to me, I was getting feverish! One foot in front of the other, at least I wouldn't have to make the next decisions this time.

Thirteen kilometres in which we were under constant attack. I had lost a close comrade and another was seriously wounded, all in one paragraph? Ridiculous! My apologies, Bill and Tug! As it turned out Tug and I had many more miles to go together in yet another campaign before sadly too much war finally caught up with him at Salerno.

As we moved more deeply into Dunkirk and towards the sea we were encountering more and more bodies, many of them French soldiers, burnt out vehicles, but something far worse that could well undo me completely, the smell of decomposition. There were quite a few dead horses lying about and this was contributing in no uncertain fashion. I still don't know why I react so acutely, but I did and I still do. The B Echelon were ahead of HQ Company and we finally stopped towards the end of a road which appeared from a distance to open out onto the quays and the sea. On one side of the road there were large and much battered warehouses, on the other what appeared to be some form of defensive works which were rather like the ones at Hilsea built up of earth and maybe thirty or forty feet high. Along the bottom at intervals were huge steel doors with smaller entrance doors.

We hadn't paid much attention to this apart from collapsing against a low wall that ran along in front of these structures. The three of us just sat there, Joe, Gaffer and I totally exhausted, and though we had shaved that morning the other two looked gaunt and their eyes were red rimmed with the lack of sleep. I suppose I must have looked the same. Add to this that we had hardly been fed for days, it was a miracle that we were still on our feet and functioning. Looking back up the road we could see Headquarter Company also at rest, but they were a good way back. All communication was being done by the ubiquitous runner and across the road the QM was sat like us probably hoping that no runner would turn up. The RQMS I saw was back in the fold and also the ration Sergeant who had struggled across to have a word with Gaffer; they were good friends (probably in crime) looking back to the days in Corruna Barracks. Tug had eventually finished up in the hands of our medics but that was all we knew.

I was contemplating the mess along the road, bodies not buried or even tidied. This illustrated more anything the débâcle of this retreat: you simply didn't leave your dead like that. To our right the road was clear except for a badly smashed 15 cwt still smouldering, We all three were beginning to sleep, I was settling down nicely when I became conscious of the QM coming across towards me with an officer in tow. Why oh why did I know this was trouble? The officer was a Major in the Royal Engineers, covered in filth, a growth of beard and I would guess in the final stages of total exhaustion. 'Sergeant!' the QM announced. I knew as soon as he addressed me as Sergeant that I was right and it was trouble. 'Go along with the Major, he has a job for you, and take Guyatt and Brown with you.' It was getting worse. We dragged ourselves to our feet, I saluted the Major, hoisted up the Bren, it was my turn, and we followed down the road towards what I thought were the quays. Nothing was said. To be truthful I was expecting the Major to keel over; he really was at the end of his physical endurance.

The Major stopped a couple of hundred yards along the road and opposite to a gap in the wall leading to one of the big steel doors. Sitting on this wall he told me to take the lads through the small door which he said was open. On the left was a water tap, so be sure to refill our water bottles then follow the stairs to the top and set up our Bren in an anti aircraft role. The bombers had been making their run from the sea along the beach very low and then banking sharply and starting to climb, still very low and almost certainly right over our position. We might just be lucky! I knew it! All he wanted was our Bren gun: no love this time we all hated the thing. I couldn't bring myself to tell him that we only had a few rounds left plus eight empty Bren magazines.

He then told us he had been the acting Beachmaster for the last five days, that there would be at least two bigger ships coming in around midnight but hoped that our Battalion would have loaded and been taken off by then. We were to leave and make our own way to the Mole to get there before ten o'clock. His company would be supervising the evacuation so there would be plenty of help as it would of course be dark. Get there in good time and just do as instructed, oh yes, and good luck. The ships coming in would be the *Royal Daffodil*, a Liverpool ferry and the destroyer *Wakeful*'. Thank you lads, good luck! And he climbed painfully to his feet, fishing out astonishingly from the officer's haversack he was carrying, two tins of bully beef and a packet of biscuits and was gone. With all our hearts we hoped that he would make it.

Everything was as he said. We filled up our water bottles, and climbed the stairs out on to the top to find that it was covered with lush grass and we had an excellent view of the beaches and the sea. Most of all, though, it was a perfect picnic area. It was another hot sunny day and we had two tins of bully with biscuits. It was late afternoon and four or five hours to wait. Marring this idyllic picture the shelling was intensifying though still very much on the south side of Dunkirk, but our main concern was that it seemed to be shifting on to the mole which seemed destined to be our lifeline home. So let's have a picnic and we did in almost total silence. I suppose at this remote time I could quote, 'Eat drink and be merry for tomorrow you…?' After the meal I took Gaffer back down into the road to see if we could find ammunition. We walked down to the end and out onto the harbour quays; there were several sea basins and troops had pushed as many vehicles into these as they could but it was all quiet now with no movement at all. God, it was a mess!

Along to our left was a badly shot up 15 cwt; funny how flat tyres make a vehicle seem somehow sad. We walked across, the only sign of occupancy being an officer's map case hanging from the windscreen frame. Round to the back and once again unreal or bizarre are the only words to adequately describe what we found. The back was full of loose ammunition, just what we were looking for. But sprawled on top of it was a very dead Sergeant. The track of the burst that killed him could be clearly seen, smashing a hole through the side panel, ploughing a furrow through the ammuniton and then through the Sergeant and on out. It was quite awful. The situation we were now in was not nice, it created problems without solution. I decided and probably wrongly, that we ought to get the Sergeant out. Gaffer agreed so maybe I wasn't so wrong but what then? We could see further bodies along the quay though some distance away and we still needed to fill our Bren magazines.

Whilst trying to sort out our thoughts a young Lieutenant had crept up on us, same old filthy battledress that everybody was wearing that year, but he didn't look right, his face was sort of set and vacant. We both saluted and he confirmed our worst fears. Staring intently into the back of the truck he simply said, 'My Sergeant's dead.' Dear God, I thought, what do we do now? What we did was to get the Sergeant out, lay him as respectfully as we could next to the truck, give his identity discs and pay book to the officer, fill our magazines, stupidly salute and leave.

There were a lot of troops to come this way in the next few hours so we trusted to them to look after him. Joe was very pleased to see us back; although it was pleasant enough on the grass nobody wanted to find himself left alone and somehow things did seem to be deteriorating. There was no let-up in the shelling which was still concentrating on the area round the mole; this was worrying, aircraft attacks seem to have stopped, though there was some high altitude skirmishing going on in which Joe said Hurricanes were involved. I suppose it was about seven in the evening when I decided to walk down and see if I could get on to the beach and maybe recce where we might be getting on to the mole. I hadn't gone far along the beach when this strange and awful day took yet another twist. I met a nurse, again in a terrible state, and I think I smelt her before I saw her but she was still wearing her badly stained red cape and cap that I remembered so well from Netley. Her badges of rank showed Captain. I saluted and said rather feebly, 'Can I help at all, Ma'am?' She replied negatively so I told her about the ships coming in during the early hours. Her reply startled me. 'I know about them, but I shall be staying, I have wounded still, and our orders are to stay.' I simply saluted again which she returned, wished her luck, and I went back to our position to wait our turn. Once more helpless and inadequate and very angry.

The day had not finished with us yet. Just after I got back and exactly as the Major had predicted a plane came in low from the sea turned along the beach and finally banked and started to climb away right over the top of us. I suppose the range would be about two hundred yards, it certainly looked big, and I emptied a full magazine in controlled bursts and without any effect at all and it was quickly gone. In spite of the other two saying I had definitely been hitting I knew that really I had simply missed. Joe said it was a Messerchmitt BF 110 and very fast; I didn't care very much whatever it was. I had missed. It was a matter of pride and despair. I did not have long to brood; about thirty or forty Moroccan troops had moved up the road

ME 110

below us and like ourselves earlier they had just collapsed with exhaustion, lying about waiting presumably for orders when suddenly the shelling moved and four shells burst in the road and amongst these soldiers. The results were devastating. The walls of the warehouse on one side and the fortifications on the other trapped the blasts. Joe simply said, 'Here we go again,' and the three of us went down to absolutely no effect. Most of them didn't have their field dressing and only Gaffer could speak to them as they spoke only French. We did our best and then I finally closed down our position as instructed and we found a quiet spot where we could settle down and wait for ten o' clock.

We dozed and I tried to get my thoughts in some sort of order, mostly trying to overcome my disbelief at some of the things that had happened. Before it got dark we made our way down to the road and settled again in the usual position, backs resting against a wall, and again slept and dozed though it was getting pretty cold as the night wore on. During this period and unbeknown to us the Battalion had come through to the mole in a different area. They had marched past the Commanding Officer closed up in threes and complete with all their equipment. How I wish now that we had still been with them!

Time to move, so doing exactly as the Major had told us to do we made our way to the mole. There were a lot of us, but again as he had said, there was plenty of help, mostly profane. I think the guides were from the Royal Engineers but it wasn't easy to tell and their line of profanity was pretty standard. It was, by now, very dark and we eventually found ourselves in a queue on the mole sort of shuffling along. This was very narrow and as I had noted early in the day very long. Gaffer was ahead of me and Joe behind but it was becoming increasingly difficult to stay together. I still had the Bren and 'Gaffer was carrying my rifle which sort of helped us to stay in touch. Meanwhile the shelling continued, mostly missing and landing on the beach or into the sea but finally a success for the German gunners, they hit the mole, This was quite a way from where we were but it had a knock-on effect right down the lines of soldiers who were trying to keep on this narrow causeway, I fear many must have gone into the sea but we did not escape entirely! I lost touch with Joe.

By this time I was really at the end of my endurance. The dark, the effort of trying to keep contact with Gaffer, was sapping not only my strength but my will and

I know now that it was only he that kept me going. My thoughts were a jumble of Girl and Tony to say nothing of death or captivity. Come on, Clem, one foot in front of the other, there must be an end somewhere, but first there was a hole in the mole to be negotiated, proof of an earlier success by the German gunners and crudely bridged by what seemed to be totally unsuitable timbers. The constant jostling didn't help but we both got over OK. I had no idea what time it was and increasingly I found myself worrying about what had happened to Joe and was it my fault? The whole thing was becoming dream-like. After what seemed like hours and by this time cold had added yet another dimension, we came to a sort of standstill and we were getting a feedback that we were finally at the embarkation point. Up to now I cannot remember anyone having spoken at all; even Gaffer and I had not said anything to each other.

THE ROYAL DAFFODIL

We were soon conscious of the bulk of a ship alongside and after a little while and several false starts we reached an opening with I think biscuit tins built up for us to scramble onto the ship. At the top were several sailors heaving people on board.'Gaffer' passed the Bren gun up to me. There was the silhouette of quite a big looking ship ahead of this one. Gaffer spoke for the first time saying, 'It must be the destroyer *Wakeful*. Maybe we should try and get on to that.' Too late, a big sailor already had me by the scruff of the neck, and I was being heaved, complete with Bren, into the scuppers so to speak. Gaffer followed, and we were herded down into what was the saloon. The floor was packed tight but Gaffer edged a space at the base of one of the supporting pillars and, clutching the Bren gun, I propped myself up against the pillar and gave myself up to exhaustion…then a sailor was shaking me awake and saying 'Come on, son, Margate'! For Gaffer and me the nightmare was over!

Back at Dunkirk the destroyer *Wakeful* had been torpedoed with fewer than twenty-five survivors and over seven hundred and eighty trapped in the ship as it went down.

The following is an extract from the Regimental History of the Second Battalion by David Scott Daniell and refers to the days following our little group's finally joining the Battalion and my elevation to Platoon Commander:

A few hours later the Battalion moved to occupy new positions, the last defensive ones in the operation. These were at Uxem and companies were posted at road junctions with one platoon of 'Y' Company with the carriers holding the bridge at Teteghem to close a temporary gap. The road running along the far side of the canal was so thick with abandoned vehicles that there was no field of fire at all. In spite of this 'Y' Company platoon and the carriers had some shooting at Germans coming up the canal. On 30th May Uxem was shelled heavily and the Battalion held the position throughout the 31st under continuous and very heavy shelling. In the evening 'Z' Company was moved up to assist the Coldstreams on the night. Enemy shelling continued all night and with renewed vigour on the morning of 1st June.

On this day of June the Commanding Officer issued his final withdrawal order. 'The Second Hampshires will withdraw to the Mole at Dunkerque for embarkation.' Paragraph 9 of this order reads 'Coys will embark fully equipped and carrying all Brens and Anti-tank rifles.' The order also stated that 'Embarkation will carry on in spite of bombing or shelling, and the flow to the boats will on no account be stopped.'

Lt. Colonel J. M. Lee DSO
Commanding Officer, 2nd Battalion, The Hampshire Regiment
At the Battle of Tebourba Gap - Tunisia, North Africa
29 November to 4 December 1942

CHAPTER 9
ALL ROADS LEAD TO NORTH AFRICA

Trying to come awake and digest the sailor's words took some time and it wasn't until Gaffer said, 'Best be moving', that I finally scrambled to my feet, slinging the Bren gun across my shoulder and joining the mass of soldiers making their way out. Funny how quiet everybody was; there had been an occasional shout but suddenly everybody was talking and even laughing hysterically. What an awful looking lot we were: dirty, unshaven, some uniforms bore testimony to what had gone before, stained and really stinking, as were ours, but we were home and already my head was filled with Girl and Tony.

Off the boat, hugs and handshakes with the crew members, we were gathered together in a large untidy heap on the quay and then onto the railway platforms where a train waited. At this point we were given printed cards to fill in saying that we were OK; these would be posted. After this we were fed by volunteer ladies and plied with more tea than we could drink then suddenly, where was Joe? I made my way as best I could to the inevitable RSM who though wrinkling his nose and moving away a little, smiled and gave me permission to work my way back through the troops to see if I could find him. It was hopeless, I had banked on Joe's height making him show more easily but it was all too much of an excited scramble so I rejoined Gaffer and we just hoped that he had got on to the destroyer, little knowing at this time of the awful tragedy that had befallen the *Wakeful*.

Exhaustion was beginning to take its toll as the waiting troops began to find space to sit or lie down on the platform. It is difficult to remember exactly how devastating total physical and mental exhaustion can be, it addles your brain and worst of all produces an overwhelming desire to give up. I suppose that I must take some credit for getting this far, 'One foot in front of the other, Clem!' I will never forget the mole. Finally on to the train, single carriages seating eight but they only put six of us in so we had a bit of room. Slinging the Bren gun and rifles on to the luggage rack and settling down, thinking of Girl and Tony and wondering how soon I would be able to get away; after all we were in England and there were buses, just a matter of timing. Yet where were we heading for? Nobody seemed to know. With a tired jumble of thoughts and trying to ignore the stench (it was hot) once again I was gone.

A crowd? And a woman trying to pull my sweat-band off, where the hell was I? Again I fought my way out of sleep just in time for the woman to succeed and disappear with the band and the sweat and the smell. Ah well, she was welcome, I had picked up this big red spotted handkerchief a thousand years ago at the farm where Gaffer was butchering a pig and had worn it round my neck ever since as a sweat-band. The carriage was full of people saying, 'Well done, lads,' and equally complimentary things, yet what had we done? We had retreated! then escaped! It's a funny world. Where were we? Clapham Junction! Will the lady who nicked my sweat-band please return it, preferably washed and ironed.

Troops finally cleared the crowd out and we were fed again, wonderful ladies, plenty to eat and drink, the tea triggering off thoughts of Joe again. After a while a major came into the carriage. I tottered to my feet and saluted; he simply said, 'My God, it is true, you do have a Bren, first one we have seen, and two rifles. Very well done!' He then took them away leaving a receipt. He had also asked if we had any ammunition and with this query, exhaustion took me straight back to standing ankle deep in ammunition with Gaffer, trying to get the remains of a Sergeant out of the truck. I am not exhausted now but suddenly I am back there again and it is still upsetting. We were soon moving, and again we all slept the sleep of the dead. Where the hell were we going and would it be near enough for me to get a bus home? Finally we stopped in a station, oh God, it's dark again but somebody located the sign and we had apparently arrived at a place called Clay Cross. A short march (shamble) through the town and into a Community Hall and a bed for everyone and yet again wonderful, wonderful sleep.

It was a typical Army morning, roused out of bed, wash and shave and then luxury indeed, it turned out that Clay Cross was a small mining town and we were marched not very far to very well equipped pit head baths; not only that but there were a couple of Army trucks dispensing new battle-dress where needed; my God, how Gaffer and I 'needed'. We were both lucky so complete with new and fragrant clothes including underwear of course, we headed back to the hall where several ladies were busy sewing on stripes and doing any other odd jobs for the lads. Though ignorant of the fact then, the beer in the pubs was being dispensed free. However, what I did know by this time was that I could get a bus to Leeds just up the road, I even had the times.

We were under orders to report to another centre and at a certain time to be processed (I love that word). This was important especially for troops like Gaffer and me who had been separated from our units. We were told that as soon as anything was known we would be returned to our units but it could be several days; meanwhile we were to report in every day, here was a pay handout (temporary). Gaffer said, 'I'll cover your back, ring the local pub for news, regards to the family, goodbye.' Minutes later I was on my way to Leeds. I didn't pay on the bus either! I suppose at this time my feelings could not be adequately described. Butterflies maybe!

The bus driver dropped me at a bus stop serving buses to Halifax, saying 'About half an hour but you can wait in the restaurant opposite, I can recommend it.' He was right but in a way I hadn't envisaged. The staff quickly identified me as ex Dunkirk so to speak (did I still smell I wondered?) from then on everything was free and people were constantly commiserating and giving me the 'Well done' treatment. I was quickly beginning to realise that we had suddenly become special and the best thing to do would be to enjoy it whilst it lasted. Remember my little quotation from Rudyard Kipling in the earlier chapters? A little unkind? I think not! What seemed hours later the bus arrived and I settled down and tried to come to terms with what was now happening to me, it was dreamlike. As the bus neared Halifax the countryside became more and more familiar. Was it only five years ago that I travelled this route in the opposite direction with my Dad? One thing, though, today was considerably warmer but I was just as nervous as on the previous occasion.

The bus station in Halifax was at the back of the Odeon Cinema with the bus stop I required at the front on the main road, Girl and I had waited at this stop many times following visits to the cinema. My family lived just outside Halifax, about two miles, and as I went to take my place in the small queue I recognised a lady who though not a blood relative had always been my Auntie Elsie from my earliest memories. I tapped her on the shoulder and said, 'Hello Auntie.' She gave a little scream, burst into tears and pretty well collapsed. It was then that I knew that my card had not arrived home and indeed she really thought I had been killed, and if so, so would Girl and Tony. This really panicked me. The bus seemed to take ages but finally I was running up the road, I just caught a glimpse of my sister flat out as she turned down my street and then I was home with Girl weeping in my arms and Tony probably thinking who the hell is this.

As I had thought, my card had not arrived which made my sudden arrival out of the blue dramatic to say the least. It was my sister I had seen and she had run down the street shouting, 'Clem's coming!' Girl promptly accused her of telling wicked lies but there I was and suddenly everything was wonderful. Sadly after four blissful days one of my phone calls resulted in a 'Best get back, Tiffy' message from Gaffer and so yet again I was retracing my steps back to Leeds and then on to Clay Cross. I was not very happy but when I arrived Gaffer said they had received our movement orders and we had to report to Battalion Headquarters at an address in Wakefield. I perked up at this. Wakefield really was just a short bus ride from Halifax. There was another reason to perk up, before we set out for our free drinks. Gaffer had handed me a sum of money, he never said where it came from and... better not ask. Remember I said earlier that I never saw the cash box again, but? Well, nor did I. The amount by the way could be described as very pleasant.

We were due to report the next day hence the message bringing me back. I remember it was early afternoon so we went round to the pub where I thanked the landlord for acting as a go-between, a couple of free pints, plenty to talk about, with Joe not long out of the conversation, I think both Gaffer and I were feeling guilty about losing him on the mole. It was a blessing that we didn't know about the *Wakeful*; we had both agreed that he must have been on the destroyer otherwise he would have finished up at Clay Cross with us. We had asked around and the Clerks who were doing our processing did a check for us without success. I spent the afternoon idling on my bed thinking about Girl and how Tony had grown and of course Mum and Dad who had suffered too as a result of the missing card. There had been a lot of visitors, friends and more of those Aunties and Uncles: indeed too many when all we wanted was to be by ourselves. Wonderful, wonderful hours but all too fleeting.

Here I was back in Leeds at the restaurant by the bus stop, Gaffer and I enjoying free elevenses before boarding the bus and heading back to the war. We arrived finally at Battalion HQ in Wakefield and before anyone could say anything at all I asked if Joe Brown was back. 'Yes,' was the clerk's welcome reply, 'I'll give you his address.' We then found out that all the Battalion were billeted with families around Wakefield and that for an unknown period we would be deemed to be at rest, no parades, no training, no bullshit and an RSM fast falling into a massive depression. We had been given the Freedom of the Town, everything was free, buses, cinemas, beer, Paradise indeed! The next day I found myself on my way to the Command Workshops in York where I would spend six weeks working an average twelve hours a day, seven days a week except Saturdays and Sundays when it was sometimes sixteen hours a day. Frankly I felt this was a poor reward for an ex-Platoon Commander. But, and I cannot express what it meant to Gaffer and me, we had found Joe! And we had managed a good chat before I had to leave.

I think it is appropriate at this point to call a roll of my own little group. Tug Wilson had got across owing to the efforts of Ben and the medics plus the unstinting bravery of the many soldiers battling their way back and sometimes carrying Tug without question. He was in hospital somewhere in UK. The three Ordnance vehicle fitters Jimmy, Frank and Harry had got back with the Battalion as had Joe Curley. Also the Quartermaster, RQMS and Ration Sergeant were safely back.

So what happened to Joe? He came over on, yes, you've guessed, the *Royal Daffodil* but a different train and a different final destination. He too had been trying to locate us and had reached the same conclusion that we were on the destroyer. Unfortunately the prospect of getting home to Girl and Tony on a regular basis and living a luxurious life for a while was shattered by this temporary posting to York Workshops. I was furious and fed up at the same time. I would have been even more so if I had known of the long hours and hard graft that awaited and even worse the limited opportunities to see Girl and Tony. But here I am like a good Soldier, reporting in to yet another Guardroom.

Accommodation was sparse but typical; we were given vouchers for food at a local café and so a small collection of Armourers paraded at the workshop sharp at eight o'clock the next morning, I wonder what the collective noun would be for Armourers? a 'Magazine' of Armourers maybe! And the job? To salvage as many weapons as we could; these were coming in from many sources. This turned into a marathon of refurbishing SMLE rifles. God knows where they came from but they all needed a complete rebuild and this meant a new fore end, which in turn requires skill and time. They never stopped; finish one there was another. By the time this job ended there was a 'Magazine' of Armourers who could fit a new fore-end in the dark if necessary and in record time and guarantee that it would pass through the range without a hiccup. We started at eight o'clock in the morning and finished at eight o'clock in the evening. On Fridays we were given a half day to get a bath.

Then the working weekends arrived and this was a miserable job. Labourers were unpacking lease-lend P.14 rifles from cases stored since the First World War. The problem was that after they had been packed into the case, the case was filled with grease. A nightmare to unpack and degrease and very difficult to work on as we checked and made them serviceable. Still starting at eight o'clock there was no specific finishing time and it was often around midnight before we crawled into bed. Meanwhile the Battalion was having a wonderful time and the odd communication from Gaffer consisted mostly of rubbing it in. At least towards the end of the six weeks I managed two Sunday afternoons off and Girl came to York but by herself. Finally it ended and I was on my way to join the Battalion who were now occupying a stretch of the East Coast at Mablethorpe in Lincolnshire. Reporting back I found that I had been promoted Sergeant (real this time); this was to fill the vacancy left by Arnold's posting.

We may have escaped from France but the war was still with us and these were desperate days. We were dug in and holding positions on the coast down to the sea line and we were desperately short of equipment, small arms particularly. I cannot remember the number of Bren guns the Battalion had but I would guess twenty or thirty at the most. No mortars but we had picked up around fifty Thompson sub machine guns from the lease-lend programme. Not really possible to work out a serious role for them. The Mablethorpe branch of Barclays comes to mind!

The accommodation was very good; we had two holiday caravans between the RAOC vehicle fitters, Jimmy, Frank, Harry and of course Joe Curley plus myself. The caravans were sited in a large empty field; the Quartermaster had his office and stores in the barns of a large farm about a mile away. This rural idyll was about three miles from Battalion HQ and six miles from Mablethorpe; it was also handily on the main road into the town and of course the sea. The fitters had a workshop set up in the parking area of a big hotel in Mablethorpe and this was a great bonus because they had to travel constantly to work and back which meant they were supplied with transport or used what they were working on and no one asked any questions. This meant of course that the 'Gang' had its own taxi service. And as we could use the hotel's bathrooms this meant a pleasant and luxurious perk.

Gaffer was back with the QM and their accommodation was spread out amongst the farm buildings so all in all we were very comfortable. It was just a pity about the War. There was a great deal of air activity as the Battle of Britain developed but for us it was a question of consolidating and training. This was throwing up the usual strange anomalies. Take motor bikes. The Battalion had been issued with seven or eight commandeered bikes and these were indeed a mixed lot. Two Triumph Speed Twins, an Arial Square four, three Matchless 500 and a massive twin cylinder Enfield with an equally massive side-car. These I can remember because I learned to ride on one of the Speed Twins. The fitters were delighted with them, particularly with their success at convincing the QM that the bikes ought to be kept in the field where our caravans were parked. For myself I knew nothing at all about motor bikes but the fitters certainly did; Jimmy in particular was quite spectacular on a bike.

The weather was still as good as ever and Jimmy began using one of the bikes to go into work in Mablethorpe, that is, until he was nicked by the Adjutant for speeding past the HQ There happened to be a very inviting stretch of road running past the Battalion HQ A little fast talking mostly to do with urgent repairs especially to HQ vehicles and Jimmy was free. At this time I started to learn to ride a bike under the skilled tuition of all three of them; they personally selected a powerful Triumph Speed Twin so my evenings spent riding around the local country lanes was exciting to say the least. Then suddenly an order arrived to the effect that all Regimental Policemen would be taught to ride and when competent they would each be issued with a bike. (I often wondered where on earth these orders came from, a bit early for the European Commission?)

Jimmy got the job and there followed many exciting and hilarious hours. Most were coping well but sadly Jimmy met his match in my old friend the Provost Sergeant, Jack Huggins. Poor Jack, he may have once been the heavyweight boxing champion of the British Army but a motor bike frightened him to death. Jimmy was very patient and finally managed to get Jack riding gently on the enormous Royal Enfield with the side car. As Jimmy said, not a good thing because a motor bike and side-car can be notoriously difficult to control but as long as they kept Jack on a straight road he was slowly mastering the technicalities, clutch, gears, braking etc.

Eventually Jack, gaining in confidence, persuaded Jimmy to let him take the bike as far as the outskirts of Maplethorpe, Jimmy agreed but only after persuading Jack that he, Jimmy, should follow closely. I remember so clearly Jimmy coming back that evening barely able to contain his laughter. Jack had gone well until undone by a bend. The bike simply went straight on and into one of the very deep dykes that lined the road. Jimmy said he stood there, no sign of bike, sidecar or poor old Jack, just bubbles!   Then suddenly a very startled Provost Sergeant surfaced blowing like a whale. Getting Jack out was easy, getting the bike out not so, not only that but the fitters were faced by having to strip it down and rebuild it. Mind you no one was anxious to embarrass Jack about his little swim. Yes he did master a motor bike in the end but as Jimmy warned, don't accept the offer of a lift.

What of my own work? This was made difficult because of the fragmentation of the Battalion; they were busy trying to establish possible defensive positions but were desperately short of weapons. As the weeks rolled by the threat of invasion increased and its possibility became a matter of when, not if. The Germans were attacking our airfields in great numbers and as August moved into September the Battle of Britain gathered pace. I spent a lot of time visiting positions and checking weapons. There were several typical sea-side kiosks dotted along the front which Platoon Sergeants (remember I was one briefly a very long time ago) had appropriated as sort of small Headquarters or really if it were big enough, a place to brew a mug of tea and forcefully discuss the ancestry of the various members of the Platoon who were considered not to be up to scratch. The profanity was again pretty standard, identical I would suggest to our helpers on the mole.

Such a Platoon Sergeant was Harry Hines, a good friend and a gifted soldier especially when the going was rough. I was on my way to his little kiosk on the front but as I approached it I thought, 'Funny, that's not right.' Lots of it were sort of lying about in smaller lumps and there was a lot of broken glass about, soldiers lying here and there some were sitting up and the air was truly filled with Harry's very special brand of profanity, now that was worth a pause to admire. I was beginning to wonder if the bang I had heard earlier might just have something to do with the state of the kiosk and of course Harry's language. The answer was yes to both.

I had noticed that amongst the debris and the soldiers there seemed to be the odd hand grenade lying about. Harry started to explain. Apparently the platoon had been practising fusing hand grenades. These came in a box of a dozen (if my memory serves me correctly) packed on each side of their box which was long and narrow and each had its own little compartment. Meanwhile the fuses were housed in a separate container and again I think there were three different time lapses, five seconds, seven seconds and nine seconds. The drill was to undo the screw cap, make sure the spring loaded firing lever was held back by the split pin, insert the selected fuse, screw the cap back on, make sure the split pin is secure and your grenade was now armed and safe until the pin was pulled allowing the firing lever to fly open and 'light' the fuse. The grenade started to smoke and depending on the timing of the fuse would explode, They had been using seven second fuses. One of the platoon had decided to perform the operation whilst holding the firing lever down by hand (very risky this as the lever has a powerful spring) and having finished putting the primer in and the cap back on he lost control of the lever and bingo a smoking grenade! I said it was risky.

Harry then said this lad looked at the grenade as if hypnotised and then very carefully put it back in the box with the other grenades where it smoked quite happily waiting for the seven seconds to pass. By this time everybody was battling to get out of the kiosk through a not too generously sized door. Seven seconds duly elapsed and then 'bang' right on time. So all was clear, and of course one would expect a modicum of hand grenades to be lying about. Fortunately, apart from a few lacerations (please note correct medical jargon) everybody was OK which just left a job for the Pioneer Platoon (remember? crosses and coffins!) and hopefully the repair of battered kiosks. Harry did say that the achievement of the entire platoon getting out in under seven seconds ranked with any of the Biblical miracles. Most of them couldn't get out of bed in under seven minutes never mind seconds.

As the weeks passed and the constant threat of invasion kept everyone anxious I became increasingly concerned about the lack of Bren guns, when visiting the various Company Headquarters which were well scattered over many miles. The Company Commanders made this point time and time again so I suggested to the QM that it might be worthwhile taking the requisition forms to the Depot at York and using my contacts from the weeks I had just spent there, and try to talk them out of ten Bren guns. This idea foundered on the explicit orders that any requests for weapons had to be counter-signed by a very senior Officer at Divisional level and accompanied by a letter with the Divisional Stamp also signed by the same officer. Apparently our Commanding Officer had already tried his luck at Div. HQ with no success.

I finally persuaded the QM to give me the baggage lorry and permission to go to the York Depot. This was based on the old premise 'Everything to gain, nothing to lose.' ('Except my Commission,' I heard him mutter.) Ah well, you can't have everything. We left nice and early with my old friend Jack Brown driving; it felt just like old times except Jack at least now knew how to start the damned truck. I had been doing my homework and a bit of map reading so ordering Jack to head for Divisional HQ, I sat back and pondered on what on earth I thought I was doing, Headquarters of the Divisional type can be extremely dodgy places to be, especially without the right pass.

The Headquarters was situated in a large old house, the lodge acting as the Guardroom. There was an armed soldier standing outside. I drove in and presented my identity, was told where to park the lorry then instructed to report back to the Guard Commander (seems a well practiced routine!). The Guard Commander was a Warrant Officer, as befits a Divisional HQ and it was now time to start digging my hole. I said, semi-truthfully, that I was on my way to the RAOC depot at York to pick up stores and had been told to call in at Div. HQ and ask for the senior RAOC Officer who would then countersign the requisitions contained in this ere envelope. All said as though it was a 'done' thing and I was just a messenger. At this time I was far from a happy soldier but I kept digging.

'Here, Corporal, take the Sergeant to the Brigadier's office and wait for him.' We set off in the direction of the large house, chatting about this and that and once inside we stopped by an imposing looking door. I was wrestling desperately with what on earth I might say; after all I had already dug myself a pretty deep hole. I gave up and decided to trust to luck. The Corporal knocked on the door and a voice shouted, 'Come in!' No! it couldn't be! The Corporal came out saying, 'Go on in,' and yes, indeed there was my old Adjutant, a very imposing Brigadier as he came to his feet saying, 'Well, if it isn't my rather small stand-off half.' He was just as big and our long ago theory that he could have amply filled in for the two missing Marine Sergeants briefly flashed through my mind along with the feeling of relief. At least I was among 'friends'. Suddenly the hole didn't seem quite so deep.

A salute and a handshake, arrange coffee and whatever for my driver and we settled down to a long chat. Brigadier Clarke was especially interested in the Battalion and our experiences in France. Somewhere along this reminiscing he asked me if Jack Huggins was still with the Second Battalion. After I had confirmed this I asked if they had met, to which he, replied, 'Yes, on three occasions, all of them painful and for him unsuccessful,' and would I be sure to pass on his regards. Eventually we got round to the purpose of my visit. Without any hesitation he signed and stamped the invoices, and had a clerk type out a letter also stamped and signed. He handed me the envelopes saying, 'I don't think it will work, indeed it might get me shot but good luck.' I refrained from saying that he would offer a wonderful target for the firing squad, don't push your luck, Clem, but my God he was big! For many years after the war this imposing physique was a common sight in the Houses of Parliament as the member for Portsmouth.

Back to Jack and on to York. After saying hello to friends in the workshops I went first to the Supplies Office where my documents were met with derision of a good-natured type. A major then sent me round to the small arms stores sheds, at the same time shaking his head sympathetically. At the stores I handed in the documents. The storeman said, 'You must be joking, is this your truck?' This was followed by an unintelligible shout directed into the bowels of the stores. A trolley appeared with ten Bren guns, quickly loaded on to Jack's truck. 'Sign here, mate,' and believe me, I was gone.

The result was a Commanding Officer, Colonel Lee, very pleased plus the Adjutant, all the Company Commanders and of course the Quartermaster who was very pleased with himself for having signed the requisitions and was not only still a Lieutenant, but being showered with praise from all sides. Myself? Well, remember I spoke in an earlier chapter of a sort of Battalion within a Battalion almost impossible to describe but where there was a strict hierarchy and to be on the right side of this was vital for happiness. All of my plaudits came from this underground source. I suspect initially the facts had filtered down from one Jack Brown. I too was well pleased with myself. I had always been good friends with Jack Huggins but after passing on Brigadier Clarke's good wishes I think Jack would have arrested the C.O if I had asked him. About the fights with Lieut. Clarke as he was then and during the Army Championships he said he was big, a hard hitter, almost impervious to punishment, but a lousy boxer. Sorry about that, Brigadier!

I should call the next few paragraphs, 'The case of the Lewis guns, the Ack Ack Platoon and the French letters.' It all started with the Battalion being issued with three Lewis guns with suitable mounts and for use in an Anti Aircraft role. These guns were of a variety where any weight had been stripped off, mainly the outer casing, so superficially they didn't look like the Lewis guns with which many of the old soldiers dotted round the Battalion were familiar. This was the gun which had preceded the Bren gun and there were still a lot about, indeed I saw only last night, one of *Dad's Army* waving one about and playing havoc with the ceiling. So time for Sgt. Clem to do his good soldier bit and not to reason why but to report, as requested, to the Adjutant's office. Did I know anything about this particular offensive weapon? Of course I did so what did I suggest? A short course by me to familiarise the Ack Ack. Platoon and then maybe a practice shoot somewhere along the beach was my reply. 'Right, get the RSM to organise something and I'll leave it in your capable hands.' Even as I saluted I thought flattery will get you anywhere.

The Lewis gun did have one characteristic suited to Anti Aircraft defence: the magazine held ninety rounds, it was possible to squeeze more but this was a good number. Against that it was prone to stoppages and needed a skilled gunner to keep it going. The course went well; I knew most of the lads who made up the Platoon going back to Corruna Barracks and the Platoon Sergeant, another of the Tacker Knights in the Battalion, had been in the Corporal's Mess with me, now, like myself, promoted to Sergeant. At the end of the course the RSM had arranged a shoot from the beach at Mablethorpe to take place the following Sunday morning. But what to shoot at? The R.S.M decided on balloons and arranged for the balloons to be filled at the local Gas Company, detailing Sgt. Knight for this particular job. Then pray for a fair wind and see how many the Platoon could shoot down…except that the RSM could not find anyone that still had balloons for sale, there is a war on, you know, was the favourite ploy by the shopkeepers and a dangerous one to an RSM fresh back from Dunkirk. The shopkeepers, survived but the balloons still remained elusive.

Sunday morning and another warm sunny day, perfect for our little shooting party, I was already on the beach setting up the guns and wondering what odds to offer on nobody hitting a balloon; after all I couldn't hit a big Heinkel at almost point blank range so very long odds were the order of the day. Whilst I was lolling about on the beach organising the betting, there was a crisis at Headquarters. The RSM had turned up balloon-less and with only half an hour or so before we were due to open fire. At this time Ben turned up at HQ and not knowing what was going on, except it sounded interesting, he hung about to listen and knowing that I was involved in a shoot that morning, soon cottoned on to the fact they had not managed to find anything to shoot at, mainly balloons which were to be filled with gas.

Even in wartime one cannot just wander onto the beach and start blazing away. All of this had been cleared with the Authorities and an appointment with the Gas Company agreed so the problem of time was becoming critical. Telling me all this later, Ben said there was an obvious answer so he popped back the to Battalion Medical Centre and picked up a box of 'French letters'. Of course, it was quite in order for Ben to use these words freely because he was a qualified nurse and it was loosely medical. But in those days nobody talked about 'French letters', at least not openly, only whispered quietly to the chemist (male of course). It seems to have changed now along with the name; my God. I saw a picture of kids at school the other day being taught to put them on a banana. I remember being whacked at school for wrong spelling and also for singing flat during music lessons but for getting a French letter twisted on a banana? the mind boggles.

I have read somewhere that they (I am not writing that name again; it might even lead to my autobiography being banned) also come in different flavours and I have also heard the word Gossamer bandied about. My God, these were Army issue, designed to keep everything out and everything in and at best could be described as 'robust'. As for flavour, 'inner tube' might get near, just a guess I hasten to say. I must add in their favour that they led the landings at Salerno rolled over the muzzles of our rifles, very heroic, the poor Germans didn't know whether we were there to f***k 'em or fight 'em, great strategy this. But I digress. Mind you, many respected friends have suggested that to increase readership I should include some naughty bits; well, I have done it! and now where the hell was I?

Oh yes, the Adjutant and RSM grabbed the box, and despatched Tacker to the gas Company with all haste. The time, I guess, would be around eleven in the morning; for what happened next I only have Sgt. Knight's version. The filling was not straightforward because basically the shape made it difficult but they finally succeeded and because of their robust design they took a lot of gas and were correspondingly quite large. This in turn meant that even from a reasonable distance there was no mistaking their real function in life. Tacker claims that he came out of the building clutching a bundle of twelve, stumbled, they escaped his grip and were off.

Probably owing to the properties of the gas they rose to a height just above the houses then steadying themselves and locating the beach they floated gently but remorselessly down the main street, still at roof top height and maintaining an impeccable formation. Unfortunately their leisurely progress coincided with what appeared to be the whole population of Mablethorpe leaving Matins, remember it was Sunday. There was a certain amount of looking away and attempts at nonchalance from those who looked, but dammit these were 'Battle of Britain' days and twelve French letters was hardly a Stuka Squadron. And so it passed; the lads got their shoot, nobody hit anything, I collected my winnings, there was a mild panic because the RSM simply couldn't stop laughing and that's not what RSMs are for, but he did eventually recover and went in search of poor old Tacker. Meanwhile the Adjutant had taken refuge in the Officers' Mess. The good townsfolk were very generous and so it was soon forgotten. I had thoroughly enjoyed the shoot and I am sorry that I used those words again.

Some time after this a tragic incident resulted in the death of one of the Signal Platoon. A young lad and one of their dispatch riders was shot and killed at a road block. It was dark and apparently he failed to respond quickly enough to a challenge. An emphasis really of how the threat of invasion was uppermost in our minds. He was buried with full honours and even now I have a very clear image of the funeral and the despair of his parents. It was all very sobering.

I had at this time a big worry about Girl and Tony, They were back with her parents in Portsmouth, a potential target if the Germans started to bomb the towns. She didn't want to move back up to Yorkshire. I think at that time she felt it would be a kind of desertion but of course ultimately Tony was the one who came first and any decision would be based on that fact. Already the Luftwaffe were stepping up the raids, many in daylight, but they were paying a heavy price. Southampton was an early target. The year was coming towards September and all the signs pointed to a 'Blitz' so we decided Girl and Tony would move back to my parents in Halifax.

Then out of the blue a rumour that had been circulating regarding a possible seven-day leave system starting came true and unbelievably on 2 September I was on my way to Portsmouth. I was carrying two items of luggage, kitbag and washing plus big pack and two large sirloin joints together with three fillets. Thank you Gaffer. The 'contraband' certainly raised a few eyebrows in Portsmouth. Wonderful to be back with Girl and Tony again and we managed to wander round some of our old pre war haunts; it was also the quickest seven days ever registered on the calendar. I did not know at the time that there would be several more fast moving seven days all equally wonderful and unforgettable.

We had taken the time together to arrange for Girl and Tony to move back to Halifax with my parents. I was relieved about this and later had every reason to be thankful. Meanwhile Mablethorpe had settled into a routine. We were still billeted in the caravans and I was finding plenty to do. Once again I was invited to present myself to the Adjutant and this I did with fingers firmly crossed. Another little job for me? Apparently one of the local Home Guard Units had been issued with six

American Winchester self loading rifles. A rifle I had no knowledge of at all and one I cannot remember well enough to name at this distance. No problem, a rifle is a rifle and the job? To supervise a range session and most importantly zero the rifles. There would be no opportunity for me to see the rifles prior to the shoot as range facilities were limited and overbooked and this Unit had been lucky to get a place at such short notice. However the Home Guard soldiers had been given instruction on the rifles including stripping for cleaning. I was looking forward to a couple of hours on the range with them.

Zeroing simply means adjusting the sights so that the bullets go where they are aimed and in turn obviously one needs a range to do this. The range turned out to be very pleasant and well kept, with an ideal range of one hundred yards. The rifles were in excellent condition; above all the Home Guard members were a great crowd and bursting to get their hands on the rifles plus of course live ammunition. I was not alone on this job. I cannot speak for other Regiments but with the Hants the Armourer was allowed an assistant, selected from the Battalion by me and subsequently trained by me. I had picked an older soldier who was at Corruna Barracks but he had only been working with me since I got back from York. He was keen and we got on well together. He also answered to the name of Donald; I never abbreviated his name but this is one of my quirks, not abbreviating first names. The Home Guard Sergeant gave Donald and me a quick run down on the gun, in turn I took it away and checked what was required to move the sights. I then addressed a question that had been troubling me. I naturally proposed to start by firing five shots but with absolutely no idea where the shots might finish up and with nothing to indicate where the shots were going, high, low, left or right I could finish up with an embarrassingly blank target.

Donald suggested an old soldier's trick, I would put all my shots off the target, preferably low so the strikes couldn't be seen and he would put appropriate shot holes in the target with a pencil. An ordinary pencil stabbed through a standard target makes an almost perfect 303" shot hole. Congratulating myself on selecting a brilliant if 'dodgy' assistant I sent him up to the butts then getting myself comfortable on the firing point I put five shots down the range as agreed, aiming well underneath and for good measure, taking advantage of the self loading characteristic. I made it a very rapid shoot.

Unloading the rifle I set off to the target followed by the entire Home Guard unit. Donald moved the target up in to view saying authoritatively, 'Great shoot, Sgt.' My God so it was, a small group of holes you could almost cover with a penny and this fired rapidly at one hundred yards with a strange rifle and to rub it in, nicely placed in the centre of the bull. Not a lot more I could say about this; we had a very enjoyable afternoon and though I never achieved the previous heights, I shot well and the whole was rounded off in the local, a pleasant boozy evening and I often wondered for how long this Home Guard unit talked about my 'Group' and, more to the point, to whom. A week later I talked the RSM into arranging an acting stripe for Donald who now became L/CorporalHarris. Oh dear, Clem, have you no shame?

These weeks were spent constantly fretting about not being able to get to see Girl. I spent a lot of time writing letters and of course received masses in return, so I was always up to date on Tony's progress but it seemed so cruel to be so near but yet so far. Everybody was in the same boat and indeed even compassionate leave was only granted in extreme cases. Childbirth for example was classed as a natural event and did not merit leave; this sparked a good deal of dissatisfaction amongst those affected. These problems aside, the Battalion had settled in well and these months provided a welcome period of rest and recovery from the traumas of France.

There was plenty of training and I managed a complete tour of the Rifle Companies and a good look at the repair situation plus a great deal of swapping yarns and bringing Company Commanders up to date on what happened to their B Echelon after Brussels. The Battalion had covered a great deal of mileage on foot as had we, so blisters were high on the topics discussed. My close friend Ben came in for masses of praise; he really was a superb chiropodist. He was also spending lots of time at our little caravan park, especially evenings, joining in the fun on the bikes. Because the Companies were so scattered there were no formal messes, Officers', Sergeants' or Corporals'. Each Unit provided some separate form of accommodation, maybe a separate room where they could gather in the evenings but it was all very much off the cuff.

The progress of the war was a constant source of concern at this time, being fought mainly by the RAF and of course, had the Germans invaded we would have been very much in the forefront of any fighting, but the weeks went by with the bombing of our towns, especially London, causing us all great distress. As the threat of invasion lessened rumours of a move began to drift through the usual channels, always a fascinating facet of life in general, this birth of a rumour and its subsequent growth, but in this case there it was and getting stronger every day. Not a lot of speculation as to where our move might be taking us but then again at this time I think there was a 'head in the sand' attitude to this aspect of the future. Joe and Gaffer, being like myself part of the QM's staff, spent a great deal of time together during the day and the occasional pub in the evening. We did have the soldier's ultimate bond, survival together when it could so easily have been the opposite; as Joe remarked one evening after a drink or two we could have quite easily be spending this evening in a prisoner of war camp. My thoughts went back to L/Corporal James Gent. 'Take it easy son!' Mostly though it was all in the past and forgotten, funnily enough until now.

Gaffer came into the barn where I had a sort of workshop set up and simply said, 'The Battalion is moving just up the road and Headquarter Company together with us will be stationed in Market Rasen.' And so it was, and this weeks before it happened. The Rifle Companies were spread around with Louth somewhere near the centre along with Battalion Headquarters and as Gaffer had predicted (or known) we were billeted in Market Rasen, a good sized market town situated about twelve miles north of Lincoln and boasting a fully fledged horse racing track, well known to the betting fraternity. The QM and staff (us) were billeted in an old coaching house, The Gordon Arms, the old stables and yard housed the business end of the Quartermaster whilst we occupied rooms in the hotel, pretty run down but comfortable never the less. A number of the Transport section also shared the rooms and I found myself sharing a room with John Harper, Transport Sergeant whose office occupied a room on the ground floor, my old friend Sgt. Joe Curley, ex horse transport, remember? And, but only for a short time, a very short time, two ferrets belonging to Joe or at least borrowed by Joe for a spot of rabbiting.

Again we settled into a routine but with a difference. First we were going to get yet another week's leave, this was phased so at the start one didn't quite know when it might happen and anyway it hadn't yet started and secondly I was starting to think about maybe trying to get accommodation in Lincoln for Girl and Tony; also as there was a bus service going through Market Rasen maybe being able to sneak in to Lincoln on a regular basis, all of this highly illegal and risky. I was already working on the idea and my first requirement was to find out if anyone in Lincoln was offering accommodation. The local paper carried this type of ad and it all seemed hopeful.

Once again we were in a strange state of suspension. The news was increasingly desperate and the Battalion were training hard but where was it all leading? For myself I had started a full inspection and this kept me busy. We were pretty well up to establishment and there had been a new weapon issued in the form of a mortar which could be carried by one man and sighting was based on the angle of the barrel to the base. There was a kind of protractor system whereby as you swung the barrel up into the firing position, a marker indicated the angle and possible range. The truth was that the soldiers using this mortar became incredibly proficient at simply estimating (guessing) what this angle should be relative to where they wished to drop the bomb.

The usual stories circulated about the ability of some to drop a bomb in a bucket at five hundred yards. Having seen some of these teams in action I have no reason at all to doubt this story. The calibre of the mortar was two inches and the bomb was quite small but it packed a punch and proved one of the success stories. The system evolved into a basic two-man team, one loading, i.e. dropping the bomb down the barrel and the other operating the trigger mechanism to send the bomb on its way. There were others involved, the bombs had to be carried and the loader kept supplied during firing but it was a popular weapon, gave very little trouble from an Armourer's point of view and was easy to carry and fast into action. Alas, soldiers are never satisfied and are always massively competitive. This led to attempts to see how many bombs a team could get into the air at the same time. This led to several fatal accidents when the bomb being loaded was hit by the bomb coming out. I remember a very nasty accident in Berlin during my service there leading to a fatality and serious wounds among the team. The practice had been forbidden almost from the time it started but was very difficult to stop.

November came with very little changing. Girl and I were still living a marriage by letters, increasingly frustrating. I was still working to arrange some sort of accommodation in Lincoln but what I really needed was transport so that I could get in to Lincoln independently, and this was proving impossible. I had a good workshop set up in what had been one of the stables with Gaffer next door sorting out the meat rations and Joe very appropriately occupying the old saddlery. The hotel had a big yard and the Signal Platoon used this yard for practising semaphore with flags. I really enjoyed watching this, sounds pretty ancient but the radios they were later issued with never worked. I think they were designed specially to frustrate the signallers and promote the hazardous occupation of Company Runner. They were to let us down badly during the North African campaign and at a time when they were desperately needed. Bring back the flags, all is forgiven. I nearly forgot, we still had heliographs, beautifully crafted and very handy for shaving.

With the battalion settled in, so to speak, with Headquarter Company, B Echelon and the Transport Section occupying Market Rasen, things were assuming a more Regimental look. The most important of these was a nicely accommodated Sergeants Mess, our own good cooks and a famous cabaret artist and band leader, Syd Jacobs, as Mess waiter. We were in, I think, a church hall but it was all very comfortable and brought the Senior ranks together on a regular basis. This mixing and togetherness can mean the difference between success and failure when the going gets rough and had been amply demonstrated during the long weary days up to Dunkirk. Not only this but the beer was cheap and like the whisky in these difficult days was always available. The Mess President responsible for this happy state of affairs was the Headquarter Company Sgt. Major, TrudgeTruran, a very good friend, with whom I, along with Joe Curley, were to face a life or death situation together during the North African campaign.

November was proving a disastrous month with the bombing of Coventry and the destruction of the Cathedral proving that there were dark days ahead. On a more personal note, but just as devastating, was the bombing of Portsmouth by 155 planes dropping 140 tons of explosive and 70,000 incendiaries. This was serious and worrying news for Girl and me, with all her family living in Portsmouth. It seemed a lifetime before we received confirmation that they were all OK There were masses of damage in the adjoining streets and this meant people who Girl knew well had been killed. It was a strange feeling. The Battalion were pleasantly billeted round the Lincolnshire countryside, it was very quiet but like me there were many whose families were living in places like London and Portsmouth. Every day was fraught with anxiety and sadly many of the Battalion lost loved ones.

Amongst all this worry and unhappiness lurked a fast approaching Christmas and the prospect of being away from our families, a prospect shared by many thousands of people, soldiers, sailors, airmen and, sadly, many evacuee children. The Battalion were planning a typical Christmas with Christmas dinner being served by officers and NCO's and entertainment from within the Battalion talent. Out of the blue Trudge buttoned me in the Mess and told me that my Christmas present had arrived in the form of another week's leave in January. It surely was a massive Christmas present, albeit a little late. This news certainly made my Christmas even though I still wouldn't be home.

Another communication from the Adjutant - as you will have gathered the Adjutant crops up a lot especially where there is something to be communicated, usually nasty! But hell, that's what Adjutants are for. Anyway this one is almost unbelievable in this age of cheap quartz watches but in effect it said that it would be a good thing if senior ranks could acquire a watch. I think at this time the only wrist-watch I had seen was on the wrist of Syd Jacobs' the mess waiter, Syd Jacobs? No, I don't think I'll go down that road. Anyway, 'acquiring' a watch was a big expenditure; once my marriage allotment had been deducted I don't suppose I was left with much more than twenty-five shillings a week even as a Sgt. Marks and Spencers did one for five shillings, too much for me and anyway where was the nearest M&S? Lincoln, I suppose. I had always managed so far without one though I did buy one in France; it was cheap and lasted about a month.

The Sergeants Mess was only a couple of hundred yards from the hotel and coming down for breakfast on this particular morning I found a covering of snow. As usual I met Jimmy Dunkley in the entrance, now Sgt. Dunkley. Jimmy was always smart and sometimes I remembered that poor bedraggled figure I first saw looking for the Guardroom. We walked down to the Mess remarking on the snow, then after breakfast as we walked back I caught a glimpse of something shining in the gutter and pretty well covered with snow. Bending down I picked up a wrist watch, Jimmy said something like, 'The Adjutant will be pleased.' I tucked it in my pocket, wondering at the coincidence; after all it had only been a couple of days since we had been encouraged to get ourselves a watch.

Back in the billet I soon discovered that I had probably picked up quite an expensive watch. It appeared to be stainless steel with a screw back and was very heavy though small. Gaffer who as a lapsed (we hoped) professional simply said, 'About fifteen quid to buy,' this equated with about ten weeks pay. 'Get thee behind me Satan', and he did. I took it to the Company Office who said they would put it on Company Orders and if no one came forward they would hand it in to the Police; meanwhile keep the watch and if any one claimed it they could come to me and subject to proof, collect it. Two days later the watch was claimed. The lad correctly identified it as a 'Vertex All Proof', and asked me if I wished to buy it. I did, he wanted five shillings and if you give me a second whilst I look, the time is 7.35! Not bad for sixty-four years in which 'time' it has seldom been off my wrist, truly an old and well loved friend.

Christmas was a great success, with everyone letting their hair down and the lads having a go at the officers and NCOs, particularly at the senior ranks in true Army tradition. There were some harsh roads ahead, far worse than France and with heavy casualties. Many at that dinner would not survive and I would lose some good friends.

Dunkley - Hoyle

On 22 January 1941 I was once again on my way to Girl and Tony but this time to Halifax. The time went just as quickly, it would appear that both Portsmouth and Halifax were using these super speed calenders. Once again a kitbag full of washing and a big pack full of the finest beef! Whose big pack are you filling now, Gaffer? I hope the meat is not coming ready roasted, though I fear it probably is. 'Take it easy, son.' Another wonderful week. Getting to know Tony was so important to me in this climate of war, because all too quickly I was back in Market Rasen, apprehensibly awaiting the next move. It was very reminiscent of the Phony War period in France.

But first how to fix a place in Lincoln. I luckily found someone with an old motorbike who was prepared to lend it to me and although the weather was very cold I set off one afternoon to hopefully visit one or two addresses in Lincoln. I was to pursue this line many times and for as long as I could get petrol for the old bike and most importantly for as long as Trudge turned a blind eye and Joe and Gaffer covered. In the end I was successful and rented an upstairs room. It was a large house nicely furnished, and Girl would have use of the kitchen. The house belonged to an elderly lady and we were very lucky in that she was happy for us to bring Tony.

Situated just a few hundred yards from the Lincoln Race course it was very handy for the bus and so started a wonderful period of sneaking off Friday evenings and sneaking back Monday mornings. We spent many hours on the Racecourse which had been covered in trenches and obstructions to deter landings, Tony loved it, just one great game. Girl coped very well with the shared kitchen and basically there were no problems. This lasted until late May when my turn came round for another seven days' leave. This time the three of us went off to Portsmouth, yet again the time simply flew but we had a wonderful time. It was decided that Girl and Tony would be safer once again in Halifax so while I went back to Market Rasen, and resumed my bachelor existence they went on back to Halifax and we all resumed worrying about the next move.

One unpleasant aspect of life turned up out of the blue. It was decided at some level, not the Adjutant this time, that all the soldiers in the Brigade would do regular route marches wearing fighting order. Thank God it wasn't full marching order. There was always one thing I hated about these marches, like the one from Arras to Tilloy, they never told you anything, no mileage information, no destination, just interminable trudging along bored to tears or if you were not blessed with good feet, then painfully bored to tears, hoping that round the next bend was the final destination. I cannot leave this subject without mention of the ten minutes halt in every hour. A doubtful blessing this, great when you collapse in a heap and ease off the weight but diabolical when you start off again; even with my feet it felt as though my boots were filled with barbed wire and though it wore off quite quickly, very painful whilst it lasted.

It was hard getting used to not having my weekends to look forward to so once again back to married life through letters. It was during these months at Market Rasen that Jimmy Dunkley and I cemented a firm friendship that lasted long after the war had finished. We spent a lot of time during the summer evenings walking the local and very beautiful countryside and along with Joe we would usually finish up in the local pub, the Aston Arms, often joined by Jack Brown still one of the QM baggage lorry drivers. The pub seemed to have been taken over by Gaffer, shades of Genech. This was pretty obvious to my old Platoon because in a time of desperate shortages behind the bar this pub never ever ran out of beer or spirits, especially Scotch. Gaffer was usually to be found in there whatever time of day. The landlord was more than happy to sit back and take the acclaim. I did hear that Gaffer was also looking after an RAF Station just down the road, well known for hospitality and no shortages.

I was pretty busy over these months with inspections and repairs, travelling quite widely to get to the Companies. We also had a lot of range time allocated and with the glorious weather I spent many hours on the range. Sadly at this time I learned that our previous Adjutant Capt. R. Humphreys had died after being severely wounded on that last journey to Dunkirk. It had been impossible to evacuate him and he died later from his wounds. Somehow it always seems to be unfair to die so long afterwards, at least it does to me. I mention this at this point because talk of ranges brings memories of many hours spent with Capt. Humphreys on the various ranges around Aldershot. He was a very good shot and firmly believed that soldiers should spend as much of their training time as possible on the ranges.

Much better news of one of my old Platoon, Tug Wilson, also wounded on the way to Dunkirk and treated and nursed to the beach by Ben together with many willing helpers. He was almost fully recovered and would be rejoining the Battalion. Ben was especially pleased with this news because at the time he was pretty pessimistic about Tug's chances. So it looked as if I would get my old driving instructor (and partner in crime back).

The year was moving along, September almost gone, must be 'rumour' time again and so it was. Gaffer was strangely silent on the subject but the rumours took us world wide and even back to Mablethorpe. I wondered if the Pioneer Platoon had put in one of their treetrunk nine-seat super latrines somewhere. Might be worth investigating, the rumours were certainly commensurate with one of these superb rumour generators. At this stage of the war it was difficult to envisage our next move and it was also easy to get misled by thinking in terms only of the Battalion whereas any move would be a Brigade move. Scattered as the Brigade was, one sort of lost sight of this aspect: not that it would have helped much. The chances are that the people who were deciding all these things in their search for the best winning formulae didn't know either. At least not at this time. I now know that at this particular phase of the war, Winston Churchill was planning to try landing troops in France for whatever reason and it would be necessary to experiment with some sort of landing craft. Now where is there a Brigade lying about doing nothing? Oh yes, The First Guards Brigade, bless em!

At the beginning of October the Brigade moved to Lockerbie, at least we did, into half finished Nissan huts in the grounds of Castlemilk some six miles outside Lockerbie. The two Guards Battalions meanwhile moved into very pleasant billets in Dumfries; we never forgave them ! The Nissan huts were stark indeed, heating was from a small coke stove in the centre of the floor, no hot water. They were situated in clearings cut out of the trees. The ablutions hut comprised a long table with bowls and odd taps here and there plus a channel cut into the concrete floor for drainage. No shower facilities. The excuse was that they had only just managed to finish them to this state in time for our arrival as they hadn't been given enough notification. There was a larger hut to serve as a Sergeants' Mess which we managed to make reasonably comfortable over our stay but all in all, our time there was uncomfortable to say the least.

We soon discovered how isolated we were. There was a village within long walking range but comprising only houses and the village hall, no shops or pub. The nearest form of entertainment was the cinema in Lockerbie, and one very good café plus the Kings Arms Hotel. This however was a six mile walk, no buses and recreational transport was so frowned upon that it was virtually non existent. The officers were well accommodated in the Castle but even this was in terminal decay. I suppose there were many soldiers and airmen living like this but that didn't make it any more palatable. The vehicle fitters and I had workshops in what had been the stable complex, the QM occupying the old estate management offices.

Two weeks after we arrived I once again went on seven days leave, this time to Halifax. On the journey home I noticed it was relatively easy to get to my local station leaving me with a five minute walk home. The route was Lockerbie Station, Leeds and then a local to Ovenden where I lived. Girl and I researched this with the local stationmaster and found it would be possible to get the six o'clock evening train out of Lockerbie, change at Leeds and be home before dawn. This on the Friday but getting back on the Sunday was much more difficult and entailed Ovenden, Leeds, Carlisle and arriving in Lockerbie at about five in the morning. If attempted, and it would be difficult to pull off, it would of course be in the middle of winter. Another fast moving seven days, packing masses of enjoyment but with always the parting looming yet again. At least Tony knew me now!

About this time the QM, Lt. Puleston, was posted away from the Battalion and back to the Regimental Depot at Winchester for promotion. He had been my direct boss ever since I joined the Battalion and we had always got on well together so I was sorry to see him go. Unfortunately his replacement would likely be the then RQMS (Regimental Quartermaster Sgt.) Northmore. This was a normal progression and he would be commissioned becoming Lt. Northmore and of course my new boss. I used the word unfortunately for two reasons: firstly Northmore and I had never really got on together and secondly Gaffer and our new QM couldn't stand each other and I can remember from months before Gaffer saying that if ever Northmore was commissioned he (Gaffer) would be posted away within a week. And so he was!

Nothing was ever going to be quite the same without Guyatt. Joe Brown and I were very upset but Gaffer went and in true Guyatt style within six months he was RSM of the Pioneer Corps, a new Corps formed during the war. We never corresponded but a few years after the war Girl and I bumped into him in Portsmouth, he looked well, a good chat and that was it. I would never forget him.

Meanwhile the new QM had made a serious mistake in getting rid of Gaffer and he found genuine cooperation right through the Battalion mysteriously difficult to come by. For myself Northmore and I existed in a state of mutual tolerance and after a certain incident later in the year or years, active dislike. It was my fault, though the incident was not originally designed to involve the QM, but more of this later.

Remember the Prime Minister and his ideas for landing troops on enemy shores? Well, here it was: we were off somewhere on what was to be called the Boating Scheme. That is the Brigade, of course, but for myself, as always I did what I was told, parading at the right time and place in full marching order and trying not to think too far ahead. Let us take a moment in time. I, along with B Echelon, am standing on Lockerbie Station with my equipment straps beginning to shut off my circulation. Borrowing a penny, I couldn't reach my pockets, I stood on the weight machine and a quick calculation before the blood was finally shut off from my brain revealed that what I was carrying in weight was in fact exactly equal to my body weight. I was glad to get on the train!

But where to? Nobody seemed to know so settle down, watch the countryside and wait for the journey's end. One worrying thing, it wasn't dark, and it was always dark when we moved, or so it seemed. Reassuringly it was dark when we got there and the place was Largs. The Battalion were being housed in Nissan huts no better than the ones we had left which in turn were situated in the grounds of a large mansion. Our ultimate destination was still a dark secret, there was not even a rumour circulating and this too can be worrying in war time, because with security this tight, it could mean something really nasty brewing. It was during the few days at Largs that the Signal Platoon had their first brush with their radio communications or I should say radio sets. I think they were called either No. 18 or No. 19 sets, doesn't matter really, they were both useless.

A range period had been booked locally but unfortunately the range telephones were out of order so it was decided this would be a good opportunity for the Signal Platoon to use their radio sets for communication between the butts and the firing points, a distance of three hundred yards. So with signallers in the butts and signallers on the firing point, down went the first shots but signals there were none. There followed a prolonged period of fiddle, even battery changes but the sets (18 or 19 who cares by this time) obstinately refused to talk to one another. The officer in charge of the range party and of course responsible for ensuring that the troops got their practice and alas faced with no communication between butts and firing points, immediately proved worthy of his rank by resorting to that age old solution…Company runner!

Chatting to the Signal Sergeant later, another good friend, he told me that the sets had just been issued as new. As I have already said they were to let us down later in North Africa when the Battalion were in a desperate situation. My friend the Signal Sergeant was spared the problem, he was already dead. But all this is for another day.

We were a little in limbo at this time; whatever we were up to it certainly hadn't leaked out not even in the form of a rumour. Time for the Pioneer Platoon to get out their latrine designs, maybe a twelve-seater might start something in the way of rumour. When this sort of waiting prevailed I just looked for work. I could usually find something that needed doing though I often finished helping out Jimmy, they were always busy. I seem to remember a very pleasant test run in the Brigade Commander's Humber Staff car complete with flag. I didn't like to tell Jim that it should only be flown when the Staff Officer was actually in the car.

Everything comes to him who waits. Attached to an Infantry Regiment during the war this varied from unpleasant through very unpleasant to bloody dangerous. In this case we set off once again by train, carrying not only full marching order but our kitbags as well. Very ominous, this; a full kitbag is a nightmare to carry and manoeuvre about when you are also carrying the rest of your possessions. The rifle especially develops a life of its own. We finally arrived at our destination and surprise it was pitch dark and ominously (that word again) it was a large port, Greenock in fact. After the usual organised milling about, it was up a gangplank, oh bugger this bloody kitbag, and down into one of the mess decks. There followed a superb meal and the information that we were on the HMS. *Eteric* and would we please go and collect our hammocks…our what? At this moment I really felt despairing; we had not been allow to write letters for several days so Girl wouldn't have the faintest idea what was happening and I was by this time convinced there was a long journey ahead of us. She would think I had dropped off the end of the earth. Learning that the *Eteric* was the only purpose built troopship ever, and had only been finished a few months before the outbreak of war certainly didn't help my feeling of foreboding. Could I wangle a posting at this late date? Hello, I'm hallucinating again.

The following morning, we were driven out of our hammocks (I had as usual slept well) by shouts of 'Lash up and stow' which in our language simply meant fold up your hammock neatly and take it back to wherever you got it. I can hardly wait for my brother-in-law to read this, an old battered regular Petty Officer: when he reads 'fold up your hammock neatly' he will go berserk. A past master of salty profanities, I suspect we shall all add to our vocabularies. And what next? Parade on the Mess deck at 0900 hrs for a briefing. At last all will be revealed, at least so we hope, and we might be allowed to post letters again. Maybe I shouldn't reveal my priorities so clearly but the news that we were to move up to Inverary on the *Eteric* from which ship we would be testing out various ideas for landing troops on enemy shores and not setting sail for some far-off shore with nothing but trouble waiting and a lousy mail service was more than welcome.

So this was 'the boating scheme': pretty innocuous, might even be fun? Come on, Clem, you must be joking. To start with it's October and it is not exactly warm out there and anyway it's always dark, at least it seems to be. So we got on with it, using the ship's lifeboats and very unpleasant it turned out to be. Everything was hit or miss and the Coxswains were finding it very difficult to get the boats inshore where it was safe to get out and wade onto the beach. The lifeboats were power driven but totally unsuitable. I was on the periphery of all this but did one trip where luckily I was not required to land. My God it was cold but the *Eteric* was warm; it was full of rationed items like chocolate and cigarettes at reduced prices and the Petty Officers' Mess was comfortable, their food was terrific and drinks were plentiful and also cheap.

Apart from the exercises most of us were stuffing our kitbags and anything else that might produce a bit of space, with mostly cigarettes and chocolate which of course were now rationed. This was the lighter side of the 'Boating Exercise' but there was a much darker side in the shape of fatalities. Although the beaches were shallow, hence their selection for training, there were unexpected holes meaning it was possible for a soldier to step off the landing craft into twenty feet of water. Assuming he was wearing fighting order and in some cases carrying heavier items like a two inch mortar strapped on, then sadly he would go straight to the bottom.

The exercise over, we retraced our steps back to Lockerbie complete with our booty and for me it was 9 October and my next seven days leave was due and I was soon on my way to Halifax, loaded with cigarettes and chocolate but this time no sirloin. Girl never forgave Northmore, the new QM, for posting Gaffer. Another super leave and Tony and I were seldom apart, Girl was still surviving and getting on well with my parents; this was important and whilst there were the odd disagreements the arrangement was a blessing for me as otherwise I would have been constantly stressed, worrying about the bombing.

Early in November I tried out my plan to get home, leaving Friday evening on the six o'clock train from Lockerbie to Leeds then picking up a train which left Leeds for Halifax at around midnight. This stopped at Ovenden, then a short walk and I was home. The real problem was getting to Lockerbie station which was roughly six miles and absolutely no transport; we were not even on a bus route. That is how I came to be crouched, shivering with cold, in a Bren carrier which Jimmy just happened to be taking on a test run after repair. I caught the train and everything went like clockwork; I was home and in bed by two o'clock. This all sounds fine now, but I was taking risks that I shouldn't have even contemplated, Absent without leave in war can result in dire consequences.

It was wonderful to be with Girl and Tony but Saturday went like a flash and now I was faced with getting back on the Sunday. It turned out to be easy, very uncomfortable but easy. A train at mid-day from Halifax to Leeds, and a long wait at Leeds for a connection to Carlisle; although the waiting room was open there was no heating, nor were there any refreshments. So it was pretty uncomfortable but Carlisle? Now there was a thing. I got to Carlisle around nine thirty, it was very cold and very dark, remember the blackout? On the station everything was closed. Groping my way into what I now know was Botchergate I found a large building that had been set up to succour cold tired soldiers, inside warmth, armchairs, tea, even food. Sinking into an armchair and with over five hours to wait for my train to Lockerbie I thought, 'This is a bit of all right, I'll get a mug of tea something to eat and settle down.' The lady serving my tea said, 'Ninepence' or something like and then, 'The RMPs check passes every half' hour in here.' How did she know? Back on the station, find a dark corner, settle down to freeze until my train arrives, then on to Lockerbie and the last leg, a six mile hike to the camp. No problem there and I quite enjoyed it, remember Clem and his good feet? Sneak into camp, a big breakfast in the mess, no one had missed me.

I cannot leave this without mention of my 'super' cover, L/Cpl. Donald Harris. (covering for his friend the Armourer Sergeant, and tight pencilled groups a specialty). There were a number of friends in the know who would cover if possible but Jimmy said that on the Saturday afternoon he was in the Armourer's workshop (a corner of an old barn) chatting to Donald when the QM obviously looking for trouble stormed in. 'Where's Sgt. Hoyle, Corporal?' Rigidly to attention and a cracking salute, 'With you, Sir!' According to Jim, the QM left with a slightly baffled look on his face and that was it. I wonder if the RSM might go to another stripe! Better not push my luck but in every way Donald was proving a great asset.

Things had settled into a routine. The lads were training hard, there were outbreaks of inter-company football and no rumours. Towards the end of November I went down with a very severe throat infection and spent a week in Jardine Hall, a wonderful and huge house belonging to the Jardine family whose millions had been made in tea. They had converted it into a hospital complete with operating theatre. I was very ill for the first few days but as I recovered I had time to appreciate the magnificent interior, Netley it wasn't. The staff were all volunteers and we were looked after superbly.

Back to the Battalion and this time no rumour, just fact. We were going back to Inverary to repeat exercise ' Boating'. This was going to be in December and that is why I am now huddled in a sort of botched up landing craft swinging on the end of whatever connects us to the davits, firmly jammed halfway down and freezing to death. Oh yes, surprise surprise, it is pitch dark. We are also under a 'quiet order': no talking, coughing, sneezing or breaking wind. There! see how refined I've become, must be the bloody cold. Apart from the sounds as they try to free the davits it is truly quiet, yet I sense an unease around me and the dark is like a blanket, I cannot see a thing. Inevitably there is a low voice somewhere in the boat having a little moan. 'Charge that man!' This in a loud voice and coming from the area of the young Naval Officer charged with steering us to a happy landing. God, it's quiet now, unbelievably so, then a loud clear voice, 'You can kiss my f......ng arse, I'm next for Rear Admiral!' We have a genius and master of the repartee on board. Everybody seems to have perked up a little.

A ghastly lurch and we are descending once again, finally slapping down in the water and we are off. I cannot describe how I felt contemplating the arrival on the shore and leaping (that's a joke, all my joints have frozen solid) carrying full marching order into the unknown which turns out to be about waist high in the water. It is only recently, some sixty years later, that my genitals have shown signs of recovery. I struggle up the beach, finally bumping into Jimmy struggling to push a motorbike to wherever we were supposed to get to. I joined in, at least it helped warm me up a bit; we eventually caught up with the rest of the lads from the boat and after a discussion decided to park the bike and press on with the lads, it would be easier. Wrong, we reached the main body and were promptly formed into a squad and began a march inland. As we squelched along in the dark to nowhere it quickly became obvious to

Jimmy and me that it would have been a much wiser decision to have stayed and looked after the motorbike. I found later we marched about four miles inland and about two miles back.

And so back to the ship. This time we had changed ships and were on the *Winchester Castle*. This was luxury. we were accommodated in cabins and the ship was still very much a liner. There were even stewards here and there. I had no doubt if Gaffer had still been with us we would by now be enjoying the exclusive services of a steward. As I came aboard wet and cold this ship had a wonderful bonus! It was hot and I mean hot; it wrapped itself round you like a blanket and after the last few hours the sensation was quite sensual. It was imperative to find Ben, Jimmy's feet were in a poor state, then into the Petty Officers' mess for a welcome and superb hot supper. A few bottles of Bass and then we groped our way back to the cabin. It was light enough but the Bass seemed to be in charge so groping our way seemed best.

After finishing the exercise five days later and with our kitbags and packs well filled with cigarettes and chocolate, we sailed (in daylight) for Greenock or so we thought; but in fact we anchored up somewhere close to a very nice looking sandy beach. There was a road running along behind the beach where there appeared to be trucks parked up. At the briefing we were told that Colonel Lee had decided we needed more practice so our kitbags would be lowered into the boats by the crew, then taken to the beach and when the boats returned we would get aboard them using scramble nets (I think Jacob's Ladder is the correct name). It's a long way down to the water from a ship as big as the *Winchester Castle*!

A lot of grumbling on the lines of 'Expect the Guards are sitting back in the train now.' It all went well, one or two moments here and there but we were soon into the trucks and on our way to Largs station. And the Guards? They were in the Customs' sheds in Greenock being relieved of their 'contraband'. Apparently Colonel Lee had wind of this and decided come hell or high water his lads were not going to lose their perks. Hairy at times and one of the physically hardest things I've ever done, but on 5 January I was due another leave and this time for nine days, no less, so my contraband was going to be very welcome. I told you Colonel Lee was a wonderful Commanding Officer. The Battalion had a great Christmas. I think this was because we were all together, the cooks did us proud, the officers worked hard all day and 'paid' for the drinks, there was even a rugby match officers versus the rest in which I stupidly played and got well bruised. What had the Officers got against the Armourer? I wondered, nursing a cut head.

I remember the Orderly Officer on that Christmas Day, a very young Lieutenant. (that's what young Lieutenants are for, Orderly Officer on Feast days) ending up in one of the swill bins. I also remember him later that year collecting a Military Cross for incredible bravery. I quote from official diaries: "'Z' Company ordered to counter-attack with one platoon, attack goes in supported by Artillery, farm retaken, but many casualties including platoon Commander, insufficient men to hold farm which is very exposed - platoon withdrawn, leaving many wounded. That night, Lieutenant E.G. Wright of 'Z' Company, already wounded in the leg, takes out patrol, extremely dark – navigates to farm – locates and brings back eight wounded men and seven previously reported missing – a dangerous and humane achievement professionally executed. For this outstanding act of leadership and courage, Lieutenant E.G. Wright was awarded the MC end.'

AIRSPEED OXFORD

The 5 January arrived and another bittersweet nine days simply flying away, lots of cigarettes and chocolates but no meat. I'll kill that Northmore, Girl was heard to mutter, and so say all of us. Tony really was growing fast and I desperately needed these brief interludes together. But it was back to Lockerbie and the already established routines; it was to a certain extent like being back in barracks. Officers', Sergeants' and Corporals' messes functioning, plenty of inter Company sport, and also intensive weapon training. I had inspected a couple of companies weapons hoping to complete them all but one just didn't know when the Battalion might suddenly up sticks and move out.

Sometime in late February I was to be posed a personal question: 'Am I in someway jinxed'? Jimmy and I were sitting in the mess quietly eating our tea and chatting about the awful fog outside and seconds later we were struggling along with the rest of the mess trying to get to the wreckage of what turned out to be an RAF Airspeed Oxford well and truly parked up, so to speak, outside the mess. None of us had heard a thing until the aircraft hit the ground, so we were all shaken to say the least. The plane had come down in an area planted with young saplings and I think these must have softened the impact but they, along with the fog, were not helping our efforts to get to the aircraft. When we finally did so it was to find a badly damaged plane but we were able to get the crew out with very little trouble. Meanwhile our first aid post had been alerted and the doctor and Ben arrived to take over.

Half an hour later here we all were back in the mess with the crew. The pilot had suffered a fair number of facial abrasions but was otherwise OK. The radio operator had broken his collar bone, whilst the navigator was simply badly shaken and curing himself by tucking into the mess whisky. It turned into a long evening for them owing to the fog; their Station was not far away but the RAF ambulance had to struggle with the poor visibility. Apparently they had been on a training flight and put very simply, the fog disoriented them and the reason they came down where they did was because I was sat in the mess. Or so Joe said, he also said: 'You've done it again, Clem,' which led to me thinking about the jinx theory. I have to say at this point I wasn't finished by a long way but once again that's for another day. The aircraft was recovered over the next few days and the Mess President received effusive thank you letters from each of the crew whilst the navigator's medical treatment was written off to Mess funds.

During our stay in Lockerbie Trudge had unearthed, if that's the right expression, a poacher. He was now a Sergeant's mess waiter. CSM Truran never missed a trick. Our location was a poacher's paradise with a famous trout stream running through the camp and the whole place alive with rabbits. The cook was good with rabbits and trout and chicken. Hang on, I had never seen any chickens about and I always presumed the eggs were normal issue though we did get a lot of them. Anyway I found myself making snares, then Jimmy and I were invited out with our friendly poacher to learn how to set them. This turned into a strange interlude in which the poacher's snares were always full and ours empty, Even though he had shown us exactly where to lay them. It was the same with tickling trout: Jimmy and I nothing, whilst our poacher was taking back enough for a banquet. I think you will have realised by now that once again this is a name that eludes me. This gentleman will turn up much later directing a lifetime of nocturnal avoidance of authority to the serious business of war. Yet another valuable friend.

I have in front of me a bill from the King's Arms Hotel Lockerbie, which shows three nights double room, bed and breakfast, two lunches, one dinner, one supper, total £2.16s. Not bad for a 'dirty' weekend. I did have one moment; coming into the lounge on the Saturday morning I found Girl chatting amicably to a Brigadier. Both had their backs to a huge fire, it was a cosy scene. I saluted, introduced myself and the three of us stood chatting until breakfast was signalled. I saluted yet again and the Brigadier said, 'Have a nice weekend, both of you,' and left. I really must try to get a pass in future.

DIRTY WEEKEND

Our stay in Lockerbie was nearly at an end and without much warning but plenty of rumour we were once again on the move and this time to Forfar, I can date this move pretty accurately to a few days before our wedding anniversary which was 6 April. I remember very clearly buying Girl a present from one of the shops on the main street. So here we were in a fair sized and very pleasant Scottish town and over the next few months were to learn the real meaning of hospitality. The Battalion were well disciplined and the people of Forfar took us to their hearts. They in turn were welcomed into our messes and, included in any of the Battalion functions and of course the Pipes and Drums were once again beating retreat every evening as they did in Templeuve, upholding yet again the Second Battalion's long tradition of beating retreat every evening when on active service.

I think the Battalion could truly be said to 'have its feet under the table'. A number of the lads became engaged to Forfar girls and I seem to remember a marriage. It is a long time ago but what I do sadly remember is that. In under a year the whole town would be openly mourning the massive losses that the Battalion suffered during four nightmare days in North Africa. Again I'm ahead but never tell a member of the 2nd Battalion that the Scottish people were anything less than generous, The wonderful people of Forfar collected an enormous amount of money and donated it to the families who had been bereaved.

I mentioned earlier an incident that did nothing to improve my relations with Northmore. At one point during our stay in Forfar it had been decided that I would attend a course on booby traps and then come back and impart my knowledge to the Pioneer Platoon whose job it was to defuse or whatever, when and if the Battalion came upon them. Not me, I hastily affirm. I arrived back, some what dry-mouthed (the same effect but pants still clean) and in possession of a few samples for my future lectures: detonators, plastic explosive (Semtex), small steel pegs for fixing trip wires; my God, it does sound macho at this distance.

To set the scene, my workshop was an old biscuit warehouse. This had a small parking area and a large gate to allow the lorries in. The gate itself had long gone to make a battleship or something so it was just a gap between the two walls. Jimmy Dunkley and I had an arrangement with a small bakery at the end of the road whereby at about ten o'clock every morning we would slip into the bakery and sit warm and cosy eating one of the town specialties, a hot Forfar bridie fresh from the oven (Scotland's more than adequate answer to the Cornish pasty). Oh yes, and drinking tea. Anyway, Jimmy would always arrive bang on time so I decided to try out my booby trap skills by setting up a trip wire between the two walls connected to a detonator together with a modicum of plastic explosive and concealed in an old biscuit tin. The tin I placed at what I guessed would be a reasonably safe distance; anyway my best mate was the Medical Sergeant so no worries there.

Yes, you are ahead of me. It was the Quartermaster who walked through. I had certainly got everything right, maybe my modicum of explosive was a touch over recipe but I think my instructor would have been well pleased; his forte was explosives especially the size of the bang. To say Northmore was not pleased would be an understatement, try shaken and furious; adding to his fury my story that I was simply setting up a demonstration for my lecture to the Pioneer Platoon was unassailable and pointing out that it was L/Corporal Harris who should have been tester could not be challenged. Mind you, I suspect Donald could have told a better story (lie) than I did given the chance. The QM left, Jimmy arrived saying, 'Christ what was that bang?' to which I replied, 'I think I've just blown my friendship with the QM'

I was very busy during these weeks in Forfar. I did a quarterly inspection of all equipment that I was responsible for and also 'suffered' a surprise AIA's inspection (AIA: Assistant Inspector of Armourers). He and his team descended on the Battalion one Monday morning from the Command Workshops at Stirling, inspected about 40 per cent of the Battalion's weapons then departed. A copy of their report arrived from Brigade HQ a couple of weeks later, reasonably complimentary: the Adjutant was happy, the Commanding Officer was pleased, and Northmore grunted.

Strange training methods were appearing; I think Platoon Sergeants had been reading the wrong books. Walking to my workshops one morning I came across several platoons scaling a wall by making a kind of ladder of their rifles then charging up them, studs and all. I was in a benevolent mood having just been told that I had another nine days leave coming up on 27 July about two weeks away. So a quick word with my old friend the Adjutant and a letter went out to the effect that this practice would cease, forthwith.

Another leave in Portsmouth. We had a wonderful time and I walked miles trying to find shoes for Tony. There were many little shops dotted all over Portsmouth selling these sort of second-hand items: clothes rationing was really biting at this time. One very worrying facet of these leaves was the undercurrent of not knowing how long it might be before we met again. We tried not to let it spoil things but the thought was always there. I decided when I got back I would try and find rooms and get Girl and Tony up; although not permitted there were one or two of the lads doing it and as long as you were discreet and careful it seemed well worth the risk.

I found a place with an elderly lady, very happy to have Tony, and this turned out wonderfully. Her son was a farmer with two children and they spent a great deal of time with their Grandma and Tony simply joined the gang. Except at some time early in their stay all the gang went down with measles; Ben and the Medical Officer were superb.

During Girl's stay in Forfar she dispensed advice on the assembly of the cocking piece to the bolt of the 'Boys' anti tank rifle. The soldiers would strip the bolt for cleaning but when assembling the cocking piece there was a very powerful spring to overcome and often they would not complete the requisite number of turns needed to overcome this. The bolt of course would look OK but wouldn't work. Though my stay in lodgings was not supposed to be common knowledge, much less my address, an Infantry Battalion doesn't work like that and one day one of the lads turned up at the door with a bolt in his hand. Girl answered the door, shouted for me and watched as I explained the problem and turned the cocking piece one turn to demonstrate. A few days later Girl told me that one of the lads had been with a bolt and as I wasn't there she had fixed it. This happened once or twice more so I thought maybe I ought to arrange a trade test for her; after all I didn't see why she shouldn't go on the payroll.

There was a strange happening whilst at Forfar. The powers that be issued the Battalion with thirty civilian bicycles, Raleighs no less, and this was to form a tank hunting platoon. I really am not joking. My reaction was to tuck them out of sight and hope that no one came to use them, Well, no one did and the whole thing was abandoned. When it came to returning the bikes it was simple, they still had their protective packing. Also they had come with a generous supply of spares which somehow didn't get returned. Gaffer would have been really proud of me. I was at this time helping the local bicycle shop to assemble new bikes (I still hated them) as there was a big demand for bikes and Mr Bruce was restricted by a form of rationing and not only were the number of bikes he was allowed rationed but they were sent as a collection of parts. Bruce was a relative of our landlady and so I went in during the evenings and helped assemble these kits, especially the wheel building; the spares came in handy too. Mr Bruce had a car plus a petrol allowance and would take Joan and the landlady out for short runs, mostly to Glamis Castle with tea to follow. This was a great treat for Girl and well worth my evenings working for Bruce.

There were a number of highlights during our stay in Forfar, not all of them pleasant, for example, 'Exercise Dry Shod'. The Brigade were to march from wherever they were, in our case Forfar, down to North Yorkshire. Again I am not joking, also there was to be a special emphasis on the types who were not normally involved in this basic type of soldiering, Members of Transport Sections, B Echelons, Clerks and so on. This really didn't apply to the Hampshires as the Battalion policy was that we all did regular route marches, and indeed, we had already done two quite taxing marches since arriving in Forfar. I cannot remember on what day this particular lunacy was abandoned, we were supposed to average twenty miles a day! I think it was probably at the end of the third. To start with the ambulances were all full, the medical services were totally incapable of coping with the masses of foot problems, Ben had many horrific stories to tell about his attempts to cope and that was just with his own blisters. The frightening thing was that the Brigade took weeks to regain anything like fitness.

The Mess managed to get Nat Gonnella and his Orpheons, together with Stella Moir, his wife, to play at a Mess dance. Girl and I were introduced to Nat and Stella and spent the evening with them; that was truly a memorable evening for the mess. I was to bump into Nat later in North Africa but that too, is another story. This of course was one of the pleasant highlights.

In terms of work the episode of the three Vickers guns stands out. Walking into the QM's store one morning there they were, delivered the previous evening by truck, These I should remind you were the famous heavy machine guns which did such sterling work during World War One. I gazed at the three guns with their huge tripods with some misgiving. I was well clued up on the Vickers gun but couldn't imagine who in the Battalion might have experience. My antenna was already indicating that I might just be getting a call from you know who. Moments later the QM clerk handed me the phone saying, 'Adjutant asking for you.' Yes sir, I would organise a training session for potential heavy machine gunners, and as soon as possible. 'Thank you, Sergeant, I'll leave it in your capable hands.' You see, even Adjutants have a need to crawl occasionally.

So to 'Trudge'. Yes, there was a machine gun section many years ago; he would try and dig up a few names. Glaring balefully at these well greased guns, I decided to leave well alone until I heard from 'Trudge. Two days later 'they' came and took the guns away.Trudgehadn't even got round to looking for names and when I went to see the Adjutant he just swore and muttered something that sounded like 'What a way to run a war,' then, 'Thank you Armourer Sergeant.' I liked the Adjutant.

The month I think would be August and suddenly there were serious things afoot. It started with a blanket ban on all letters in or out. One cannot stop people posting a letter when they are stationed in a town the size of Forfar but the threat was sufficient to inhibit people; this was war and our own lives might depend on total security. Sadly it was time for Girl and Tony to go home, this time back to Portsmouth; it was a big wrench and who the hell was going to fix those recalcitrant anti tank rifle bolts?

During this short period I received instructions along with a gallon of nitric acid to black all the bayonet blades. The method was to degrease the bayonets using boiling water then wipe them with dilute nitric acid. I have no idea what the proportions were but I managed nicely using old biscuit tins which held just the right amount of water and acid and boiling in one and dipping in the other. I achieved this rather ghastly looking grey black. For heat I used one of the petrol cookers that were issued to the cooks and it all went very well. Donald and I whilst doing these bayonets spent a fair amount of time trying to fathom what it was all about at such short notice.

Very shortly after, we loaded the QM baggage lorry, still driven by my old friend Jack, now LCpl. Brown. I was allowed the usual Armourer's tool box, a crate for spares; very useful to Donald and me, tea-making equipment seemed to be a high priority spare. I also included a spare blanket and ground sheet. Clean up the warehouse and here I am once again on a strange station (Forfar) and as usual it is bloody dark. Onto the train and even as we rattled along none of us had the slightest idea of where we were going. There had been several lectures on this issue and the need for absolute silence about our move though it must have been obvious to the townsfolk that the Battalion were certainly on the move somewhere.

Wherever or whatever, one thing was certain: no one on the Planet Earth must know where the Second Battalion The Hampshire Regiment were at this particular moment in time. During the day we had stopped for food at various places but were not allowed off the train. There were times when one of the Pioneer Platoon's Specials (at least a twelve seater), would have been welcome. All things come to an end and at around eight thirty in the morning we pulled into our final destination, detrained and where were we? Portsmouth Central Station. So much for the hush-hush aspect of our next job. Even as we formed up on the station platforms civilians were diving into the ranks with cries of 'Hello John, Harry, Fred, Ron and so on, we'll let your wife, mother, girl, uncle etc. know you are here.' Indeed unbeknown to me a message was already winging its way to Girl.

All quite simple really, The Regiment was a Hampshire County Regiment and had always recruited extensively from the County towns, especially Portsmouth, Southampton, Winchester and the Isle of Wight. And where was our final destination? The Isle of Wight, Shanklin to be precise. By the time we got to Shanklin I would guess everybody in Hampshire knew where we were. And the task in hand, nasty and dangerous, was to provide cover and specifically a distraction in support of a Commando raid into France. Our own landing was to be noisy and very visible in an effort to draw off German troops and thereby give the Commandos a better chance of success. Casualties would not be evacuated! Any volunteers out there? No, I thought not. The next few days were very comfortable; the QM staff were billeted in a hotel and Joan, unfortunately without Tony, managed a day in Shanklin with me: please don't ask.

So load up onto the ships, yes, yes, it is dark! Black up, this fortunately matches the dark; now I'm a bloody Commando. In the ship's mess there is a definitely ration-free supper. There was a barrage of last meal jokes; none of us were laughing. The whole thing was very scary though we had of course done some training. The ships ploughed on, then turned round and ploughed back, we disembarked, took off our make-up in the hotel and went to bed. What was all that about?

We are well into September and once again I am due to go on leave on 5 October. A quiet period this, enlivened for me by the case of the Purdy shotgun owned by a young officer and one of a pair that probably cost around five thousand pounds pre-war. Returning through the woods after a night training exercise the officer spooked a young deer and without thinking clobbered it with the butt of his lovely Purdy. Oh dear, when I saw that beautiful shattered Caucasian walnut I could have cried. 'Anything you can do, Armourer Sergeant?' Not really, I thought to myself, but foolishly said I would try. Once alone it quickly became evident that repair was impossible; it was going to need a new stock: this I could make but where to get suitable timber?

From the local auctioneer's! I often wandered in to watch and a few days after I had agreed to try a repair I found a large round table, very old and with a huge centre leg. I bid two shillings and sixpence and it was mine. A local carpenter stripped out the leg and trimmed it down to the correct size, perfect? Well, yes and no, the timber was mahogany. Ignoring this I carried on and carved out a new stock, matching it carefully to the old one. The mahogany proved easy to work with and even took the chequering well; I had expected the wood to be harder and tougher than it was. The main problem was weight and I couldn't really reduce this but there was a bonus; it polished beautifully, lacking the grain of walnut, nevertheless it looked good.

Strangely the balance felt comfortable and the Lieutenant was delighted with it. I was a bit pleased myself and I wonder sometimes whether there is a pair of Purdys somewhere, resplendent in a beautiful Purdy box, one gun stocked with Caucasian walnut and the other gun stocked with mahogany.

And so, to what was to prove my last time with Girl and Tony for some three years another wonderful nine days which simply flew. I was certainly pretty miserable when I got back. It was also the last time she would see me as a soldier of the Royal Army Ordnance Corps. On 1 October 1942, the Royal Electrical and Mechanical Engineers were formed and they embraced all of the old RAOC mechanical responsibilities: Armourers, Vehicle Mechanics, Gun Fitters, Instrument Mechanics etc. all moved into this new Corps. It was a massive change and though we didn't like it at the time it has worked very well. So there I was, back with the Battalion, Armourer S/gt C. Hoyle, REME (attached) but was I yet a soldier? The future stretched ahead, happily an unknown quantity. I was to find further and worse nightmares during the next two years. I was also full of despair at having left Girl and Tony behind yet again.

Strangely at this time the Battalion was very quiet. I seem to remember there was a definite feeling of foreboding about, unusual, as there had been a lack of rumours. I suppose we all knew deep down that our time in England was coming to an end.

And what of my friends? I had lost Gaffer of course, and was about to lose Jimmy Dunkley. Jimmy had been taken in to hospital suffering, and I mean suffering, from haemorrhoids. It had been a problem for a few months and finally they had decided to operate. I visited him in hospital and he was looking forward to rejoining the Battalion. In the event the Battalion moved before Jimmy was fit and it was a few years before we met up again when Girl, Tony and I spent a weekend with him and his wife at their home in Christchurch, near Bournemouth.

Joe Brown, now Corporal Brown, had been occupying a corner of my workshop. This had further cemented our friendship. Best of all, though, Tug Wilson was back and driving the QM 15 cwt., Jack Brown of course still driving the QM baggage lorry.

There were three additions to our little group, L/Corporal Donald Harris of course, and at long last, a shoemaker, Corporal William Holden: no, not the film star. Bill had been running his own business before being called up and was certainly a very fine craftsman, As soon as he reported in to the QM we took him under our wing and arranged for him to be billeted with us. Joe of course was delighted because he had been filling in for the shoemaker and could now concentrate on his forte, producing mugs of sweet tea when all seemed lost. There was one very interesting thing about our new shoemaker: his sister Beryl was married to George Formby.

We had lost the other two vehicle fitters from our Aldershot days, Frank Day, posted for promotion and Harry Drew posted to a Command Workshops also with a view to promotion. They had not yet been replaced. One important addition to the QM staff was Headquarter Company Sgt. MajorTrudgeTruran, promoted to Regimental Quartermaster Sergeant and becoming Northmore's number two. This rank, RQMS, was always the stepping stone to RSM and so it proved later in North Africa. It was pretty obvious at this time that the Battalion would soon be moving; apart from anything else we had been in England nearly two years, training most of the time with only the Boating Scheme and our abortive trip to Shanklin of any consequence. I had made it clear to Girl (and Tony as best I could) that in the short term we could be moving. There wasn't the slightest hint when or where we might go, it was a big war and so it could be almost anywhere in the world. Time to pray and keep the fingers crossed.

And so we moved, once again by train and once again in the bloody dark. We were certainly in the dark about where immediately or in the future we were ultimately bound, but there were signs in the weeks leading up to us moving that this time it was serious. Small things like inoculations, the packing of vehicles, the massive checking of equipment, particularly small arms, which involved me in many late nights, Everybody getting their personal lives in order. This was a period filled with worry and apprehension; everything seemed to pick up a momentum towards what? Most of us had endured a morale-sapping baptism of fire and it was too recent to be pushed to the back of our thoughts. We just didn't know and my goodness with hindsight we didn't want to know.

We were soon to know our immediate destination as we detrained yet again at Greenock but none of us dreamed for a moment that this was another boating exercise. It was grey and miserable and very soon we were being formed into files then up the gangway and onto a large ship. At this time, although it was after dawn (just), the light was poor so it was hard to make out what type of ship it was but as we collected cards detailing our accommodation and were shown where to go it was obvious that the ship was crewed by American civilians. All would soon be revealed. The first and apparently pleasant surprise was being shown to a nice cabin on the deck. There were three bunks and a washbasin but it wasn't very big. The sailor said, 'Pick a bunk, stow your kitbag and I'll be back later,' and so he was, first with Sgt Raddon, the QM clerk, next my old mate Joe Curley, then Ginger Salter, the Transport Sgt. This made up four of us but only three bunks. I had just found out what the odd mattress propped up against one of the bunks was for. Lucky I was first in.

This was going to be a pretty crowded trip no matter how long it took, but we were really comfortable compared with the lads who were occupying rows of narrow bunks, three high and with a narrow passage running along down the centre, These were running along the two decks below our deck. I have no idea how many of the Battalion were accommodated in these bunks, but the ship was packed to the brim.

I seem to remember there was a company of the Royal Engineers on board. This packing of troops boded ill and ill turned out to be the word.

The four of us got ourselves sorted out. Don Raddon had volunteered to occupy the floor, following promises not to tread on him. One thing, drink was not going to be a problem: this was an American ship and as such 'dry'. Our guide came back to take us for a meal and although we didn't realise it at the time we had been very lucky in that we had been allocated to the Gun Crews' mess. These were American soldiers manning the anti aircraft guns. As there were only about fifteen of them it was a very small mess but very luxurious and after months on rationing we found the food beyond belief. I remember that first morning as if it were yesterday. Our guide introduced us individually to everyone, we were given places at a large table complete with all the usual condiments and as we sat chatting to our new American friends a waiter came round asking us what we would like. A sort of funny question, the Americans had obviously finished their breakfast, the table had been cleared and they were just sat drinking coffee.

Someone, probably Joe Curley, asked politely what was available. 'Cereals with cream, eggs any way you want them and as many as you want, bacon, sausage; tell you what, as there are only four of you I'll bring it in and you can help yourselves.' What a feast it proved to be and we certainly did it justice. We were soon swapping yarns with the GIs and the voyage began to seem more than bearable. Arriving back at the cabin I went on deck. The ship was well under way and after standing at the rail for a while the cold forced me to set off back to the cabin. I was puzzled to see a long queue about two deep trailing round the deck until finally disappearing below; they were all carrying mess tins, mugs and 'eating irons'. This was about eleven in the morning. Apparently there were so many troops on board that there would only be two meals a day. The first would start at nine o'clock in the morning and the second around one o'clock. Throughout the voyage this system was a nightmare.

So there were two eating arrangements but lurking in the wings was the sea and a ship which from the day it was launched had pitched and rolled in a very unpleasant manner. The civilian crew had proved to be superb, nothing was too much trouble and their skills and devotion to helping the lads was to be sorely tested in the days ahead. The ship was the Coama, and many of the crew had been with her from the time she was launched. New York registered she had operated between there and Coama and according to the crew their main cargo was New York weekenders cruising down to *Coama* and back, mostly business men and as one of them delicately put it, with their secretaries. Others used a less delicate description I remember, 'Floating Brothel being one description. One thing they were all clear about, it had been a cracking ship to be on and very, very lucrative. As the days passed and we began to make firm friends amongst the crew their stories were really worth listening too.

Back in the cabin the four of us decided to spend an hour or so trying to get our bearings especially between the cabin and the Gun Crews' mess: always one must look to priorities: my goodness, was that a U-boat periscope? Never mind, at least we know our way to the Mess. As the others went off to find the Mess I decided that I ought to locate Ben. I think the last time I had spoken to him was when he stuck a needle in my arm and all I said was 'Ow'. Our friendship had become very close over the years so how to find him on a strange ship teaming with troops? Before I could set off a crew member popped his head round the corner asking if Sgt. Raddon was one of us and if so could I tell him to report to a Lt. Northmore. He gave me the Deck and Cabin number and in turn I asked if there was any sort of medical centre on the ship. A little huffily I thought he replied, 'If you mean a fully equipped hospital then we certainly do, Buddy, let's go, you feeling unwell?' I reassured him and sure enough, after diving hither and thither there we were in what was a superb, though small hospital. Our own medical team were there and Ben and I had a catch-up chat. I told him about our mess arrangements and Deck and Cabin number and that was the last I saw of Ben until we left the ship.

I told Don about the QM wanting a word; he went off and Ginger Joe and I went on deck. There wasn't much daylight left but it was soon obvious that we were part of a large convoy with accompanying frigates and destroyers and that we were well into our voyage, making steady progress but still without the faintest idea of where we might be going; at least we hadn't been issued with tropical kit. I seem to remember that we all remarked on the movement of the ship. The sea looked very calm but it was the first time I had really noticed this movement! What on earth did Northmore want Don for? This was sure to be unpleasant but what? It was beginning to get dark and we knew that the ship would be blacked out so back to the cabin and wait for Don then on to the mess for our evening meal.

Don arrived back with relatively good news. There was an American type NAAFI (Shop) being opened whilst the journey lasted and the Purser had been looking for volunteers to run it. Don had been volunteered by the QM and was quite happy about it especially as it included accommodation, which meant more room for us. Also, whatever was being sold we would have a friend in the right place. Whether or not the Purser had got a friend in the right place gave me pause for thought; after all, Don had worked closely with Gaffer for many years.

Arriving at the Mess we found that there wasn't a set time for anything but when you wanted a meal just turn up and literally ask for what you wanted. This system was due to the erratic hours of the gun crews. We thought it was a bit out of this world and I wished Girl and Tony could have sat down to the food we were being served, I remember one of the GIs recommending the turkey which appeared, together with a large and delicious ham, slice it yourself, this was getting ridiculous. By the way was it my imagination or was the boat moving about a bit more, especially up and down. Anyway we sat drinking coffee and chatting to our new found friends who, once Dunkirk was mentioned in the context of our having been there, dominated the rest of the evening.

I slept well but lying in bed thinking about getting up I became more and more conscious of the ship's movements, especially the seemingly long climb up and the long drop back. It was very smooth but disconcerting. I got up, but suddenly realised that it might be advisable to get up on deck. I abandoned my ablutions but once on deck I was literally surrounded by soldiers being sick; this didn't help my own unhappy stomach. I had no idea how long I was going to be able to survive without being sick but I battled on, walked around a lot and gradually began to feel better, finally returning to the cabin. My mates had disappeared but thankfully there was no evidence of a disaster so still having to exert some mental effort I finished washing and shaving and from that moment never looked back. I wouldn't dare offer this as a solution to avoiding sea-sickness but for me it was exactly as written. The other factor which I think was crucial, none of us in the cabin suffered with sickness. I had one more moment of doubt when I went in for breakfast next morning but I forced myself to nibble and with plenty of coffee things settled down. Only Joe Brown didn't make it for breakfast that morning but he was there for lunch and tucking in as if there was no tomorrow.

But there was a terrible tomorrow and the rest of the voyage was a nightmare of sea-sickness. With the troops packed in the mess decks, three bunks high and with only a narrow passage between the bunks, heaven only knows where the toilets were relative to the men. Within three or four days the decks were awash with vomit and the stench was indescribable. We were all working down there, but it was the Herculean efforts of the American crew members that kept the situation even partly manageable; they were truly magnificent and many lifelong friendships were forged during this time. Later, back on terra firma, Ben told me they had been battling in the hospital with three potential fatal cases plus many others who were seriously ill. I remember Syd Jacobs (Sergeants' Mess waiter) was one whose sickness was life threatening. The smell was again my biggest problem but once more I battled on and although all we could do was try and clean them up, fix changes of bedding and dispense medicine where appropriate there was for me a huge satisfaction in sticking it out. Six or seven days out from Greenock and the Battalion was indeed a sorry fighting force.

Writing this and remembering, there are no words that I could put together which would convey the suffering and indignity many of those lads suffered.

The journey was coming to an end and although we didn't know it, the gun crews certainly did and they were pretty certain which port we were heading for. Whether they had been told or simply worked it out I don't know but we were still kept in the dark. The convoy had suffered casualties but the only sign had been the frigates and destroyers suddenly bursting into action and dashing about. I cannot remember ever worrying about being attacked or sunk, we were so busy and preoccupied and at the end of the day, tired. I slept well.

Whenever I have been in a situation where facilities for washing and shaving were, shall we say, 'cramped', it has been my habit to get up early thereby avoiding the worst of the crowd. I had been doing this throughout the voyage and once finished would walk out on deck and look around, trying to recognise other ships in the convoy that had been there the day before. It was probably the eighth or ninth day and I was leaning on the rail watching what was obviously a tanker. It appeared to be a fair distance away from the *Coama* but the ship was big and near enough to be clearly seen. Suddenly, with no sound, the ship was obscured by a huge black cloud of smoke, no flames, just the smoke which climbed into the sky and where the ship had been there was nothing. All of this in seconds. The deck soon filled with troops but there was nothing to be seen until the Navy appeared. The destroyer flat out was certainly a wonderful sight but too late, too late. Soon we had moved on and the incident had assumed a dreamlike quality.

The following day we were alerted for disembarkation and late evening we docked just outside Algiers. So that had been our destination and so 'Operation Torch', the invasion of North Africa, had begun. I wondered how long it would be before it was reported at home and when they did, I knew Girl would know instantly where I was. It seemed a bloody long way and we had only just started. Though dark, (please believe me) it was a mild balmy evening and we began to form up. We were carrying full marching order less our kitbags which we had previously piled neatly on the docks; these were to come later by truck and would meet us wherever it was we were going, sounded good. We never saw them again!

B Echelon formed up and bringing up the rear were Joe Brown, Don Raddon, our new friend Bill the shoemaker, always referred to as Shoey, myself and of course, Donald Harris. We didn't need to be told what was next though how far would have been nice. I had some concerns about Shoey; he said foot slogging was something totally new to him so we quickly worked through the jokes about the possible advantages of being a shoemaker when faced with a long march, offered some very sound practical advice and promised to look after him. How did I know it was going to be a long march? Simple, they always bloody were! I should have said earlier that I always carried more than anyone else in the shape of the 'Bags Tool Armourer'; this was a small leather bag containing as few so called necessary tools as I could get away with. Remembering that I'm still a small package I should miss being able to hang it on Gaffer; indeed we all would because he never refused an extra burden when our little group were slogging it out. Equipment straps were my Achilles heel; not having any real sort of covering of muscle or fat they soon began to cut into my shoulders and this became very painful!

So we were formed up, shuffling about waiting for the starting gun, when the first bomb dropped, not close but there were a lot to follow. We dived for cover, my mouth dried up and Joe offered the opinion that they were Junker 88s. I thought he was just showing off, it was pitch dark! He turned out to be right; nevertheless, I ought to have known by this time that when Joe pronounced on an aircraft he was always right, even in the dark. Oh shit, welcome once again to the real war. The raid didn't last long and we were soon on our way, quickly settling into the rhythm and in my case blocking everything out thinking of Girl and Tony and our last leave together. I also found time to wonder how my other friends were getting along, being Transport they were probably on another ship but I hadn't seen them since leaving Forfar. I am of course referring to Jack Brown and Tug Wilson.

We had quite a bit to chat about. How had Don got on in the shop? We had noticed his kitbag was very heavy, indeed, at one stage I had helped him with it. Whether it was stuffed with goods or money I never found out but anyway it was academic, as I said we never saw them again. After Don left the cabin we had sort of smuggled Donald, my erstwhile assistant, in to take his place. I say smuggled because it was a 'rank thing'. The cabin was allocated for senior ranks. It didn't matter as long as Ginger and Joe Curley were happy and indeed he also ate with us in the gun mess and certainly no one there ever noticed his lack of three stripes. He was also more than happy to sleep on the floor and like the rest of us he wasn't sick.

By the time we were at the stage of simply concentrating on the next step we had learned most of Shoey's history. At about five miles Shoey had begun to flag; luckily his feet weren't too bad, Ben, who was travelling in the Battalion first aid lorry, caught up with us to see how our feet were holding out and it was good to see my closest friend again. We had a good chat whilst he did a few running repairs especially on Don Raddon who was already suffering with blisters. One good thing, Ben could tell us was how far it was likely to be; they had to tell the medics so they could prepare properly. A pretty complicated thing this soldiering and one thing I had learned, making the right friends in the right places (as for instance my friendship with both the Adjutant and the RSM and not least having the ear of the Commanding Officer, who genuinely admired my batting), meant I was getting close to being able to call myself a soldier…really?

What about Stukas and the nasty things like that you might ask. Unfortunately the only help from a Stuka was a short cut to the Pearly Gates. I never heard of one sewing stripes on your arm. Improving your sprint time maybe but stripes no. But I digress, How far was it? Nine miles! Not a particularly spectacular distance as I look back but at the time a killer. So where did it end? Surprise surprise, in a bloody farmyard.

Morning revealed we were being billeted in the general outbuildings of a large and very well equipped farm. It didn't take us long to make ourselves reasonably comfortable and get our kit together but where were those kitbags? None of us were happy at the thought of losing them: never mind things like spare clothing, we had all stocked up on the luxuries from the *Coama* shop and for smokers this meant masses of Chesterfield cigarettes. As a non-smoker my own was pretty well stocked with chocolate and funnily enough tins of salted nuts, delicious.

I had never stopped writing letters since leaving. The drill was to write it, and hand it into the Company Office or equivalent where it would be censored and hopefully dispatched in the general direction of UK This writing letters to a loved one knowing it would be read and censored took a bit of getting used to but I was well practised by this time. What I and everyone else really wanted were letters arriving. No sign yet. CorporalTim Budden, the post Corporal, came in for a lot of pestering at this time but I clearly remember Tim having a very equable temperament and believe me there were times when he needed it.

Once again we were in limbo, not a decent rumour in sight. I think the trouble was that the Pioneer Platoon when faced with the small numbers of a B Echelon had gone off multi-seaters and we were managing with a miserable two-seater, a decent rumour never came out of one of those. On the second day we were on the move and it had a distinctly urgent feel about it, which is never reassuring. The transport mind you was more than a little familiar as in France, ten horses or forty men. We had marched to a small station and with very little warning so it had been a bit of a scramble and when you have just landed with the object of clearing the Germans out of North Africa one cannot escape wondering what the hell has gone wrong. As so often happens in war, we were being rushed to plug a gap, though history showed us much later that it was a much more complicated cock-up than just a gap. In the next few days it was going to turn into as nasty a gap as can be imagined, a nightmare in fact, and many many of the Battalion now settling down into what was a long journey would not survive.

Our own little gang settled down, plenty of straw and plenty of room. As the day wore on it became hot and the journey was comfortable. We sat with our legs dangling out and the mood was very relaxed. The countryside was mostly pretty flat and barren looking, though much later there were massive cornfields and equally massive looking farms. We stopped for food and the mugs of tea were more than welcome but I cannot remember the timing. We certainly spent a full day and night on the train until we stopped just outside Constantine where facilities for washing and shaving had been provided but no provision for bowel movements. Come back, the Pioneer Platoon, all is forgiven! I have a lasting image of looking across the railway line to a bank of earth where a long row of white bums were doing what bums are for. I suppose it could have been described as a mass evacuation.

Once again there was the unmistakeable feeling of haste and we were soon off again. Bill (Shoey) had settled into the group and it all ready felt as if he had always been there. We were an odd assortment to be setting off to clear the Germans out of North Africa: a Shoemaker, Equipment Repairer, Armourer, Assistant Armourer and the QM clerk. Still enough to make up four for the inevitable Solo, known in posher circles as 'poor man's bridge'. Nevertheless it was a very demanding game and faced with big money in the kitty, required the utmost concentration. Making a mistake that allows someone to take the kitty was not a way to make friends and influence people. A little research has suggested this must have been somewhere around 25 November.

We stopped twice more, once at Souk El Arba and once at Souk el Kemis. Here we stopped for a brief while, enabling us to stretch our legs. Wandering around we found ample evidence that Germans had rested up in this area very recently. We were soon on our way again. Our next stop saw the end of our train journey at Medjez el Bab; we were to get to know this place well, a relatively small town with large railway sidings. Once off the train we moved out to a wooded area. It was noticeable by this time that we were no longer at Brigade strength and indeed the Guards Battalions had been left behind in Algiers to perform some form of ceremonial for one of the French politicians. So here we were at Battalion strength, resting after our train journey in a wood a mile or so outside Medjez el Bab. Almost the first thing we found was a mass grave where members of the Northants Regiment had been buried, and very recently. This had a profound effect on us all. We still did not know what our ultimate task was but this evidence of what had gone before was massively sobering.

Once again, welcome to the real war, Clem! Nothing to do but make ourselves comfortable and wait. An hour or two later I had a message to go and see the Quartermaster. I found him the centre of some sort of excitement. This turned out to be a senior French officer complete with staff car which showed every sign of having tangled with an aircraft cannon; noting the big holes here and there I had instantly and quite brilliantly diagnosed this. The QM was trying to talk to the officer in English and in turn the officer was replying in French, there was a certain amount of frustration involved. I didn't help by suggesting to Northmore it was a pity Gaffer wasn't there. He sort of wiped the smile off my face by taking me round the other side of the car and pointing out an explosive cannon shell lodged in the door panel. I had been wondering why he had brought me in to it rather than one of the vehicle fitters. I knew now. Our French friend wanted it taken out so he could push on.

At no time during my training had I practised taking a live explosive cannon shell out of the door of a car. They always forget something! The one thing I had learned on my booby trap course in Scotland was to keep well back, the further the better. I had already noticed the QM was almost out of shouting distance so he was fully aware of this maxim. Why the bloody hell had it failed to explode? There was a crowd by this time so I was in a hopeless position made all the more difficult by our French Officer hovering around expectantly at a safe distance. Ignoring my dry mouth I walked over to the cannon shell and for want of a better idea, I very gingerly got hold of the end sticking out, it was loose! A slight pull and the shell was out. The lads cheered, the officer shook my hand and thanked me and I hurried away and buried it, at the same time trying to stop shaking whilst adopting an air of casual indifference. A strange interlude at this particular time but very vivid in my memory.

CHAPTER 10
TEBOURBA GAP 1942

Just after dark, we climbed into lorries supplied by the RASC and moved out through Medjez el Bab, over a recently erected Bailey bridge and into the darkness. No one was talking. We had been briefed during the afternoon and our task was to press on to Tunis. Intelligence had said that the Germans were moving back to Tunis and were looking to evacuate their troops. We were to dig in at a place called Tebourba ready for an assault on what was a German Headquarters at the small town of Djedeia. This would open a clear run into Tunis. We were well protected along our flanks by the River Medjerda, a deep gorge river, on one side and on the other the Jebel Munchar range of mountains. Both of these natural objects had prevented the Germans bringing up tanks or Infantry.

Well, well! Intelligence is only as good as its accuracy and if it isn't accurate then it is rubbish and more often than not deadly rubbish for the troops who must act on it, and so it turned out to be for us. We sat there listening to the awful whining of a Bedford RL transmission, all of us busy with our own particular nightmares; meanwhile the Germans were reinforcing Tebourba with Infantry and tanks, even the dreaded 'Tiger'. What on earth had happened to the River Medjerda and the Jebel Munchar mountains? Ignorance is quite definitely bliss. Things began to go awry almost immediately; the truck carrying elements of 'W' Company went off the road and turned on its side, as a result of which the Company lost two platoons. Travelling like this, in the dark with no lights, was always fraught with difficulty and danger.

To disperse a Battalion of some eight hundred men into position, in the dark and eventually to get them into the best formation for whatever is planned is as near impossible as makes no difference. Add in the necessity to supply them with food and drink during this deployment ensures that only a disciplined force could even attempt it. We got on with it and finally in our own little area prepared to dig in. We were immediately faced with a disaster of massive proportions, it was impossible to even break the surface of what was basically a clay soil baked hard until it resembled concrete. We only had the normal entrenching tool, a kind of combined spade and pick. This proved to be hopeless and only a pick-axe made any impression on this ground. How many did the Battalion possess? I hadn't the faintest idea, each Company had its entitlement and the Pioneer Platoon had one per man but already the QM was coming under pressure to provide more and this too was impossible, we simply didn't have any more.

Here we were, starting under a serious handicap which ultimately would contribute directly to many deaths and injuries and in its own way affect the efficiency of everybody. Trying to find positions in the dark, relative to the other soldiers in your Platoon and also relative to the whole plan, is very difficult; the darkness alters your judgement of distances so much that I learned early on never to trust this judgement but always to pace it out. Irrespective of the battle situation it could be just arriving at a position in the dark and as always digging your own personal slit trench against possible air attack then finding come daylight that everybody has dug in almost next to each other. This time I along with Shoey and Joe dug in between the railway lines which were running alongside a wood which seemed to be the focus of our deployment. At least until we could find a 'pick' it seemed to give the best protection. We then located Battalion HQ and reported our position, followed by an uncomfortable night trying to sleep; it was very cold. With our briefing still fresh in my mind I slept dreaming of thousands of German soldiers pouring up the gangways as they set sail from Tunis back to Italy.

The morning brought a rude awakening along with the bombing and shelling of our positions and suddenly the Battalion really was at war, X Company had been attacked by Infantry brought into battle in a half track vehicle, the half track had been destroyed and the position restored but here again I was on the fringes and this information came from a visit to Headquarter Company. My problem, as well as survival, was to find a role for myself and the other two. At this time I was totally out of communication with the Companies who might possibly have needed my assistance; meanwhile the three of us improved our position, managing to dig in a little deeper with our trenching tool and discussed what form our defence would take if we were attacked. During the afternoon it became very obvious that on our front somewhere there was a battle going on, the slow fire of our Brens mixed with the fast spurt of bursts from the German MGs. There were occasional periods of what I thought was artillery shelling but which I was to learn later were German 88 mm mortars.

A wide awake night. It was relatively quiet but with the odd burst of fire or mortar shell somewhere down the railway line. Just after midnight and hopefully during a lull I took my dry mouth back to Headquarters and was told to stay put and if attacked, resist and report as soon as practical and anyway we were to join Headquarters as soon as things quietened down. We had no communication (I didn't do flags) but we would be contacted by a Company runner. I was told that the lads were giving a more than good account of themselves and indeed one of the rifle companies had prisoners to show for it. Some how this reassured me a little but from what I had picked up unofficially from some of the lads the big worry was supply. At this time we had none, no food, no ammunition and more seriously no water. Fortunately the water bowser was tucked away somewhere as were the ammunition trucks but how to get them to where they were needed? I reported to Joe and Shoey and so we decided to make a big effort to build ourselves a really good defensive position. Joe disappeared and came back with a pick-axe; amazingly the baggage lorry was still there and Jack Brown had been vigorously wielding what he claimed was the only pick axe left but the Armourer Sergeant was more than welcome to it, a little favour long ago still paying dividends. Aldershot, cricket, tennis, shooting, snooker in the Corporals' Mess and a driver who had never driven before, God, how long ago it seemed and even longer ago Girl and Tony, at least blissfully unaware of what the old man is up to at this particular moment. God, who's this dodging his way down the rails? A fraught moment turns into an Assistant Armourer. Where the hell have you been, Donald? As the JU 88s turned lazily in our direction and dropped their bombs I never did get an answer. At least there were four of us now that is four rifles and one hundred rounds of ammunition each. I must make an effort to pick up a Bren gun and ammunition.

We were becoming conscious of another problem, food and drink, and as the day wore on and the temperature climbed, water became urgent. The only food we had was our emergency ration, something like a chocolate block which could only

FIFTY YEARS ON - THE BATTLE OF TEBOURBA, TUNISIA

This is a condensed account of the extremely gallant action fought by the 2nd Battalion, The Hampshire Regiment, in Tunisia in November/December, 1942.

It was fought at a time when the newly hatched North African Campaign was suffering little but discouragement in its efforts to reach Tunis. The 2nd Battalion's stubborn determination to stand and fight the enemy was said to have had an infectiously inspiring effect through the whole of the First Army. Not only did the action merit a separate despatch in a contemporary edition of the Times, but it was also cited by no less than King George V when addressing a military parade at Aldershot, (Quote) "I recommend you to read the story of the 2nd Battalion The Hampshire Regiment in Tunisia. That was a triumph of individual leadership and corporate discipline" (Unquote).

First Day - 30th NOVEMBER

The Battalion is in position along a strip of eucalyptus wood 30-40 yards wide, alongside a railway line. Two companies are forward, on the right, X Company, covering the end of the wood and the right flank. On the left, Y Company, on a feature running at right angles to the wood. Battalion HQ and the remaining two rifle companies, W and Z, are positioned in echelon along the wood covering the flanks and rear. W Company is already deficient of two of its platoons through sheer bad luck. Considerable air activity during morning - occasional shelling by the enemy - our own artil'ery ranging for defensive tasks. During afternoon - ground activity on right front beyond X Company - infantry-carrying half track knocked out - enemy withdraw. Night fighting patrols from Z Company reach out 1½ miles to Djedeia - no enemy contact - return safely.

Second Day - 1st DECEMBER

Morning - OP's report enemy activity along whole Battalion front, enemy starts attack, supported by artillery, in front of Y Company - considerable small arms and automatic fire - attack peters out - enemy clearly seen off by Y Company. Early p.m. - OC X Company reports enemy infantry attacking from his right front across railway line - enemy get into position forward of X Company - immediate counter attack by X Company with bayonets fixed - enemy driven off - German paratroopers taken prisoner. Late afternoon - enemy occupy farm buildings in front of and between both forward Companies - Z Company ordered to counter attack with one platoon - attack goes in supported by artillery - farm retaken, but many casualties, including platoon Commander - insufficient men to hold farm, which is very exposed - platoon withdrawn, leaving many wounded. That night, Lieutenant E.G. Wright of Z Company, already wounded in leg, takes out patrol - extremely dark - navigates to farm - locates and brings back eight wounded men, and seven previously reported missing - .a dangerous and humane achievement, professionally executed. For this act of outstanding leadership and courage, Lieutenant E.G. Wright was awarded the MC.

1

Third Day - 2nd DECEMBER

Enemy MG's in position firing on both forward companies - enemy attacks with infantry, supported by tanks - own artillery brings down defensive fire - Y Company on left under heavy pressure - enemy tanks in right forward platoon locality, firing directly into slit trenches - platoon decimated. Tank now between two forward companies - fires into Battalion HQ area - direct hit on Battalion Signals carrier - Signals Officer killed together with five signallers - rear radio link severed to Brigade HQ. Severe and bitter fighting now raging in X Company's position - enemy infantry attacking - repeated counter attacks - many led personally by Company Commander - casualties mounting - 2 pounder anti-tank gun supporting X Company receives direct hit - crew killed - tanks now in X Company area, slewing over slit trenches trapping occupants - X Company rallied by Company Commander - counter attacks through tanks to enemy beyond - possibly now five or six men left, including Company Commander and his CSM - German "Tiger" tank now identified in action for first time - X Company now virtually non-existent - OC X Company hit by two separate bursts of automatic fire. For his display of outstanding leadership and fearlessness in the face of most discouraging odds, Captain C.L. Thomas, OC X Company, was later awarded the DSO.

W Company now ordered forward to cover gap left by X Company - Battalion second-in-command killed in Battalion HQ area by MG fire - OC W Company reports enemy infiltrating down wood towards his position - OC Z Company ordered to counter attack with one platoon - up the wood they go, bayonets fixed, tails up, right through to X Company's old position - back they come - Platoon Commander, Platoon Sergeant, and four men wounded - six enemy paratroopers captured.

Lull now occurs in vicinity of wood, but Y Company forward on the left still under artillery and mortar fire - out of radio contact - enemy infantry seen beyond Y Company's left flank - their situation obscure - OC Y Company sends runner with message to Battalion HQ - shot by MG fire as he tries to traverse open ground - two more runners sent, who manage to reach Battalion HQ - Y Company still holding position - heavy casualties - ammunition running low - no water left - plight desperate.

Commanding Officer orders vehicle carrying ammunition and water to get to Y Company - hit as it starts to cross open ground - an Officer now ordered to take a carrier, suitably laden, and relieve the beleagured company - takes circuitous zig-zag course - successfully reaches Y Company - returns with wounded.

Situation as darkness falls on this third day - W Company has one platoon - X Company non-existent - Y Company perhaps one and a half platoons - Z Company two weak platoons - Battalion anti-tank guns two left out of four - Battalion has had no sleep, and is beginning to wear a bit thin at the edges.

2330 hrs - Officer from Brigade manages to reach Battalion HQ - Battalion to move 1½ miles to new position at rear, and be dug in by dawn.

2

Fourth Day - 3rd DECEMBER

At 0130 hrs Battalion starts what was later described as an "immaculate withdrawal" - complete silence - companies thin out - disengagement from enemy complete - reach new positions - start digging - discipline unchanged - morale remarkably high.

Battalion now positioned between a river on the right, and high ground, including point 186 on left, which dominates Battalion area. W Company is on right, covering as far as the river - Z Company on left occupying high ground and Point 186 - Y Company at rear, covering gap between W and Z Companies.

Early morning - infantry and tanks held off in front of W Company - attack develops on Battalion's left flank - and high ground held by Z Company. Noon - OC Z Company reports enemy established on high ground further to his left, previously held by neighbouring Battalion - Z Company's left platoon on Point 186 now under MG fire - Z Company position now threatened, and with it the Battalion's left flank - Z Company attempts to retake high ground - driven off by MG fire - more casualties - very few men now remaining on that hill - Major H.W. Le Patourel, OC Z Company, personally leads five or six volunteers towards Point 186 in a desperate attempt to silence the enemy MG's - he attacks three separate positions - each assault exacts inevitable casualties - finally, with no men left, he goes forward alone with pistol and grenades, to put in final assault - he does not return.   For this most gallant action, Major Le Patourel was awarded a posthumous VC.   (Later reported badly wounded and a prisoner of war). Situation now becoming confused - by late afternoon W and Y Companies have held off repeated attacks - at dusk enemy supported by tanks breakthrough on right - W Company restores position with resolute counter-attack, led by Company Commander - infantry now attacks Y Company from front - driven off - under failing light not easy to tell friend or foe.

Darkness sets in - Battalion strength now about 10 Officers, and less than 200 men - forms enclave around Battalion HQ - all ranks arm themselves with weapons and ammunition taken from casualties and dead - Battalion breaks out of enclave - sporadic and confused fighting in dark - continues along line of railway towards Tebourba outskirts - they were there.

Unfortunately the remaining troops of the Brigade had been withdrawn from Tebourba, and the final escape routes were now blocked off with enemy tanks straddling the roads, and MG's firing on fixed lines.   It was a bitter disappointment.   The Commanding Officer ordered those remaining to organise themselves into small groups, and to work their way back as best they could.   Two days later the last remnants of the 2nd Battalion assembled at a "Collection Point" some twelve miles to the west.   There were four Officers and just on 120 men.   For his action at the Battle of Tebourba, Lieutenant Colonel J.M. Lee was awarded the DSO.

Total awards for Gallantry were - one VC and two DSO's. Five MC's; four MM's; and a number of Mentions in Despatches. Inevitably and regrettably numerous acts of courage went unrecorded.

3

1

THE VIEW FROM THE OTHER SIDE

EXTRACTS FROM THE DIARY OF LEUTNANT HANS HOLLER (PANZER JAGER)

A report on his squads participation in the battle of Tebourba Gap.
1st and 2nd December 1942.

FEBRUARY 1941 :-   Commenced Military Service with Panzer Jager Abt.
33 (Anti-Tank Battalion, 15th Panzer Div. Africa
Corps.)

JULY - OCTOBER 1941 :- At Tobruk - Sollum - Haifaya Pass - then returned
ill to European Hospital.

OCTOBER 1942 :-   Attended Weapons School, promoted to Leutnant.

NOVEMBER 1942 :-   Sent to Naples, and then by Junkers 52 to Bizerta,
but the landing field had been badly bombed, and we
could not land, and were diverted to Tunis.
Myself, and 35 boys were equipped with MG42 machine
guns, and were sent to the Railway Station at
Jedeida, Tebourba, on the right side of which was a
Eucalyptus wood.   The battlefield, from the
previous days fighting, showed all destroyed, shot
to pieces.   Dead and wounded were found from both
sides.   During the next day we got into position,
the "Tommy" shot all day with sweeping artillery
fire.

DECEMBER 1st :-   We attacked, we had one Luftwaffe 2cm. cannon, and
some Paratroopers from Battlegroup Koch, (Paratroop
Regt. 5) supporting us.   The farmhouse on the
right at 300 metres was burning.   The "Tommies",
tucked away behind the hill, prevented us going any
further.   The situation was very sticky.   In the
evening we dug in, each man separate, and the
artillery was always shooting.   A wounded "Tommy"
was laying 50 metres in front of us in the branches
and leaves, but only when it was getting dark was
it possible to fetch him, he had a shot through the
lung.

DECEMBER 2nd :-   I had orders to start an attack at 0700hrs. after a
barrage from our artillery - Panzer support was
also promised.   At 0700hrs we were at the bottom
of the hill, our artillery fired only ten shells,
all falling much too short, but we were lucky, but
had to attack without the artillery support, but to
get over the hill was not possible, so I then
ordered to deploy to the left, cross the railway,
and attack from the side, to gain the hill.
During the crossing of the railway we suffered
casualties, but we did get nearer.   On our left
again was a field and a lovely house, which had
British "Tommies" inside, but they were virtually
surrounded.

be eaten when authorised by the CO and of course we each had a water bottle. Time for Donald and Joe to find the water truck and fill our bottles, except moving was becoming dangerous to say the least. They went anyway, returning after a worrisome wait with the bottles filled and three bandoliers of ammunition, another hundred and fifty rounds. I warned, using my rank, that the water must be conserved, at any time a mortar shell or bomb could destroy the water truck. Though I had no idea how long we were going to be here I already knew deep down that the Battalion was in very serious trouble. Little did I realise.

The next day we reported to HQ as ordered. Donald and Joe were to act as Company runners for the time being but my old friend, Company Sgt. Major TrudgeTruran, Sgt. Joe Curley, myself and strangely a Boys' anti-tank rifle which had been brought in with a 'faulty' bolt. Where was Girl? We were being sent to recce the ground beyond the trees and west of the railway line. Well, I did have first choice all those years ago and I had chosen the 2nd Hampshires so just get on with it. I picked up a magazine of five rounds for the Boys' anti-tank rifle and got on with it. After carefully picking our way through the trees and surviving a nasty hazard in that mortar bombs dropping amongst trees exploded at tree height, the bombs just kept coming and we needed all the luck to get through.

We finally broke out into open country. There was nothing to be seen except to our left a clump of bushy trees. The ground was flat but sloped away markedly on our right. Trudge decided we should press on and check the bushes but he also expressed a worry about how quiet it was. I had already said this to Joe. I had also expressed concern toTrudgeabout how exposed we were. Within minutes our fears were realised as we heard the unmistakable noise of tanks coming from our right where the ground sloped away. The tanks showed almost immediately, three cresting the rise in line astern and unquestionably with us in their sights. I recognised them as Mk IIIs and what a big help that was. I suppose as they came into sight they would have been some three hundred yards away. The tanks changed to line abreast formation and opened fire and to use a cliché, they were closing fast. I write this and wonder: did this really happen? It did. We had gone to ground pretty quickly and their fire was strangely inaccurate.Trudgeseemed to be unbelievably composed, taking the anti-tank rifle and the five rounds and ordering us to engage all three tanks with rifle fire. This would have absolutely no physical effect on the tanks but it kept them closed down, severely limiting their vision. So here we were,Trudgewas striking sparks off the tracks of the nearest tank with his five rounds and Joe and I were banging away with our rifles to absolutely no effect. The tanks just kept coming. I remember how desperately frightened I was when the tanks first appeared and again when they opened fire but as I settled to the futile task of engaging them with rifle fire, I felt strangely calm, a sort of flat feeling, maybe it was resignation.Trudgeas far as I could judge might just as easily have been on the range. I suppose he was frightened but he never showed it. I never ever forgot the strength he showed. We had always been good friends but I never look back without thinking ofTrudgeTruran, Company Sgt. Major, as the epitome of a British soldier, courageous and calm.

At this point Joe was hit,Trudgetook his rifle and I started to try and help Joe; the tanks were now only some thirty yards away. Suddenly there was a loud thump from the cover behind us and the tracks on one side of the leading tank were torn off in a cloud of dust, as spectacular as it was unbelievable. A second shot hit the turret of the second tank, richocheting off in a shower of sparks. This tank and the one not yet hit simply turned and retreated. Suddenly it was quiet and nothing was making any sense until three gunners appeared cautiously out of the cover where they had been nursing a sick 25-pounder gun, with just two rounds of armour piercing ammunition.

There was a lull whilst we all gathered our wits and speaking personally, a faint hope that my heart might return to a more normal rate. Meanwhile nothing had moved on or around the disabled tank.Trudgethen decided that he and I (sorry heart) would approach the tank to check whether the crew were wounded and in need of first aid. Myself, I felt it was more likely they were lurking behind it somewhere waiting to open fire at point blank range. The fifty yards we had to cover to reach the tank was the longest fifty yards of my life and seemed to take an age. We were of course carrying our rifles at the ready but an empty rifle is strangely useless. NeitherTrudgenor I had said anything, it was ominously quiet then suddenly the crew appeared from behind the tank, hands in the air and anxious to surrender.

The Gunners took Joe and the prisoners; they were going to spike the gun and then get back in their truck which meant Joe could get treatment to what was a nasty bullet wound just above the hip. We didn't know at the time that the Battalion was virtually cut off and the Gunners didn't make it, Joe eventually turning up months later in a POW camp. Once the crew had been secured Trudge and I had a look round inside the tank. Somehow a camera stuck to Trudge's fingers, and to mine, with Joe in mind, a very nice pair of Zeiss binoculars

'Trudge' and I cautiously and slowly made our way back to HQ to report. It was obvious to us that the situation must be deteriorating; mortar fire followed us all the way back plus air attacks from the Ju.88s HQ was a mess. A tank had penetrated between the Companies and attacked the Signals Platoon carrier, killing the Signals Officer and five Signallers including my friend the Signal Sergeant. Our direct radio communications were completely severed but the Intelligence Sergeant told me the sets, true to form, hadn't functioned properly even before the attack. Joe and Donald had both been sent, one to contact X Company Commander and the other to try and reach Y Company. They had not returned and this concerned me greatly, Trudge promised to keep their non appearance in mind but nothing was coming out of X Company at this time. They were very heavily involved and finally the Company Sergeant Major, Lew Garlic, though wounded, arrived at HQ to report that X Company had been over-run by tanks suffering heavy casualties and were virtually non-existent as a Company. His report was horrific. The tanks had broken through then returned driving up and down the trenches using the tracks to crush the soldiers who were still firing at them.

During the time I had been away Shoey had been making himself useful trying to fill water bottles for the lads at HQ. This simple chore was in itself worth a medal; reaching and getting back from the water truck had become almost suicidal. About this time an attempt to get the water and the ammunition truck to Y Company resulted in them both being destroyed. Sometime during this period that I was at HQ the Battalion Second in Command, Major Chamberlain a was killed just outside the Headquarters by machine gun fire. I asked permission from the Adjutant to take Shoey and try to reach the Battalion first aid post. I was sure I could be useful there, I did have a first aid qualification so on the strength of this we were sent off. First we had to cross the ground where Major Chamberlain had been killed but it was quiet. I also wanted to contact Ben who I hadn't seen since the march from Algiers and I was worried as there had been no communication with the Aid Post.

We were all becoming very ragged both physically and mentally. This was the third day without food and only a little water and the constant noise, and most of all the permanent state of fear, were taking a heavy toll. A report was received that a Platoon of "Z" Company had put in a bayonet attack resulting in the capture of six German paratroopers but at a heavy cost. And so Shoey and I set off to find the first aid post. It is impossible to describe what was happening; one thing was certain: we were trapped in a tight perimeter, not able to get anything in or out, and to move at all was to invite wounding or worse. The Germans had kept up a steady and unremitting barrage of mortar fire. It was impossible to decide the better option, wooded or open ground, but either way they were exacting a heavy price in casualties. Our morale was badly hit by the feeling of being trapped, this was a battle we were not going to win but I know now that at no time did the Battalion stop fighting. This was the end of the third day and the light was fading as we tried to locate the farm building where they had set up the first aid post. We desperately needed any Company soldier who would be certain to know; alas, we found two but they were dead. I had known one of them by sight. We found a half dug slit trench and with the mortar fire increasing I decided to wait until it was darker. We had what looked like Ju.88s overhead. At this moment a crouching figure running hard appeared, well, well, if it wasn't Tacker Knight, he of the broken football trophy. Before we had a chance to exchange pleasantries a bomb arrived, blowing Tacker off his feet. We got over as quickly as possible but when Shoey and I turned him over I could see about five inches of his spine. Almost a final straw. I dressed the wound using his field dressing whilst chatting about football. He seemed remarkably unperturbed but he did direct us to the First Aid Post. I made him comfortable and Bill and I set off for the First Aid Post and some professional help

The truth was that neither of us was in a fit state to move quickly but we needed to move and move we did, not only move but luck took us into the First Aid Post or what was left of the building. Ben was virtually at an end, wounded early, and he was working with a piece of shell stuck out of his skull. The Doctor had decided the best thing was to leave well alone and excuse him wearing a hat. Like Ben, Sgt. Rogers was still battling on but also like Ben stumbling and falling over from time to time. The inside of the building looked like a slaughterhouse; there were a number of wounded lying among the debris. Some had obviously been treated but only with their field dressings. Ben took me along to the Doctor who had collapsed not long before and was sitting propped up against the wall and looked like death. The place stank of fresh blood, sweat, faeces and fear. We went outside; mercifully it was dark by this time but outside were the wounded who could not be treated but had been made as comfortable as possible except they had no cover and were being wounded again and in some cases killed. So much for professional help. Ben said it would be better if Tacker was brought to the Aid Post; at least they had water and an odd soiled blanket and I mean soiled. Two of the stretcher bearers offered to bring Tacker in after I assured them it wasn't very far. I shamefully asked Bill to show them where he was.

Ben said they had run out of all medical supplies early on the second day and had been resorting to using anything to hand, this basically meant field dressings. It was a Court Martial crime to use your own field dressing on somebody else; harsh as this sounds the wisdom of it was all around me. Ben said there had been one blessing in all this: the Doctor, a young surgeon in a previous life, had been so disgusted with the contents of the medical pannier that he had brought a large quantity of morphine with his own kit. This had finally run out a few hours previously but had provided the stretcher bearers and the medical staff with a morale boost that was incalculable. We made Tacker as comfortable as possible outside and Bill and I simply crashed out.

Later on this third day during the night or early morning the Battalion pulled back to the rear. It was well done though for what reason I'll never know but we of the First Aid Post didn't move, for several reasons: we could hardly stand on our feet, the Medical Officer was still in a state of collapse, we were surrounded by seriously wounded soldiers and we had simply collapsed into an exhausted sleep, and we were still being mortared. It is a measure of our physical state that we slept through the mortar fire.

So dawned the fourth day. It was obvious there was no let-up in the battle so I decided that Shoey and I would attempt to get back to Headquarters, not easy as they had moved during the night, Ben and Sgt. Rogers could not of course leave the wounded, which now included the Medical Officer, so along with two stretcher bearers they stayed. After a fraught struggle we finally contacted HQ and reported in, where we found the position was dire. Throughout the afternoon an occasional report would filter in courtesy of one of the very brave Company runners; these reports consisted almost entirely of small but desperate battles being fought with diminishing ammunition and no water and with heavy casualties. The first use of Tiger tanks was also reported. The day wore on and every hour you survived was a bonus. As darkness set in, the Commanding Officer, Colonel J.M. Lee, formed us into a Company; by this time the Battalion strength was down to ten officers and fewer than two hundred men. Following the line of the railway we literally fought our way into Tebourba only to find the Brigade had withdrawn the remaining troops and our final escape routes had been blocked off by German tanks and machine guns set up to fire on fixed lines. We had already in our desperate attempts to reach this far been caught by those machine guns and they claimed many lives. We really had reached the end. At this point the Battalion had been reduced to four officers and fewer than one hundred and twenty men.

I have, all these years later, tried to recapture the way I felt at this moment but it is impossible. From the morning of the first day I had been subjected to a mental and physical battering without let-up, one terror led directly into the next. Added to this was the lack of food and drink and always not knowing what the outcome would be, I was still on my feet, still moving and working as a soldier, carrying a rifle but no ammunition and trapped! Yet here I was listening intently to Colonel Lee ordering us to break out on an every man for himself basis, warning us not to attempt to swim the River Medjerda, which it was deep and fast and not swimmable. And please be lucky.

I gathered Shoey, so to speak. He had simply followed me without saying a word throughout the fighting as we struggled towards Tebourba. Once we had been told to make our own way out I headed back down into the wood as far as I dared, then turned right alongside a tank that had been knocked out early in the battle, keeping very low. By this time it was dark and I told Bill that we might be walking into captivity, still no word. I have no idea how long a time elapsed as we carried on through the wood. We were increasingly having to stop to rest, but the battle had stopped, especially the mortaring. Eventually we came on to a main road and I simply, and for no reason I can remember, turned right. Staying in the ditch we kept going along the road, resting ever more often, until suddenly out of the dark I was challenged by an Artillery Officer. We had made it.

Instructions regarding War Diaries and Intelligence Summaries are contained in F.S. Regs., Vol. I. Monthly War Diaries will be enclosed in A.F. C.2118. If this is not available, and for Intelligence Summaries, the cover will be prepared in manuscript.	WAR DIARY *or* INTELLIGENCE SUMMARY *(Erase heading not required).*	Army Form C. 2118.

Month and Year................DECEMBER, 1942.   Unit...2nd B^n The Hampshire Regiment.

Commanding Officer Captain J.W. Brehau...

Place	Date	Hour	Summary of Events and Information	References to Appendices
TUNISIA.	1		The enemy made contact with the forward Coys by M.G., and light automatic fire at approximately 1100 hours, from positions occupied during the night on the high ground quoted in War Diary for 30.11.42. In the early afternoon the Commanding Officer decided to attack and capture a small village on the right front of "Y" Coy, from which the enemy were directing strong M.G., and L.M.G., fire on the forward troops. No. 16 Platoon, "Z" Coy was ordered xx to attack and capture this village, and their attack went in atx approximately 1400 hours that afternoon. The approach to the position was down a very exposed forward slope and the platoon suffered severe casualties from mortar and L.M.G., fire. The village was set on fire by the enemy. The Commanding Officer decided that the position was untenable by such few troops and ordered the Platoon to withdraw to Battalion reserve. This was carried out by dark that evening. During that day one Platoon of "X" Coy, was ordered to occupy the forward edge of the wood to their immediate front for observation purposes. This platoon was withdrawn p.m. Casualties for that day's fighting were as follows:- "W" Coy........ Nil. "X" Coy........ 7 Other Ranks killed, 18 Other Ranks wounded. "Y" Coy........ 12 Other Ranks wounded. "Z" Coy........ 1 Officer wounded, 3 Other Ranks killed, 15 Other Ranks wounded or missing. "HQ" Coy....... Nil - as far as is known. Night quiet.	
	2		Battalion engaged on all fronts by the enemy commanding at approximately 0845 hours. Fighting continued throughout the day.	

WI.41820/1900 600,000 12/41 W.H.& S. 51-4070

Instructions regarding War Diaries and Intelligence Summaries are contained in F.S. Regs., Vol. I. Monthly War Diaries will be enclosed in A.F. C.2118. If this is not available, and for Intelligence Summaries, the cover will be prepared in manuscript.	WAR DIARY *or* INTELLIGENCE SUMMARY *(Erase heading not required).*	Army Form C. 2118.

Month and Year................DECEMBER, 1942.   Unit...2nd B^n The Hampshire Regiment.

Commanding Officer Captain H.W. Brehaut

Place	Date	Hour	Summary of Events and Information	References to Appendices
TUNISIA	2		7 tanks were seen, 4 of which were knocked out. One infantry gun and carrier was also knocked out. Shortly after mid day "X" Coy and supporting arms were overrun by 2 tanks and some infantry. "Y" Coy were completely cut off by fire from the Bn. Situation at 1400 hours as follows:- "W" Coy, less 2 Pls plus personnel of Bn H.Q., less Command Post in original Bn H.Q. positions as forward troops. "Y" Coy less 2 Pls still in position. "Z" Coy less 1 Pl still in position. Enemy infantry made contact with "W" Coy through wood, and in reply to information received from O.C. "W" Coy the Commanding Officer ordered one Platoon of "Z" Coy to fix bayonets and to clear the wood. The attack was carried out immediately and was completely successful. 5 German prisoners were taken and an estimate of from 40 to 60 Germans killed. This platoon then withdrew to its original position. The situation was therefore temporarily restored, but it was feared that "Y" Coy had been overrun as communications had completely broken. 2 Runners reported from "Y" Coy just before dusk giving their position. The Commanding Officer ordered that the remnants of "Y" Coy withdraw to the wood occupied by "HQ" Coy after dark. Contact with Brigade had been broken since midday, but a Liaision Officer visited the Battalion after dark bringing orders for withdrawal, and for the Battalion to, take up a defensive position on the SOUTH EAST of TEBOURBA, with left occupying hilled called Point 186 and right as near as possible to the river.	
	3		Battalion withdrew at approximately 0130 hours and positions were occupied with supporting arms in position by dawn.	

WI.41820/1900 600,000 12/41 W.H.& S. 51-4070

Instructions regarding War Diaries and Intelligence Summaries are contained in F.S. Regs., Vol. I. Monthly War Diaries will be enclosed in A.F. C.2118. If this is not available, and for Intelligence Summaries, the cover will be prepared in manuscript.

Month and Year....DECEMBER, 1942.

WAR DIARY
or
INTELLIGENCE SUMMARY
(*Erase heading not required*).

Army Form C. 2118.

Unit. .2nd. Bn. The. Hampshire. Regiment.

Commanding Officer ...Captain. J.W. Brehaut.

Place	Date	Hour	Summary of Events and Information	References to Appendices
TUNISIA	3		Positions were as follows:-	
			"W" Coy and 2 Sec Carriers right forward.	
			"Z" Coy left forward.	
			"Y" Coy along line of railway slightly back in centre.	
			Bn H.Q., in rear of "Y" Coy.	
			"HQ" Coy in olive grove in rear of Bn H.Q.	
			Enemy attacked this position at approximately 0900 hours.	
			The high ground on the left after fierce fighting was occupied by the enemy and in spite of 2 counter attacks by "Z" Coy this ground remained in enemy hands. Throughout the day enemy pressure by both infantry and tanks was sustained, and by 1500 hours 2 tanks and some infantry had infiltrated behind "W" Coy on the right of the river.	
			Situation at 1600 hours was as follows:-	
			"Z" Coy less 2 Pls and Coy H.Q., forced down to line of railway NORTH of "Y" Coy, and put under command of Officer Commanding "Y" Coy.	
			"W" Coy withdrawn to form semi circle with "Y" Coy and Bn H.Q.	
			Bn H.Q., incl carriers and mortars on line of railway in rear of "Y" Coy.	
			The Battalion thus occupied a semi circle round the railway.	
			At dusk the Battalion was joined by the remainder of "HQ" Coy.	
			Contact with Brigade had not been gained since the Liaision Officer had left at approximately 0330 hours that day. Repeated efforts had been made both by D/R and supporting arms wireless to get through to Brigade with the situation.	
			Just after dark the enemy attacked with both tanks and infantry and reached the railway on both flanks.	
			The Commanding Officer ordered "W" Coy to drive the enemy out on the left, some men of "HQ" Coy to drive them out from the centre, and some men of the carrier Platoon to drive them out on the right.	
			Heavy casualties were inflicted and the position remained with the enemy	

WL.41000/1000 500,000 12/41 W.H.& S. 51-6070

Instructions regarding War Diaries and Intelligence Summaries are contained in F.S. Regs., Vol. I. Monthly War Diaries will be enclosed in A.F. C.2118. If this is not available, and for Intelligence Summaries, the cover will be prepared in manuscript.

Month and Year..DECEMBER, 1942.

WAR DIARY
or
INTELLIGENCE SUMMARY
(*Erase heading not required*).

Army Form C. 2118.

Unit. 2nd Bn The Hampshire Regiment.

Commanding Officer ...Captain J.W. Breh...

Place	Date	Hour	Summary of Events and Information	References to Appendices
TUNISIA	3		temporarily beaten off.	
			The Commanding Officer then decided that the position, without ammunition or water and without any anti tank weapons, was untenable and would only result in the complete annihilation or capture of the remainder of the Battalion, which then consisted of approximately 10 Officers and 150 men in these positions.	
			He therefore ordered all ranks to arm themselves, for bayonets to be fixed and for the Battalion to move out in extended order down the railway due WEST. This was duly carried out with the left flank making direct contact with an enemy tank and some infantry.	
			The Battalion formed up on the outskirts of TEBOURBA and marched to the eastern end of the village with the intention of reporting to Brigade H.Q. On arrival on the outskirts of TEBOURBA it was discovered that all troops had been previously withdrawn and that the main road to MEDJEZ-EL-BAB was cut. The enemy had placed machine guns to fire on fixed lines across the hills and over the road, and tanks were situated directly on the road. After reconnaissance the Commanding Officer decided that all troops would make their own way back to MEDJEZ-EL-BAB in small groups. Rations and such water as there was was issued and the order to disperse given.	Appx.1. Report by Adjt, 2 Hamps on Battle of TEBOURBA.
			The Battalion was ordered to collect and regroup on the road 5 miles NORTH EAST of MEDJEZ-EL-BAB (6545).	Appx.2. Report by O.C. "Y" Coy 2 Hamps on the Battle of TEBOURBA. Report by an cancanapt of O.C.p. Appx.3. Report by an artillery F.O.O. on the Battle of TEBOURBA.
	5		After collecting some men the Battalion was ordered to amalgamate temporarily with the 2nd Parachute Battalion and guard a landing ground due EAST of MEDJEZ-EL-BAB. This position was taken up after dark this evening.	

WL.41000/1000 500,000 12/41 W.H.& S. 51-6070

1162

NO. 2 ARMY FILM & PHOTO SECTION (PR)

Neg. Report No.(Not received) EJ. **SECRET DOPE SHEET** **1162** Date 6 Dec. 4?

Cameraman CAPT. GLENDINING   Soundman _____ Length 200 feet

Story ACTIVITY AT MEDJEZ EL BAB, typica Tunisian village.

Location MEDJEZ EL BAB _____ Unit, Brigade, Div. Paratroop 2 nd. Battalion and

Also covered by _____ 2 nd. Battalion Hampshires.

NUMBER		FOOTAGE
/3/1	Long shot of ALGIERS HARBOUR enveloped in smoke screen.	30 feet
	Street scenes MEDJEZ- EL BAB.	
	Panning shot showing BAILEY BRIDGE over original bridge	
	destroyed by Germans.	30 feet
	Jeeps etc... crossing bridge.	15 feet
	Scenes various.	25 feet
	Total of Roll 1 –	100 feet
/3/2	Close up of NOTICE BOARD to TERBOURKA.	15 feet
	2nd. Battalion Paratroops and Hampshires crossing bridge *	
	through streets preparatory to taking up defensive positions	45 feet
	Pan withntroops passed bombed houses.	15 feet
	Low angle shots of Tanks approaching village of MEDJEZ-EL)BAB	25 feet
		100 feet
	* ... whole	
Remarks—		TOTAL

(1254) Wt.30294/4898 25 Pads 10/42 C.& Co. 745(8) J5914.

\# The Crayon is Censors' marks
and deletions

One copy please as indicated
enclosed £25.

Quote from the *Portsmouth Evening News* :

Under overwhelming enemy pressure the Battalion was forced back on the night of December 2nd and during the following morning, until at last, after smashing a number of frontal attacks with further bayonet charges it was encircled by three enemy Infantry companies supported by tanks. A last charge of all available forces-riflemen-cooks and clerks was led by the Colonel, and the Germans were driven back in complete disorder. This great charge carried the Battalion almost into Tebourba, from which position they were ordered to withdraw, an order that was obeyed with regret.

For this four day action, 1 Victoria Cross, 2 Distinguished Service Orders, 5 Military Crosses, 4 Military Medals and a number of Mentions in Dispatches were awarded. How many other acts of courage went unrecorded? Every time a Company runner set off with a message this was courage of the highest order and at Tebourba they paid a heavy price.

Once the Artillery Officer had cleared our identity he told us that us that there had been a few of the Battalion through, also a number of Paratroopers. He directed us onto the main road, pointed us in the direction of Medjez el Bab, told us a collection point had been set up and left us to get on with it. No one ever tells you how far it is. Neither Bill nor I was in a fit state to go very far even on a one foot in front of the other basis so after a very short time I moved us off the road. We stretched out, or more like collapsed, and in spite of the cold we both slept the sleep of 'survivors'! Unbelievably, Bill still hadn't said a word.

Getting onto my feet in the morning was both painful and difficult. The huge fact of my escape had not really registered. My worries were not over. Bill was still not speaking; it was almost trance like. I set off down the road and I prayed it wasn't going to be far because Bill was limping badly. We were passed at intervals by American half track troop carriers, unfortunately going in the other direction. The collection point wasn't in fact very far, and we eventually reported in. Food and tea were ready, we found a quiet spot. Neither of us had any appetite in spite of four days without food but the tea was a blessing. After our second mug I suddenly couldn't stop Bill talking! The morning brought a welcome wash and shave courtesy of a water truck that arrived from the RASC Bill had his feet done by one of two RAMC medical orderlies who had been sent from a nearby Field Hospital. They took away several of the walking wounded; meanwhile our lads were still coming in.

After a good meal I settled down to try and rest but everybody was drifting round looking for friends and I was getting more and more concerned about Joe and Donald. I was still very shaky and I remember that I had a terrible headache and my ears were still dull and ringing. The general situation was becoming more confused as increasing numbers of the Parachute Regiment began to arrive. They had been part of a force commanded by Colonel Frost who were to have been dropped on or close to Tunis Airport to secure it for the Allies; unfortunately they had been dropped miles short and by the time they reached their objective they were without ammunition. The Airport was well defended and the operation was aborted. They too had then been ordered to find their own way back. I suppose by early afternoon there were around a hundred troops in this small holding area, a roughly even mix of Hampshires and Paratroopers.

Girl and Tony had never been far from my thoughts and I was looking forward to writing letters again. I had taken the time to sort out my kit. We had been wearing fighting order and I was short my big pack, groundsheet and blanket so the nights looked like being uncomfortable to say the least. I am finding it difficult to write about this period, I have no particular focus; one thing that sticks in my mind was the faces of the Hampshire soldiers, a sort of grey disturbing colour as I suppose was I, certainly Bill was. Nobody had anything to say, an occasional 'Glad you made it,' from someone whom you might only have known by sight. In truth we had all withdrawn into our own little world and were waiting for the next order.

I must pay a sincere tribute to Shoey. Here was an older man, certainly some ten or more years older than me, who one minute was sat comfortably cobbling shoes, relatively newly married and with his own business, then suddenly he finds himself in the middle of the Tebourba Gap battle, following, and obeying without question a terrified twenty-two year old boy with three stripes who, he presumes, knows what he's doing. Dear Bill, none of us did. And here we are still together wondering what comes next and I think Bill looks a bit better than I do. What came next was Colonel Frost and before we could gather our wits what was left of the two Regiments had been formed up together and we were marching back or at least partly back to prepare to cope with any follow-up attack and bizarrely once again Sgt. Clem Hoyle REME Armourer (attached) was a Platoon Commander, my Platoon consisting of four Hampshires, three Paras, one Bren gun and, you have guessed it, a Shoemaker! Oh yes, and a dry mouth.

I wonder what Gaffer would have made of all this? Heaven only knows because as we rounded the corner into Medjez el Bab with myself leading the Platoon, there, large as life, was a film unit busily filming, which is of course what film units do. Which of my favourite words would you prefer - bizarre or surreal or dammit, why not both? The very brief film was ultimately shown in UK cinemas as part of a newsreel, which Girl and Tony and of course all the family saw and of which, courtesy of the Imperial War Museum I now have a video copy. My appearance runs for approximately ten seconds so don't settle down. The previous page shows a much censored copy of what was presumably the paperwork accompanying the film to London or wherever.

We didn't march far, thank God, and started to dig in just north of the railway yards, but very shortly Colonel Frost ordered us to stand down and rest. Food and drink was brought up to us and resting into the late afternoon certainly started to have its effect on me physically but my mind was lagging behind this recovery and to the fore was the worry about Joe and Donald. It got dark and I was trying to get comfortable when Colonel Frost and a Para. Sergeant dug me out and I spent the night with them laying anti-tank mines, I was also given the responsibility of logging where they were. So in the end the only cold that troubled me was the one in the pit of my stomach as I dropped a mine into the hole and scraped the earth over it. Until the Para.Sergeant picked one out of the crate I had never seen a British anti tank mine much less primed one and buried it. Fortunately the Sergeant did the priming and I did the logging and burying whilst my nerves did the twanging.

Nothing happened, plenty of tea but no Germans. With the morning the Royal Army Service Corps turned up and this time took us in the opposite direction and somewhere near to Souk el Chemis they turned up a road running between acres of cornfields. The corn was about two feet high and looked really good. Finally we turned off and climbed out - into a farmyard! I kid you not, however, this turned out to be a sort of luxury farmyard, part of a superb farm complex. There were plenty of empty, comfortable barn buildings and I even found a well equipped workshop with ample room for me to live in. Another bonus: we had caught up with B Echelon and the Transport section who had been outside the perimeter of the battle: this meant the QM baggage lorry and all the personal perks I had stashed away and of course Jack Brown. A bigger and an even more pleasant surprise, Tug Wilson was back and driving the QM15 cwt.

I quickly settled down to make myself comfortable and Bill got himself installed in a nice barn, like myself with plenty of room to bed down as well as work. We had two or three quiet days and then they started to build up the Battalion to full strength. This kept me pretty busy as the small arms began to be delivered. There were still a number of stragglers coming in; after we broke out the Germans apparently withdrew and amongst other things treated our wounded. Some were taken prisoner but some, after treatment, were made comfortable and left to take care of themselves. These were the ones straggling in and I was delighted when amongst them Joe Brown turned up, limping but OK and also out was Ben minus his bit of shrapnel. The Medical Officer was also out but sadly, after getting back, he collapsed with a nervous breakdown and was taken back to a Base Hospital. Joe had seen nothing of Donald after they were both sent off to contact 'X' and 'Y' Companies. Joe had been wounded in the heel and lost touch with Donald. When I gave Joe the binoculars he was totally bereft of words and so I said fatuously, 'I suppose you are really glad you got out now.'

Much later I was to learn that after the battle the Germans behaved impeccably, treating our wounded exactly as their own and many of our Battalion were to survive serious wounds as a result. The prime example was Major Le Patourel who after being reported as having died as a result of serious wounds having been awarded a posthumous Victoria Cross, weeks later was reported by the Red Cross to be in a German Military Hospital and though very ill he eventually made a full recovery.

Then right out of the blue, Corporal Budden, the post Corporal, turned up with the mail and there I was with a big fistful of letters from Girl. Another of those moments that cannot be put into words. A good percentage of my letters had been getting through which was a big relief and at least I could now look forward to getting letters on a reasonably regular basis. Joe moved in with Shoey. The Pioneer Platoon had come up with a very comfortable two-seat rumour generator. At this time we were introduced to 'Compo' rations. These were very new and so expensive that ultimately they were stopped but they were undoubtedly the best field rations I ever encountered. Contained in a wooden box they supplied a Platoon with rations for one day. Mostly of course tinned but containing items such as John West salmon, bacon, and the most superb steak and kidney puddings. A fifty tin of cigarettes, chocolate, toilet paper, matches, tinned fruit, reasonable biscuits and of course tea, milk and sugar. No wonder they didn't last.

Headquarter Company was about two miles away in another farm. This was at the end of a straight track through the wheat. Once settled I was anxious to see Ben so I set off mid morning to walk to HQ, carrying just my rifle I was really looking forward to the walk. It was a pleasant day and all the more enjoyable as I had pretty well recovered from our desperate days. I had moments when I felt totally overwhelmed by the experience and it would leave me feeling sick and strangely disorientated. After a little while I was conscious of an aerial battle developing and although it was very high I was sure the planes involved were 109s and American Lightnings (P38s). The Germans certainly had air superiority during this period and the Americans were just coming into the battle with their Lightnings and sadly the Lightnings or their inexperienced pilots were suffering badly at the hands of the experienced Germans.

As I carried on a 109 appeared low down and some way off but apparently looking for a spot to put his plane down. He headed remorselessly in my direction dropping ever lower in what appeared to be a controlled attempt to land. He certainly had acres of wheat to put down in and this theory was reinforced when he was near enough for me to see that he was not under power, at least the propeller was not turning and of course the whole thing was eerily quiet. But acres of wheat or not, by this time he and I were on a collision course and Clem, putting all of his considerable experience into action, flung himself flat. In the high wheat everything disappeared from sight but I heard the 109 hit the ground and go sliding along, hopefully not in my direction. It went very quiet and getting to my feet I found yet again a crashed plane only a few yards away. The 109 looked pretty well undamaged and its progress through the wheat had left a clear straight track; the nose was down and the propeller bent with the tail in the air. Seemed a good landing though and I made my way through the wheat as quickly as possible to see if I could help, I might even capture my very own prisoner.

As I got close I began to pick out cannon fire damage, some on the tail but the worst around the cockpit especially to the cover. Finally managing to scramble up I found that the pilot's head and upper torso had been completely destroyed by cannon fire. A very unpleasant ending to what had started out as pleasant stroll to see a friend. I had thought that at least the pilot had made a good landing but it was now obvious that the plane had landed entirely by itself. Whilst I was still pondering how to get at the pilot, troops began to arrive from HQ and 'B' Echelon led by my best mate Ben who in the way of medical people said, ' I see you didn't bother with a field dressing.' I enquired after Ben's head wound, we congratulated each other on survival, made arrangements to meet and then he went back to the problem of getting the pilot out and sorting out his identity documents. The pilot was buried the next day in a corner of the farmer's kitchen garden. There was a proper burial party and all the usual honours were accorded. Ben who had recovered the documents said there was the usual wallet with family photos and a letter would be sent. How sad it all is.

That evening Ben arrived driving a very pretty horse and trap together with the new Medical Officer, Captain Murphy, and a couple of bottles of wine. We both found later that using a pony and trap was a favourite way of getting round these big farms. Ben and Spud (it was inevitable) had been doing a bit of doctoring for the farmer and his family hence the wine and trap. Ben and I had a lot to talk over along with Joe and Bill. Still no news of Donald. They presumed that Sgt. Rogers had been captured and so it eventually proved. Ben and the Medical Officer had followed more or less the same route as myself, keeping going in the dark until overcome with exhaustion; they had then just collapsed and waited capture which turned out to being located by a British patrol and as the saying goes, 'the rest was history'.

I remember we had a long and interesting discussion on survival. Friends in the Battalion were already beginning to look like 'survivors' and the three of us, Joe,

Ben and I were looking like prime examples but this was not a subject that any of the three of us wished to discuss, it seemed like tempting fate, and I for one was not going to stop digging deep slit trenches, survivor or not. But one fact that was fascinating Joe, and which I was more than ready to discuss, was my apparent propensity for occupying spaces just prior to aircraft crashing into them. Ben brought up the Gloucester Gladiator at Feltham during our cricket match; the Fairey Battle just as we set off for the real war, the Lysander probably the nearest I ever came to being killed; the Airspeed Oxford at Lockerbie; and now this '109'. Coincidence I protested and I would have protested much louder if I had known then that I was far from finished with this strange phenomenon. There was still another 109 and a Wellington bomber to come of which the Wellington could certainly have terminated my war.

This evening started a little card group including Spud the MO, who strangely enough had managed to drag a wind-up gramophone together with a few classical records around with him and was more than happy to while away the time, especially when he was alone, just listening to them. Funny old war sometimes. Another good friend who survived and came along from time to time was Trudge Truran, soon to be promoted RSM I was assembling a good solid core of important friends. Moving round the Company' inspecting the small arms I certainly missed faces and friends especially officers: their attrition rate at Tebourba had left huge gaps among the old familiar faces.

The Battalion gradually came up to strength and I remember how quiet and sort of restful the farm was; even the bull, just as they said, turned out to be a pussycat and liked nothing better than a good scratching. There was plenty of air activity and it appeared that the Lightnings were continuing to get the worst of it. I had arranged with the Battalion Intelligence Sergeant to try and find what might have happened to Donald but as the days passed it began to seem that he might not have survived and it would only be a matter of time before he was officially posted as missing believed killed. I had settled into a letter day rhythm which lasted until I was back with Girl and Tony. At some point in North Africa the powers that be introduced an air letter, which was rationed, I think it was three a week, but it went by air and was very popular. This changed my system to a letter a day and three air letters a week. Girl was pretty prolific too and I could always look forward to the Post Corporal arriving. We were into the first weeks of February, Girls birthday was 16 February, Tony's 16 October. This had passed during the days on the *Coama* and so another birthday approached but at least this time I would be able to communicate.

During this period we were all taking a regular guard duty. These guards were quite properly 'prowler guards' the usual two hours on and four off but different in that the two hours were spent prowling round in pairs. After finishing a two hour stint I was dosing off when I came alert to the sound of a motor-bike. Dispatch rider, I thought; I was right, and as so often happened a few hectic hours later the Battalion were once again on the move and as always happened we who were going to be directly involved in whatever nastiness was at the end of the move were completely in the dark. Yet again and frighteningly we were in a great hurry. My premonitions were once again accurate and it would soon be dry mouth time again.

CHAPTER 11

KASSERINE SBIBA AND A VERY BRAVE AMERICAN LADY

So here we were once again making ourselves comfortable in the back of Jack Brown's three-ton Bedford. There was plenty of scope for comfort as the Battalion had recently been issued with a new type of two-man bivouac and the QM naturally carried spares and so provided us with a comfortable packing for our weary bones. I must say these bivouacs were a great success keeping out the worst of the weather and providing warmth; unbelievably I have been part of a four-man card school complete with candles in one of those bivouacs. We had simply got used to living dangerously, mind you being a Yorkshireman any game that might involve losing money qualifies as living dangerously. In the back then were Bill Holden, Joe Brown, Don Radden and myself. In the front were the RQMS and of course Jack Brown, driver *extraordinaire*. Thus we lurched off into the dark, sorry, Jack, we took off smoothly into the dark and I lay there nursing this nasty emptiness in my stomach. I was also having bad patches thinking about Donald and hoping for news. I just couldn't shake off the feeling of responsibility. I wasn't being fair to myself but this black feeling persisted. Sixty years on and I am still upset by it.

There never was any news!

As we settled into the journey I thought that at least our mugs of sweet tea would be coming along. Firstly, my Boxes Tool Armourer or at least its replacement was sitting in the truck with us, complete with blowlamp specially modified for boiling water, Joe was definitely back on form and whilst Don and Joe had supervised the loading of the truck ensuring plenty of tea, milk and sugar, when I asked where the rum jars were hidden I got a very short answer, especially when I said, 'Come back, Gaffer, all is forgiven.'

We finally arrived in the late afternoon, pulling off the road onto what was just desert, sort of hard, rough, stony ground and with nothing visible whichever way you looked. Mind you it turned out to be home to more scorpions than I had ever seen before. A two-man bivouac can be very comfortable but add five scorpions and it becomes much less attractive. Where are we? God only knows. We had come quite a distance south but it had been mostly dark and the land was featureless but we were on the fringes of a battle which led to major criticism of the Americans. The area which the Americans had deserted….new Sherman Tanks fully loaded for action and which were promptly taken over by a delighted Rommel who was making a successful thrust south of the British Armies, was Kasserine. The German concern had been lack of reserves and the Shermans, with black crosses hastily painted on, solved this problem for them and they were soon in action against us.

Rommel's thrust from the south was aimed at a key town called Sbiba. He seemed to be using classic *Blitzkrieg* tactics combining Armour and Infantry. Somebody had to stop him and here we were. Again I have tried to set the scene but I am not writing history. This has already been covered by military historians but my concern is simply what happened to myself and I suppose at this precise moment Joe and I were probably setting up our bivouac, we had teamed up as a pair whilst Shoey had paired up with Jack Brown.

    The Quartermaster had by this time been issued with a small Utility truck which he shared with the RQMS. This was proving very useful, when what was left of us were going back into action with the Paras. At Medjez el Bab, Northmore had gone off back to an Ordnance Base sixty or seventy miles away to pick up stores. After looking for him at Battalion HQ I once again found he had gone off for stores taking the R.QMS. with him; this sort of left me in charge along with the ration Sergeant but at least I found out what it was all about and that we wouldn't be long before moving again. So I made a meal top priority and with the Ration Sergeant joining us we broke open a box of 'Compo' rations and settled down to eat and await orders.

    There was a great deal of military activity going on all around us including a Squadron of Crusader III tanks. They had been badly mauled tangling with a number of German Mk.IVs. This meant they were hopelessly out-gunned and from long range. Chatting to one of the Tank Commanders we learned a great deal about the situation, none of it good. The Brigade was back to almost full strength; our two Guards Battalions had finally left the 'Algerian Ceremonials' and were once again back with us making up the Guards Brigade. I was not alone during our ordeal at Tebourba in wondering why, badly outnumbered, we were fighting for our very lives whilst the rest of the Brigade were performing Ceremonial Parades in Algiers. There was more to come but our situation this time turned on the toss of a coin; during the night the two Guards Battalions moved out their CO having won the toss and we moved out at dawn and in daylight.

    At first light we were eating breakfast when the order came to move out and within minutes the B Echelon together with the Transport Section were trundling along the road in convoy. I did know where we were going to this time, Sbiba. I had also been told that under no circumstances were we to stop. But as a well seasoned veteran by now, I knew that, with air superiority, the Germans were not going to let us breeze up to Sbiba in broad daylight without doing something about it! Funny but there was only one simple thing that I could do about this frightening prospect, let the tailboard down and lock it then ride with our legs dangling out of the back ready for a fast exit. We were wearing fighting order so at least our important possessions would go with us. There were the usual gang in the back, Joe, Bill, Don Raddon and the Ration Sergeant; we were already laying bets on a time for the first attack. Meanwhile Joe had his tea making facilities laid out, converted blowlamp freshly filled with paraffin, water cans handy and of course mugs. Who was riding up front with Jack? Strangely, we couldn't find a volunteer.

    There was indeed a panic on, our Brigade Commander was driving up and down the convoy in his open staff car exhorting us to keep moving and the convoy was I suspect, travelling faster than regulations were supposed to permit. It was getting hot as the day wore on, Bill was running the book and I had got my money on an hour and a quarter from the time the convoy started moving. The finishing post would be on Joe's first shout; we didn't worry at all that Joe might hang around a little just to further his own chances. So which word would you like this time? Bizarre, surreal or maybe 'It's a funny old world'?

    We had been running for about an hour when a small utility truck (not the QM) pulled into the convoy behind us and settled to maintain correct convoy distance between vehicles; not to worry, we had plenty of tea, milk and sugar. After a while it

Helen Kirkpatrick in England with Lee Miller of Vogue

slowly dawned on us that the passenger was a lady (don't forget we had been away from the fair sex for some time) and the driver an officer. The lady was wearing an American uniform and a military cap and from time to time she would give us a wave. Without comment Joe put out another mug and we settled down to try and resolve this strange turn of events. This didn't last long. Joe shouted, we frantically signalled at our new convoy friends but by this time the convoy was slowing but not stopping. There were six 109s quite a long way back and fairly high and as we sat facing the back of the convoy they were on our left and obviously closing fast. The convoy kept moving so we could only sit tight and wait for the inevitable.

The aircraft changed their direction and attacked the convoy at an angle but across it and I suppose about a mile further ahead from where we were positioned in the convoy. It was, as usual, noisy and frightening and we could see smoke from at least one burning truck and the convoy had finally stopped. We had lost sight of the planes but we could certainly hear them. It was vital to locate them because we had no cover, no ditches, just a flat barren landscape and in this situation the only cover at all are the wheels of your truck. They offer a solid resistance to machine guns if not so much to cannon. Mind you, it might leave the truck burning round your ears but you can't have everything. Shoey picked up the 109s and they were on the other side and heading in our direction. We gathered up the lady and the officer and crouched behind the wheels of our truck. Again we were lucky; they made their pass at least five or six vehicles behind us and they then started to leave fast. Joe quickly spotted the reason for this as a considerable number of American P.38s appeared high up. So we were going to get some cover, thank God.

Our little group gathered at the tail of the truck, joined by Jack, all of us shaken and feeling that funny sense of relief which manifests itself as feeling a little sick. The lady was visibly shaking, no colour left in her face and suddenly she grinned and said very memorably, 'Shit, I've wet my pants! call me Helen.' We left Joe with Helen. Her driver, Capt. Johnson RASC came with the rest of us to where the attack had been made to offer help. There were a couple of badly shot up vehicles but as so often in these potentially desperate situations the thing you least expect, no casualties. We certainly appreciated the tea when we got back and Helen was still shaking but was getting stuck into Joe's prizewinning beverage. Unfortunately before we could find out what was going on, our Brigadier appeared, still exhorting us to keep moving, and indeed the convoy started to move shortly after.

So, Joe, what's the story? Her name is Helen Kirkpatrick, she is an author and journalist and now an accredited war correspondent. The Captain has been given the job of driving her wherever she wants to go. Looked to me as if the Captain was in for a rough ride. It was nothing to the rough ride meted out to the American forces when her articles on Kasserine eventually appeared in the American press and for which she was severely disciplined.

And the rest of our traumatic race against time? The convoy was attacked constantly but again and again our little group survived; there was plenty of evidence of the damage and casualties as we kept doggedly moving until slowing down dramatically. Sections of the convoy were hived off and we were turned off the road into what was grassland. There was some sort of battle going on further to our left and as we got out of our vehicles we came under air attack from Ju.88s but this was very shortlived and things started to quieten down. So what of our two guests? They were still with us, Helen by this time very frayed to say the least but feisty as ever and it was with great reluctance that at the Captain's insistence she agreed to leave. A hug all round and this very brave American lady was gone.

For us there was a nasty nightmare awaiting. 'B' Echelon and the lads of the Transport Section were given the task of trying to help where possible the casualties from the Crusader tanks of the 5th Armoured Division. This had been the battle we could hear as we left our vehicles. The Crusaders had once again been badly mauled by German Mk. IVs who could just sit out of range of the Crusader's six-pounder guns then reply with deadly effect with their 88mm guns. When we got there the surviving crew members were working hard. Two of the tanks were burnt out; tanks are not the easiest of vehicles to try and help anyone wounded or trapped inside but fortunately for us the Tank Squadron's recovery vehicles turned up very quickly with lots of expert help. We made our way back. I was feeling pretty grotty, it was the smell that had done for me yet again. One needs a great deal of courage to crew battle tanks in war, they are not for me!

Shortly after getting back, an officer from Brigade came and told us to stand down and organise a meal. Apparently the problem had been contained and Rommel's thrust stopped, but we were to make sure our vehicles were ready to move and with full fuel tanks. Before we could eat we dug slit trenches against air attack (this was standard procedure) then settled back to enjoy a meal. I knew the meal would be enjoyable because of its simplicity. We in 'B' Echelon had instigated a system of collecting the tinned steak and kidney puddings from the 'Compo,' rations, please don't ask, so that in a situation like this instead of organising meals for seven men from the rations our elected cook simply boiled up the tins and we picked one up... delicious! wonder if there's a spare.

Then it rained and rained and kept on raining. Yes, I'm still in North Africa. We simply scrambled into the trucks to wait for it to stop or for 'orders', whichever came first. It was 'orders'. Simple orders really, form up into convoy on the road ready to move off: sting in the tail, the battle situation had deteriorated and if we didn't move our arses we could well finish up chatting to Rommel's lads. Nasty. Big scramble, trucks starting up, Jack asking if we were ready to move except the truck wouldn't move, not in a forward direction at least. The grass had become a soft mud and none of the trucks could move, the wheels simply wouldn't grip. It really was farcical. Twenty or more trucks slithering about, groups of troops pushing and pulling all to no avail. Ah well, I had heard nothing but good about the way Rommel and his troops treated prisoners, very soldier to soldier and a bad luck mate attitude. Officers from Brigade began to appear in larger numbers than I remembered seeing before, all very cool but showing certain signs of anxiety. You will note that. Officers anxiety; me panic. Jack very cool, though also very cross with his truck, had disappeared, finally arriving back in the passenger seat of a big American GMC truck. The American, after finding it hard to believe that British Army trucks only possessed two-wheel drive, ably assisted by Jack, proceeded to tow all our trucks out onto the road.

Jack had spotted a gaggle of U.S. trucks parked up one of the side roads into Sbiba much earlier and could now claim to have saved the day. We were already on the move. Days later I exploited my friendship with Trudge Truran, soon to be RSM, and he shortly became Corporal Jack Brown. We had come a long way together, Jack and I, since that trip to Winchester and as I would sometimes remind him, long enough for him to learn to drive, after a fashion anyway. The reply was unprintable. I would have put it in but my laptop absolutely refuses.

Where the hell were we going now? I assumed the flap was over and as we trundled along, now in the dark, we all settled down to sleep. This is one night I can recall very clearly. As I have said previously, sleep always came easily to me but prior to settling down we had been talking about our attempts to help the tank crews and suddenly I could smell the burnt-out tank. It was a long night and by morning I felt ill enough to seek out Ben. He suggested I see the doctor, 'Spud', who said I was OK physically, I just needed to try and ride it out. If the feeling persisted I was to go back to him. We finally arrived at our destination, a village called Beja which was badly knocked about but we drove along a sort of sunken road with wheat fields on one side. The other side was a built up bank which we later learned had been the start of a railway track.

It was dark by now and pouring with rain. Joe and I tried to find a decent spot but everywhere was wet and muddy. I decided to go back and try and find the baggage lorry where I could pick up a few extra ground sheets and an extra blanket or two. It was very dark and so I had stayed close to the bottom of the bank until I came to the baggage truck. I decided to go back close to the fields as I felt it would help me locate where the bivouac was. As I fought my way back to the surface of a deep gully filled with water and scrambled out still clutching the soaked blankets and ground sheets I thought, mistake! Arriving at the bivouac I flung the ground sheets in, dumped the blankets, crawled in alongside Joe, managed to wrap my own dry blanket round me and slept like a log.

The next morning I crawled out, scrounged a mug of tea then praying for the sun I wandered back to see what I had stumbled into the night before but the first thing I stumbled in to was Tim Budden, the Post Corporal, with a big fistful of mail for me. The sun would surely follow and soon. How important letters are to soldiers, especially so far away and not enjoying the safest of environments cannot be exaggerated. Wet through and cold, I clutched my letters and the sun was soon out. What had I fallen into? A deep gully which was only on one side of the track. I had missed it going up but changing my route back and in the dark I simply walked into it. Quoting our old friend Captain Mannering…'Stupid Boy!'

B Echelon and the Transport Section were parked up along this track almost stretching back to Beja. As the sun came out it began to prove a pleasant enough location and indeed we were to be here for several weeks. We were at this time being issued with what were titled 'Tents 180 pounds'. These were quite large tents and if used strictly for accommodation would hold six people. These were being used strictly as offices and stores, the Battalion First Aid Post had two complete with Ben and my converted blow lamp, oh yes and Joe Brown had right of way! As we settled in there was a small group of these large tents together; the Quartermaster (now restored to the bosom of his family? I wonder where he finally got to? the R.QMS. claimed Algiers but I always doubted that) also had two of these tents, one was office and accommodation and the other stores.

I nearly forgot my workshops, a small patch of firm level ground and my trusty Boxes Tool Armourer all set up and waiting for me to burst into action. This action was delayed quite a while whilst I got the design of a windproof cigarette lighter to be made from a rifle oil bottle and using only the tools available to me, finalised and tested. I have always felt that it is very important to get priorities right. There was another delay, my Dad had made up about thirty suitable flint wheels. These I couldn't do, they needed to be very hard with sharp teeth but they were on the way, suitably drilled for the steel bar I was going to use as a pin. I'm sorry if I have previously led you to believe we were out here fighting a war! Also as part of my workshop complex I had constructed a test range for Bren guns. This was a nicely dug slit trench and by poking the muzzle in the general direction of one of the bottom corners one could blaze away quite happily. The QM hated me doing this, oh dear! any Armourer will testify that test firing a machine gun after repair is an absolute necessity, just as my lighters also had to be thoroughly tested after manufacture though not necessarily on, or is it in the range. The QM said that I timed these bursts of Bren gun fire for maximum annoyance, it's a lie. Never bothered anyone else.

So we settled down and eventually my lighters came off the production line and were a great success, I could make one from scratch in less than half an hour. I wonder if there are any out there somewhere. I certainly made a lot of them, the officers were particularly keen but not being equipped with a rifle they didn't have a oil bottle to lose. Somehow it didn't seem to slow them down and who was I to ask questions? I would simply say, 'Give me an hour and you can collect' after all it was everybody's duty to maintain moral. My first recipient of one of these lighters was the Adjutant; is there no limit to your crawling, Clem? Not really, anyway the Adjutant was a perfect test bed….he was a pipe smoker. Crawler, maybe, but cunning with it; anyway I was at this time lobbying for Tug Wilson's first stripe and with success. I was delighted.

I was really working hard at this time. The NAAFI had set up a large store in Medjez el Bab. They were selling luxuries and necessities, cigarettes, chocolate, razor blades, beer, spirits, writing materials etc. Once a week the Companies would collect the cash and a list of requirements from the lads and it was the QM who was then responsible for collecting it from the NAAFI Joe and I had taken on the job of taking a truck into Medjez el Bab complete with a considerable amount of money and a long list. L/Corporal Tug Wilson was our driver, Shoey often came along for the run. I think it used to take about five hours all told. We often had to wait quite a while to be served so that added to the journey. Fortunately there was very little German air activity, which of course disappointed Joe but it was always reassuring to know that Joe was stood up in the back of the truck keeping a sharp eye on the sky. There had been a sharp change in the control of the air with the introduction of Hurricanes and Spitfires. The other niggle for Joe: he wasn't getting to use his nice new Zeiss binoculars, believe me they never left his side.

I was also sharing a difficult job with the ration Sergeant and the RQMS. The Battalion were dug in on the reverse slopes of the Jebel Munchar mountains harassing the Germans and sending out reconnaissance patrols at night. Our job was to deliver the rations every night to a selected Company by mule, yes this is still me, Armourer and Muleteer! Actually the mules and their handlers were part of the Royal Army Service Corps. If you needed to move anything they would do it for you and very obliging they were too, no matter how dangerous. A note here, remember our poacher, he was doing sterling work as a one man recce. patrole on Jebel Munchar but sadly they caught him.

So here I was on a black filthy night, rain pouring down, huddled in my poncho trying hard to concentrate my thoughts on Girl and Tony while I hopefully followed a mule's arse along this narrow mountain track to a rendezvous with the Company Quartermaster Sergeant of 'Z' Company, one of the replacements after Tebourba and we had not yet met. Arriving finally at the rendezvous point, a junction of three tracks, I shouted into the darkness.' 'Z' Company?'

A muffled figure shouted back 'Yes!' and groping under his poncho handed me a wet piece of paper.

Thanks,' I said as the mules took off with this figure and I began my own journey back to one of Joe's welcoming mugs, little realising that I had just given 'Z' Company 2 Hant's rations to the CQMS of 'Z' Company the Sherwood Foresters. Only a very few Battalions use the letters W, X, Y, Z to title their Companies but I had just found one.

My friend the Adjutant had some hard words the following day as he lit his pipe with one of my lighters but strangely the 'Z' Company Commander never said anything and he was a non smoker. A couple of days later I was on another of these mountain paths making my laborious way, with a guide, to one of 'Y' Company's forward positions. My journey was to look at a bolshie Bren gun that was refusing to fire. It was urgent, they always are, but they had not been able to replace the gun with the appropriate number of riflemen so quite naturally they wanted the gun back in action and quick. Eventually we arrived at a straight piece of different track, different because it was pockmarked with mortar strikes. It was about thirty yards long and the position I was seeking was at the other end.

'So what now?' I asked my guide.

'Well,' he replied,' there is a 88mm mortar ranged on this path so you need to hurry.'

You will notice it was only me that was going to hurry along this track, hoping that at least he knew what to do with a field dressing, I dutifully dashed along this track and unmolested fell into one of 'Y' Company's forward positions. I was at this time thinking that the fault had better be worth my long climb and my dice with the mortars. The Platoon Commander and I had never met so after introductions, I put a full magazine on the gun and squeezed the trigger. The action thumped forward, nothing! Extracting the round that should have fired, a quick look showed no strike at all. Any Armourers who might be accidentally reading this will probably be ahead of me already.

'Has the gun been stripped recently?' I asked.

'Yes.'

'Where?'

'Over there.'

I walked over, picked up the firing pin from the ground, handed it to the Sergeant, reminded him to stick to field stripping then stood looking at the little stretch of track, made a dash and just as I reached my guide, 'bang'; missed me, I thought but I was still pretty pissed about the whole thing and already composing a nasty letter to Company Commanders to be signed by my old friend the Adjutant. I must remember to get him a packet of flints on my next NAAFI trip, still, no shame.

There was a sort of amusing incident at the main crossroads which were situated on the main road just out outside Beja. This road came from the direction of Tunis and went on to Medjez el Bab. Joe, Bill and I knew it well. On this particular morning about eight o'clock, the Royal Military Policeman, who was on duty at the crossroads and wearing all his finery, immaculate battle dress with creases, white webbing, red hat and boots to die for, wandered into our area trailing a couple of German soldiers. The MP had not even bothered to draw his pistol. I think his opening remark should go down in history, something like, 'Could you find a cup of tea for these two German lads, I think they are lost.' And the story? They had appeared on a motorcycle and sidecar complete with machine gun, they arrived at the crossroads at a fair old speed and from the direction of Tunis. Ignoring the RMP's white gloved hand, indicating please stop, they sped on past, braked hard about fifty yards further on then turned round, came back and surrendered.

Basically life was fairly calm and restful, so much so that in between cigarette lighters, I made, entirely by hand, a change lever for a Thompson sub machine gun. This component was of course round and comprised, I think, three separate cams: what one might describe as a tricky little machining job but impossible by hand! I was quite proud of it and it worked. Then there was the day that a mysterious largish box turned up labelled Projectors Infantry Anti Tank. On opening the box there were three very strange looking contraptions, round, about two or three foot long with a tray at one end with a long spigot sticking out of the main body and at the opposite end a primitive sort of butt. Yes, but what the hell was it for? I know, the anti tank bit struck a chord, maybe we were going to rush around knocking out Tigers with it. I really shouldn't joke about these things. But much more to the point where were the bloody instructions? Nothing.

Taking one out I walked around it for a while and decided to have a look at the ammunition that had arrived with it. This was a pretty standard bomb shape but with a spike-like protrusion on the business end and from the other a long tube. All my laborious training and should I say experience plus my sex life indicated that the spigot might well fit down this tube and so it proved. Never mind the tanks, there's potential for breeding here. The reality was that half an hour later I was no nearer working out how to operate the damned thing. I had tried putting my feet on the butt then pulling hard with my hands round the trigger guard; this moved the spigot and seemed a promising start but there was an enormous spring to pull against and I simply couldn't move it very far. Still a small package! I was quickly galvanised by the usual message from the Adjutant. 'Heard about the anti tank weapon, could you run a little course on them this afternoon, thank you, Sergeant.' That's nice, it's almost 'this afternoon' now and I haven't had my lunch yet. In desperation I looked round for a big lad and there was Shoey; asking him to put his feet on the butt and keep pulling till something happened; he grabbed the trigger guard, feet on the butt, straightened his back with little effort, the spigot disappeared there was a satisfying click…so that's how it works.

Knowing how it worked I found I too could cock it without too much effort: bend the knees and just straighten up. So who was going to be the first to fire this awful looking contraption? Well, well, here is truck full of my students just arriving and who is that getting out of the passenger seat but none other than my old mate Sgt. Harry Hines, remember? Battered kiosk on the Mablethorpe front, and I think I said something about my regarding Harry as one of the best soldiers I ever knew. Here was Harry's chance to prove it. He was far from enthusiastic but flattery and the offer of one of Clem's cigarette lighters clinched it and there he was lying down, butt well pulled into his shoulder, front end pointing vaguely across the adjacent field of wheat, bomb lying correctly (I hoped), eyes tight shut I swear, and woosh, away went the bomb over the wheat and woosh away went Harry backwards about three feet. As he got to his feet I said, 'Bit of a kick, Harry!' To which he replied, 'Don't forget that bloody lighter.' Brilliant soldier with a wonderful gift of repartee? By this time the following day Harry was dead, killed in a solo attempt to take out a German machine gun post on Jebel Munchar. It took me a long long time to get over this, if indeed I ever did; as I type the upset comes welling back.

A footnote to this new weapon: one of the young 2nd Battalion lieutenants was awarded a Victoria Cross later in Italy attacking a tank and unbelievably firing it from the hip. The name of this moderately successful weapon was abbreviated to PIAT Mortar. All the soldiery who may read this will recognise it ndimmediately with maybe traces of panic if they had ever been called upon to fire one. What else was new in this little rest area? Churchill tanks grab you? Three of them had turned up further down the road, brand new! Forty tons of armour with a two pounder (toy) poking out of the front to say nothing of a useless gearbox. I reckon the German Mk IVs could hardly wait. Even later when equipped with six-pounder guns the Churchill was still a sitting duck for the German tanks.

Speaking of six-pounder anti tank guns, three of these turned up one evening brought by a full contingent of Artillery lads towed (guns not the lads) behind fifteen cwts. And left, handily pointing across the wheat field as per the PIATs. The QM had signed for them and probably owing to the fact we lived together in mutual dislike left me to sort of fall over them, muttering where the bloody hell did these come from? And, more to the point, why? Answer: they were to provide the Battalion with its own effective anti-tank weapon. Summoned to the QM's office I was informed that I would be joining a REME workshops for a two-day course designed to familiarise myself with the six-pounder gun. Not normally part of an Armourer's brief, too big? Anyway it was logical that I should know my way around them so I looked forward to the break.

Two days later I returned with a good but superficial knowledge of the workings of the six-pounder. In the morning, much to Northmore's annoyance and ably crewed by Joe and Shoey, I managed to bang off a couple of rounds, very enjoyable. Following this we dashed off on our NAAFI run and when we got back the guns were gone; the same Artillery lads had turned up and taken them away. That was it, I do hope you are all managing to follow this; believe me it's true. Another little thing, whilst at the workshops, and having time to fill in one morning I sat a second class shoemaker's trade test, passing with excellent marks. Shoey was delighted. There were times when Bill was snowed under with work and Joe and I would help out. In my case Bill taught me to sew on soles and other more advanced techniques and for my trade test I had been asked to sew soles on to a pair of officer's brown shoes. Easy! So I went off to become a gun fitter and came back a qualified shoemaker.

During this relatively easy period for us it must not be forgotten that the Battalion were in action every day trying to soften up a possible route when the main attack began to take Tunis, with constant patrols and actions such as the one which had cost Harry his life. Each day with the arrival of the dispatch rider bringing Battalion Orders for the Quartermaster there seemed to be yet another loss. Some I knew: the Carrier Platoon Sergeant who was caught by a rare air attack was a good friend. Whatever you are doing or wherever you are, there is nastiness just round the corner. And once again my jinx struck. Joe continued to blame me. We had been watching an air battle involving 109s and Hurricanes, I was trying to write yet another letter, the planes were very high and only Joe could see them properly through his binoculars and anyway the odd air scrap was not infrequent. I was alerted when Joe shouted that two of the planes had collided which he identified as a Hurricane and a 109. Still tracking the planes through the binoculars he said the Hurricane had turned away and was dropping further over to our right and the pilot had baled out.

He then said quite calmly that the 109 had broken up and the bulk of what was left was going to hit the ground not far from where we were. He also said there were two large objects that seemed to have broken away from the main body of the plane. By this time a little group had gathered and then scattered as the plane and the two objects were obviously going to hit very close to where we were. They did, into the wheat field about a hundred yards away. By this time there were quite a number of us running towards the plane. Not all of them stayed the course; when they found that one of the falling objects was in fact the pilot, there was suddenly a lack of volunteers to help. Joe and I sorted out the remains as best we could, recovering identity and documents and organising the digging of a grave. The QM got a message to the Padre and that was the end. The reason for the pilot's death was simply that his parachute harness had been partially shot away and when it opened the straps had parted. The other object that had come down was the engine.

Joe and I were a little unlucky to have to cope with the practical side of this tragedy but Ben and the doctor were at this time attached to Headquarter Company complete with the Aid Post Staff. They sort of moved between Beja and Jebel Munchar. Annoying really, it disrupted our card school.

Tragedy seemed to be stalking me at this time. A few days later I had gone up to one of the tents which had been used by the Rifle Company's as accommodation, should one of their Officers need to stay with B Echelon for a couple of days. At this time one of the Company Commanders, a Canadian who was attached to the Battalion, was in residence and my visit had been requested to talk about PIAT mortars. I also knew that the dispatch rider would arrive about this time with Battalion orders but that he would also be carrying the mail. As I stood outside the tent, entirely by myself and sort of deciding when to barge in to see the Major, the dispatch rider arrived, put his bike up on its stand near enough for me to reach and touch him, swung one leg off the saddle, sat sideways and never, speaking, pulled out his revolver and tucking it under his ribs, shot himself! Looking at him lying there I simply could not believe what I had just seen, even less so when I checked and found that he was almost certainly dead.

The Major who had been fast off the mark when he heard the shot, said immediately it must have been an accident but of course, as I pointed out, I had witnessed it from no more than a couple of feet away and there was no doubt he had intended to commit suicide. At the Court of Enquiry a couple of days later the Canadian Major who was senior officer was very keen to return a verdict of accidental death and had already approached me to offer evidence as to how it could have happened: technically impossible with the type of pistol he was carrying this was the modified type with no single action as the comb on the hammer had been removed. Further evidence had come to light showing that he had that morning received a 'Dear John letter' to say his wife had left him. Add to this my evidence as a witness and much as we wanted to spare the wife and the relatives it was presenting a problem.

The Major and I solved it simply. The letter in question was mislaid, and on the day of the enquiry I was with Joe and Shoey collecting stores from the NAAFI and so unavailable. Verdict. 'Accidental death'. Another life lost and just as much a victim of the war as Harry Hines.

Things were moving to a climax. The Eighth Army were moving rapidly and we were expecting them to link up with us, for the final push to Tunis. Once again we were on the move and once again it was during the hours of darkness. 'B' Echelon's position was eventually to be on the side of a hill over looking the Goubelat Plain; called by the troops 'Gab Gab', this flat land dotted with small hills stretched out to Tunis. This move took us to a staging position, again on a small hill at a place called Oued Zarga. The rule when first arriving was still to dig your slit trench but there had been almost no German air activity, it was dark and we were tired so Joe and I got about six inches dug, put our bivouac up, had supper and went to bed.

The following morning, another lovely sunny day, found me sat by the front of the bivouac writing to Girl and Tony and idly contemplating making a start on finishing the slit trench. Joe had gone off with Bill on the NAAFI run a little to our left and down the hill was a Company of Artillery and about fifty yards away behind me was the Aid Post. I could just hear Spud Murphy's gramophone and I suppose it was sort of idyllic; there was a lot of light broken cloud quite low all adding to this pleasant feeling of euphoria. I picked up the sound of aircraft diving and came alive but too late, I looked up straight into the nose of a Me.109 aimed at me personally or so it seemed. I saw the bombs leave the wings, and made a frantic scramble for six inches of slit trench. I eventually recovered consciousness to the sound of a large bell ringing in my ears and Ben saying, 'Come on, Clem, it was only a little bomb.' Checking later, this 'little bomb' had picked me up and dumped me nearly nine feet away from where I had tried to reach my six inches of slit trench, I must admit that the bomb hadn't made much of a hole.

I was again lucky, The artillery lads had taken a bad pounding, losing three of the Gunners, and once I came to, Ben dived off to help cope with one of the Gunners who had lost both legs, and several others with serious wounds. Several hours later I was sat in the first aid tent with Ben picking odd small pieces of bomb out of my back and Joe moaning about me not having finished the slit trench. There was a serious lesson here about counting chickens before they are hatched or something like that. At our final destination on the hill overlooking the 'Gab Gab' Joe and I gave a good illustration of something to do with shutting stable doors; we dug a magnificent trench, indeed so deep was it that we had to sling a rope from the olive tree under which it was dug to enable us to get in and out. At the time we were digging this, the Quartermaster had gone off to somewhere near Algiers to try and pick up a few nipples for the petrol cookers. This had been agreed with the Commanding Officer because we were having very serious problems with the cookers

These cookers were in effect huge blowlamps, working in exactly the same way but burning petrol instead of the usual paraffin. Unfortunately they suffered the same terminal problem once the hole in the nipple got beyond a certain diameter and this it does quickly owing to the constant necessity to clear the accumulated soot away using a little tool called a 'pricker' They simply don't work. The only repair is to replace the nipple. This problem was compounded by a failure right at the start of the campaign to anticipate the trouble and so the quantity of spares that might be required was grossly underestimated. At this time I would guess we had at least twenty cookers out of action. I suppose it sounds a small thing in the context of supplying spares for vehicles or tanks or the supply of ammunition but it was a problem out of all proportion and it was genuinely serious.

At this time I needed a job welded and decided to seek out a REME Field Workshops which I understood was not too far away. I was always very self sufficient and rarely needed to seek out a workshops so I looked forward to making contact and catching up on REME news. As always the Transport Section Sergeant sent me a 15cwt driven by Tug Wilson and it didn't take long to locate the workshops. It was a pleasant run with a good friend and though I was still suffering from extensive bruising after my brush with the Luftwaffe I was enjoying the day. Once at the workshops I introduced myself to the ASM who arranged my welding. Tug and I then enjoyed a good lunch and because the workshops looked very well equipped and looking to the future, after all who knows what one might need, I climbed up into a large machinery lorry where a turner was busy on a lathe. Chatting to him, I remarked on two large tea chests tucked away in the back of the lorry to which he replied in perfect King's English: 'Oh they're filled with those f******g cooker nipples, I've been turning the bloody things out for four days and I'm sick of the sight of them, seems there is a big shortage.' To my immediate answer he simply said, 'Help yourself, Sergeant'. Scrounging a box from the cookhouse, Tug and I really did help ourselves; the count when we got back yielded well over fifty.

I dished them out to the cooks (personally of course and accompanied by a small lecture on the correct or at least careful use of the prickers) and then feeling pleased at my luck I forgot about them. A couple of days later my relations with the QM took another nosedive. He had managed to get ten nipples out of the Ordnance Depot which under the circumstances was pretty good and I would have been well pleased with ten. Unfortunately, instead of asking for me to come and pick them up he took them straight to the Adjutant where he then found out that I had already solved the problem. I got a nasty ticking off for not keeping him informed. I had just got back to Joe and Bill when there was an alert for a possible air attack. In these circumstances we all dived into our respective slit trenches but the QM, not having dug one, jumped into ours, dropped the six feet odd to the bottom and broke an ankle. I tried later to explain that there was a rope arranged to help you get down and also out. To no avail. I knew then it was possible that I might follow Gaffer out of the Battalion and back to REME At least any relationship which we might have had was gone.

As I have said we were positioned on the side of a hill, quite high and overlooking the 'Gab Gab' or Goubelat plain. Almost underneath us was a huge flat area maybe half a mile long and almost the same wide. During the second night we were fascinated to watch a Battery of the Royal Artillery moving into the area and eventually setting up camp at the left hand end of this area but our main interest was when we identified the guns as the new anti-tank seventeen-pounders. This believe me was a truly great gun capable of taking out any of the German tanks and at long range. Even though it was dark we could keep up with what the RA lads were up to and by this time it was cooking, getting bivouacs up and settling in for the night.

So we followed their example and settled down for the night. I haven't mentioned it before but in any active service situation especially as we were now, waiting for the final attack, there is a ' Stand to' procedure in force which simply means turning out at dawn and taking up defensive positions. Strangely, not a popular 'Parade'? On this morning I lay there thinking, 'It's time Joe moved and produced a mug of tea' but suddenly, along with everybody else on the hill, I was outside looking for the source of the terrifying and unmistakable sound of tanks and a lot of them and there they were, coming in to this flat area from our right where a road crossed the plain, Mk IVs and in a seemingly endless convoy, turning on to the plain in slightly staggered line abreast. This even from the safety of the hill was an awesome and frightening sight and also pretty worrying: where the hell had they come from and more to the point where were they going? As they fanned out and moved rapidly down this flat area the Gunners on our left were frantically coming awake and desperately trying to get their guns into action.

It seemed an age before they got the camouflage netting off the guns, and by this time our area was crowded with troops watching this drama unfold. The tanks pressed relentlessly on towards where the Gunners had holed up for the night. There was only the distinctive sound of the tank engines and their tracks but it was obvious that the tanks had no idea that there were troops ahead, much less that they were Gunners equipped with the British Army's latest anti tank gun. They were due a terrible shock as the first gun into action opened up and the leading tank was hit with a tremendous shower of sparks. It just stopped dead in its tracks and almost disappeared in a dust-cloud. By this time the Gunners were really into action and the tanks were shifting formation and firing back at where they judged the shells were coming from. The noise by this time was horrendous and already one tank was burning with its ammunition exploding and adding to the noise. The tanks were in a hopeless position. They had not expected this sudden resistance and they are very 'blind'; once under fire they have to rely on periscopes so their return fire was simply in the general direction of the guns. The seventeen-pounders were proving superb and the shoot must have been easy: very flat trajectory, open sights and a whack fully equal to that of the German 88 mm, a gun that had already entered history in its duel role of anti-tank and anti-aircraft. I cannot remember how long this action lasted; I know there were two tanks burning plus a good number not moving and crews beginning to get out and take cover behind their tank. Casualties were mounting and from a German point of view the whole thing must have been their worst nightmare. Very shortly the tanks began to withdraw, the Gunners still engaging them at extreme ranges and still scoring hits.

Then it was over. The quiet was physically awful; I remember feeling sick and I certainly wasn't the only one. Troops were beginning to pour onto the plain to help the German casualties, ambulances began to arrive and if there was any redeeming feature for the Germans about this action it had been fought within a stone's throw of one of our large field hospitals. Writing this has brought the whole drama back to me. I can almost smell it, and it did smell. How could it be summed up from our grandstand seat? Maybe 'Savage Theatre' might be appropriate.

History showed that this was a disastrous climax to a brilliant tactic by Rommel who brought the tanks up during the night and was aimed at a Hurricane Squadron who were operating from an airstrip several miles to the south of us. Had he succeeded our campaign would have been seriously compromised. The staggering thing about this late thrust by Rommel was that he had brought the tanks up through our lines without being accosted in any way and using the main road from Tunis. Many heads were to roll for this! The whole thing foundered on a quite accidental decision to stay the night in that particular location by the Royal Artillery seventeen-pounder troop.

We were seeing the final days of the campaign to drive the Germans out of North Africa. The Battalion continued to contribute to the final advance. They were no longer part of the First Guards Brigade. Earlier at some stage and whilst waiting to be brought up to strength after Tebourba the Battalion had been a sort of spare, used wherever needed and as we had learned, usually in a hurry with something nasty at the end. But now they were bringing out two Battalions of the Hampshires and forming a Hampshire Brigade. Meanwhile the two Guards' Battalions had been joined by the Irish Guards and were now a Brigade of Guards. I do hope you are keeping up with all this.

The collapse of the German Armies in Tunisia, and the resultant thousands of prisoners has all been well documented and as I have previously said this is not a history of war, just my own story, and all this involvement is just as my service unfolded. After all, I had chosen this wonderful Infantry Battalion, and even if my motives were selfish at the time I had so far stayed the course and am more than a little proud of that, and more and more I am identifying with the Battalion. Just a little more history. The Hampshire Regiment had a very distinguished association with India, serving for many years in that country and had adopted the tiger for their cap badge, A Hampshire soldier within the Battalion was always known as a 'Tiger'. Myself! who knows?

B Echelon were briefly laid up in the suburbs of Tunis and we were able to watch the low key Victory Parade but quickly we were on the move again and this time back to very familiar territory, Medjez el Bab. Here the Army had constructed a large Prisoner of War camp. I don't remember how many prisoners there were, something like a thousand, mostly from the Herman Goering Division. At the start there were also some two hundred Italian soldiers but they left very shortly after we took over the camp. So this was to be our new role. And a very unhappy two weeks it proved to be; we were sleeping in the large 180-pounder tents and I even had a camp bed courtesy of an American and fifty cigarettes.

The German soldiers were a revelation and more than equalled us for both individual smartness and the way they behaved in their compound. Parades, kit inspections, tents lined up, kit laid out at all times; in fact they were making our own RSM, my old friend and tank fighter Trudge Truran, restless. Trudge and I had discussed the possibility of running a trial game of football with a view to getting a few names together for a future Battalion team. This had been prompted by the area we were in possessing a very good football pitch. A problem immediately cropped up: should the POWs be allowed to watch? The Adjutant decided why not, so there we were kicking off in front of a good crowd of our own lads and almost a thousand very critical Germans and what a reception every little mistake got. I never realised how loud whistling could be from such a crowd nor how it encouraged self analysis. It was great fun and was really our first easing of the stresses that had built up during the campaign. The next problem for the Adjutant was a suggestion from the senior German Officer that a football match be played between us and the Germans but this quite rightly was considered a step too far.

At the rear of the Germans' tented area was a stretch of the camp that had no fencing. This was not really necessary because beyond was a minefield and very prominently signed as such. Who had, laid this minefield and subsequently produced the map showing the layout? Why yours truly, aided, and abetted by a Paratrooper Sergeant. What goes around comes around!

Our little gang had settled down very well and most evenings were spent in the Aid Post tent with Ben and the lads of the Medic section, to say nothing of Doctor Murphy. A beer or two, drop of Scotch, it was all very cosy. Joe was still deep into aircraft recognition and seemed to have a constant supply of new cards coming in through the mail. Myself? Well, my supply came from Girl and Tony. Surprisingly enough, nothing much in them about aircraft recognition.

It never pays to be complacent. The campaign was over, the prisoners were quiet and well behaved, food was good; then a different sort of disaster struck. Just about the whole camp went down with firstly a sort of general feeling of being unwell and a strange kind of depression which Dr Murphy diagnosed as delayed shock from our experiences. Speaking personally, after a night in which I had been sick twice, I woke up shaking and I just couldn't stop. I felt truly awful and just stayed in bed hoping Ben might come round. This he did and said I was far from the only one in this state: nothing to be done, just stay in bed and ride it out and he would pop in from time to time. This I did and the next day I felt a little better. This lasted a couple of days then I went down with dysentery and on my first sprint I found that the Pioneer Lads had built a massive latrine complex and that the whole camp, Germans included, were falling like flies with dysentery. We were being treated with one of the new sulphur drugs, I seem to remember it was called Sulphur Guenadine and came in a long strip, about three feet, of tablets. The drugs certainly worked and gradually the epidemic died down and the camp started to come back to normal.

It was a shaking experience and took a lot of getting over, 'Spud' always maintained that the whole thing was a reaction to our experiences, I suppose today it would be described as 'trauma' but as I said once before, our nearest Councillor was the RSM (my good friend Trudge not such a frightening thought now) but the whole thing passed quickly enough and apart from producing a few sore bums didn't seem to leave any lasting problems. Certainly the Pioneer Platoon were to be highly commended. Their handling and construction of the latrine facilities under the most appalling conditions was superb. A further but sad word on my old friends the Pioneer Platoon. Four of them were the only ones to ignore Colonel Lee's advice not to attempt to cross the River Mejurda and they were all drowned.

Once again we were all wondering what the future held. They were beginning to reduce the prisoners as they were taken off to what would eventually be prison camps in England. One thing we would miss was the choir, they had formed whilst with us. This was huge and they would perform during the evenings. I don't think any of us would ever forget their beautiful rendering of Brahms' Cradle Song; this of course was bound to strike home to all the parents, like myself, missing their children; nevertheless, enemy or not it was beautifully done and generously applauded.

I wasn't doing any sort of work at this time. We were all supposed to be resting and trying to recover and speaking for myself I spent a lot of time writing letters and of course reading Girls replies. I think, too, it was about this time that Tony began to write. Of all the letters that passed between Girl and me, well over a thousand, these from Tony are the only ones that survived; how I wished that I had our letters now. I had during this spell at the camp acquired a very good Bessa camera, no questions please, but whilst at that time I had no interest in photography this acquisition sparked off an interest that has lasted to the present day.

There were many signs beginning to show indicating that our stay at Medjez el Bab was coming to an end. For instance, the Royal Engineers were busily digging up all those mines I had helped to lay a thousand years before. The German area of the camp was practically dismantled and there was a general air of waiting for what comes next. This turned out to be a holiday break by the sea at a place called Hammen Lif; I doubt very much that that is the way to spell it but it sounds right. B Echelon were occupying a orchard, mostly citrus fruit, which was part of a Sultan's Palace, and very grand it was too, the Palace I mean, and though empty we made good use of its sumptuously equipped toilets. The orchard itself stretched down to the beach and underfoot it was just loose fine sand. It always surprised me that the trees seemed to thrive in it. It wasn't ideal for our needs, we were still using bivouacs and trying to keep the sand out of your blanket was a problem.

They were running trucks into Tunis so I managed to spend a day there and even saw a film, well remembered, James Cagney in *Yankee Doodle Dandy*. During our stay there George Formby was appearing in Tunis, part of his tour of North Africa entertaining the troops. Unfortunately our stay had come to an abrupt end and after only two days we were standing by to move. On the day before we were due to move, Bill asked the Adjutant if he could go into Tunis to see his sister Beryl and his brother in law George Formby. After duly reminding Bill that the Battalion would be moving very early the following day he arranged a truck and off Bill went. Joe and I were very intrigued and though we had never doubted it when Bill told us that his sister was married to George Formby, well, it sort of seemed unlikely.

Well, we were soon to learn. Around eleven o'clock that night when Joe and I were beginning to get concerned, Bill came back with his sister together with George Formby who apologised profusely to the Adjutant because of the late hour, but he had to finish the show he was doing at the time Bill turned up, but was entirely at the Battalion's disposal from then on. He found a spot on the outskirts of the orchard, word soon got round, and the lads came pouring in. George played and sang for almost four hours with only short breaks for rest and refreshment. During this time Bill introduced Joe and me to Beryl and George and they expressed thanks for the way we had taken Bill under our wing. Apparently Bill had been singing our praises. I couldn't help thinking about Tebourba and Casserine and thinking, if only they knew.

And so our brief stay by the sea came to an end and at first light we were once again on our way, courtesy of the RASC and of course our own transport, Joe and Bill in the back of the baggage lorry and myself riding up front with Jack Brown. It was a large convoy so progress was steady but slow, plenty of stops for food and drink but nothing is ever straightforward. Sometime during the afternoon of the first day the convoy ran into a massive bush fire, there were hundreds of gendarmes, and civilians all battling desperately to contain the fire. Eh, look over there! hundreds of troops have just arrived and so we had. This struggle was not to my liking; the fire kept shifting and the whole thing became very dangerous. I suppose we must have been there two or three hours before we were able to leave.

The convoy stayed the night by the roadside and close by an Arab village enabling us to stock up on eggs. We were still on 'Compo' rations so the food was good. We were also told where we were going and why. Our destination was a tented camp on the outskirts of a town called Djidjelh; this was a harbour and we were to practise landings with the Navy. Whoops! doesn't sound good and where the hell will we be eventually landing? No answer was there to that question.

The camp was well set up and very comfortable. Joe, Bill and I were sharing a tent which doubled as a workshop though we all three were working outside most of the time. Joe and Bill were very busy catching up with the boot repairs and I was at last getting round the Companies and mostly establishing an introduction and wherever it was needed inspecting and taking the repairable weapons back to our little base. Evenings we were joined by Ben and set up a regular card school. During this period my Solo improved though not my bank balance but by far away the most important thing was the regular mail, letters every day and it was wonderful to be keeping abreast of Girl and especially of course Tony's progress. We were well into 1943 so he was fast approaching three years old and I sometimes despaired, wondering how old he was going to be before I saw him again.

During what was a long stay at Djidjelh the Battalion were due to celebrate one of their Battle Honour dates, Minden Day. This normally starts with a full Battalion Parade when a rose is issued to each man to put behind his cap badge. After this there is a day of inter-Company sport, Mess dances and a general merry making, most of it drunken. This is fine at home in Barracks and the whole thing is very well done but as we were at Djidjelh and in the middle of a war the celebrations were a problem. It all finally boiled down to a massive Inter-Company Sports competition. We had access to an excellent football stadium and also a large theatre in which the lads were organising a variety show. The Adjutant, still a good friend, approached me to try and make some sort of trophy.

I decided on a shield as the simplest and most practical, always providing I could find some suitable timber and brass to form a centrepiece. Of course my other problem was tools but I felt confident I could manage with what I had. Where to look for timber? We had been using the harbour for swimming and I noticed that the Navy had a workshop set up to repair landing craft which were essentially wooden. Poking my nose hopefully into the large marquee where the workshop was housed I found they were using sheets of beautiful, mahogany faced, nine-ply timber for patching. A quick word and they had cut me a piece just right for what I had in mind. This timber was about three quarters of an inch thick and perfect for the shield. The brass I had found in the form of an old shell case but it required cutting and flattening and as always with shell cases it had been heat treated and was very hard.

I hacksawed a suitable length off but found I simply couldn't flatten it because of its hardness. I needed a substantial heat source to anneal the brass and so back to the Navy where I was introduced to the Blacksmith - job done! A nice piece of soft flat brass. Cutting the shield to shape was not too difficult but hard work; the brass centrepiece was straightforward. At the top corners of the shield I mounted two Hampshire Cap Badges and at the bottom under the brass centre piece, a REME Cap Badge. This centre piece I engraved suitably but I cannot remember exactly what the inscription said and finally a plain brass plate engraved with 'North Africa 1943', along the bottom of the shield.

A word about this engraving. Shortly after joining the Battalion, Sgt. Arnold's grandfather, an engraver by trade, died and left a beautiful set of engraving tools, Arnold had no interest in engraving but I did; as a result of this interest he very generously gave them to me. I searched out books on engraving and started to teach myself becoming reasonably proficient. Had not the war intervened I fully intended to find a source of hands-on teaching, I really enjoyed this craft. Hence the engraved shield and though I needed a bit of practice before I embarked on the final lettering it came off very well. The Adjutant was delighted and said he would include it if possible with the Mess silver. Sadly, unlike me, it apparently didn't survive; at least the Regimental Museum has no record of it.

'Minden Day' went off very well indeed, plenty to eat and drink and the sports were a big hit with everyone. Ultimately the day ended very strangely for me and not a little frightening. I was very involved physically and started by representing HQ Company in a couple of short water polo matches down at the docks. One didn't need to be able to play this game just so long as you could swim; a lack of volunteers had resulted in my being picked. The next item I did know something about, tug of war, all those hours spent watching the Hilsea team suffering at the back of the block. I had actually managed a little training with HQ team and couldn't wait for it to start. Mind you, this was the first time I had actually captained a team but in the event we wiped the floor with everybody. Sgt. Ollier, you should have been here! Surprising how tiring it was for me although all I did was shout but my exertions in the water polo match were beginning to catch up and it was a hot day.

Next up in the afternoon was the six-a-side football. Led byTrudgewe had a pretty good side which included Pugh, the current Stoke City left back, and we were pretty confident of winning this particular competition and so it proved but it took a long time and several matches resulting in the final being played in the late afternoon. I was by this time really struggling, as we all were; for me it had been a long day and I just don't how I finished the final but we won and I staggered back to the tent to try and get my wind back before we all went off to the theatre in the evening. I only remember seeing the first couple of acts and then once again Ben was bending over me reciting my name. Apparently I had collapsed completely at the show and been brought back to my bed. Spud had diagnosed exhaustion and suggested a surfeit of beer and rest would soon have me on my feet again. Turned out to be spot on but I had missed the presentation of my trophy to HQ Company (who else) but I did have the satisfaction of engraving our Company name on it.

There was one more sporting occasion worth a mention: a football match with the Royal Air Force who were going to experiment using a bombing raid with Lancasters which instead of flying back to England were going to carry on and land in North Africa. This landing turned out to be at an airport close to where we were. I cannot remember whether the intention was to do a bombing run on the way back or simply to enable the aircraft to fly back at leisure and safely. In the event our football team lost to a combined RAF team made up of crews and maintenance staff. It was a great game. War produces many strange twists and turns not, all of them bad.

The next turn was all bad, indeed as bad as it ever gets. The troops had been on exercise all day and in the early evening were returning in small groups to their tents. These were laid out in rows and ours was part of one row. Joe, Bill and I were just packing up and as the lads came past passing the time of day, suddenly from the tent on our left there was the sound of a small explosion, a lot of smoke and the most awful and intensive screaming that was to live with me for ever. I can still hear it and feel the horror. Parts of the tent were burning but as we dived over to it as fast as we could there was nothing that could have prepared us for what we saw. One of the soldiers had been sat taking a phosphorous grenade out of one of his equipment pouches. These pouches rested on your chest and served as general ammunition pouches but were specially designed to carry two Bren magazines. The bomb had exploded in his face and from the waist up he was covered in burning phosphorous. This generates tremendous heat and cannot be stopped by any conventional means. Usually it throws the phosphorous off in small pieces and any of these would burn through a limb without you being able to stop it; even totally immersing it in water has no effect. In this case I think the equipment had contained it a little but the pouches were fast being destroyed.

Very quickly after we arrived Ben and the doctor got there plus several of the medics with stretchers. Whilst the three of us organised efforts to isolate the pieces of burning tent, the medics were helpless and though they eventually got the lad onto a stretcher and over to the Aid Post he died shortly after.

I always thought that Ben was immune to the traumas of his job but he never got over this and was a changed personality. Bill, Joe and I were never again quite the same, I could never shake off the sound of those screams. I think being first on the scene was a trauma too far.

We were quickly on the move again and once again courtesy of the RASC I didn't like moving because the mail tended to dry up and one never quite knew when it would appear again. I had been kept very much up to date with young Tony and I continued to write every day. One effect the incident above had was to make letter writing more difficult. I was pretty low at this time. Our destination this time was Bizerte and the rumour was that we would be leaving there to invade Italy. What! just like that? Oh God, here we go again.

We staged on the way, pulling in for the night and this led to a strange but very lucrative interlude. I was returning from whenever and was between the RASC vehicles when one of their Sergeants asked me if I would like to make up a hand of five card brag, Not thinking too clearly I agreed, and climbed up into their truck. Now our own little gang, though playing mostly Solo, often played brag for a change but we played basically just for enjoyment and the money side of it was not an issue. Because of this if you lost a hand then you simply paid the kitty this amount having previously agreed, we didn't go in for large amounts. Once the cards have been dealt certain of the higher value cards will remain in the pack and it is possible to make a bid which depends on one or other of these cards being in this pack and not in one of the hands dealt. If for example winning your call depended upon say a Jack of Hearts being in the pack and you made the call this is known as betting on a bare Jack. Not done! But in our little school if you lost it didn't matter with only a small amount of money to pay into the kitty.

I sat down and as is normal it was decided what the stakes would be. I quickly realised I had joined a serious school of gamblers. Firstly buying into the kitty was expensive, then finding that if I went down on a call I would have to pay not only the kitty but the whole school, this would be quite a sum based on the agreed stakes. Another little snag, I didn't have a lot of money on me. What to do? I decided to just play my normal game, betting on bare cards as I would do in our own little school; the result of course would be that I would soon be out of money and back in my bed. It didn't work out like that: much to the disgust of the RASC lads I just kept winning and when they called it a day, muttering about luck, I found that I had more than quadrupled the money in my pocket.

By the time we finished I was feeling hungry so wandering over to the cookhouse I grabbed a loaf with the object of making a bully beef sandwich and in doing so managed to inflict a very serious gash on my hand. I expect I was carried away by the money in my pocket. I walked over to First Aid dripping blood and munching a very messy sandwich. I dug Ben out of bed and as he stitched up the gash I told him about the evening. 'If you'll stop eating that ghastly sandwich I'll prove it's your lucky night. From midnight the currency exchange rate has been changed and it will double your winnings.' Well, well, well!

I never saw Ben again; along with Spud Murphy he was killed at Salerno a few weeks later.

Arriving in Bizerte, B Echelon had been allocated two large marquees and the three of us settled ourselves into a corner using odd boxes to give ourselves a bit of privacy, I needed the privacy to count all my money! The Battalion were busy gearing themselves up for the landings and I in turn was busy inspecting and checking their weapons including making sure that everybody had a War Department French letter guaranteed to be robust enough to stand the rigors of leading the troops ashore located on the muzzles of their rifles, and hopefully keeping the sea out. It was very quiet really, Ben had disappeared on some sort of advanced medical training, the mail was coming through steadily and it was easy to be lulled into a sense of security.

I was also pretty apprehensive about the immediate future and one of my previous expressions comes to mind, 'Oh no! not again!' but that is the Infantry during a war. One job finished, on with the next.

There was a wonderful moment just round the corner. I had been out all day and when I walked into the marquee there were Joe and Bill chatting to Tacker Knight, remember he of the broken football trophy and last seen showing me his spine at Tebourba, at least a big lump of it. It truly was a great joy to see him and to find that he had been passed fully fit again and posted back to the Battalion. Bill and I spent some time admiring his scars: how on earth did I cover that lot with a Field Dressing? His story confirmed a lot of what we had heard about the aftermath of the battle and the behaviour of the enemy. After the battalion pulled out Tacker had been picked up by German medics and taken to a small aid post where a doctor gave him first aid and morphine. He was then put into a queue along with German wounded and eventually evacuated to a small Field Hospital where they carried out preliminary surgery and there he stayed, well looked after until the Germans pulled out and handed him over to British Medics.Then to one of our large Field Hospitals and from there to the Base hospital near Algiers. More surgery and a long convalescence. And here he was looking forward to reclaiming his rightful place in the battalion Football team and glad to be back. I still didn't tell him the truth about my miraculous repair to his trophy and never did.

About this time the Battalion were entertained by the Pioneer Corps Band which was touring with ENSA The band leader was my old mate Nat Gonnella, how long ago it seemed back to Forfar. The troops went wild and kept the band on until the musicians just had to give up. The officers had laid on refreshments in their Mess and excusing myself to the Adjutant who was by this time well oiled I grabbed Nat and we settled down with Joe and Bill in our little corner of the marquee and with a couple of bottles of Scotch, spent the evening clearing up the Scotch, munching bully beef sandwiches and listening to Nat playing all our old favourites softly, sometimes with a mute, but often reducing us to tears. As I have said before it's a funny old war.

It became even funnier (or not) a few days later, when the QM told me that I had been posted to the 30th Searchlight Regiment at Bone. This truly was out of the blue and I was quite shaken by it. I was to see the Adjutant as soon as possible. This revealed that I was being posted for promotion and that he had insisted on a replacement before this move could take place and on the instructions of the Commanding Officer, he had been ordered to ask why I couldn't I be promoted and remain with the Battalion. This was very flattering but foundered on the sacred altar of the 'Battalion Establishment' which only allowed one Sgt. Armourer, REME attached.

Anyway, since the terrible tragedy at Djidjelh I had begun to feel that it might be a good idea to try and get away from the Battalion, Girl too at this time, was putting a lot of pressure on me to try and get myself posted. The Portsmouth newspapers always carried accounts of what the Hampshires were up to, even though it might be long after the event owing to censorship. I suppose that deep down I was suffering from a feeling that I was a part of the Battalion, a sort of family member. I had been with them more than three years, traumatic years to say the least, and somehow there never seemed a right time to approach the Adjutant with a request to move on. Even now the Battalion were waiting to start the landings in Italy and I would have been conscious of that fact. So there never was a right time. Well, it had been taken out of my hands and so I prepared to move on.

Mentally at least, but before then it seemed there was a little matter of Salerno to be faced unless of course my replacement arrived first. Unlikely I thought, and I was right. So here I am once again but this time on a proper landing craft together with B Echelon and on what the Army refers to as 'D' +3, i.e. three days after the initial landings, the idea being that B Echelons' 'Transport Sections' etc. would be able to land unopposed. In this case it was pretty well as it was supposed to be and although the Brigade was still involved in a vicious battle to achieve their objectives and once again the Battalion were taking heavy casualties, we made it without problems to the inside yards of a warehouse complex and dug in whilst I tried to get rid of my dry mouth. Here we stayed as the Battle turned our way and things began to return to normal.

Maybe a week or more later and I was stood, together with Joe and Bill and all my kit, at the entrance to this complex waiting for a truck to take me into Salerno and then on back to North Africa. We weren't a happy trio. I was still very distressed at Ben's death as were Joe and Bill and of course I was leaving two very dear friends. A motorcycle drove up. Oh no! but it turned out to be RSM Trudge Truran. We had been good friends since I first joined the Battalion and he had discovered that I was the left half back he was looking for. After our brush with the tanks at Tebourba this friendship always had a special edge to it and I was moved that he had undertaken what was not an easy journey even at this late stage of the battle to see me off. He also had a message of good luck from the Adjutant which, too, set the seal on what had been a well understood relationship. Handshakes all round. I walked to the bike with Trudge and as he prepared to kick it into life he simply said, 'Tug Wilson was killed yesterday' And so there was an end!

CHAPTER 12
MOVING ON

Back to Bizerte, miserable, and fretting as to when I might get letters again. Once on the move by yourself goodness knows how the mail would catch up; the Battalion Post Corporal would send any mail on and I had already given Girl my new address but it seemed a bleak future. I was really low. Tug's death I find deeply upsetting, somehow different to all the others; we had covered many miles together. There was something special about Tug, everybody liked him and after recovering from serious injuries when he turned his truck over in Palestine (just another war) and the quite serious wounds he sustained on the way to Dunkirk it just seemed cruel.

I reported to the Mobilisation and Holding Centre in Bizerte. These were large camps scattered about any large theatre of war like North Africa and their job was to process soldiers moving about, either singly as in my case, or in groups, and sometimes reinforcements from UK Their main task was to sort out where they were going and see that somehow they got there. These centres could be looked at as either a good rest or a pain in the arse. At this one I was beyond caring but it provided good food and rest so I just had to be patient. Eventually they found a small REME workshops set up three or four miles outside Bizerte and who from time to time sent vehicles down to the REME Base Workshops at Bone. They said they could fix me up and the Searchlight Regiment I was joining was virtually next door to the Base Workshops.

And that is why I'm sitting in the cab of a seven ton Leyland recovery lorry, next to a REME L/Corporal who will drive me down to the Searchlight Regiment, a nice long run. We had stacked up with rations, time was not an issue. The Corporal had done the trip twice before and indicated our route would run parallel to the shore with bags of swimming opportunities. I was beginning to warm to this lad and indeed the whole thing was very pleasant indeed, picnicking here and there and a swim. Already the war seemed a long way behind. There was a great deal of American traffic both ways and we stopped a couple of times to swop rations and yarns; well, well, so this was life away from the 'Poor Bloody Infantry'. So far I hadn't even had an aircraft fall out of the sky on top of me, things were really looking up and then, and then! we were passed by an American Jeep with a trailer full of tyres, travelling much too fast as he swung round a sharp bend leading on to a railway bridge and the trailer, taking the Jeep with it, went straight through the parapet and on to the railway line some twenty feet below It happened right under our noses, the L/Corporal needing to brake pretty smartly.

Diving over to the hole I could see the Jeep on its wheels and with the driver sitting, gripping the steering wheel and parked neatly in the middle of the railway line. The trailer was on its side some distance away but ominously still and lying next to the trailer was an American soldier. I told my driver to try and get the recovery truck on to the track whilst I scrambled down to have a look at the casualty who sadly was dead, somewhere along the way he had, I suspect; been trapped by the trailer which had broken away and rolled down the embankment. The driver said later that he had jumped when they went through the bridge. Whatever had happened his head had

been badly crushed and he was certainly dead; the casualty was a young Lieutenant. I quickly went to the Jeep and as I got there the driver sat up, pressed the starter and the engine sprang into life, then he just sat.

It was obvious that he was just stunned so I chatted him up until the recovery truck appeared, backing carefully down the rails. The American driver soon began to come to and start to talk, I didn't tell him about the Lieutenant but took my driver over to see how we were going to deal with the situation. The Lieutenant was lying face down, so we turned him over carefully which exposed the injuries this upset my L/Corporal and I was reminded of Gaffer and myself all those years ago. He quickly recovered and I sent him back onto the road to stop the first vehicle that came along. Meanwhile the American driver had got out of the Jeep and I told him about the Lieutenant, then suggested he join my driver. Eventually they stopped a small American truck driven by a Major and with several soldiers in the back. They quickly got the Lieutenant back up to the road and into the truck. I said I would look after the driver and the Jeep, profuse thanks and they left.

My L/Corporal and I, with the help of the driver, recovered the Jeep; after all that's what recovery trucks are for and I was able to use my camera to get the photo on the previous page. We took the truck and driver back to his unit and after a big supper stayed the night and were quickly back on the road next day.

Finally I reported in to the Headquarters of the Search Light Regiment, was allocated a tent complete with bed, and introduced to the Corporal Armourer who had been with them for a long time (sadly names elude me yet again as they have with the L/Corporal who drove me down). I really should remember the Corporal's name because we were to get on together superbly and between us write a Technical Manual for the Oerlikon Gun. This was printed and circulated amongst Armourers with the First and Eighth Armies and Eureka! His name was Anderson, my good friend Corporal Anderson. This unit were very settled and were even producing a small news sheet as and when. A feature of this little paper was a small item tucked on the end and called 'Flipovers' written by the Chief Clerk to welcome newcomers. I have always cherished mine which very simply said:

S/Sgt Hoyle,
Drinks rifle oil,
And pulls himself through,
With four by two.

Any old Serviceman will instantly recognise 'Four by Two' as the cleaning material for rifle barrels and issued by the Services. Please note that no time had been lost in promoting me.

I remember during this period feeling very tired and sort of lethargic when out of the blue I was summoned to the CO's office where he told me that he had been looking at my previous Service with the Hampshires since arriving in North Africa, and that he had a close friend here in Algeria, a wine grower, a friend of many years, stretching back before the War, and I was being dispatched, so to speak, to go and stay with this family for a week on the basis that I probably needed a good rest and that I had earned it. Almost before I had digested this wonderful prospect I was being introduced to the lady of the house and shown to my room. There was just Mum and Dad and a boy of twelve who spent a great deal of the week driving me round the huge vineyards using the inevitable pony and trap. Although they did have motor vehicles there was no petrol.

It was a wonderful week made even better when my mail caught up with me courtesy of the unit dispatch rider. I earlier criticised French cooking and still think it is much over rated but during this week it was superb though I suspect there was a conscious effort to tailor it to my English taste. I lazed about, wrote lots of letters, there was always a bucket of iced grapes available which the family grew specially for dessert and were really delicious. I remember each evening we dined formally outside, usually as it was just getting dark; normally this would present an insect problem, especially mosquitoes but it had been solved by using four large hanging baskets suspended over the table in which lived a colony of chameleons and lizards. These beavered away, very happy in their work, mopping up these pests. A very neat and simple trick, fascinating to watch and believe me very effective. The wine of course was superb with seemingly endless variety.

So back to work and first a visit to the Base Workshops, which occupied an old factory complex. I was surprised at the size and capability of the various workshops but my main interest was with the Armourers' section and this too was big with just one main workshop area plus secure storage for the small arms, an in the centre a good sized office. The AIA in charge was Captain Gilmour and a nicer person would be difficult to find. Some six years later he was to be my boss at 21 Command Workshops, Burscough. After a long chat in which I moaned about my first class trade test going astray at Dunkirk he said he had been pressed to produce a Technical Manual for the Oerlikon and how would I like to put it together? I pointed out that I had only ever seen an Oerlikon from a distance so that I was hardly qualified. Ah, but the Searchlight Regiment had twenty Oerlikons and more importantly nobody knew more about them than Corporal Anderson. The sting in the tail, 'It would make an excellent trade test.' And so it turned out. I did the writing and Corporal Anderson supplied all the technical details and I became First Class. The manual turned out very well and was printed in a small paper backed book and widely circulated.

By the time it was finished I had become very familiar with the gun, including test firing on the beach. I enjoyed that. I found the gun itself very efficient but the magazine less so. One nasty snag was the ease with which a round could be toppled over when loading against a powerful spring; this resulted in 'us' Armourers having to strip down the magazine, a tedious business but as a certain percent of the rounds were high explosive with a sensitive nose it wasn't wise to drop one. The exercise turned out to be academic because without warning the Regiment was disbanded along with my promotion and both Andy and I were left waiting for a posting. This was October and again Tony's birthday came and went without his Dad; indeed I have a feeling I might have been in hospital at the time with a recurrence of the throat infection I had had at Lockerbie. This base hospital was superbly equipped, and with discipline and a suitable Matron who struck fear into everyone it was very much a carbon copy of Netley; it certainly brought back memories. This time, once over the initial stages of being unwell, it was a pleasant enough stay.

I eventually found myself posted to the REME Light Aid detachment attached to the 39th Royal Artillery Light Anti-Aircraft Regiment, (Bofor Guns). This unit was based in Bizerte so here I was on my way back to where I had just come from. This was the start of a mostly unpleasant period which lasted several months. The first nasty surprise was finding that the LAD only had an establishment for a Sergeant Armourer, so bang went my promotion and when I raised this forcibly, maybe a little too forcibly, with my new Officer Commanding (OC), a young Lieutenant, he was totally indifferent and from then on our relationship went downhill. I really was furious and couldn't see a way out. Somehow this new Unit seemed strangely disjointed. The Sgt/Major (AQMS), who was really running it was a strange character; he had at some time been referred to an Army Psychiatric unit who had issued him with a certificate which in effect said he was sane. As it had been the OC who was responsible for the referral, here again there was an unhappy relationship. The AQMS was prone when stressed or drunk to pull out this certificate and demand to see your own proof of sanity.

But compounding my feeling of depression was a lack of mail; this was due to my moving about, and had dried up. The situation couldn't have been more miserable, Additionally I didn't have the faintest idea what I was supposed to be doing. There didn't seem to be any sort of connection with the Regiment except when they brought an item in for repair, usually a truck, a Bofor Gun or a 'Predictor', which worked out the height and course of an aircraft. Meanwhile I had been busy talking to the craftsmen who made up this unit, not a happy crowd at all even though they had been together a long time. Besides myself there was another Sergeant a vehicle mechanic, a Corporal welder whose first name I do remember, 'Danny', and L/Corporal Instrument mechanic. Although the Army had insisted on enrolling him into REME as an instrument mechanic simply on the grounds that his previous employer had been 'Elliots' who manufactured instruments, the Army then steadfastly refused to listen to him when he said that he was a cabinet maker and though he did work at Elliots his job was making boxes for the instruments. Another disgruntled soldier.

The other factor that worried me, I was going to be spending Christmas with this unit; I nearly typed 'lot'. This would have been unkind because I spent a long time with them and they proved to be a great crowd and we had a good Christmas. I had during this stay been trying to contact the Hampshires through Brigade but without success. I was going to try and get back to them seeing as my promotion had fallen through but anyway I didn't succeed in making contact, so I soldiered on.

All of this time the Regiment, along with us of course, had been marking time before embarking for Italy. Finally, we climbed aboard a large LCT (Landing Craft Tanks). My second time in just a few weeks but this time our destination was a normal port at Taranto, where we convoyed up to Foggia which became our home for the next couple of months. There was a Commonwealth Bomber Squadron operating Wellington bombers from Foggia Main, the local Airport, and looking back I presume that was the reason for the Regiment to be there though by this time we had almost total air superiority and the Regiment was slowly becoming superfluous in it's Anti-Aircraft role. This was to be resolved in the not too distant future.

Meanwhile I had tried to get some sort of contact going with the Batteries but they only seemed concerned about their Bofors which were the responsibility of the Gun Fitters not Armourers. I had acquired a motor bike ostensibly to get round the Batteries and have a look at the small arms situation but apart from enabling me to get about a bit I allowed myself to become disillusioned. I was still angry about the promotion, and as no one seemed to care I attached myself to the vehicle recovery section and the Corporal Recovery Mechanic, a young lad from Southampton, first name John, very good and conscientious at his job. Our truck was a Leyland seven ton recovery vehicle (remember my sad episode with the jeep and railway bridge, same type poking it's nose into the photo). John always said he would pull anything out with this truck, I had no wish to contradict him and later he was to prove his skill in no uncertain way. I also learned to drive this truck, not easy, a beast of a gearbox but John, once I had mastered it, was always happy to let me drive.

There was of course one huge plus at this time: my mail had caught up and was arriving regularly so I was keeping abreast of Tony's progress. We were comfortably billeted in a large block of empty flats and another little plus turned up: one of the cooks was a baker in a previous life and providing you could supply him with yeast (easy, our American friends were issued with tinned yeast), we would wake up to the smell of baking bread and hot rolls for breakfast. How long ago it seemed that I was splitting and cooking Compo Rations, always careful not to move far from my slit trench. In many respects life was becoming much more comfortable; the Army had opened up one of the cinemas in town and there was the prospect of regular film shows.

About this time I acquired an official job, not of my choosing but one I was happy to take on. A group of officers from the Regiment had formed a Bridge club and used one of the spare flats in our block for their bridge games. We knew that one of these was the Medical Officer. A group of us were having a sort of social evening but mostly a 'fry up' when Danny the welder started to choke on what turned out to be a piece of bacon. Funny how everybody just sat making suggestions like, 'come on, Danny, cough it up', somebody banged him on the back then suddenly he fell off the bed and instantly I could see he was in serious trouble. One of the lads was already on his way to find the doctor. I didn't really know what to do but his mouth was open as he struggled desperately for breath so I wrapped the handle of a table knife with a handkerchief and forced it between his teeth. I didn't really know why but it seemed the right thing to do. The whole incident was assuming frightening proportions and these were magnified when Danny lost consciousness. Where the hell was the medical officer? Actually he arrived pretty quickly and using the gap I had wedged he quite brutally forced open Danny's mouth until he could wriggle a hand in and luckily he got a finger behind the obstruction and was able to clear it.

A couple of days later the OC told me that he had been told to nominate someone to be responsible for First Aid in the LAD I was it and would I report to the MO as soon as possible. I did and he confirmed the job and said any problems I was to refer directly to him. So there it was, I had at last been given a job. A cut finger or two certainly, the odd hangover, sounded good, you must be joking, Clem, messy disasters seemed to follow you around.

Not long after settling in at Foggia I bumped into Bill Causon, another ex Hilsea boy; he too was with an Artillery Regiment and had a workshop in the airport area and was able use the Wellington Squadron's mess. Bill had been engaged to Alec's (remember my best man) sister and they had just broken up; sadly Bill never got over it. We enjoyed one or two wild evenings in the crew's mess after Operations had just been cancelled. I was great friends with one of the Canadian Pilots, Sgt. Blackwell, known as Blackie, who offered to take me on one of the bombing raids over Berlin. 'Great,' I said but my OC would never permit it. I certainly made sure of that but the aircraft returned safely and I often regretted being 'Chicken'.

So to my last aircraft disaster. The cinema was up and running and a group of us were settling in to enjoy the film when everybody became aware of one of the Wellingtons very low and with the engines labouring badly as if desperately trying to gain height. The cinema was deathly quiet as every one wondered where it was going to come down. Not for long, it hit the houses in the same street as the cinema but about one hundred yards further along, the explosion was terrible and we were showered with bits of the cinema roof which had only been patched up. Once more there was no way any of us could get near the aircraft or what was left of it and there was the added hazard of the houses brought down and along with the aircraft they were on fire and the heat even at a hundred yards was searing. We moved away and took cover behind a block of flats, a wise move as one of the bombs exploded and the cinema collapsed, fortunately empty. None of the crew survived along with several of the occupants of the flats; the fire was eventually brought under control by RAF fire crews who arrived within minutes of the crash. War never gets any better! Months later I caught up briefly with my old Battalion and told the story of the Wellington to Joe and Bill, Joe simply said 'I don't believe it!' maybe not, but it was true.

I was settling into a steady routine, and with the odd recovery, I really was learning but nothing to do with small arms. I kept very busy, wrote stacks of letters; mail was coming in regularly and we still enjoyed our hot bread rolls truly you really can get used to a soft life. Somewhere up the road the war was grinding on and though we were not far removed it seemed very distant. The second Battalion were much in the news but it just seemed to get harder and I often thought about them and the contrast with my present Unit. John and I were given the job of taking the Leyland down to the big Ordnance Depot at Salerno to pick up spares. Load up with rations, bedding, and other earthly comforts, no time limit what more could you want. We planned a stop off at the REME Base Workshops in Naples and a very pleasant trip it was until climbing a steep hill in the direction of a village situated halfway up where the road levelled out and then after meandering through the village continued to climb with a formidable gradient.

As we breasted the hill into the village, careering down this gradient and in desperate trouble was a Royal Artillery Quad truck towing a huge 5.5 gun. This type of truck was designed for this gun and in addition to its basic function of towing it was equipped with seats to carry the gun crew and there was stowage for ammunition. The driver was frantically trying to get a gear which of course at this stage was impossible but the noise was sickening. Arriving at the level road through the village where it turned quite sharply he went straight on, burying the Quad and the gun deep into the first house. We had stopped as soon as we saw the tragedy unfolding and here I was again the sound of the crash ringing in my ears and the inevitable cloud of dust covering everything.

We both sat stunned and I remember feeling desperately tired as I tried to envisage what possible action we could take, then as the dust cleared we saw that there was a long convoy of vehicles which had been following the Quad down the hill and they were already deploying, with troops pouring out of the vehicles. By this time I suppose we were about half a mile from the accident when the Convoy Leader in a jeep came rushing up and told us to just keep going past the pile up and they would take care of it. Astonishingly 'they' turned out to be a complete Base Hospital on the move to a new location. As we passed truck after truck I would guess the convoy was well over a mile long. Although the trucks and the convoy were well marked I couldn't help thinking that they certainly presented an easy target until coming up fast and low nine Spitfires appeared, now that's what I call an escort. I presume the dust cloud had prompted a close look. We pressed on feeling helpless and distressed but I was shaking with relief at having the problem taken out of our hands.

In the end, although we called in at the Base workshops I decided to just park up for the night, top up our rations and after scrounging a hot breakfast press on to Salerno. Here I found a REME workshops where they gave us lunch and also told me that the RAOC we were looking for was a few miles down the road at a small place called Pontecagnano. Well, well, well, this was where we landed all that time ago and was one of the Battalion's main objectives. The Depot proved to be in the large warehouse complex and after parking in the huge car park running down to the beach I was able to pin-point the exact spot where Joe, Bill and I had sheltered from the German guns. John was mightily impressed, ah well, here I am, still 'swinging the lamp'.

Another quiet lazy evening, myself in the Sergeants' Mess and ditto John in the Corporals' Mess. Next day load up and set off back. A couple of hours into the journey and I found myself climbing gingerly back into the truck with a very fine crop of blisters on my hands and John pointing out that after all I am responsible for the LAD's First Aid so not to worry! Thank you John. So how did it happen? well I suppose it was all down to John's ego. Driving along a narrow dirt road we came up to a big American G.M.C. lorry, partly on its side in the ditch. There were a couple of Americans sat by drinking coffee so we stopped and joined them. They were not best pleased with their predicament and having passed a message back to their unit, were facing a long wait for help. I was sympathising when John said, 'Not to worry I'll pull you out.' Oops.

The Americans had already tried to winch themselves out, fixing their winch to a small tree which on the first strain had simply left the ground. I couldn't see any thing else that might provide an anchor and oh yes, the truck was filled with scrap metal. To say the Americans were sceptical was an under statement. John disappeared into the cab with paper and pencil and came out saying, 'No problem.' Thinking it was time I had a word with him I was greeted with the words, 'We are going to have to put all our ground anchors out.' Now I did know about ground anchors, one comprised a steel hexagon bar about five foot long with a loop and striking head at one end, sharp at the other. For some-one my size picking one up was a fair strain and scattered strategically in boxes round the Leyland were what appeared to be dozens of them. Additionally there were steel bars with holes set at an angle through which these hexagon bars were driven; these also carried fittings to fix the truck to enabling the ground tackle to take the strain.

Standing neatly in their allotted place were also several sledge hammers, John kept a very tidy truck. To complete the equipment we were going to need were a number of diabolical items called 'snatch bocks', very heavy and awkward to handle. These were in fact pulleys allowing the cable from the winch to be passed through in different combinations creating different ratios and so multiplying the power of the pull. There is a formula for this but it requires knowing the weight of the load you are trying to pull out, in this case according to our American friends and with the size of our recovery truck. Impossible! John didn't like that and kept them quiet by handing out sledge hammers. As I boasted at the beginning I enjoyed blacksmithing and could handle a sledge hammer; an hour later we were all exhausted and blistered and I was drifting away from the idea of a blacksmith's life. The problem was that the earth road was hard and it took a lot of 'sledging' to get one of the bars in never mind the twenty or so that we had actually driven in.

More coffee, a long rest, drag out the snatch blocks, take the cable through, let the Americans drag it over and fix it to their towing ring, wait for them to sort their bets out then John muttering something about either the American truck comes out or our winch gets ripped out he starts up engages the winch, the GMC starts to move, tips back over on to its wheels and moves slowly and easily back on to the road. A good moment indeed; fancy me doubting a recovery driver of John's caliber. The Americans were both flabbergasted and delighted, nearly back slapping John to death. A pity we weren't back with the Battalion, John, I reckon I would have squeezed another stripe out of the Adjutant for you. One thing that had bothered me, when we were finished how the hell were we going to get the bars out of the ground, simple, push one of the bars through the ring, twist it and the hexagon loosened the earth and out it came.

We pushed on back to the workshops where we were again fed and watered, fuelled the truck and left early in the morning. I was thinking earlier before I dropped off to sleep, about the terrible accident we had witnessed on the way down to Salerno and I couldn't help wondering if these sort of things did really follow me around just as Joe had suggested all those months ago. Well, climbing out of the truck to go and get some breakfast I found that Vesuvius had started to erupt after all these years and already a fine ash was beginning to settle. Honest, it wasn't me! I had decided earlier to detour and try and call in to look round Pompeii but this dramatic turn of events cast a doubt but I thought, what the hell, let's give it a try. John was very keen so off we went. By the time we arrived the ash was quite thick but we were shown round by the one curator who seemed to be on his own and it was well worth the detour. It really was mind boggling and certainly lived up to what I had imagined it to be. I also got a good photograph of Vesuvius in action, a troubling sight but the guide seemed unimpressed so we just pressed on.

And so back to Foggia. At the top of the hill leading down to the site of the accident they had erected a large sign detailing the number of fatal accidents and saying, 'Stop, change to a lower gear before proceeding.' John was asleep and I crawled down in bottom gear, Later I told him about the sign and that I'd had no trouble coming down in top gear, that woke him up!

When we arrived back in Foggia the dispatch rider must have visited, we were on the move.

Once again I had no idea what the Regiment's ultimate destination was but it turned into a long journey in terms of time. We kept stopping and bivouacking for three or four nights at a time and mostly I didn't care very much: the weather was great, plenty to eat and drink and no work. There was virtually no air activity and although the troops at the sharp end were finding progress slow and costly, somehow we seemed to be fighting a different war. Most importantly, during this long move the letters kept arriving so I was as content as it was possible to be so far from home. Having been issued with a motor bike I was expected to do convoy duties which meant rushing up and down the convoy making sure no one had legged it back to UK I really enjoyed this, though it was very tiring; I estimated that I always covered twice the mileage of the convoy. Add to this the odd recovery job which I enjoyed and I was of course, learning all the time. Anybody out there looking for a key to good sure recovery work then John's golden rule: 'Never take short cuts,' is as good as it gets with our success pulling the Americans out a fine example.

Once again the Regiment finished up guarding an American airfield. We were there several weeks though it is difficult for me to remember the exact time scales but what I do remember was being part of the American Army during this period and it was a very good period for our LAD We were billeted yet again in an old farmhouse with our trucks and workshops set up in the yards. Nearby were the American Airforce tents which ran parallel to the long runway from which they were operating Lightnings (P.38). We were attached to this Unit for all purposes, rations, fuel, medical etc. and we soon became very much a part of the Unit making many friends amongst the Americans who treated us right royally at all times. Their photography unit made up a few films for my camera, cut from the huge rolls of film used in the aircraft cameras.

I was at this time acting as the ration Sergeant and this was very illuminating in the context of the supplies. I had to fill in an American form detailing how many men we had in the unit and based on that I would be issued with the appropriate quantities of whatever was available at the Depot. I filled this in very meticulously, got it signed by the OC and set off to find this American supply depot. This turned out to be a large field the centre of which was piled high with rations. Boxes of tinned foods, sacks of sugar but no fresh rations except for bread and these loaves were again just piled on the ground. On my form the amount of each item, say sugar, that I was entitled to was listed according to the number in the unit; with fewer than thirty men my quantities hardly registered.

Arranged round the rations were tables and radiating back to these rations and supported on steel framework were steel rollers. At the start point, so to speak, was an American 'Top' Sergeant behind an enormous high desk (I wonder where that had been liberated?) Leading up to this from the road was a queue of large American trucks, GIs were wandering around and the air was filled with banter, mostly profane. When I turned up with my slightly smaller truck I was immediately cleared and sent to the front of the line of trucks with shouts like, 'Let the Goddamned Limey through, where's your manners?' I finally pulled up by the desk leaned through the window and with something of a flourish, handed in my form, The Sergeant looked at it, screwed it up and threw it into a large waste basket saying, 'Just move along the line, tell them what you fancy and how many cases you would like and I'll see you tomorrow—no form!' Normally with our own ration system they would only be issued, say every three days, and your form had to be correct.

I remember I started with sugar and they delivered down the rollers two sacks. I asked for milk (tinned of course) and finished up with four cases and so it went on. The Americans had a very good tinned bacon, another four cases, tinned turkey ditto and cases and cases of various tinned fruit. Fortunately there was a large American fatigue party to load all these goodies and when I arrived back there was no lack of volunteers. Two sacks of flour and a case of tinned yeast certainly impressed the baker; it wasn't long before bacon buried in fresh hot buttered rolls were on offer, definitely to die for. Did I mention the two cases of tinned butter?

We were all developing some very firm friendships with our American Allies and I spent quite a few evenings in one particular tent watching the regular poker game; the amounts of money that changed hands was a bit startling at times. I remember one of the regular players being introduced to me as the son of a full blooded Indian Chief. I can't remember his tribal name but I do remember that he always carried a superb pair of leather working gloves, that he was a welder by trade and according to his fellow poker players a very good one. He was no slouch at poker either, that was for sure.

There came a time when an air of excitement and tension became very apparent especially among the air crews. I knew several of the pilots, indeed I had picked up another invitation to fly with them and once again to my shame I had turned it down. Probably the odd bottle of Scotch that I was able to produce helped lubricate my own particular friendships. So what was the excitement? The Squadron was about to lose their Lightnings which were being replaced by the latest American fighter-bomber, the Thunderbolt. Radial engined, very fast, weighing in at something like nine tons and hardly a pretty aircraft but it was to prove a deadly fighter. I couldn't imagine how this change over would take place: the two aircraft were diametrically opposed, the Lightning light, agile and very pretty and the Thunderbolt all brute force and menace.

I was well up with the game at this time and keeping an eye on the Squadron Orders, just like ours, posted everyday on a suitable board and just like ours detailing the minutiae of every day life, mostly duties including who would be flying what and when. Suddenly there it was! In two days time the Squadron would take delivery of the Thunderbolts and surrender their Lightnings. We of the LAD couldn't wait. One of my pilot friends on being asked had said the planes would arrive, the crews would take the Lightnings back with them, leaving behind the Thunderbolts. These would be checked and serviced. He would get some sort of handbook and away he would go. Regaling this to my mates we agreed it was going to be an interesting week. I think had he been there, Joe would have insisted that I left, at least until it was over. I subsequently learned that it wasn't quite like that, in fact three instructors had been with them for two or three days doing classroom work with the pilots and they would be sort of hanging about when the moment arrived to climb in and take off.

The Thunderbolts arrived and were parked up in the dispersal area. The following day the Lightnings left, the ferrying pilots ensuring quite a display before finally settling down and disappearing into the distance. So far so good a couple of quiet days and then the great day dawned. We knew it was the day because the Americans had put in to operation stage two of the conversion course. Along the sides of the runway, appearing as if by magic, were a large number of ambulances and fire-engines. This would of course offer great reassurance to the pilots who would now set off confident of the quickest treatment possible.

The next few days provided plenty of entertainment, but no drama and the 'just in case' backup left and a week later the Squadron was fully operational again. The Regiment too was on the move: having now lost their Bofor guns they were moving over to the American side and would be operating with them and as Infantry. I think at this time the main objective was Florence. The Anzio debacle was over and Rome had been liberated. Strangely a lot of these events sort of passed us by, they happened and we heard about them but I suppose we were more concerned with our own future and I was certainly concerned at being back with the Infantry. There still didn't seem to be any real connection between myself and the Regiment and certainly my OC didn't seem bothered so off we went and I was once more dashing up and down the convoy and I must confess, really enjoying myself on the bike, a Matchless, for the record. The big thing for us all really, the mail service was proving to be superbly reliable thanks to the Royal Engineers who operated the Field Post Offices.

Before I left I went back to the Ration Depot and dropped a case of Scotch, Haig, if I remember rightly, onto the Top Sergeant's desk. This really flattened the Sergeant and his face was something to behold. The lads had all chipped in and why not? We had been hard pressed to find enough room to get our rations on to two big trucks before we moved off. Spares? What spares? We never really knew where we were during these moves, an odd village name or signpost but mostly we seemed to meander through the minor roads in the countryside, staging for the night. The LAD didn't require much room, we were a small unit so there was always somewhere. The summer was fading but the weather was good and only the separation from our families intruded on what was a quiet and pleasant period. We had total air superiority so even that menace had disappeared.

So after a long day and a lot of miles we turned off into what was a field at the bottom of a large garden. I was pretty tired; after all I had covered twice the mileage of the others. A superb meal, then bed with a little prayer for mail in the morning, Santa Claus had assumed the guise of the Post Corporal We had been following a coast road for some time before staging and the sea was at the bottom of the 'garden' so, with no early start, writing letters, idling and swimming quickly became the order of the day. Letters were assuming an important significance at this time as Tony was approaching his first school days to start at the Copnor Road Junior School, so far and so long away it seemed sort of unbelievable, but I was still on my feet and battling on so count your blessings Clem!

It was mid-morning, that is certain, but apart from idling I can't remember what I was doing. At the top of the garden there was a rather nice looking bungalow which we had assumed was empty. I was suddenly conscious of some of the lads running past me in the direction of this bungalow and more urgently the cries and shouts of a woman in some distress. Quickly following the lads and the shouts I intercepted a lady in great distress carrying a young boy of six or seven who was bleeding profusely from the face. A couple of the lads grabbed her and when I checked the damage, the boy's face had been sliced to the bone and into the mouth, the cut running from just below his right eye to the edge of his mouth. It was so clean it could have been done with a scalpel but it was gaping open and pouring blood. I realised immediately it required pulling together but how was I going to even treat it? The first thing was to separate mother and son; the lads did this beautifully and already somebody had brought my first aid case. The Doctor had made it up for me and it didn't lack anything, ultimately

I simply covered the laceration with a large dressing fixed firmly with bandage, trying to keep the edges of the cut together and most importantly slowing the bleeding. What the hell now? The young boy was in shock his mother was hysterical, God knows where the Regiment is and with it the Doctor.

'Santa Claus' arrived in the shape of the Post Corporal who had passed a small American Unit about two miles away. He dashed off to see if they could help and came back with directions to an American Field Hospital some ten miles away. Carrying the boy with great care in the front of one of our 15 cwt trucks we found the Hospital. Their casualty staff quickly took the lad and shortly a Major came in, examined him carefully and within minutes they had wheeled my casualty away. Already Mum was being looked after, a big mug of coffee and one of the American nurses chatting fluently to her in Italian. This inability to talk to the boy's mother had indeed been a big handicap to me and at this stage I still hadn't any idea of how the accident occurred. Mum came rushing over to me, weeping and hugging me. The nurse said she was just trying to say thank you but was overcome with emotion. I needed a coffee!

I was also by this time beginning to feel a glow of pleasure at how things were working out. All this was nothing compared with what was to come. The Major came back and having complimented me on my first aid said he would be operating on the boy in half an hour or so and could I bring his mother back tomorrow. Still trying to get my breath back another of the nurses came over and said, 'It is unbelievable, the Major is a leading plastic surgeon and is just visiting to tidy up a couple of severe facial wounds before the soldiers are moved to a Base Hospital.'

I gathered up Mum, and found from the nurse that the boy had been rushing about and put his head through a pane of glass. The bungalow turned out to be quite big and comfortable, the offending glass a flimsy patio door. There was nothing flimsy about the wine store. I can't say I remember leaving or what the hell happened to the Post Corporal, he was with me to start with.

Back to the hospital with Mum; a long chat with the Major and instructions typed for them. A nurse would be sent in a weeks time to remove the stitches and report on the healing, two huge boxes of food to make sure the boy was nourished and finally an ambulance to take us to Frascatti where the family lived. Well, what else would you expect from the Americans? The Major had also told the boy's mother that given time it would be impossible to find a scar. That was quite a day. The family owned a large transport firm based in Rome, the bungalow was a holiday home. Their gratitude was overwhelming and I left with the promise of a permanent welcome when the war was over and of course their Rome address. I also intended to bike over the next day to see how the lad was. Unfortunately the next day I was once again shuffling up and down the convoy as we moved on, but worst of all I lost the address. I have always regretted this. I never got to see the family again but most of all I would have dearly liked to see the result of the Major's handiwork.

I certainly recognised the next town we passed through, there was this tower sort of leaning over at a funny angle; not only that but there was a sign on the road which said Pisa. We finally turned off into what turned out to be an almost finished school, set in a very pleasant wooded area; the buildings were bungalows and with water laid on and our own generator giving us plenty of power, plus a liberated oven to keep our Baker happy and at least two truckloads of American rations still left, the future looked set fair. The place we had arrived at was called Marina de Pisa and across the road was a very nice beach well planted with German Teller mines. These were anti-tank and would take the tracks off the biggest tanks. Ah well, can't have everything, there were a lot of glum looks from the lads as they put away their buckets and spades.

The day after our arrival we found that the Americans were bringing in Italian builders to alter some of the buildings further into the wooded area. I think they were planning a more permanent staging area for their own troops. The workers would arrive in an American lorry with usually around twenty or so in the back. The first lorry would arrive punctually at nine o clock in the morning followed by a second usually about lunch time. They followed a well used track stopping at what was a large concrete 'raft' previously laid to take future buildings. All our lorries had used this track regularly; I know I had been round it a few times in the Leyland. The Americans were using this concrete raft to stack materials and I suppose it would be about a hundred yards from the building I was using as a billet. I was sat with the OC drinking coffee and signing requisition forms for spares, believe me I can picture the scene as if it were yesterday. We heard our lunch time lorry go past followed by an enormous explosion which shook the building.

We were both out of the building like scalded cats to face a scene of carnage. As we ran to the smoke cloud I can remember groaning to myself. I already knew what it was and this was confirmed when I saw the truck pitched over drunkenly and resting on what was left of the near side suspension. It had pulled in close to the concrete raft and detonated a 'Teller mine'. Apart from the damage to the truck it would not normally involve casualties as the Americans had their trucks well sand bagged against mines, just a good shaking and hearing loss for a while, but disastrously in this case we arrived to find a quite indescribable scene. The workers had been in the habit of grouping round where they felt the truck would stop and a small group of them had taken the full force of the blast, one of whom must have been almost standing on the mine.

I could see there were three further back who were dead so ignoring them I set about trying to help the injured whilst the OC went to organise help. He was quickly back to help me and though struggling desperately to keep himself together he never backed away. Some of the lads too were gritting their teeth and getting on with what instructions I was giving. Finally we got the casualties away in two of our trucks, the three dead had been covered and I was faced with the remains of the one who had taken the full force of the blast. I managed to cover the remains using ground sheets. At last I crawled away, was violently sick and then I spent a long time under the primitive shower we had rigged, fully dressed, boots and all.

Some half an hour later a team of American medics turned up. As I watched them, their professionalism and the respect they showed to the awful work they were doing was a revelation. At the end the Corporal in charge said, 'You did a good job Sergeant, I reckon you've been there before' I nodded and there was another end.

A few days later we were once again on the move and our destination this time turned out to be Torre di Lago, the birthplace of Puccini; indeed the entrance to the small boatyard which the LAD moved into was exactly opposite Puccini's house.

Using offices and what had been some form of accommodation we made ourselves comfortable and waited for the smell of baking bread. Life was indeed hard? Sadly, no matter how comfortable the billet might be, nothing helped the heartache of separation from our families. I was sustained entirely by mail from home, a strange distant form of being a husband and a father. Over the months Girl had been a prolific letter writer. I owed her so much and of course she kept me up to date on Tony's progress.

Just adjacent to the boatyard there was a lake. The following day I found that Puccini's house was in fact kept as a museum and the Curator was only too happy to show me round. The main room had supposedly been kept just as Puccini left it and with a partly finished manuscript on the piano. It was all beautifully kept and very interesting. Even more so the story about the supposed madness of Puccini: apparently when things were too difficult and inspiration dried up, he would rush out of the house and row out to the middle of the lake and just sit there for hours.

A few days after we arrived I was told that the Medical Officer wanted to see me and with some trepidation I set off on my trusty Matchless. After remarking that he had heard I'd experienced a 'bit' of bother at Marina de Pisa he got down to explaining what I was there for. Apparently all the Allied medical facilities, which in our case were the Doctor and his merry men, were being used to fill the gaps in Medical Care for the Italian civilians. As the Regiment moved on they were to take over treatment in the various districts or towns they might pass through for so long as they were there. The emphasis would be people who had been treated for wounds suffered during any fighting and the object to see they were progressing all right, replace dressings where necessary and for the medics to take out stitches if required.

Why did I know what was coming? 'Here's a list of eight addresses in Torre de Largo, I will send a truck with odds and ends you might need, any problems refer them back to me, don't attempt stitches and oh yes, your bit of bother! The Americans were very impressed.'

Ah well, Clem, maybe it's time to go back to the Armourer's trade? Meanwhile back on your bike, with a bit of luck we might be on the move tomorrow. So what happened? Firstly the OC loaned me the Italian who had been translating for the LAD We had always called him Benito, very clever this, remember Benito Mussolini? A cheerful personality always anxious to please and I suppose in his late twenties. We had a great time together, and for the patients it paid to be early on my list; the hospitality was such that at the end of the day I only had a hazy recollection of my last visits and at the start of the next, a fearsome hangover. Benito sometimes didn't even make it. Yes, I enjoyed this period.

I was well aware at this time that my old Brigade were still in the thick of the fighting and that of course meant the Hampshires and indeed the war was still very much with us though far enough up the road to offer insulation. Even so I had been savagely reminded only a few days previously that complacency was a dangerous luxury. Here I am, once again sat drinking tea with the boss plus the ASM (remember him of the certificate proving sanity) when a very interesting signal arrived from GHQ inviting workshops like ours to send a truck to a town, which had been liberated a couple of days earlier, the name of which eludes me. Here we would find a large factory which in better times built luxury railway rolling stock for 'Wagon Lit'. and the famous Simplon Express. This might yield useful items in the way of tools and materials. I fancied this little job and the following morning left in a three ton Bedford driven by a L/Corporal George Mussen. George was one of the older members of the LAD and we got on well, indeed this wasn't the first job we had done together.

I said in the second paragraph of 'Tebourba Gap 1942' and I quote, 'Well, well! Intelligence is only as good as its accuracy and if it isn't accurate then it is rubbish and more often than not deadly rubbish for the troops that must act on it.' So here I was, a pleasant day, good company and about a forty mile run in front of us. Looming up eventually the opportunity again to sum up the war in those two words 'bizarre and surreal'. I really should have paid more attention to the words in the signal, which said, 'Liberated a couple of days earlier.'

We were approaching our destination in the late morning, and could see the town ahead or at least where the suburbs started. Approaching a fork in the road I decided to turn off to the left and find a place to park and organise our lunch. Two or three miles along there was a large house set well back with a very inviting drive up to the front door. Getting George to back the truck into the drive, I told him to stay in the driving seat whilst I went to see if it was occupied. I was very uneasy, it had been very quiet over the last five miles or so, no traffic at all, not normally a cause for worry but I was a different animal these days and my senses were telling me to worry.

I reached for the door handle and froze at the unmistakable sound of a German mortar bomb heading in my direction. Not possible I thought as I fled for the truck whilst three more bombs arrived dropping well short. George had obviously taken a very quick course on survival because he had the truck moving almost before I had scrambled in. There were no more bombs so I turned left at the fork and once again headed for the town. I was wide awake now and George was a bit startled by the sudden introduction to enemy mortar fire but as I pointed out he certainly had a good story and so far no harm done. As we drove slowly towards the town we passed a field with a Squadron of Sherman tanks dug in, obviously in an Artillery role. Nothing was moving except the nasty feeling in my stomach. I was determined by now to at least reach the town before we turned back. Ahead of us was a crossroads almost shrouded in dust, come on Clem, listen to your senses, then there he was right in the centre of the crossroads, a Military Policeman, white gloves, red hat, creases and I had no doubt that under all that dust a wonderful pair of boots.

So that's all right I thought. We drove up to the policeman and although he was signalling for us to go straight on I needed some information. Window down, I pulled up next to him whereupon he said very calmly and quietly but very forcibly, 'I should move as quickly as possibly Sergeant there is a 88mm gun ranged on this cross roads.' We moved and quickly; sure enough we were followed by the sound and fury of an armour piercing 88mm shell hurrying on its way over the crossroads and into the wreckage of the building already suffering mightily from previous salvoes. I had pulled up about twenty yards further on from the RMP. He quickly emerged from the dust and just as if nothing had happened asked me where I was hopefully going. Well well, he said laughing, we were the third that day and that never mind the signal he could assure us that they were still fighting for the town although it was expected to be in Allied hands 'Any moment now'.

It is well beyond my literary skills to adequately describe this bizarre episode and totally impossible to do justice to the courage and total imperturbability of the Royal Military Policeman. Even long words don't help. I have already used my favourite short word 'bizarre', so, for the earlier episode and the mortar bombs I think it is back to 'surreal'. George was delighted with events and just couldn't wait to get back. Naturally we never saw the factory which was a disappointment.

Shortly after this nonsense we were once again on the move and though we were all sorry to be leaving Torre del Largo our next stop was at a spa town further inland called Montecatini and this was indeed a great billet, quite a big town and still relatively unaffected by the war. Being a spa it was geared for visitors and we finished up occupying a very nice hotel, though not functioning. We were certainly comfortable and soon settled in. Many of the spas were functioning so we could enjoy the benefits, wonderful showers good for our aches and pains and Spa water to drink which would cure everything. Not for most of us, I'm afraid; it was so vile tasting that we decided to keep our ills.

Sadly for me it didn't last. I had set up a nice little workshop in a small furniture factory. Very comfortable, I might even organise a few small arms to work on. Unfortunately the Regiment had other ideas like sending me back to war. 'Not fair, I said to the OC I've done that bit! 'then you will know what to do' was his witty reply. Anyway they haven't said when so it might be days yet. The next day I went out with John on a small recovery job to bring in one of the Regimental vehicles and on the way we stopped to help a small utility truck that had broken down. John set up a brew and I sorted out the engine problem. There was a driver and a Lieutenant and as we sat and chatted the Lieutenant remarked somewhere along the line that he was an AIA this made him one of my real bosses, Assistant Inspector of Armourers to give him the full title. I introduced myself as an armourer and indeed an ex Hilsea boy. He replied, 'I'm an ex Hilsea boy myself, Alfie Wyatt! and what the hell are you doing as a mere Sergeant?' I got it all off my chest and as we shook hands before he left, he said, 'Don't worry, I'll sort it, Clem.'

Travelling back with John I was intrigued by the meeting but much more intrigued and worried by thoughts of what the Regiment had in mind for me following the OC's remark about them sending me back to war. I just couldn't imagine. The following morning the LAD clerk said I was to report straight away to Regimental Headquarters and with all my gear including tools. They were about fifteen miles away and when I asked how I was to travel he said they had sent one of their Bren Gun Carriers for me to use. I would find it in the vehicle park, it had been filled with petrol and no, he hadn't the faintest idea what was in store for me, and would I please sign for the Carrier as it had been issued to me. He expressed a hope that I could drive one and good luck. So now I'm a bloody Bren Gun Carrier driver. That's it then, I have finally been chosen to end the war in Italy by charging at the Tigers in a Bren Carrier.

I decided that 'straight away' would be early the next day, give me time to get my gear together, say a goodbye here and there and find out whether or not I could drive this strange beast: this part I was looking forward to. So the following morning, just getting light, a slight frost and full of hot bacon roll I climbed into the driving seat, started up and aimed myself roughly at the entrance or exit, who cares when you are driving an armoured vehicle, out into the road. A touch on the right tiller (nothing as sophisticated as a steering wheel on this Carrier) and shit, I was spinning like a top on the icy cobbles. It was, as I said, about fifteen miles to the HQ and God, I enjoyed every minute of it finally parking up with quite a flourish. I hadn't killed anyone either.

So report to the Chief Clerk. I was being sent to join an Italian Mountain Resistance Group operating about forty miles away and who had requested the services of an Armourer. Oh God, I thought, no mail! except said the Chief Clerk I have a signal here from GHQ, no less, which states that you have been posted to Eighth Army Troop Workshops, at present stationed in Rimini, you have been promoted to AQMS (this was a two rank jump to Warrant Officer) and the posting is to be treated as immediate. I was stunned and after lunch and a little celebration in the mess I once again climbed into my trusty but very cold Bren Carrier and prepared to enjoy myself but this time in a very different mood. Not only that, but I had even collected my new badges of rank from the Quartermaster, where's that bloody housewife?

Dear Alfie Wyatt, we served together some twelve years later in yet another campaign, the Mau Mau troubles in Kenya. He was again my boss, this time as a Major and AIA Kenya. I was, surprise surprise, back with the Infantry as Thirty Nine Brigade Armourer. His wife Jean and Girl were good friends and our families enjoyed much time together. Shortly after returning to UK Alfie was killed working under his car when the jack collapsed.

The following day and I was on my way to Rimini. We staged overnight in the yard of a deserted house and I finally reported in to the Chief Clerk at Eighth Army Troop Workshops and was accommodated in a one of the rooms of a large house, indeed the Chief Clerk, Sgt. Siperius, was one of my room mates and we became good friends. I had no conception of what exactly a Troop Workshop was or even what it did but I soon began to realise that it was big. The house I was in as well as providing accommodation also served as the Sergeants' Mess, cosy I thought at the time and so it was.

Almost the first person I saw in the mess was an old friend from the Aldershot days when our Battalions occupied adjacent Barracks, Frank Passingham! He was also the one I was replacing; having just been Commissioned to the rank of Lieutenant he was moving on. Cause for a long chat and an even longer celebration. The next morning a desperately hung over Frank took a desperately hung over Clem to meet a desperately hung over Commanding Officer; his excuse was some sort of celebration in the RAOC mess just up the road. We shook hands and having assured him that I had reported to Siperius it was left to Frank to introduce me to the rest of the workshops and report back for drink and a chat in the evening.

Any attempt to describe this Workshops just has to start with the Commanding Officer. Major Vollum a very distinguished Electrical Engineer in a previous life, had a hand in the design of the Battersea power generators and was the author of several electrical engineering text books. Also and much admired by the lads he was a seriously practical engineer who would be more likely to be found at any given time of the day in overalls busy on some project are other. I would describe Major Vollum as a civilian running an Army Workshops. You were expected to be good at your job and happy to work long hours. The working day was eight o'clock to near enough dusk and we worked a seven day week with only Sunday afternoons off.

Eighth Army Troop Workshops started in life as a small LAD not unlike the one I had just left and was formed in Scotland. I believe there was both a Reserve and a Territorial element to the original personnel and I am almost certain that Lieutenant Vollum, Officer Commanding, was ex TA. The unit numbered about twenty five which included an AQMS. as number two, a couple of Sergeants, and the odd Corporal. Shortly after getting themselves organised, sorting out equipment, vehicles etc, they were moved to North Africa and joined the Eighth Army where they were upgraded to a small Field Workshops, picked up a few extra Craftsmen and from then on they moved with the Eighth Army through the trials and tribulations of Tobruk, the Western desert, Tunisia, Italy and here they were in Rimini.

As they moved they grew. Their civilian OC, cleverly disguised as a soldier, acquired, Italian machinery lorries, various recovery Scammels, a superb American Ford Staff Car. Even a one ton Ford, identical to his Staff Car, for the Armourer Warrant Officer. Not one item of all this could be held legally by a small Workshops but when I joined them at Rimini it was all on the Workshop books and accounted for. Along the way Lieut. Vollum had not neglected his own acquisitions. Now a Major and not an OC but a fully fledged Commanding Officer, still basically a civilian, mind you.

I suppose when I joined the Workshops they would be about eighty strong, I see from the photo of the Sergeants' Mess there were thirty Senior ranks. My own particular serfdom, the Armourers Section, comprised myself, a Sgt. Bill Bartholemew, a Corporal Jonah Jones and nine Craftsmen, which included a Lance Corporal. Oh, and a one ton Ford utility truck, nearly forgot that. How did all this work with such long hard hours? Apparently Major Vollum had laid out a simple ground rule: whilst the lads are fighting we will work hard to support them but the moment the battle for Italy is won we all down tools, absolutely no more work and a good time for everyone. This is exactly what happened, but more later.

Nothing was too much trouble or even good enough for Vollum's Lads. A typical example: an Army Mobile Cinema unit was being sent out to provide the Eighth Army with entertainment. Major Vollum sniffed this out long before the Unit arrived in Italy and who were they attached to for all purposes. Us of course. I was way ahead of Girl when it came to the latest films. ENSA shows always seemed to finish up as guests of the Officers' Mess.

Another important component of Major Vollum's philosophy was that accommodation was as comfortable as possible. All the Tents were heated, food was superb and did someone mention parades, or even duties, they must be joking. The result, Major Vollum asked and the unit delivered. The Army were shaping up for a final push to Venice, the weather suddenly deteriorated and the heavy rain posed a possible problem with the Sherman tank tracks losing grip in the mud. Our Blacksmith Sergeant designed a track fitting to solve this problem, but it was a heavy attachment and required all the resources of our extensive equipment. The Major undertook to produce a hundred of these fittings in two days. We worked continuously for thirty hours, taking breaks when exhaustion set in. Nobody complained: indeed I for one never thought about it, we just pressed on and the job was done. The fittings were delivered bang on time, the weather cleared and the fittings were dumped! I personally paid a heavy price. I had joined the blacksmith's team and my job was to forge a bolt head on a piece of round steel, about a foot long whilst the fitters and turners threaded the other end. I don't remember at what point I retired from the fray but it was to go to hospital to get my lacerated hands treated and they took a couple of weeks to recover and heal. What a problem toilet paper was. I was not the only one taking a long time to recover, the Sergeant Blacksmith was having the same problems wiping his backside.

Sometime later in the year the Unit was awarded an MBE to be awarded at the discretion of the Commanding Officer or so Major Vollum said. He gave it to the Sgt. Blacksmith. Sgt. Siperius always disputed this account of the award and said the award had, in fact, been made directly to Major Vollum. Chief Clerks always know everything.

The original members of the LAD had become a sort of exclusive group within the Workshops with the Major of course the senior member. This group were known as 'The Dodgy Boys', and carried this title in big white letters on the back of their overalls. There was no animosity towards this privileged group, indeed they were held in some awe. I think a lot of the lads had discovered it was a good idea to acquire one of The Dodgy Boys as a friend, the closer the better. It has to be remembered of course that this group had come along way together, Scotland, Tobruck, the Western Desert and Tunisian campaigns and finally Italy.

All this leads me to the General's visit. I can't remember his name but he had a reputation of being an inflexible disciplinarian and given to flinging nasty reports about. Absolutely no preparations were made for this visit and we were told about it on the normal orders. Date and approximate time, nothing else. The General arrived with his large entourage some time during the morning and Major Vollum was dutifully showing him round and with the Workshop's spy (Sgt. Siperius) trailing closely behind but in the middle of the party. Inevitably a couple of the Dodgy Boys wandered into view wearing overalls and of course carrying their privileged insignia emblazoned on the back. The General blew his top and ordered that all these 'Dodgy Boy' markings would be removed and immediately. Major Vollum saluted and excused himself, reappearing a few minutes later wearing his own overalls emblazoned with Dodgy Boys on the back.

Sgt. Siperius said this was the best moment of his Army career so far, The General and his party left without a word nor was anything ever heard about the visit.

The Major's interests revolved around A, the Workshop's football team, B the Generator driven by a large Lister diesel engine, designed and built by Major Vollum - housed on a big flat bed Fiat lorry, it was a superb piece of equipment and purred away twenty four hours a day supplying all the domestics plus the workshop machinery and with power to spare, and C the enormous amplifier built and incorporated into a fifteen cwt truck together with two turntables, two enormous horn speakers and around three hundred records. Only the Dodgy Boys knew where the two enormous horn speakers came from; these were always set up on the highest building around. Funny how we just happened to have a General Duties Corporal posted in who just happened to be a steeplejack before the call up brought him to earth. Oh yes, D, I nearly forgot the Major's strange fascination with explosives. More later.

The power of the Amplifier can be judged by the requests we got during the evening from an American Bath Unit some three miles away. The Americans would pop in from time to time to gaze in awe at the set up and offer their supreme compliment - 'Jesus'! I suppose it is true to say that the sound system was the source of the only serious 'Duty' in the workshops; at least the duty 'disc jockey' for the day was always listed on orders. For the rest of us requests for the evening in by four o'clock.

Life was very orderly at this time: regular letters and Tony was beginning to put the odd letter together which was eagerly looked forward to. The Armourers Workshop was running very smoothly and we were taking in small arms from the RAOC Returned Stores Depot, and refurbishing them to a good standard ready for re-issue. This unit was also in stationed in Rimini accommodated in a badly damaged theatre, lot of debris about, I never really felt at ease when sharing a cup of coffee with the OC, a Warrant Officer, Paul by name; we became good friends, mind you coffee wasn't the only beverage on offer. Possible collapse or not Paul had made himself very comfortable in what had been the Manager's Office.

The Workshops had 'acquired' a superb collection of machinery, because none of it was written into the 'Establishment' which dictated down to the last screw what a unit could have but more importantly what it could get from the RAOC In our case measuring instruments essential to the machinery section, not allowable. Considering that after months of scheming, offers of bribes etc neither the Major or indeed the Dodgy Boys had managed to liberate even one small micrometer. Well, well well!, AQMS Clem Hoyle (relatively recent addition to the Workshop staff) knew where there was a large steel cupboard every shelf bulging with micrometers, clock gauges, Vernier-calipers and every measuring goody imaginable.

This cupboard, alas resided in Paul's office, and the contents were documented officially as valuable and attractive: this meant keep firmly under lock and key and to be issued only on the authority of the King or equivalent rank, more or less anyway. Crawling, I always maintained, was the best way to get on anywhere so how was I to liberate this lot and bask forever in the approbation of my Commanding Officer to say nothing of the S/Sergeant in charge of the machining section? A few drinks there I reckon. Unfortunately I hadn't reckoned on Paul who stuck to the book and don't get me wrong, very admirable indeed. Shit, I thought as I lay in bed wrestling with this problem.

Time passed and I still hadn't got anywhere, in fact I was resigned to joining the rest in failure. Then one morning at breakfast Siperius passed a message to me asking me to go and see Paul at the RSD. I realised as I approached that all was not well, the old familiar dust cloud sent out a clear message and when I arrived it was to find that the concrete roof had collapsed into the centre of the theatre. This had been the auditorium where Paul employed lots of Italians sorting uniforms and clothes in general. Paul was fine and there had been no casualties but sadly the valuable and attractive items cupboard standing in the corner of his office was lying buried under tons of concrete and impossible to recover so he had written it off, together with the contents. Would I like to take it away?

No one ever knew where the cupboard and its contents came from or how I had liberated it, a bit like my football trophy. My new best friend the machine shop section S/Sergeant couldn't wait to get the drinks in, whilst my own section improved by one new L/Corporal and the previous L/Corporal became a Corporal. Best of all I now had real clout with the Dodgy Boys.

Suddenly Christmas was here and nothing was spared. The Commanding Officer and Adjutant along with us Senior Ranks served the dinner, and our own personal film unit produced a film that hadn't even been on general release in UK *For Whom The Bell Tolls*, Gary Cooper and Ingrid Bergman as I remember. For the rest I suppose we got quietly drunk. The amplifier had done sterling work over the whole Christmas period and we had been surprised how far away were some of the units requesting carols. Of course this period was also miserable in that it was a constant reminder of the separation from our families so there was a lot of hope that the new year, 1945, would see us home again. New Year's day was simple, back to work.

The main workshops were involved in converting a three ton Bedford into a caravan fit for a General but who this was I cannot remember, and superb it was when finished. The workshops seemed to be full of fine Craftsmen none more so than the

Corporal Welder. Welding can be of two kinds, good or an art form, and this welder was an artist. You would never dream of trimming back a run of weld by him, it was a finish in its own right. I suppose modern motor cycles illustrate this type of weld but of course machine generated. There was a problem, the Corporal was an aggressive Communist and virtually impossible to get on with. Tolerated because of his skills we all suspected that, come the end of the Battle and our move into recreation mode rather than work mode, he might just be moving on.

My own section were busy enough and there was a steady flow of weapons coming in from units for repair plus our RSD commitments. Whilst we were settled and comfortable the sharp end were still fighting, often ferociously, and the Major never let us forget this, any forward Unit asking for help got it without compromise.

It was about this time that I met Major Peniakoff, known well enough by every soldier as 'Popski' and his gang of soldiers were titled 'Private Army', hence the famous or notorious 'Popski''s Private Army' and what a record they had from the Desert, through North Africa, and Italy. Never numbering much more than a hundred, most of their quite astonishing actions used only a handful of men. Late in the Italian campaign twelve men in five Jeeps (I hope at least one of the Jeeps was mine) captured a German position comprising seventeen officers and 670 soldiers, who were operating three batteries of 88mm guns, one hundred 20mm guns and supplies for three months.

One morning Major Vollum brought 'Popski' round to my workshops and introduced us: quite a moment, not every day one meets a legend. I don't know quite how I had imagined 'Popski' but he was physically small and a quiet man, very deceiving this, once he had decided on something that was it. We argued a lot and mostly I managed to complete his requirements, together with the rest of the workshops who were soon falling over themselves to make this or that or attempting to design something that was an engineering impossibility. We became firm friends and he spent many days in my workshops and mugs of tea in my office whilst I would spend the interval between slurping sweet tea, saying and sometimes shouting, 'It's not Bloody possible!' And the reason for all this? Well, here is a list of items he wished to carry on or in a Jeep, some mounted and to be operated from the Jeep, others carried but very specially stowed so as to be quickly into action.

.50 ins and .30 ins Browning Machine Guns, mounted. Two Bren guns with ground tripods to be designed and built. One 'Bazooka'. One three inch mortar capable of being fired from the jeep. Smoke generators fixed at the rear of the Jeep operated electrically from the dashboard. Finally a 'Wasp' Flame Thrower. 'Come on, Popski, you're joking it's not bloody possible. The mortar weighs a hundred weight, it's only a Jeep where the hell are you going to stow little things like ammunition, grenades etc? Ah well, waste your breath, it was possible! The lads were very proud of this and it's maybe not very military but they loved Popski they were also awed by the odd characters he brought with him from time to time, awed or frightened I don't know which. So if you have ever met a Jeep with its springs bending the wrong way it could well be one of mine. So Major Peniakoff, 'Popski', I, and I suspect many of the lads, were very disappointed not to get a mention in your autobiography. All those arguments, all that work? Shame on you, but never mind, you are in mine!

Bill Bartholemew, my Sergeant Armourer, had been pressing me for a chance to upgrade to First class. He was an excellent Armourer and seeing no problem I headed off to GHQ and my old friend Alfie Wyatt, AIA because there were formalities like getting his signature on the relevant documents. I had been to see him several times and at this time I also had an application to be allowed to take photographs lodged with GHQ so I thought I might chase it up. It turned into an interesting morning.

The most senior Inspector of Armourers in the Army at that time was Colonel Gundle. Throughout his career he had been a pain in the arse to Armourers, a serious pain because of the damage he could do and often did to a young career. He had built up a fearsome reputation in India in the years prior to the War and was intensely disliked. Any of my contemporaries reading this will be nodding their heads. His trademark trick before visiting an Armourer was to mug up some obscure technical niceties then early in the inspection he would spring a question about whatever it was he had mugged up. In the normal run of our job it was impossible to counter this, the area of small arms was much too wide.

So Clem knocked on Alfie's door, breezed in and there was Colonel Gundle sat in my chair guzzling what was probably my coffee. Of course I didn't know who it was until Alfie introduced him. I shook hands, he didn't frighten me, well only a little bit. After chatting amicably for a little while, out of the blue and apropos nothing we had been talking about he said, 'what do you know about the Oerlicon gun, Sgt. Major?' A nasty question this as most Armourers never saw an Oerlicon and like myself when I joined the Searchlight Regiment knew absolutely nothing about them other than what they looked like.

Yeah, he didn't scare me! So popping in a couple of minor technical details about what is known in the trade as 'Field Stripping', guns not birds, I expounded at length on the vissitudes of the magazine and its potential to knock the foot off an unwary Armourer should he drop one of the explosive rounds. 'Ah' said the Colonel. 'I see you have had a copy of the excellent technical instruction book we've had printed.' What to say? Tread carefully here, Clem.

'Beautifully printed and laid out, Sir, I never dreamed my scribbled notes would be cleaned up so well.'

How about that? Alfie did then say, 'Actually Sgt. Major Hoyle compiled the original instructions along with a Cpl. Anderson.' I can vouch for the fact that Colonel Gundle is or was a pussy cat and before we parted he had promised to have a look at a suitable promotion for Corporal Anderson and had signed Bill's upgrading personally.

Oh yes, I got my photographic permit too and a map reference for my old Battalion, who were out of the line resting not too far away. Quite a fruitful morning, you always need luck. I lost no time in finding my old Battalion and the next day located them without trouble. People say that it is always unwise to go back and basically so it proved, there had been so many changes. Bill had left in the natural order of things for a better job and promotion. Sgt Raddon was still there and was now RQMS but one reunion made it worthwhile, my old mate Trudge Truran was there, now commissioned as Quartermaster and best of all my real mate Joe was there, I couldn't wait to tell him about the Wellington but I don't think he really believed me.

We spent a couple of hours together swapping stories and he brought me up to date with what had been happening. My old friend the Adjutant had gone to one of the other Hampshire Battalions as Second in Command. I didn't get to meet my replacement but Trudge spoke highly of him. The visit was worth while but still an anti-climax. I suppose my real hope was that Joe and Bill would be there but it didn't happen. 'Ships that pass in the night.' I wonder what happened to Bill after he left the Battalion, I bet it was nothing like the Tebourba Gap!

After a couple of trial games I had become a fixture in the football team and this was something to look forward to on Sundays. We really did have a good team but with Major Vollum issuing challenges right left and centre often carrying big side bets, indeed one game against an Eighth Army Team was reputed to have netted our boss three thousand lira, no wonder we had a good team, we dare, not lose. The war was remorselessly grinding on and it was felt very strongly that a big and hopefully final offensive was near. Rumour was not what it was in the old days when my old friends the Pioneer Platoon were putting up six seaters, they could really generate a rumour to say nothing of enough methane to power a small factory. Missed Gaffer too; he would have known exactly what was going to happen and when!

The push finally came and was going very well, and then suddenly it was over. The German and Italian troops surrendered on 2 May, and Major Vollum, true to his word, stood the Workshops down. Would we be moving? Mixed feelings about that, we were pretty comfortable here in Rimini especially now we weren't accepting any work but it finally happened; we even knew where we were going, Mestre at the end of the Causeway running into Venice. I was about to be introduced to the 8th Army Troop Workshops method of convoy. Rules for Convoys are well laid down in Army Regulations, a specific number of vehicles per mile, a strict speed limit, vehicles to keep the spacing etc, etc. a convoy leader and a tail end Charlie and so it goes on.

Workshops however always start with the problem of what vehicles are still awaiting repair. Other items like my own, small arms that are awaiting repair, simply have to be carried to the next site, just work really though we finished as many as possible and returned them to their Unit. The same effort to return vehicles to their Units was made by the Vehicle Repair Workshop section but they were left in this case with five vehicles, three Bedford three tonners and two Bedford fifteen cwts. These were not driveable but could be towed. For the rest there were our own vehicles, each with an allocated driver plus the Transport Section S/Sergeant whose job was to keep both trucks and drivers happy and unfortunately also to see we convoyed properly and arrived at our destination in good order and somewhere near the time expected.

A couple of days before the move the Transport Section S/Sergeant grabbed me in the mess and asked me what I would like to drive on the move as they didn't have enough drivers for all the trucks, I said quick as a flash, something big: after all I was an experienced Leyland recovery driver. Actually I hadn't taken the question seriously. The day before the move the convoy list was circulated showing what vehicle everybody would be driving and where they would be in the convoy. There I was somewhere in the middle and opposite my name simply 'Mac'. I dived off quickly to have a look at this truck; it truly was a monster. I stood under the radiator and I swear I couldn't see the top. For the rest it was just a huge cargo truck and loaded with what seemed like the entire workshops. It certainly wasn't one of our trucks but not to reason why, just turn up in the morning and get on with it, always supposing I can climb into the cab. I never was much for heights.

Sitting in the cab, with three of my Armourers, Armourers are always fearless? seat adjusted, everything very comfortable, a quick look through the convoy orders and we were off, certainly Major Vollum was! According to what I had just read he was convoy leader and so it proved. He arrived at our ultimate destination about five hours before the rest of the convoy staggered in. That's what comes of having civilians disguised as Majors running the War; like Popski they please themselves. The one ton Ford that I had as my workshop vehicle was mechanically identical in every way to the Major's mysteriously acquired staff, car only the bodies were different, his a comfortable saloon and mine a working load carrier with a canvas cover over steel tubing. I pondered this over the coming days and felt that suitably modified with canvas and tube off, I might just be able to give the CO a run for his money. Dark thoughts these!

Our destination this time was really just a staging post between Rimini and Mestre. But everything had not gone smoothly. At the rear of the convoy had been two big Scammel recovery trucks, one towing three non runners, the other towing two. Quite illegal Army-wise, fair enough but where the hell were they? The drivers and passengers were all Dodgy Boys and the favourite assumption among the lads was that they had pulled off somewhere and flogged the lot, Scammels and all. The Transport Section S/Sergeant was running about a bit but the Major was quite unfazed on a 'They'll turn up' basis. Mind you he didn't know at this time that the Corporal (a carefully selected 'Dodgy Boy' quiet type) driving the truck with his beloved amplifier, two turntables, two huge horn speakers and some three hundred records had been nicked by the RMPs for speeding. The Corporal not the gear.

And the Scammels and assorted trucks? Trailing a bit, they had turned down a narrow road, no one ever claimed that the Dodgy Boys could read a map. This road was built up with steep dropping banks either side and as they quickly discovered, led nowhere. A Scammel, three trucks on tow another Scammel, two trucks on tow, nose to tail, a narrow road, steep banks dropping off maybe ten feet, absolutely no way to turn round and as far as the Workshops was concerned incommunicado. Or, as I said earlier, 'Where the hell are they'? Did you like 'incommunicado', good eh? Very Italian.

Some very fancy backing up to be done, but the Dodgy Boys could magic four new tyres to fit almost any truck you could name out of thin air so this problem should be within their capabilities. Took three days! Our Corporal of the Amplifier truck got a real roasting from the CO then a letter to the RMPs saying he had been demoted to L/Corporal and all was well. Nothing seemed to change 'arm wise', still two stripes, but Siperius assured us that he had typed the letter personally; mind you he never said who'd signed it. Ultimately Major Vollum got out his little box of explosives and successfully blew down a wall that he claimed was in the way and his mood brightened in proportion to the size of the bang.

Whilst in this location it was decided to celebrate the 'Victory in Italy'. Unfortunately the NAAFI had let us down and drink was in short supply. The Dodgy Boys had picked up a reasonable supply of beer for the lads but the Sergeants' and Officers' mess were very low. It was decided to trust myself and my very good friend Ron Copperwheat, a vehicle Artificer and like myself an AQMS. He also ran the football team and was no mean performer. Helping ourselves to a three ton Bedford and three cases of 'currency' from the cookhouse then fortified with almost the last of our Scotch, we set off. As we moved along the road I was trying to think like Gaffer! He would have honed in on the drink with no problem, of course: find a farm and as isolated as possible, don't forget the Germans have already passed this way.

After what seemed like hours and a million miles of likely looking tracks we found our farm and liberated four huge jars of reasonable Italian wine, using our three cases, one of stewed steak and the other two the inevitable corned beef to speed the liberation. After much back slapping and lots of 'salute' we were helped up into the truck. Ron happened to fall in the driver's side, I curled up on the other side, fiercely clutching my St Christopher medal whilst Ron wrestled with various items, gear lever, hand brake, pushed pedals in and out how the hell could he forget so soon? Suddenly the engine burst into life and to a chorus of 'Bravos' we lurched down the track. I was worried, Ron had started singing! but I found it strangely easy to join in and now I had Ron worried.

As we wandered along, eventually finding ourselves back on the main road and hopefully moving in the right direction, half dozing I was aware that Ron had stopped. 'What are those?' he said pointing to a neatly stacked pile of Teller mines. We had been passing these mines for some time; obviously they had been lifted by the Royal Engineers at some stage in the fighting, neatly stacked just off the road and were awaiting collection. Before I could answer, Ron had sort of fallen out of the driver's side and was walking in that special way we all have when alcohol dictates, towards one of these piles. As he did so I was conscious of a truck pulling up behind us and I quickly came awake as a young officer and a Sergeant walked towards Ron who by this time was hugging a 'Teller' mine to his chest and walking his 'Walk' towards the back of the truck and straight into the arms of the Officer and his Sgt. By this time I had recognised a Royal Engineers cap badge and being without any documents for our journey I sat quiet as a mouse.

'So, Sergeant Major, what are you going to do with that, they are not normally worn on the chest?'

Thank God I thought, he's got a sense of humour so come on, Ron, what the hell are you doing hugging a Teller mine to your chest?

'I was hoping to find out what it was. What's a Teller mine anyway, sir?'

I think I heard the Sergeant mutter 'such innocence' but I'm not sure.

'Will blow the tracks off a tank, even a 'Tiger', Sergeant Major.'

Ron promptly dropped the mine, the Sergeant picked it up and flung it on the pile whilst the officer was killing himself laughing. 'Better get on your way,' he said and off we went.

I hadn't said anything about these mines as we passed them because, even under the influence, the memory of that awful day at Marina De Pisa still haunted me and even as I wrote about the incident earlier I realised, even at this distance, it still does!

By the time we got back we were both sober and ready for something to eat and then of course there was the wine to take care of, it was a good night. A couple of days later we were once again moving out onto the main road heading for Mestre; this time I had swapped my 'Mac' for a Scammel. I reckoned by the time the last of the convoy got on to the main road, Vollum was probably in Venice. Mestre is situated at the north western end of the 'Causeway' that runs into Venice and we were all hoping for a decent stay there with plenty of chance to get into the city. The Workshops finally deployed into a large aluminium factory. This was in the form of powder ready to be smelted into the aluminium that we know.

The factory was about eight miles out of Venice and still keeping to his word about not working we most of us piled into a truck next day and set off for Venice. I suppose we all have mental pictures of places like Venice, and are often disappointed when we finally get there but to me I found Venice exactly how I had imagined it to be. Alas, three days later and we were on our way to Udine, further north, and Clem was driving his own truck, stripped down and with the engine breathed on by a couple of my vehicle friends. The Transport Section S/Sergeant had placed me well up the convoy, about four vehicles behind the CO . I had carefully planned a route of my own (I wasn't the holder of a First Class Certificate in Map Reading for nothing). I handed over the wheel to one of my young Armourers. And with me clutching the map we were off.

The precise location had been ringed for me by Siperius and ultimately turned out to be a large area of fields and very pleasant it was. Some half an hour after we arrived the Major came through the gate at a fair speed to find me stood to attention and saluting as befits an 'Old Hilsea Boy'. I also knew that the Major would exact revenge as befits a civilian disguised as a soldier. For the moment he went away and blew a hole in yet another wall: frightened me to death, I thought he had committed suicide.

This location proved to be only a staging post on our way to Udine, pleasant enough but one gets tired of putting up the same old tent then taking it down a few days later and so on ad infinitum. Two days later the convoy lined up again for the last leg to Udine. For some strange reason my ex-friend the Transport Sergeant had me down to ride an old battered BSA motor bike with the suggestion I might do a bit of convoy work. Somebody knew a thing or two. I spluttered along for a few miles then stopped at a junction to do my guidance bit and the blasted bike wouldn't start. Not to worry, last in the convoy was the recovery Scammel and he was there for just such a situation, the recovery lads would get me going or just stick the bike in the truck. So why was the Scammel beatling straight past me and disappearing up the road ? I sat there for about an hour thinking dark thoughts about the Major's revenge until a passing Gurkha in a 15 cwt. picked me up and cleverly found my new location. Not long after I arrived back the Major blew yet another hole in yet another wall.

Girl died at home and in my arms in the early hours of this morning, 13 December 2004 after a courageous battle with cancer. Her family were with her. I'm distraught.

February 2005. During Girl's last few days she made me promise to finish this autobiography, I will but it is hard!...

So where was I? We had arrived just outside Udine and settled our workshops in to a large field. This was to be home for a quite a while and we quickly settled in. The Major had broken his promise about work by undertaking to fit an engine into a German launch that had been acquired by a South African Air Force Squadron who were wanting to use it at their rest centre down the coast. This was done and in return Major Vollum was being taught to fly in a small spotting aircraft. Our perk was to fly any time in one of the Boston Bombers who were by this time just doing training flights. Oh yes, they were also doing a regular trip to Florence to pick up ice cream. I never did this trip but I certainly enjoyed hedge hopping whilst laying in the nose, mind you 'dry mouth' was back in moderation at times.

Sport picked up, and we played a representative Eighth Army Team, in which a certain Tom Finney scored four goals. We lost. But for myself, after playing cricket against a South African team I found myself selected to travel to England as part of a Services team which would be playing several County sides on a kind of end of the War tour. The team would be captained by Athol Rowan, one of the pre-war South

African Test side. Siperious was absolutlely bursting when the letter arrived. Myself? I was stunned, I would be going home! Visions of seeing Girl and Tony after all these years, it was beyond belief.

And so it proved. The Tour never took place, something to do with administrative problems, it was very cruel and I took some time to settle again. We were all getting edgy at this time and rumours were flying round, the strongest one to the effect that soldiers who had been abroad for more than a certain time (never specified) would be getting a month's home leave. Oh dear, where was Gaffer or even the Pioneer Platoon and one of their multi seaters?

About this time I began to feel strangely unwell and after a while I started to develop a terrible headache. Sod's Law decrees that under these circumstances work that must be done will turn up and sure enough it did. A Corporal serving with one of the local units had shot two soldiers dead, apparently at random and for no reason. He had used a Sten gun (sub machine gun) and I was asked to inspect the gun and be prepared to give evidence at the Court Martial as to its serviceabiliy. This I did but I was really ill by this time and the Judge Advocate having taken my evidence suggested I be taken off to hospital. I spent two days in bed. My chart said Pyrexia of unknown origin. This frightened me a bit so I asked one of the nurses and she said it simply meant a high temperature and they didn't have a clue why. Well, whatever caused it soon disappeared and I was quickly back into trying to find out whether any of the rumours were true.

We were not short of things to do at this time. The Major had acquired five superb ex German Army horses, again don't ask, plus an ex-cavalry Corporal who had been a riding instructor in better days and yet again don't ask! These were at our disposal and it was a fine chance to learn to ride. Additionally we were able to borrow tanks from the Return Stores Depot next door and we soon created an exciting run. Trying to drive the various types was great fun and pretty difficult. So eventually moving time came round again and this time it was to Bruch in Austria. Another convoy and I was back in the 'Mac'. Uneventful this time and we finished up in what had been a German Arms Factory; the main workshops were all underground cut into the side of a hill. Very big too. We never did find out for certain what they made, but we were told that it was the 88mm all purpose gun. Anti-Aircraft, Anti-Tank and in turn fitted to the 'Tiger' tank - a truly remarkable piece of weaponry.

There was no reason to doubt this, although all the machinery had been removed by the Russians. It was obvious from the huge concrete bases and the size of the holding bolts that this machinery had been massive. We were told that this had been done manually by hundreds of labourers brought in by the Russions and of obvious Asiatic origin. They had been accommodated in three huts, no beds just the floor, and above this two large slightly sloping platforms. Certainly smelt like it. Anyway the machinery was loaded on to flat railway trucks and taken off to Russia except the trucks were parked up in a siding about fifty miles away and are probably still there rusting away.

We were well accommodated in what had obviously been the Senior Engineers complex and probably also used by officers. Very comfortable it was too, excellent beds, proper linen, hot water, superb kitchen and very welcome, showers.

So what interrupted this idyll? LIAP! It is stamped in my trusty old Pay Book, '13 September 1945. LIAP. Leave in UK to 17 Oct 1945.' So the rumour was true and as Sipirius said enviously when he brought me the news, you are top of the list and first to go from this Unit. As the rumour had indicated it was decided on length of service away from home and in my case this amounted to some three and a half years. My feelings at this time cannot be described but predominately fear that something would stop it. I cannot remember how long I had to wait for departure day but it was like being a child again waiting for Santa.

Eventually the day arrived, all the farewells said (and drunk) and here I was sat on one of the bench seats in the back of a Bedford 3 ton lorry on my way across Europe to the Hook of Holland. Quite a journey in the back of a truck; there had been some attempt at padding the seats but it was pretty ineffectual. For some strange reason nobody seemed to be complaining. For myself I was content to nurse this knot of excitement that had settled in my stomach; it was wonderful and certainly a change from that knot of fear that I had become only to familiar with over the years.

There were several overnight stops, but I can only remember Klagenfurt, Innsbruck and Cologne. I especially recall standing on the steps of the main entrance to Cologne Cathedral, which was almost entirely unscathed, and not being able to see one other building standing, just total devastation. I stood in exactly the same spot some twenty-eight years later and looked out onto a magnificent city.

The journey was completely uneventful, that is to say not one aircraft fell on me, are you listening Joe? I told you I wasn't jinxed. It finished for me on Victoria Station in the arms of Girl !